T0304318

In this book, Kazimierz Z. Poznanski offers an integrated study of institutional change in the Polish economy since 1970. He examines the economic peak of the communist phase, the decline of the system, and the post-communist transition since 1989. Taking his analytical framework from evolutionary economics, he provides a complete reevaluation of conventional views of communist economies and the post-communist transition. The book presents the communist economy as subject to major changes, particularly due to political pressures, and interprets its economic difficulties as related to underlying systemic decay. The economic 'shock therapy' of 1990 is seen as very much a continuation of earlier trends and pressures, which has led to probably an even deeper, though brief, economic collapse. This book will be of interest to economists and political scientists concerned with institutional transitions, as well as to students of East European and post-Soviet studies.

POLAND'S PROTRACTED TRANSITION

Cambridge Russian, Soviet and Post-Soviet Studies

Series list continues after index

POLAND'S PROTRACTED TRANSITION

Institutional change and
economic growth 1970–1994

KAZIMIERZ Z. POZNANSKI

CAMBRIDGE
UNIVERSITY PRESS

CAMBRIDGE
UNIVERSITY PRESS

University Printing House, Cambridge CB2 8BS, United Kingdom

Cambridge University Press is part of the University of Cambridge.

It furthers the University's mission by disseminating knowledge in the pursuit of education, learning and research at the highest international levels of excellence.

www.cambridge.org
Information on this title: www.cambridge.org/9780521553964

© Cambridge University Press 1996

First published 1996

A catalogue record for this publication is available from the British Library

ISBN 978-0-521-55396-4 Hardback
ISBN 978-0-521-55639-2 Paperback

Cambridge University Press has no responsibility for the persistence or accuracy of URLs for external or third-party internet websites referred to in this publication, and does not guarantee that any content on such websites is, or will remain, accurate or appropriate.

Contents

Preface

This book has taken a number of years to finish and in retrospect, it is hard for me to recall when the whole project began. It goes back at least to my days at Cornell's Economics Department. At that stage, when I was doing my visiting lecture on communist-type economies, my insights were mostly straight out of a textbook, but the research that I was doing was drawing me away from the conventional thinking. I have continued my search for a fresh look at the system and, since it collapsed, have applied the same approach to the post-communist transition. My book presents this alternative view through an in-depth examination of Poland's economy during 1970–1994 period. While at Cornell, I gained greatly from close cooperation with Jan Svejnar and Kathy Terrell, colleagues on a joint project about Poland's economy during Gierek's reign. I made another major step in my research along the same lines while on a fellowship at Stanford University. My efforts gained from encouragement and comments by Ellen Comisso and Laura Tyson, who published my research results in a book collection printed by the Cornell University Press. Invaluable has also been help from Paul Marer, with whom I have worked on a number of projects, including a study of the impact of foreign debt on Poland's economic growth after Gierek (this during my brief teaching appointment at Northwestern's Economics Department). I am also much indebted to Michael Montias, whose fine art of comparative economic analysis inspired a number of my own empirical tests of Poland's economy (whose early postwar decades he examined in a seminal volume published by the Yale University Press). I benefited enormously from my many exchanges with Janos Kornai, whose work seems closest to my alternative framework for studying communist and post-communist economies. While developing this, as I call it, evolutionary, framework, I have drawn from my frequent discussions with Peter Murrell. Josef Brada has critically read a number of my drafts, since incorporated into the book. Jacek Kochanowicz has commented on parts of my manuscript, as has Stan Gomulka, always eager to pass on a valuable comment. Grzegorz Kolodko and Danuta Gotz-Kozierkiewicz have been most helpful in leading me through the vagaries of Poland's most recent economic developments. My faculty colleague at the University of Washington, Dan Chirot, and Ken Jowitt of UC-Berkeley have been helpful, particularly with regard to my forays into political issues. But, by and large, this book has involved a lonely struggle with the rapidly changing and complex picture of the Polish economy. For this I have needed a lot of persistance and peace of mind, both only possible because of the support of my wife, Joanna, who collaborated on two smaller themes touched upon in my book. And now that the book is finally finished, I hope we can go for longer walks with our brown-haired dog.

Introduction

Research agenda, conceptual model and principal findings

This book argues that the post-1970 period in Poland's economy has been characterized by the relatively slow, often inconsequential, disintegration of the planning regime and the parallel reemergence of capitalist markets. Much of this systemic transition has been brought about unintentionally by the communist leadership responding to a variety of pressures coming from a disaffected society. The mid-1989 negotiated relinquishment of political control by the communist party did not mark the end of this institutional transition, but it did accelerate it by opening additional avenues for reform. The lengthy, still unfinished, process of remaking the economic system has weakened the mechanisms of coordination and ownership structure through most of the period in question. This institutional deterioration in the dominant state (= public) sector is here found to be one of the main reasons for Poland's volatile pattern of economic development, marked, among other things, by severe crises in 1979–82 and 1989–91.

Our particular interest is in explaining the period between 1979 and 1991, when Poland's economy experienced severe imbalances, extensive aging, and no real growth. We consider this general condition one of the most intriguing features of the whole period studied and also one that distinguished Poland from the rest of the region. We call this phenomenon 'growth fatigue' to separate it from other types of economic adversities that are either cyclical or caused by external shocks (e.g., in bank credit supplies, commodity prices). Growth fatigue is defined as a combination of economic stagnation and internal instability (manifested in shortages and/or open inflation) resulting from a serious decline in economic institutions, i.e., incentive structures and information quality. It is this institutional nature of growth fatigue that accounts for its durability, because restoring systemic efficiency is typically very time-consuming.

We also argue in this book that the post-1992 economic recovery that seems to finally be taking the economy out of its growth fatigue condition, can similarly be explained in institutional terms using a conceptual model applied to analyzing the previous years. While the transition process to capitalist markets is not yet finished, there has been a major shift in the direction of this change. After years of institutional deterioration, Poland's economy has recently begun improving its institutional setting. The public sector has seen its system solidified, but far more important has been the rapid replacement of that sector with the private one. While the system has remained mixed, the private sector, with its superior set of economic rules, has become dominant, and, as such, and largely by itself, this sector was capable of lifting the economy out of the 1989–91 crisis.

With its focus on systemic factors, our analysis could be considered an exercise in institutional economics, or, given our interest in the plan-market alternative, a study in comparative economic systems. By economic system, on which such analysis concentrates, we understand here the rules by which principal agents abide in their pursuit of economic objectives. The rules can be best viewed as constitutive constraints on choices and actions taken by agents when coping with production processes, themselves subject to their own constraints – related to scarcity of physical factors. One component of rules refers to the coordination mechanism – linking individual agents – and the other to property rights, which provides the motivation matrix for those actors. The systemic rules of the game can be either formal (= impersonal) or informal (= personal), the former forming a structure and the latter representing what could be called the meaning of a given institution.

The pattern of Poland's institutional development uncovered in our case study contradicts on numerous accounts the conventional thinking on communist-type economies, in particular the prevailing paradigm offered by the so-called totalitarian school. The core ideas of this basically political theory were formulated mainly by Arendt (1968), and Friedrich and Brzezinski (1956). But our findings also seem to depart from another prevailing approach, that of the modernization school, which can be linked to the works of such political scientists as Black (1966) and Jowitt (1971, 1978) (who in his later work on what is called Leninist-extinction took a different position; Jowitt, 1992). While formulated as political theories, they have also greatly influenced economists' thinking on institutional analysis – particularly with respect to totalitarian arguments on the nature of communism.

This study, in particular, contradicts the totalitarian argument on the static nature of the communist economic system, i.e., on that system's nonreformability (which applies even more to the communist political system). Rather than finding the system unable to afford any substantive change, we show the system as slowly moving through a number of major modifications. In terms of the totalitarian paradigm, it would follow that since the communist system supposedly caused social problems to infinitely compound, its collapse had to be revolutionary in character, most likely with elements of violence, but the transfer of power in mid-1989 was orderly and peaceful. Rather then seeing some momentous change in the aftermath of that transfer, one finds the postcommunist economic system changing at a relatively slow pace, with many elements of the past still in place or just marginally altered.

Unlike the other major current in communist studies, the modernization school views the whole system – including its economic component – as dynamic and moving towards a state of normality, seen as a routinized communism (or some sort of more efficient mixed system of neither communism nor capitalism), but we offer here ample evidence that the economic system was instead deteriorating, or becoming increasingly dysfunctional, while at no point of its whole long existence representing an efficient alternative to the capitalist-type order. When extended to the postcommunist stage, this key approach does not stand up well to empirical tests either because, rather than to see further progress in moving to a normal state, the Polish economic system almost immediately experienced further degeneration, particularly in the still dominant state-owned (although now only nominally state-controlled) sector. And it is exactly this institutional deterioration that became one of the critical sources of the second – 1989–91 – economic crisis.

Our empirical findings are consistent, however, with the evolutionary approach – with its roots in economics – which views social systems as complex or living structures that are permanently undergoing change and which, indeed, exist because of change. Since the communist order falls in that category, one is not surprised with the large amount of substantive change that happened throughout the years of its existence. Within the evolutionary paradigm, any change – including this, entailing economic systems – is assumed to be an open-ended process that can either take a progressive direction or lead to a regression. This open-endedness would account not only for the installation of the state-managed system as an inferior alternative to the market-type system, but could also explain what we have discovered to be the regressive trend in system's evolution under communism, as well as the fact that in the first postcommunist years, the economy went through another loss of systemic efficiency as well.

It is not that we have taken a finished paradigm and applied it to our case study, since this approach is still very much in the making. Nor have we been able to build heavily on the existing comparative literature, because to date there has been little effort made by the economic theory of communism and postcommunism to absorb evolutionary ideas or concepts (while some of the successful applications have not explicitly referred to the paradigm). Thus, in great part, we had to develop the theoretical model for our study, and the study, in turn, provided a test of its validity. We outline that general approach to institutions in this introductory part of the book and then make various methodological statements later in the book. But we offer no exhaustive review of the evolutionary perspective and instead refer interested readers to our other recent work dealing more extensively with that subject (for instance, see Poznanski, 1995c).

Evolutionary approach

Many elements of the evolutionary approach relevant for students of the communist and postcommunist economies were formulated in the twenties and thirties, when economists such as Mises (1920) and Hayek (1935) tried to prove that the state-controlled economy is infeasible (with Lange (1935) and Dobb (1935) taking an opposite stand from neoclassical and marxist perspective respectively). This argument was grounded in a broader framework, whose original intent was to correct mainstream neoclassical (= liberal) economics rather than to confront Marxism, which claimed that the state-only (no-market) system is not only possible but also of superior efficiency and higher justice. Another key contribution to that broader body of theory came from Schumpeter (1939, 1942), though while in agreement with the main tenants of the evolutionary argument developed by Mises and Hayek, Schumpeter – not a party to the original debate – was of the view that, though inferior on both these accounts, a state-controlled system is feasible.

It should be kept in mind that while Hayek and Mises were primarily addressing the question of the feasibility of state planning as attempted by the Soviet Union, Schumpeter took a broader view. His prediction referred to various forms of state-dominated systems, i.e., that of the Soviet state-bureaucratic system, as well as the national-socialist model tried in Nazi Germany, and also the welfare state evolving at that time in Great Britain. The real focus of Schumpeter's work was the lattermost model, where, as he saw it, labour unions captured state power and used it to forward their own interests. The decline of the Soviet version partially vindicates Mises and Hayek by showing that at least in the long run, the system was not viable, while the demise of the national-socialist model does not support any of the positions, for it was caused by external factors (losing the war), and the durability – and popularity – of welfare states in the contemporary world directly supports Schumpeter's position.

The ideas outlined by these first evolutionary scholars have been expanded upon by a score of contemporary theorists including Nelson, who, among other things, has developed (in tandem with Winter, 1982), a formal model of an evolutionary enterprise, one which is assumed to be constantly searching for relevant data rather than passively using information for decisionmaking (this integrated with a macroeconomic model of evolutionary growth, where diffusion of information – technology – is a prime driving force). In this line of work, drawing mostly from Schumpeter and the organizational theorist, Simon (1947, 1957) (with little mention of either Mises or Hayek), Nelson has concentrated on the capitalist system. For a long period of time, the potential validity of that model for studying the real communist system – its state enterprises and national growth – has not been widely tested (early exceptions include Murrell's (1990b) study of foreign trade patterns, and Poznanski's (1989a) research on innovation aversion under a state-planning regime).

Evolutionary economics entered the field of comparative studies more broadly only after the collapse of the state-planned system. The main reason for this wider reception, however, has not been the application of this economic paradigm to studying communism itself, i.e, its past, but rather to analyzing its aftermath. We are referring here to the then raised main question of an optimal – in terms of both time required and costs to be incurred – path of transition from communism to capitalism. The evolutionary perspective has been employed by a group of economists arguing for a gradual programme of economic reforms, one that would rely on voluntary – spontaneous – actions taken by individual actors and against radical methods based on the forceful application of abstract, blueprint, ideas by a state committed to mass-scale and short timetable reforms (for such an evolutionary perspective, on reform see Murrell 1991, Poznanski 1992a; 1995a, Stark 1992).

But the evolutionary paradigm can also be used to examine the communist period, a good, if rare, example of such application being the work by Kornai (1990a, 1986) on the late so-called reformed communist (or, as he prefers to say, socialist) economy, where the spontaneous nature of systemic change is stressed. Such affiliations are also visible in Kornai's recent summary work on the communist system, including his redefinition of economic systems as being deeply embeded in the political structure (see Kornai 1992b). While only in this late analysis Kornai directly refers to the evolutionary framework, it might be argued that the bulk of his work on comparative systems is crafted in that economic tradition (see Poznanski 1995b). This includes his anti-equilibrium argument against neoclassical understanding of how market operates (Kornai 1971), as well as the related theory of shortage economy (Kornai 1980).

Economic institutions

To further clarify, the evolutionary theory is one that – following classical economics – considers the single individual as most central to economic analysis (rather than class, as in the anti-classical Marxist approach, or the nation/state, as in pre-classical mercantilism, for more see Poznanski 1995c). But, unlike in classical economics, the evolutionary ones does not assume that the individual is perfectly rational and thus that economic processes are totally deterministic. While in the classical formulation, individuals make choices on the basis of perfectly clear options – and opportunity costs involved – in the evolutionary approach, it is more legitimate to talk about human actions, through which much necessary information is discovered. Within the evolutionary model, an individual operates, as Hayek stresses, in an intentional rational way under conditions of incomplete information with the result that actions are only quasi-deterministic (with eventual success reflecting effort as well as luck) (Kirzner 1992).

While in the classical model, the greatest barrier to the individual pursuit of economic objectives – profits, wealth, or happiness – is a shortage of productive factors such as labour and capital, in the evolutionary approach, it is lack of full information. It follows from that above proposition that it is not so much the effective allocation of physical resources, as understood by classical economics, but rather informational efficiency that primarily concerns the evolutionary theory. When information is scarce, then the individual agent is uncertain and this uncertainty influences the valuation of alternative courses of action. Indeed, at certain levels, this uncertainty may cause the individual to entirely forego an opportunity to mobilize his productive resources for some practical use. In this sense, possessing good information – and bringing uncertainty to tolerable ranges – constitutes a more fundamental economic problem than having access to productive factors.

Evolutionary economics also assumes that most of the information is possessed by individuals and in a form that makes it often impossible to communicate (Lavoie 1985). This type of information, often called technical or tacit, cannot be properly communicated because it is not easily separable from an individual's experience and the specific conditions under which it was accumulated. Certain nuances of this private knowledge are easily lost when articulated by the source person, but these details can also be missed through improper interpretation by receptors. To be more precise, such type of idiosyncratic information can be transferred but only under very special circumstances, where intimate personal contacts are allowed to develop over an extended period of time and where frequent observation – rather than instruction – helps to reveal the contents. Consequently, the best application for such tacit-type knowledge is for individuals to use it by themselves whenever they find it appropriate.

One principal method, or instrument, for maximizing the stream of information is to build economic organizations that can be viewed as entities for processing information, or, more specifically, for both retaining useful information and finding additional information. Their principal role is to economize informational processes, a point reflected, for instance, in Nelson's definition of an enterprise as a set of so-called routines. Routines are the established rules of decisionmaking that allow members of an organization to reduce the costs of processing information for each choice faced in their daily affairs. These routines are cost-reducing since they operate as subconscious patterns of behaviour that help individual members respond to changing conditions without overloading their limited computational capabilities. As such, routines can be fairly considered the most essential organizational asset and thus the one least amenable to change as well.

While organizations are players, it is institutions, as more general unintentional arrangements, that provide the rules by which organizations play. Similar to organizations, institutions are information processing devices, and this applies as much to the capitalist system as to the communist one. As a coordinating mechanism, the capitalist system serves as a devise for processing information, or, as Hayek (1988) calls it, is a discovery process. Coordination under central planning serves same purpose of bringing information into economic decisionmaking, though here the major vehicle for relevant information is not competitive prices, as in the market economy, but bureaucratic commands (= directives). The function of the other systemic component of the capitalist economy, i.e., private property, is, in turn, to provide incentives for both searching for information as well as releasing it to other economic players, and a very similar role is played by public property in the state-controlled economy.

With this difference in informational procedures – horizontal flow under the market as opposed to vertical flows under planning – comes the difference in the cost of processing information. Similarly, with various types of property rights – private property under capitalism and public ownership under communism – comes disparity in informational costs. Since processing information is the basic function of any economic system, it follows that systemic differences can be best measured in terms of their respective information cost, and the evolutionary theory claims that the capitalist system is superior to the communist-type economy exactly in those informational terms. While the competitive market is the least costly coordination procedure since it automatically engages all players at their source, private property produces the strongest incentive to share information (as such release is a precondition for concluding any voluntary commercial contract).

Institution building

While classical economic theory does not explain how social institutions emerge, change, and decline, evolutionary economics does offer such an explanation. In fact, classical economics has no true theory of institutions at all, because they are assumed perfect, meaning that information – on producing and transacting – is complete and cost-free. Such a theory is provided by the neo-institutional approach, which builds on certain classical assumptions (including the concept of rational agent responding to resource scarcity as it is reflected in relative prices) while also assuming that economic institutions matter, since information is scarce and it costs. But only most recently has this theory moved beyond the question of the role institutions play to begin looking into their dynamics (for instance, see North 1990). Interestingly, in this attempt, the neo-institutional theory has borrowed heavily from evolutionary economics.

The central evolutionary thesis on the dynamics of institutions is that, as a rule, economic – as well as political – institutions come into existence, evolve and sometimes undergo a demise through the actions of single individuals. This assumption is thoroughly consistent, of course, with the underlying methodological individualism of the evolutionary approach. While institutions come about because of individuals acting on their initiative, they do not build institutions with well-defined and calculated end-goal or vision of their exact shape. Such complete – and optimal – vision is simply not possible because social institutions are too complex for anybody – even a group – to figure out in all details. Given this general lack of information, the whole process of institution-building proceeds in a largely unpredictable – trial and error – fashion.

For the same reason of complexity, institutions are formed at a relatively slow pace, often unnoticeable to a given generation of individual actors, and they undego transformation in the same slow manner – such changes invariably being complex as well. Altering formal arrangements is less problematic than developing a proper informal setting, in other words, laying down a structure is less complicated than establishing a proper meaning (values, expectations, and habits of those working within a formal system). While the essence of any institutional decay is the breakdown of this informal setting, it is the development of new meaning that is at the very core of any substantive institutional building. The lengthy nature, or slowness of such rebuilding relates mostly to this resistant nature of the informal aspect of any social institution.

It follows from the above characterization that any attempts to radically remake institutions are potentially destabilizing and thus costly to an economy. Such attempts are called in evolutionary economics 'constructivism', or 'radical engineering' as opposed to 'spontaneous' or 'organic' process which we described above. The essence of costructivism is an attempt at wholesale replacement of an established institution with an untested design (= project) preconceived by the state. These are dangerous attempts in part because they assume that no elements of the existing system are usable, even after adaptation – which seems impossible, since, if not useful, they would have been removed, or altered on their own prior to such a state-led institutional overhaul. And when newly introduced elements prove unworkable, it is impossible to correct the errors at low cost by falling back on just removed elements from the preexisting institution.

Since constructivist attempts by the state are highly impractical, they always are executed in a downsized – compromised – version. Deradicalization is typically the first thing that happens to radical systemic attempts, and this gives them a chance of temporary survival. Leaving in place certain workable elements from the past helps to stabilize the imposed system before it destroys itself. If the design is well-directed, then, through progressive adaptations, it can evolve into an effective economic system, but even then it won't be totally free of elements existing prior to its imposition. If, however, the project is ill-conceived, then its evolution basically means that various components of the destroyed predecessor system are systematically reinstalled, though it is not possible to recreate the past with any great accuracy. Following the logic of the evolutionary argument, one would have to argue that dismantling such an impractical system should proceed spontaneously rather than through another constructionist attempt.

Growth fatigue

Our application – and test – of the evolutionary model begins with the analysis of the 1971–75 burst of production, unmatched by almost any other East European economy, except possibly Romania, notorious for overstating its own achievements. This upturn was fuelled by a sharp increase in the share of capital outlays in the national product, with a considerable part of this investment increase paid for, however, with a large-scale foreign debt exceeding that of most countries of Eastern Europe. To gain control over the debt, Gierek, in 1976, initiated investment downsizing and wage corrections, but this policy was not able to protect the economy from a production crisis and high inflation. The crisis ravaged the economy from 1979 to 1982, so that by the end of 1982 the national product had fallen to its 1976 level. While many other East European economies registered relative production slow-downs at that time, no other suffered a similar absolute decline – not even the other large-scale borrowers.

Positive growth was resumed by Poland in 1983, but it was an anaemic recovery with little restructuring – a situation which contrasted, for instance, with the other slowly growing economy of Hungary. Investment was not revitalized enough to facilitate stronger growth combined with a fair measure of structural adjustment, nor was the government forceful enough in resetting production priorities. Inflation – after the 1982 price correction – subsided, but shortages were still pervasive, and rationing of many goods was necessary. Trade deficits were turned into surpluses, mostly by keeping imports down, while export revenues remained too low to reverse the increase in the foreign debt. Sooner or later, the economy was certain to show the effects of lack of proper adjustment, and indeed, in 1988, major macroeconomic indicators worsened. By 1989, before the economy was able to fully recover from the crisis of 1979–82, another crisis was underway, with industrial output registering a moderate fall.

In 1990, Poland's economy witnessed an even deeper decline in industrial production, which continued in 1991 and then through mid 1992 when the cumulative loss of national product was about one fifth (and industrial output down by almost a quarter). The scale of the 1989–91 economic crisis was comparable in depth to that of 1979–82, though this time it was all of Eastern Europe that suffered a slump as bad, if not worse, than Poland's. Unlike the first crisis, the 1989–91 downturn was accompanied by production restructuring, mostly because of the relatively healthy activity of the private sector. Poland's economy, however, remained deeply imbalanced, so that rates of inflation, after peaking in 1990, fell, although only to high double-digit levels which exceeded those recorded during 1983–87 (though this time, shortages were almost absent as was the phenomenon of so-called shortageflation). External imbalance worsened as well, and the outstanding debt increased, due to further accumulation of all service payments.

At the end of 1991, the combined impact of these two economic crises, separated by a period of elusive recovery, translated into the loss of more than a decade of economic growth. By then, the national product – measured in constant prices – was close to the 1976 level and, if one bases the comparison on per capita indicators, quantitative decline appears yet more drastic. In qualitative terms, this period of, as we call it here, 'growth fatigue', seems to have caused even more economic damage. With relatively limited capital expenditure in the preceding years, production in 1991 was more obsolete than in 1976, when the economy was nearing the end of a several-year investment bulge. Moreover, this economic retardation took place without resolving two serious macroeconomic problems: those of external imbalance and domestic instability.

The economy began recovering from that low point in mid-1992, though initially the growth momentum was rather timid, particularly given the depth of production losses incurred a few years before. At that time, while the state sector continued to be stagnant the private sector showed strong, though uneven, expansion, concentrated mostly in services and to a lesser degree in industry. Investment activities during this early stage of recovery were, at least in light of the official data, very modest. This indicated that substantial restructuring of production – other than through trimming the labour force and shifting among exisiting products, including phasing out some of them – was still limited in scale. The level of inflation was further declining, though price increases remained relatively high, suggesting that inflation might be a chronic illness. In part, inflation was fuelled by raising prices of the few remaining state-controlled goods, though a return to budget deficits put additional pressure on prices as well.

Only in 1994, did the economy show visible signs of moving out of the growth fatigue syndrome and assuming a path of self-sustained growth instead – signs which by 1995 were even more evident. At this stage, the recovery was mainly driven by expanding industrial production, in both the public and private sectors. For the first time, investment showed high increases, particularly in the private sphere, where, as in 1995, capital outlays almost doubled making further gains at the expense of the state sector. Helped by recent tax reforms – the simultaneous introduction of income and value-added taxes – budget deficits were prevented from widening, despite increasing budget expenditure (for bank recapitalization, delayed wage increases for public sector employees). The rate of inflation was brought down in 1995 by another few points, even though capital inflows made it more difficult for the government to control the domestic money supply.

Foreign-debt hypothesis

The standard explanation of the 1979–82 crisis and the troubles which followed it is that Gierek, having inherited economic stagnation from his predecessor and afraid of genuine reform, turned to foreign credits. The traditional economic system which under Gomulka produced stagnation by wasting domestic resources was now allowed to waste imported capital. While this capital embodied technology superior to that internally available, any advantage was cancelled out by inefficiency. When debt payments peaked, the industry lacked supplies of goods which it could sell on hard-currency markets. Poland had to default on its debt, which led first to a decline of imports and then to a loss of output. As it borrowed more extensively than the rest of the region, it also suffered a deeper crisis of production.

We find, however, no strong evidence to support an argument that there was massive misuse of imported capital. While Poland, under Gierek, did indeed dramatically increase imports through deficit financing, it also modernized its industry rapidly. This upgrading of domestic production was combined with a visible structural shift (e.g., towards durable consumer goods) which further helped to strengthen its competitive standing. Although Poland borrowed more, its economy also made much greater progress in entering these markets and earning higher unit-values than did most of Eastern Europe. Thus, according to our data, Poland seemed prepared in export terms, if not to prevent a crisis, then at least to avoid so deep a fall as in fact occurred.

Problems stemmed not so much from the deficit financing of growth as from the fact that Poland's export capacity was immobilized during the critical period of 1979–81 by massive strikes unknown to most of the other East European economies at that time. At some point involving a majority of the state enterprises, these stoppages drove production below the level to which import decline was dragging the economy on its own. Even industries not particularly dependent on imports, such as mining, experienced large output losses. These reductions in output often hurt exports, mining again being a case in point. In fact, the losses in energy exports – the main source of hard currency – happened to be particularly detrimental, as unearned income from coal sales equalled one fifth of the dollar debt payments due in 1980–81.

We also provide ample statistical evidence that, beginning in 1982, under Jaruzelski, the communist successors to Gierek, the economy again did not fully utilize the export potential created during the period of import-led growth. The debt servicing policy was intended to generate the minimum hard-currency revenues needed to avoid default, rather than maintain, or even upgrade, export potential to arrest the foreign debt. The priority was to supply goods domestically to meet consumer demand, so that exports of products not particularly sensitive to imports often did not show substantial recovery, as was the case with energy and foodstuffs. The shares of many export sales in domestic production, whether dynamic or stagnant, fell significantly, indicating economic inversion – closing – as well.

The export potential was not fully mobilized until 1990 under the impact of reforms introduced by the Mazowiecki cabinet. Even then, however, neither stimulation of exports nor servicing of foreign debt were high among governmental priorities. The government suspended payments with the acceptance of the lenders who, in a sudden change of heart, also agreed to open talks on debt reduction. Exports to hard-currency markets increased sharply, almost by one-fifth, this mostly in response to the domestic crisis that caused a sharp fall in domestic demand. Many producers also tried to redirect their trade to these markets from the rapidly shrinking regional trade centred on the Soviet economy. That the national economy was able to mount such an export surge – and relocation – spoke not only to the adaptability of state enterprises which dominated exports, but to the availability of saleable outputs as well.

The 1990 export surge subsided in 1991, and only in 1994 did the economy again engage in a rapid expansion of exports, to report another record in 1995, when foreign sales rose by more than a quarter. While in 1990–91, exports cushioned the recession, this time they seemed to be the primary driving force behind production growth. Since exports far outpaced production, the economy was able to mobilize for foreign trade more effectively than under the threat of recession, this causing a rise in currency reserves, which reached one third of annual import expenditures. A sizable debt reduction – through a Brady-type facility – made Poland's financial situation even more comfortable, and with this its credibility was regained (as reflected in the first placement of government bonds on the international market). Thus, moving out of the growth fatigue has paralleled an end to unmanageable payment problems, though the final test is still to come when larger payments are resumed after 1997.

Domestic Imbalances

Rather than seeking the economic roots of unmanageable debt solely in the wasteful importation of capital, this book stresses the distractive role of domestic imbalances. These imbalances had already emerged at the beginning of Gierek's tenure, when real wages were allowed to outstrip yearly productivity increases, causing diversion of exportables to the domestic market. The 1976 'economic manœuvre' reduced the pace of real wages, but increasingly stiffer anti-wage measures were clearly needed to fully mobilize exports. When tried in 1979, such an austerity policy provoked mass-scale strikes, which culminated first in 1980, and then again in 1981, all of this causing real wages to further outpace labour productivity than before the 'manœuvre,' so that conditions for debt stabilization worsened.

The price and wage operation executed by Jaruzelski under the shield of the 1981 martial law, helped to create domestic conditions more favourable for debt repayment. A substantial decline in real consumption allowed the economy in 1982 to produce its first trade surplus in many years – a situation which continued through 1987.

Remaining pressures on wages forced the regime, however, to rely more heavily on cuts in domestic investment than on trimming consumption. With reduced capital outlays often insufficient for replacement of retired equipment, the export capacities created under Gierek were soon allowed to deteriorate. Consequently, while experiencing short-term improvement in foreign debt servicing, the economy was less and less prepared to cope with the long term payments on its persistently increasing debts.

The period of relatively reduced domestic imbalance – and certain progress in debt stabilization – came to an end in 1988, when workers won some major wage concessions, among them a remuneration parity for industrial workers, civil servants, and farmers. Provoked by the price reforms of Messner's cabinet, the gains made by workers pushed wages far ahead of inflation, aggravating domestic shortages. The next wave of real wage increases came in early 1989, when the free unions concluded their roundtable talks with the communist party (e.g., generous indexation of nominal wages on a monthly basis). Expectedly, this relaxation of income policy was followed by drastic deterioration in the foreign trade balance (and in an alarming increase in the current account deficit).

The 1990 reforms helped to restrict real wages through regressive indexation, which only partially covered the effects of price increases in that year. This reduction in real wages – by about a quarter – marked a sharp turn in a lengthy trend, particularly given the fact that real wages were not allowed to increase by any significant measure until 1994 (though they gained in dollar terms – not an insignificant fact given the increasing trade opening and thus greater reliance on imports). That such wage losses were tolerated by the workers whose unions brought the Mazowiecki government to power might seem odd. But the unions were not indifferent or unaware, rather, it had taken them a long time to gain any major concessions, such as the removal of crude wage limits, because with great uncertainty over the future of their enterprises and stiff competition from the rapidly expanding pool of unemployed, workers were reluctant to take on any more radical measures.

To the critics of the 1990 reform programme, the wage reduction was simply too severe, since bringing inflation down could have been accomplished with less wage reduction, particularly if more prices were left under state control for a while. By releasing most of the remaining state-fixed prices in 1990, inflation was temporarily accelerated, thereby wiping out household savings. This only added unnecessarily to the decline in domestic demand and made the production contraction far worse. There is no doubt, however, that this reduction in real wages and their relative stability since greatly helped to energize exports (other positive factors being the temporary under-valuation, or greater flexibility allowed in spending foreign currency revenues). This becomes particularly obvious if one considers the fact that real wages have been relatively stable despite steady increases in labor productivity since 1992.

System reformability

Linking debt problems with domestic imbalances offers only a partial explanation, for the question arises as to why such imbalances occur in the first place. Given the critical role of systemic factors in determining the state's ability to control wages and prices, one might first consider an institutional explanation. But here we are confronted with the enigma of imbalances happening in a central planning system that was originally well equipped (better than the market system) to prevent instability (see Portes 1983). There is little doubt that prior to Gierek's leadership, this systemic design proved quite effective in holding real wages under strict control and restricting price increases. It could be, for instance, that – as the totalitarian school suggests – the system did not change but that the economy did, meaning that one and the same system, though effective at the early stage when the economy was relatively simple, became ineffective as the economy grew more complex.

Of course, this argument on systemic fixity (= rigidity) could be used for explaining issues besides the foreign debt. Presumably, leaving the economic system unchanged would not only undermine the state's control of wages and prices, but would actually make other aspects of economic life less governable as well. Following this line of reasoning, one could then argue that such a deterioration of efficiency by a frozen economic system could lead not only to domestic imbalances that made arresting the foreign debt crisis impossible but it could also cause the overall decline in growth momentum that coincided with the crisis in external debt servicing. Using our terminology, we would then have to say, or hypothesize, that the claimed lack of any substantive adjustments in the traditional economic systemic could possibly be seen as a key factor responsible for the occurrence of the growth fatigue.

But our analysis of the post-1970 evolution of the system's property structure and coordination procedures suggests that, quite to the contrary, the communist economic structure was dynamic in the evolutionary sense. It passed through its first important transformation under Gierek's regime, when an attempt was made to reform the middle level of the economic structure. It was then that the real locus of control over resources shifted from the narrow centre – under party supervision – to industrial ministries and associations. Simultaneously, the discretionary power of regional authorities over resource allocation was increased. Since this delegation of decisionmaking did not empower enterprises or localities, contemporary critics have argued that Gierek's reforms were meaningless. We claim, however, that this was a significant change in the property regime, as it involved a power transfer from a relatively unified centre to a number of generally disjointed, self-centred industrial lobbies.

The next major change in institutional structure (= order) came under Jaruzelski, in 1982, when he introduced a package of legal measures largely patterned after the 1968 Hungarian model, which is known as the 'new economic mechanism.' This reform, received with great scepticism by the opposition as another empty gesture, was critical, as it shifted the locus of power from industrial lobbies to worker collectives. Workers – acting through councils and general assemblies – became the dominant stakeholders and supervisors of enterprises. For all practical purposes, Poland's economic system assumed the shape of labour-management, representing, of course, a fundamental departure from the original Hungarian model, which gave the major say at the enterprise level to managers (a situation not altered even by the 1984 rules giving more control to the workers, since they did not make use of these rules).

Beginning with the policies of the last communist leader, prime minister Rakowski, the economic system entered into yet another major phase in institutional transformation. Critical here was a series of decisions by Rakowski in 1988 to allow privatization of public capital assets by state-enterprise managers and party apparatchiks, a form of so-called political capitalism (or corrupt market where public positions within power structure are used to acquire advantage in amassing capital for private uses). This phase represented the logical next step in a long process in which private activities were allowed to expand (including through leasing state capital and licensing of certain imports to private parties from within the political elite).

The wave of reforms executed by Rakowski's cabinet was followed by Mazowiecki's programme which envisioned even broader – and bolder – systemic changes in what was offically termed the transition to capitalism. An argument is often made by the authors of that reform package that in contrast with their stabilization measures, the systemic component – including asset privatization – mostly failed to materialize. It is true that this ambitious programme called for converting most of the state-owned enterprises into private entities within three to four years and that very few conversions took place during that period. This apparent slowness in privatization is then blamed for the 1990–91 production losses, which came as a major surprise to the reform team, for they expected only a short-lived production loss that would be more than eliminated within the first year (for instance, see Sachs 1993).

But the way we see it, the economic system under Mazowiecki's government underwent quite radical changes, including the status of the ownership structure. While it is not debatable that only a few assets were privatized in the sense of full title transfer – except for services – this does not mean that the announced intention to privatize had no impact. When assets are said to be put up for sale at some, even not precisely specified, point in time, this by itself affects the status of property rights. And in this narrow, though not practically insignificant sense, the reform steps taken by Mazowiecki's team were truly radical. One should also keep in mind that systemic reforms were not limited to reconfiguration of property rights but involved coordination procedures too. By almost full elimination of the remaining directives for state enterprises and suspension of the majority of subsidies, the government did nothing less than to radically alter the coordination mechanism in this sector, and, given its dominant weight, in the whole economy as well.

Political dynamic

Not only have reforms in the economic system during the communist rule proved possible, but so have reforms in the one-party political system, this providing an even more formidable challenge to the totalitarian argument on nonreformability (which claims that even if the communist party would reluctantly permit economic reforms, they would serve as a substitute for political change). As we demonstrate, reforms were taking place in both of these elements of the overall social system of communism, and, importantly, in relative synchronicity, or, as we would prefer to call it – in a coevolutionary way, as was the case, for instance, during the Gierek period, marked by a considerable increase in intra-party disunity. It was this inner disunity which facilitated the formation of powerful special interests, as well as of well-organized labour. The latter further benefited from the fact that Gierek, unlike his predecessor Gomulka, was ready to accommodate extra-party political forces. The reality of power rather than the ideal of communism was what mainly concerned the Gierek regime – with the power not exercised unilaterally but instead 'contracted' out with the workers.

Nor did the post-1981 period lack political reform, though the trend is not easy to follow. An intriguing aspect of martial law was that, rather than restoring the party to its previous standing, it only assured its survival in the face of increasingly militant unionism. The 'state of war' provided a mechanism for Jaruzelski to shift the power base to the state apparatus, i.e., from the cadres to the bureaucrats. Moreover, rather than remove the oppositionists, military rulers ended up only restricting their space, with the intention of bringing them into formal political channels through selective inclusion. The parallel depoliticiza-tion of the party and 'politicization' of the opposition – with the state as a mediating force – was intended to create conditions for finding a lasting solution to the all too obvious political crisis.

As a logical outcome of years of inclusion policy, Poland, before any other communist country, in 1989, entered into power-sharing negotia-tions between the communist party and anti-communist forces. Early that year, a group of mainly military and police officials – supervised by Jaruzelski – brokered a compromise between the two political forces. This peaceful retreat by the communist party – under pressure from the opposition – opened the door for further major political changes. The two sides agreed to semi-free elections and a number of other arrangements (often seen as temporary) to allow for the orderly redistribution of power. This political experiment proved successful, for, though the communist party lost the elections, the power locus was indeed transferred in an orderly fashion.

While the mid-1989 removal of the communist party from centre stage greatly helped accelerate change, the public at large has con-tinued to be politically withdrawn and suspicious of politicians – whom they judged mostly by moral criteria. Nor has the style of political discourse radically changed, with a number of the old symbols still visible. After adopting a socialist stance, the former communist party gathered one of the largest single blocs of seats in the 1991 elections, and went into the late 1993 race as the sure winner. The once reformed communist unions – a product of the 1981 state of war –

have emerged as possibly the strongest single representative of labour. With their backing, reformed communists, in alliance with a less numerous but very well-organized peasant party – also with communist period roots – formed a government led by Pawlak.

The regaining of political control by the communist-period official parties is particularly instructive, since similar 'returns to the present' (rather than to 'history', i.e., pre-communist politics, dominated by conservative forces) have taken place in many other post-communist states. In Russia, the communist party was forced out of formal existence by a decree in 1991, but it soon came back to retain control over parliament despite formidable obstacles (forceful dissolution of communist-dominated parliament, near-exclusion form the media, to name a few). In Hungary, where the communists had left a power monopoly through negotiated settlement, the 1994 return of their successors, engineered through local level vote getting, was decisive too. (Seeing this continuity throughout the region, one is better prepared to appreciate the pace of political change under communism.)

Paradoxically, in certain cases, it has been the rules established during – or right after – the negotiated transfer of power by respective communist parties that have prevented ex-communist political formations from exerting more political influence. In the case of Poland, such an obstacle has turned out to be the division of powers that gave great prerogatives to the presidency office (originally meant to secure a power share for the communist elite even if they were to lose the first open elections). The office – under Walesa – has been the single most formidable obstacle faced by the coalition, despite the very low popularity of the president himself. In Russia, to give another example, despite their control of the parliament, the ex-communist forces have had limited influence on governing, for the executive branch has been controlled by the new highly independent office of the president (which, under Yeltsin ironically, recreated the old Politburo structure).

'Real' interests

The fact that the original centrally planned system went through many intermediate forms following a rather clear pattern, would suggest that some groups or individuals could have had a hand in it for a considerable period of time. Since so much change has taken place, both within economic and political realms, this would contradict the conventional view, expressed in the past, that under the political rule of communism, there was nobody who could benefit from substantive economic reform or political change. In this static view – which can be linked to the totalitarian paradigm – party leaders were said to be most content with their power monopoly, enterprise manages with the automatic bail-outs, while the workers are seen as fully pleased with their low-pressure and secure jobs in state-owned enterprises. Similarly questionable in this light is the frequently made claim that the state, driven by theoretical interests, was solely responsible for advancing market reforms in the post-communist period, because there were no other groups who had an advantage and/or 'real' interest in rebuilding a capitalist economy (see Staniszkis 1991; for critical analysis, see Poznanski 1995d).

However, as is shown, 'real' interests can be found though at the individual – not collective – level, and not in one specific segment of society but rather throughout it. This includes the communist party, which was as much weakened by the internal disintegration caused by actions of its members as by openly hostile attacks from the political opposition. The party lost its cohesiveness in large measure because its members began putting their personal welfare ahead of the advantages of a collective hold on power. While individual actions were initially not intended to undermine the party, they ultimately had this effect and during the final stages of communism, under the pressure of a self-interested membership, growing segments of the cadres consciously engineered their party's demise.

Many in the state apparatus, including managers, contributed to the undermining of the traditional system, for much the same reasons that caused corrosion of the party. While the rigid central planning system offered job and wage security, state officials, as utility maximizers, were increasingly ready to trade these economic advantages for opportunities to better themselves financially as individuals. A rapidly growing illegal sphere – state corruption – was less a reflection of increased moral decay than of unchecked natural instincts to improve one's own wellbeing. Less and less manageable by the party, state officials found themselves in growing conflict with the cadres, as each group tried to obtain the best access to limited resources – power and wealth. Given the strategic location of the state apparatus in the political structure, their actions had to have great consequence.

The 'individualization' of the party membership and growing lack of discipline within the state apparatus were not the only factors that contributed to the expansion of the private domain or civil society.

With a gradual weakening of party–state cohesion, ordinary citizens were increasingly able to carve out private spheres for themselves as well. This was made possible mostly through informal arrangements of patronage, ignoring orders, and theft, but also through 'escape' to the second economy – often without severing all ties with state jobs. By their actions, workers, purposely or not, paralyzed the very system which was designed to protect them, and in 1990, when the mega-welfare system was about to be scrapped, they put up limited resistance even though economic reforms generally called for the surrender of much of the workers' control.

Very much the same 'real interest' – those in expanding the private domain, with adequate protection – have been the driving force behind ownership changes since 1990. The interest in privatization, as well as expansion of the private sector through entries, has continued to be strong, with spheres of disagreement among major players – now the state bureaucracy and managers and workers – centred on control of asset reallocation. Like in the past, when managers and workers struggled to gain control of their enterprises from the party, this time they engaged in taking control of divestment away from the state. The state has tried to monopolize privatization decisions in the name of a radical timetable, though in reality largely to maximize its own gains. Bottom-up pressure has derailed this effort, with managers and workers setting the pace – a slower one – for themselves as well as deciding on the particular form of divestment.

To avoid possible misunderstanding, these various manifestations of private interests should not to be seen as mainly the product of steady economic progression and a related increase in education and shift to nonmanual jobs. This is the position the modernization school would take but we feel it is not necessary to refer to these forces to explain the above described spread of self-interest. Our view is that the real interest in privacy is fundamental enough to eventually prevail even without any development (= modernization). This interest is natural to human beings, not in the sense that men are born with it, but because it serves them well, if not best. In other words, under conditions of privacy – personal freedom and property – individuals perform best, i.e., are most economical. Such interest may be supressed through some kind of collectivist myth, such as the communist idea of a perfect economy, but once its futility is realized, at any level of economic development, people soon return to their natural condition of privacy (Kolakowski 1971 and 1992).

We also argue that among the possible motives for systemic change (besides privacy) is nationalism, in this the desire to free the economy from Soviet domination. This feeling arose when, at one point, the system was discovered to be a tool of foreign control, more specifically that the system imposed on them after the war by the Soviet Union served the primary purpose of subordinating Poland economically and facilitating her exploitation (such as the alleged draining of the most valuable goods manufactured with imported technology at subsidized export prices). As a defender of that exploitative system, the communist party of Poland has been found by the public to be an accomplice to the Soviet elite, even though the party members have also grown uncomfortable with foreign dictates. Since this widespread nationalist mood can be quite properly viewed as a force of traditionalism – similar to the other powerful anticommunist current, i.e., religious revival – this would further contradict the model of communist dynamics offered by the modernization school.

Transition crisis

Having demonstrated that the economic order, as well as the political structure, has been undergoing substantive, if largely random, change under communism – and that for that reason the system should be viewed as dynamic – we cannot logically put the blame for the growth fatigue on any absence of reforms. That leaves only one reasonable explanation, which is that the poor economic condition must be somehow related to the direction – or nature – of the actual reforms. In the book, we document that, while reformable, the economic system has assumed a pathway of reforms that caused its basic elements – ownership structure and coordination procedures – to severely deteriorate during most of the period analyzed. Thus, we are not dealing here with a case of systemic crisis, as it is understood in the usual static argument on nonreformability, but rather with a crisis of reform (or even better – transition), and it is the latter, dynamic phenomenon, that should be seen as the true source of Poland's growth problems.

To capture this regressive aspect of Poland's institutional changes, one would have to recognize that in its traditional version, as under Gomulka, the centrally planned economy represented a 'strong' economic system. Not only was it internally consistent, combining public ownership with state coordination, but both these elements were 'strong'. Public ownership was reasonably well protected, given the wide acceptance of the myth of common property and the serious threat of punishment for any misuse. State coordination – through directives – was also in its strong form, since managers, supervised by local party units, were obedient, while commanding control over workers. These are the features which made the economy, in general, resistant to major fluctuations, and even more to crises marked by overproduction and unemployment.

That the economy – after a brief surge – has entered a lengthy period of 'growth fatigue' can be attributed to the fact that, since Gierek, the system has assumed a number of 'weak' versions of property structure. During the years of Gierek's leadership, workers continued to view the party/state as the guardian of national, common assets. The party/state was relatively diligent in executing its ownership function through lower level (enterprise) units, i.e. enterprise and municipal party organizations and top management, both subject to a rather strict nomenklatura system. However, while public ownership continued to be strong, coordination became weak, for the locus of power shifted in favor of special interests built around sectoral and branch ministries. Two basic instruments for managing the economy – wage limits and product targets, were greatly idled and it is this institutional change that explains, to a great degree, why the early rampant expansion occured and also why the 1979–82 production downturn and price acceleration were impossible to avert.

During the Jaruzelski/Messner period, the economic system assumed another weak version, this one far less effective than the last. State coordination further deteriorated when workers' collectives were provided by the 1981 reform programme with considerable authority over enterprises. This version of the economic system can best be viewed as a form of labour-managed system, where property is in state hands but decisions are left mostly to workers and managers of individual enterprises. Under such a model, maximization of wages is the objective function and therefore profits are sacrificed, along with expansion of capital stock. As managers became more responsive to workers' collectives and enterprise-level party units became less loyal to the central apparatus, its ability to enforce public property rights was diminished. These systemic changes could well account for the post-1983, as we call it, illusory recovery that the two governments managed to accomplish.

The next stage in the history of weak systems occurred during Rakowski's cabinet, when a further reduction in the state's coordinative functions was permitted, mostly because this cabinet lost interest in effective management of the economy. With little concern for the possible negative consequences, the government – staffed mostly with lesser known and less experienced party/state officials – executed such long resisted steps as elimination of price control for foodstuffs, reduction of subsidies to farmers, and legalization of internal currency sales. Direct intervention in production through special programmes that the Jaruzelski/Messner governments had initiated was partially suspended as well. Parallel launching of wild sales of public-sector capital and greater tolerance for private illegal uses of such capital further undermined the property structure, only adding to the disorganization that triggered both the decline in production and near-hyperinflation in 1989.

The further, more pronounced, fall in production in 1990, which lasted until mid-1992, can be viewed as the consequence of yet another wave of systemic changes, which produced possibly the weakest economic structure of all. The point that we are making is that by cutting off most of the remaining direct links with enterprises – budgetary subsidies and credit guarantees in particular – the traditional methods of coordination were marginalized, while market-type coordination was emerging too slowly to provide an effective replacement. The announcement of a rapid state-led privatization of public assets made the legal status of state-owned enterprises instantly more ambivalent, and because the actual process of divesting turned out to be ambivalent itself, this condition continued for some time. We find these changes responsible for the 1990–91 economic crisis, which, at least on paper, proved worse than that of 1979–82. Consequently, the Mazowiecki period could be considered the lowest point in the prolonged, as we prefer to call it, transition crisis.

That the economy entered a recovery in mid-1992 can also be traced to institutional change, which, this time, produced the first improvement in many years in the property and coordination structures. In the public sector, these improvements became possible only after withdrawal into a more decentralized – voluntary – formula for asset divestment. By gaining more authority over privatization of their enterprises' collectives, managers and workers, became more confident about payoffs, either in terms of securing jobs or stock acquisitions. Even more important has been the fact that the private sector – greatly, though sometimes in a perverse way, helped by the 1990 reforms – had reached a critical mass. With this, the overall property structure began rapidly shifting in favor of superior private property and more efficient market coordination, putting greater competitive pressure on producers in both sectors, private and public, and supplying them with more accurate signals (= prices) as well.

Hidden path

In our effort to establish possible patterns in Poland's institutional change, we have also found that much of that truly substantial systemic change has come about in an unintentional way, or spontaneously. This is evident even for the early stage of our analysis, the Gierek period, when the party still had rather clear ideas of where it wanted the planning system to go and when it possesed enough power to give some direction to reforms. At this point in time, the political leadership was looking for a perfect planning system and references made to the market had nothing to do with endorsing the market economy, i.e., capitalism. The market was understood in a purely instrumental way as something that the planners could use – or, better, simulate – to make their management of the economy more effective. This was very much in line with the concept of market socialism, where prices follow a supply and demand equation but are set by the state (as developed by Lange (1935) in his famous debate with the evolutionary Mises and Hayek).

It is to that effect – a desire by the state to improve the planning machinery – that sectoral ministries were given more power under the 1971 reforms, and that more use was made of aggregate – financial – instruments of control. Ministries were expected to solve their own algorithms of cost/product structure, taking into account macroeconomic requirements, and then translate them into financial targets (= parameters) for enterprises to fulfill. In reality, the whole process of economic control was in large measure taken over by narrow sectoral interests with little concern for general economic welfare and the setting of targets was turned largely into a game, in which enterprises had a clear informational advantage. As a consequence, at both levels of economic organization, ministry and enterprise, those with access to authority managed to create enough space for themselves to engage in uncontrolled actions, or, as one could say, a real (rather than simulated) market of sorts.

During the Jaruzelski/Messner leadership, there was still no desire to abandon the state-controlled system, though this time a bolder departure from the original arrangement was entertained. Inspiration was sought in the reformed model operated at that time by Hungary, where real market forces were expected to drive short-term actions, while long-term plans were left to the party/state. While the product and labour sectors were permitted to operate more freely, with managers having the greatest say in that respect, the capital sector was to remain mostly under state control. In reality, the power over short-term decisions shifted to workers, marking an important departure and another one was that while in the Hungarian original, the party/state retained many indirect, often very effective, influences, in Poland, the political leadership was much weaker – unpopular and divided – so that even greater niches of self-interested – market –exchanges emerged.

To strengthen the ailing public sector, the government also allowed more room for private activities keeping close watch on their size so that they posed no threat to state-owned enterprises. This concept was again brought in from reform-minded Hungary, where regulations were passed to encourage the formation of private businesses, including by utilization, for a fee, of idle, or partially employed, capital resting in the hands of state enterprises. But once these ideas were transplanted, it became clear that opportunities for the government to control this sphere were very limited, even more so than in the state sector. Taming private businesses by limiting their unit size, banning them from certain lines of business, or taxing them excessively turned out to be impossible. Also, contrary to expectations, rather than assist the public sector, the private sector became a parasitic companion, syphoning illegally derived – speculative – incomes as well as transferring assets to help set up private operations.

In a most serious departure form the communist reform practice, Rakowski's government engaged in further systemic changes, though erratically and without any well articulated programme. What was clear, however, is that the government was giving up the idea of any further improvement, or defence of the state-controlled system. It was ready to abandon direct controls within a short timespan but in dispensing with public property prepared for a lengthy process, in large part because nobody had a good sense of what such a divestment entailed, given both its enormous scale and lack of real historical precedents. The spirit of Mazowiecki's was not much different, for they also wanted to quickly phase out direct control, but with respect to divestment declared not only a readiness to assume a very short deadline for completion but also their preference for certain procedures – techniques – of transferring assets to private owners that would allow for a concrete model of capitalist economy to be introduced or reintroduced.

Institutional Radicalism

With this boldness and specificity – exactness of the end-vision – the attempt by Mazowiecki's reform team exhibited a number of features that evolutionary economists would categorize as constructivist. They would also expect that most of the programme would fail to materialize even if allowed to be curtailed and rearranged. And we find this to be largely true, as in the case with the expressed desire to ensure that privatization break up the extreme concentration of production. So far, divestment has not really served that purpose well, as many traditional monopolies have been recreated, as exemplified in foreign acquisitions (primarily seeking state enterprises with a dominant market position). In many cases, privatization has even helped to strengthen these preexisting production concentrations, as evidenced in the activities of many newly established – mostly with domestic capital – holdings.

This is not the only way in which the emerging capitalist system has taken on characteristics of its predecessor, another example being the formation of capital markets. The early articulated intention of post-communist reformers was to move away from discredited banks – viewed as mechanically financing projects with little oversight – and make the securities (stock and bond) market the core element of the financial sector, this following the Anglo-Saxon practice. To facilitate that course of systemic change, it was envisioned that after rapidly divesting, state enterprises would be brought directly to the secondary market. Hovever, while only small amounts of equity have entered the emerging securities market, banks have managed to modernize their operations and retain their dominant role as supplier of fresh capital (as well as deeply penetrate the securities market with their own shares and as equity holders).

Another feature from the past is that much of the fast growing private sector has remained hidden, causing the size of the second (= grey) economy to expand, possibly even to double its share in the national economy. These activites have been driven underground for the purpose of tax evasion, this leading to an unequal distribution of the tax burden across the economy (resulting, for instance, in excessive taxation of the state-owned sector already burdened with problems inherited from the communist past). By staying in the second economy, private entities also avoid the labour regulations, such as minimum wage, as well as the heavy burden of social security payments. Furthermore, keeping private activities hidden has helped some producers to bypass quality control, thus leaving consumers with inadequate protection. Not to forget, the vast scale of un- or under-reported activity has greatly complicated government's job of managing the economy.

Possibly the most striking evidence of how slow the parting with the past has been is the extensive presence of the state, still, at least nominally, remaining the owner of most of the industrial assets, though its equity positions are unevenly distributed across sectors (almost none are left, for instance, in consumer chemicals, passenger cars and power engines but the state has majority stakes in steel-making or machine-building). The state has also retained considerable ownership in recently privatized enterprises, including those that are listed on the newly created securities market (and account for about a fifth of its capitalization). Most of the financial sector, particularly the largest commercial banks, are still owned mostly by the state (= Treasury), and public ownership extends also to numerous non-financial entities that these banks control through shareholdings. But public ownership is on the decline and with the several large-scale privatization programmes underway this large equity exposure may rapidly shrink in the near future.

State control extends beyond ownership titles. It also entails various forms of direct involvement, as is the case with wages in the state-owned enterprises. Until very recently, the state continued the pre-1989 practice of controlling wage funds through the annually set indexation formula combined with progressive taxation of wage payments. This old-fashioned wage system was abandoned in 1994 for tripartite negotiations, where the state commands a clear leadership position. The same state-owned sector continues to benefit from various types of subsidization, often in the form of large-scale nonpayments (= arrears) in taxes, social security premiums or cost charges owed to the state. Another – hidden – form of subsidization is the tariffs that have been raised on a number of products up to one-half of their import price, if turnover tax and import surcharge are added (widely used import contingents, as well as licencing of production, are another avenue for state intervention in enterprises' activity).

The state has mostly withdrawn from direct allocation of capital for investment purposes, while keeping a relatively small number of projects funded from the budget (to support so-called central projects aimed mostly at infrastructure), but at the same time it has assumed a powerful role in supplying existing capital assets, this for the purpose of privatization. In this function, the state retained much of its decisiveness, though not as much as originally intended because insiders – managers and workers – proved difficult to sidestep. Consequently, the state has been in a position of great influence over both the pace and nature of divestment process. In fact, the disposal of public assets has provided the state with an opportunity to exert more impact on the economy than at the time when the last communist leaders were still channelling some quantities of fresh capital into the economy – this being one further paradox of the institutional transition.

Part I

Imperfect decentralization, broken political contracts and foreign debt crisis

1 Import-led growth policy under 'soft' planning

The Gierek period has been typically analysed from the point of view of why his economic policies ultimately failed, i.e., what specific forces were responsible for the economic crisis of 1979–82. The period of extremely rapid growth in investment combined with unprecedented gains in real consumption, lasting from 1971 through 1976, and the following years of more modest output growth and wage increases, are usually viewed as a prelude to that crisis. The most common explanation for the economic downturn is that the foreign credits which made the early expansion possible were also responsible for the crisis. Poland borrowed too much, given its absorptive capability and low overall production efficiency. The above view is examined in this opening chapter and throughout the rest of the first part of the book.

The opening of the economy by Gierek's government at the end of 1971 is viewed here as a key element in his ambitious programme of growth expansion, driven not only by a desire to upgrade the ailing national economy but also to quickly raise the standard of living. However, the strategy of active imports – and Western credits, which made them possible – does not seem to be the exclusive, or even primary, cause of the subsequent crisis. Ineffective aggregate demand (income) management – wage-rate and price policies – are identified as additional, possibly more critical, factors responsible for the onset of economic difficulties in 1976, and for Poland's inability to soften the 1979–82 collapse (with some decline in production almost unavoidable due to shocks coming from world markets) (Poznanski 1986a).

In retrospect, the policies of Gierek's government, assessed at the conclusion of his tenure as basically a failure represent an important stage in Poland's reconstruction of an open – we stress, open – market type economy. With the benefit of hindsight, we can look now at Gierek's import-led strategy not as an episode but as a possible phase in a sequence of related events. Although Gierek's decision to 'soften'

3

the planning system contributed to the ultimate failure of his ambitious growth programme, it also made it difficult, if not impossible, for Poland to restore the old-fashioned, 'hard' planning regime. While the opening of the economy resulted in an ungovernable foreign debt, it also permanently integrated the country into the world economy. It is in this way that Gierek's policies and reforms set the path for many years to come.

The import-led expansion programme of 1971

When Gierek took over as First Secretary of the Polish United Workers' Party (PUWP) at the end of 1970, Poland's industrial output was both stagnating and visibly falling behind the world technological frontier. Moreover, years of deflationary income policies had had a detrimental impact on labour productivity and work discipline. Gierek's immediate response was to establish limited corrective policies, primarily in the agricultural sector. This was followed by a set of far more radical measures which formed the foundation of the economic expansion of 1971–75. In many respects, Gierek's policies represented a bold attempt to invigorate Poland's economy through a series of interrelated measures – economic and political.

The investment programme

The outstanding feature of the new economic policy was the decision to accelerate investment through an unprecedented buildup of production capacities. By 1975, the volume of investment exceeded the 1970 level by 133 per cent. The share of investment in the national product soared to 29.0 per cent in 1975 from an average of 19.4 per cent for 1965–69 (table 1.1). This spurt was much faster than that of any other East European country at the time. In comparison, Romania, with its very aggressive growth policy, reported an increase in total investment of about 72 per cent over a similar period. Only in Hungary did the share of investment in national product approach that of Poland. Nevertheless, Hungarian investment increases were much less drastic than those of Poland[1] (with Hungary starting from relatively higher investment shares).

Gierek's decision radically to accelerate investment reflected in part his major goal of upgrading and stimulating the stagnating economy.[2] It also reflected his acquiescence to strong systemic forces, whereby industrial units – from enterprises to sectoral ministries – continually

Table 1.1 *Macroeconomic indicators, Poland, 1970–1979 (annual rates in percentage)*

	Net Material Product produced	Total output		Gross fixed investment	Share of investment in NMP utilized
		Industry	Agriculture		
	(1)	(2)	(3)	(4)	(5)
1970	5.2	8.1	2.2	4.1	20.5
1971	8.1	8.5	8.3	10.2	20.6
1972	10.6	10.4	5.4	26.7	23.3
1973	10.8	11.6	3.4	27.7	25.9
1974	10.4	12.0	−2.9	22.3	28.3
1975	9.0	11.4	−8.1	12.1	29.0
1976	6.8	9.1	2.0	−.9	27.0
1977	5.0	7.6	.2	2.7	27.1
1978	3.0	2.7	7.3	−4.0	25.9
1979	−2.3	−1.7	−5.6	−15.4	22.7

	Inflation (CPI)	Real wages	Real consumption	Productivity of	
				Labour	Capital
	(6)	(7)	(8)	(9)	(10)
1970	−	−	−	−	−
1971	−1.2	5.7	7.0	6.9	1.8
1972	.0	6.4	8.8	8.6	3.8
1973	2.6	8.7	8.6	9.0	3.0
1974	6.8	6.6	6.8	8.2	1.0
1975	3.0	8.5	11.2	8.3	−1.1
1976	4.7	3.9	8.6	7.7	−2.5
1977	4.9	2.3	6.5	5.0	−4.3
1978	8.7	−2.7	1.1	3.3	−5.3
1979	6.7	2.4	3.3	−1.5	−9.6

Source: Rocznik Statystyczny, Warsaw, GUS (various years); Government Report on the State of the Economy, 1981, Warsaw (July).

seek investment. In the past, Polish leaders succeeded in restraining the 'expansion drives' and 'investment hunger' of the industrial units by ensuring that the economy faced relatively 'hard' budget constraints (e.g., shortages of hard currency to pay for foreign equipment and limited physical capacity of the construction industry). In contrast, Gierek did not restrain the investment pressure and in fact allowed foreign financing to be used for this purpose.[3]

Acceding to administrative pressures for higher investment also permitted Gierek to obtain support among important political actors in the state bureaucracy. When Gierek assumed the post of the First Secretary, a large number of activists with strong industrial backgrounds were in fact elevated to high political positions. This group showed much less concern for balancing the budget than had previous leadership elites. Almost none of the top leaders under Gierek stood for the same fiscal restraints as did the old 'watchdogs' of balanced plans under Bierut (e.g., Minc and Szyr) or Gomulka (e.g., Jedrychowski and Jaszczuk). The major investment drive of the early 1970s had, therefore, the backing of the top leadership, the state bureaucracy, and the industrial units.

Income policy

Another important policy change was the decision to accelerate the growth of real income in the 1970s. This policy had the dual goal of placating workers and eliciting greater work effort and labour discipline. By offering a 'social compact' – that is, trading a promise of continuous wage improvement for political compliance – the party hoped to buy political stability. Theoretically, the compromise was to be the ideal solution, since higher wages would also increase worker productivity – which, of course, would be crucial for the success of Poland's drive to revitalize its fledgling economy.

During the 1966–70 period, real wages grew more slowly in Poland than elsewhere in Eastern Europe, and Gierek felt compelled by the demands of industrial workers to achieve income growth with relatively stable prices. Ironically, although the unpopular price increase which Gomulka imposed in 1970 was a prime factor in Gierek's rise to power, Gierek had initially resisted workers' demands to roll back the price increases. However, when faced with massive strikes in Lodz in February 1971, he restored the old prices and promised not to raise the price of necessities over the next few years. The 1971 decision in fact marked a turnaround in traditional labour policy, under which decisions on wages/ prices were made unilaterally by the party.

The actual increase in income levels greatly exceeded the earlier plans for rapid growth in the level of personal consumption. Between 1971 and 1975, nominal wages increased at an average of 9.6 per cent a year, or more than three times the original plan figure. The annual rate of growth of real wages was around 6.8 per cent, several times above the level permitted under Gomulka. It was also more than twice the rates in the two other East European countries that had adopted models of 'consumer socialism', East Germany and Hungary. The main mechanism for transmitting the sizeable wage increases was the unexpectedly high rate of growth in revenues of industrial associations. The other factor was the centrally instituted reforms in the wage schemes of particular trades and in the retirement system.

Gierek's willingness to allow rapid income expansion clearly differed from the behaviour of other incoming party leaders in post-war Eastern Europe. New regimes, of course, often attempted to gain popularity by temporarily allowing incomes to grow faster while allocating more resources to the consumer goods industries. For example, Gomulka followed this strategy during the 1956–57 period. However, in the case of Gierek, the decision to allow consumption to increase was (or was perceived to be) a long-term commitment, partly intentional and partly forced on him by the political leverage of the workers at the time.

The intentional aspect of the income policy reflected the new political philosophy of Gierek and his entourage. The new approach called upon the party to 'earn' its authority not through political indoctrination and threats but rather through the satisfaction of consumer preferences. Gierek had tried this approach successfully in Silesia long before his appointment as PUWP First Secretary. Under his jurisdiction, Silesia boasted both the best-supplied shops and the most disciplined workforce in the country. Hence, Gierek's wage and price policy through the mid-1970s represented an attempt at instituting a type of 'efficiency wage' economy – improving the living standard of workers in the expectation of eliciting greater work effort.

Western assistance

Unlike his predecessors, Gierek did not hesitate to open the economy to outside contacts. The principal purpose was to engage Western economies in Poland's expansion programme by increasing supplies of imported consumer goods for which society was hungry, but even more (or predominantly) by raising the share of imported capital equipment in total investment. In the short run, the economy was expected to benefit from larger consumer imports as a means of motivating labour to work more productively, while in the long run, the success of the rapid-growth strategy relied mostly on the ability of the government to channel Western imports into the capital sector (which was in great need of modern technology not available in the Soviet bloc).

There were two basic options available to the communist leadership of Gierek. The first was to increase the share of export revenues which was allocated to imports of Western machinery and equipment and increase this category of imports in absolute terms, when exports, hopefully, had expanded. But there were rather serious limits to this type of strategy, since most of the hard-currency imports were already directed to these goods (and related supplies of intermediate products). Moreover, the government could hardly expect hard-currency exports to rapidly expand in the short-run due to supply constraints (i.e., low quality of goods).

Another solution was to increase resources for imports through external borrowing. In this case, Poland would allow its imports to exceed its exports and finance the resultant trade deficits with foreign credits. These credits would then have to be paid back through additional exports created with the help of imported machinery and/ or by directing more of the existing supplies of exportables to the world market. This strategy of import-led growth was promising, provided that sufficient external funds were not only made available to the country but also were offered at a reasonable price, i.e., at a good rate of interest, and with a sufficient grace period for investment projects to be finished before payments culminate.

Gierek's government decided to choose this second option as promising faster results, even though relying on large-scale foreign credits as an engine of growth carried a higher risk. To begin with, if external financing were allowed to support domestic consumption (including a welfare programme), then the national economy could end up unprepared for debt repayment. Similarly, if imported capital were applied inefficiently, then production potential built with foreign credits would not be sufficient to pay in full the cost of borrowed money. It follows that for a credit-driven strategy to work, the economy would have to be able to resist excessive wage demands while providing strong incentives for capital users to apply imported inputs most effectively.

If foreign credits were not properly utilized, the country could find itself in a 'debt trap', where even the utmost effort to mobilize existing export potentials and to execute drastic import reductions would fail to stabilize the level of outstanding payments, far less to lower them to an acceptable size. With an insufficient trade surplus, the national economy could be forced to roll over part of its foreign debt again and again, while lenders grew increasingly reluctant to lend money and, if they opened fresh credit lines at all, would charge higher interest rates. The costs of servicing such an uncontrollable debt burden might exceed the benefit of the original foreign credits, thus making the import-led strategy counter-productive.

Geopolitical aspect

The normalization treaty negotiated with West Germany by Gomulka and signed in early 1970, helped to create a more favourable political climate for borrowing. Importantly, when Gierek assumed power in 1970, the Soviet Union was already in its fourth or fifth year of trying to gradually reduce political tensions with the Western powers. The Soviet leaders needed this improvement as their economy was in great need of modernization, which required increased supplies of advanced Western products. To maximize the benefits of such an opening, the Soviet leadership instructed its East European partners to also engage in more intense economic exchanges with the West in order to upgrade East European exports to the Soviet economy.

An important internal reason for adopting such an intense borrowing policy in Poland was that Gierek was attempting to use economic ties with the West to emancipate himself somewhat from Soviet control. Unlike many leaders in Eastern Europe, Gierek had not been mandated by the Soviet Union but rather had been internally elected by the Polish party. His ability to build a strong domestic base enabled him to pursue a more independent political line, freer of Soviet interference. Such a shift had the advantage of appealing to the traditionally strong nationalist currents within the Polish party. Increased political independence was also helpful in building broad support with the public, which exhibited strong anti-Soviet feelings.

The above features of Poland's political scene made the country particularly attractive to Western governments seeking ways to weaken Soviet control over Eastern Europe, but, economically, Poland appealed to the West as well. With the largest single East European market, Poland seemed most suitable to Western investors, and her strong sympathy for Western culture – and its consumption pattern – was seen as a positive factor as well. The extensive presence of private activities, basically in the agricultural sector, made Poland far more desirable than most of the other East European economies. Poland also had an advantage in possessing minerals and fuels sought after by manufacturing industries in the Western world. With large deposits of sulphur, copper, and coal, Poland could be expected to readily mobilize hard-currency revenues if its trade balance got out of control.

Gierek's interest in opening up the Polish economy coincided with the effort by Western countries to stimulate the sale of their products in Eastern Europe and the Soviet Union. Consequently, Western countries adopted a policy of liberalizing restrictions on the transfer of technology while providing generous credits.[4] These efforts of Western countries intensified after the 1973 oil price shock as the search for export markets increased and the need to recycle petrodollars emerged. Neither oil countries nor Western economies were in a position to absorb the excess money supply, so that credits were made available to others on attractive conditions (see Tyson 1985).

The Polish government took full advantage of these external opportunities. Whereas Poland showed a positive balance of trade with Western countries in 1971, a year later, it incurred large trade deficits: the largest increase in its deficit occurred in 1973, reflecting the sudden increase in the accessibility of Western credits. The gross debt to the West increased rapidly from a manageable 1.1 billion dollars in 1971 to an already worrisome 8.4 billion dollars in 1975 (and then to a crisis-genic 23.7 billion dollars in 1979). Although similar strategies of deficit financed growth acceleration were adopted by other East European countries (and to a lesser extent in the Soviet Union), none except for Hungary and Romania pursued foreign borrowing as aggressively and as early as Poland.

Technology switch

These developments in the external sector were accompanied by a sharp increase of technology imports from the West, particularly from Western Europe. Polish imports of Western technology resumed in 1958, intensified around 1965, and then experienced their most rapid acceleration in 1971. This surge in technology imports from Western economies is well reflected in licence statistics, showing that Poland purchased mostly from Western sources about eleven licences annually between 1958 and 1964, approximately twenty-two licences a year during the 1965–70 period, and an average of forty-four between 1971 and 1976.[5] The peak occurred in 1974, when fifty-seven contracts were signed (see table 1.2). Between 1972 and 1978, the total royalty payments on licences virtually tripled from $28 million to $81 million.

A similar pattern can be observed in many other Eastern European countries, although the data are too fragmentary to allow a precise comparison.[6] In Hungary, as in Poland, the number of all (not only Western) licence agreements tripled in the seventies (from eighteen per annum in 1970 to around sixty-two during 1975–77). In Czechoslovakia, imports of licences increased significantly in the late seventies as compared to the first half of the decade (i.e., an average of thirty-six contracts in 1970–74 against fifty-six agreements signed annually during 1975–79). However, the Czechoslovak figures for the late seventies exceeded only by one fourth those for the last few years of the sixties (an average of forty-three contracts in 1966–69). In contrast, no significant upturn in East German licence imports took place in the 1970s.

In the late 1960s, Poland was one of the least active East European countries in terms of attracting (being granted) Western patents. With an average of 350 patents granted in 1967–69, Poland was well behind East Germany with 1,245 patents, Czechoslovakia with 737, and Hungary with 513. With the acceleration that took place in the 1970s, Poland reduced its gap with the leaders as the cumulative number of patents granted to Poland in 1973–78 amounted to 8,318, which was still less than that granted to East Germany (12,660 patents), though very close to Czechoslovakia (9,104 patents), and more than Hungary (5,462 patents). However, even during this period of acceleration, the number of Western patents per capita was lower in Poland than in the other three countries (though above that reported by Romania).

Almost simultaneously with the aforementioned acceleration of licence agreements in 1971, Poland began to expand rapidly its purchases of Western machinery and equipment, a major source of embodied foreign technology.[7] In fact, a large fraction of the machinery and equipment imports was needed to implement the acquired licences.[8] This acceleration is reflected in the statistics on Polish imports of machinery and transport equipment (SITC7) from the OECD countries, and in the data on purchases of specialized machinery and metalworking machinery (SITC7.2 and SITC7.3) (see appendix 1). The latter may be considered more accurate since they represent active capital – unlike some other product categories which are broadly classified as machinery and transport equipment.

During the 1970–75 period, Poland increased its imports of specialized and metalworking machinery from the OECD countries by 760 per cent, which is more than double the 288 per cent increase in similar imports for all of Eastern Europe. Second to Poland was Bulgaria with 503 per cent, followed by Hungary with 288 per cent. East Germany was at the bottom with an increase of 157 per cent. With this very rapid expansion, Poland quickly became the major recipient of this type of OECD machinery. Whereas Poland accounted for about 20.2 per cent of all specialized and metal working machinery bought by Eastern Europe in 1970, its share increased to 44.8 per cent in 1975. Czechoslovakia, the leading importer in 1970 with a 27.4 per cent share, accounted for only 16.8 per cent of 1975 imports.

Economic reforms

Systemic reforms were to be the final element that would help to achieve the full potential benefit of the large-scale investment programmes, the modified labour policies, and the technological modernization aided by Western capital. Gierek's regime also turned to economic reforms as part of its commitment to remove the bureaucratic barriers which were widely criticized by workers, state officials, and even the party itself. His expansion programme therefore perceived the systemic reforms as a means of strengthening incentives for improving productive and allocative efficiency, as well as buying broad political support. By 1972, a broad package of systemic changes in the economy had been developed and, in 1973, consecutive parts of industry began adopting the recommended changes. Given the enormous magnitude of existing systemic inefficiencies, the package of reforms launched by Gierek seemed relatively limited but were of substance anyway.

The actual modifications consisted of important organizational changes, namely the amalgamation of enterprises into product-based associations and their conversion into 'accounting units' with greater authority over labour, investment, and production decisions. Not only were price controls loosened (e.g., by allowing managers freely to set prices for new products), but wage regulations were also modified, giving managers more discretion in this respect (e.g. in term of intra-enterprise wage differentiation). The government hence greatly consolidated the industrial structure but failed either to introduce foreign competition or to strengthen supervision of associations by their respective ministries. The new associations (officially also called 'large economic organizations') therefore provided managers with increased opportunities to exploit the potential for monopolistic practices. All these new measures were aimed at reaping the benefits of a market economy, but in practice they introduced strong monopolistic tendencies and weakened incentives for efficiency. Politically, however, the greater power of the industrial associations provided significant momentum for the expansionary drive of Gierek's political leadership.

The reform package in agriculture constituted a bold attempt but, as in industry, the economic underpinnings were questionable. Polish agriculture had been dominated by small private farms, and the Gierek regime initially pursued policies aimed at improving the performance of these farms. However, in 1972, the government shifted to a different development strategy which gave preference to the state sector and the concept of large specialized state-owned farms. This strategy mirrored the earlier concentration of agricultural activities attempted elsewhere in the Soviet bloc and of course, paralleled the ongoing reforms in Polish industry. The declared economic rationale for the strategy was the desire for cost-rationalization and rapid modernization of agricultural production.

These reforms did not bring a genuine market to either industry or agriculture, but this does not mean that no important institutional changes took place. There was a partial delegation of central authority which stopped at the lower level of central bureaucracy, i.e., the sectoral, or branch, ministries and their industrial associations (or agricultural combinates). At least initially, the lobbies operating at this middle level also gained considerable authority at the expense of individual enterprises (or farms). The reverse pyramid was turned into a trapezoid decision-making structure with some important practical implications which were difficult to appreciate at the time. It was a significant change because it meant that power shifted greatly from the upper-level bureaucracy – naturally concerned for macroeconomic balances – to lobbies pursuing their particular interests.

The new systemic arrangement could be described as 'soft' planning to contrast it with the 'hard' planning of the Gomulka period (Montias 1962), but even more with that of his Stalinist predecessor, Bierut (and Ochab as an interim figure). 'Soft' planning is not a system of central plans that are frequently changed, since that is a reality of any plan-based economy. It is not a system under which plans are subject to bargaining between the central organs and subordinate enterprises, since such 'trading' is likewise a reality of any planning. A 'soft' plan is rather one where central planners are the weaker side in the conflict over targets, so that changes in those figures are imposed on them rather than reflective of their own preferences for allocating public assets and distributing gains from their application.[9]

The economic adjustment of 1976–79

Judging by the economic results since 1971, the above mentioned 'softening' of the economic system did not prevent the economy from taking off with the help of imports. The unquestionably unprecedented surge in output (almost 9.8 per cent average annual rate of increase in 1971–75, see table 1.1) did not, however, outlast the first world oil-price shock and the resulting recession in the West, both of which started to affect Poland around 1975. From 1979 on, external shocks in the world market included a sharp recovery of the dollar value against other major currencies, this combined with an increase in real interest rates from a mostly negative level before 1980 to a high level thereafter (about 15–20 per cent). At the same time, energy prices rose sharply again while dollar prices of many export products declined, which increased the cost of servicing debts as well.

Debt immediately became the principal economic short-term problem, or threat, faced by the government (with potentially devastating long-term consequences). Many observers have argued that Gierek's response to the increasing danger of default on foreign debt was not to put a halt on foreign borrowing but rather to continue his expansionist programme with the help of increased flows of Western credit. However, a careful look at the actual record shows that such an assessment is far from accurate, since the policies adopted in 1976 (the so-called 'economic manoeuvre') entailed significant structural adjustments aimed at putting external imbalance under control, and thus avoiding a 'hard' landing. This policy package was a clear sign that Gierek's government continued to actively respond to changing economic conditions rather than to be simply driven by events.

The investment slowdown

Bringing the foreign debt under better control necessitated the curtailment of investment projects – particularly those using hard currency – as well as some scaling down of investment outlays to relax the extreme demand on the strained domestic construction capabilities. To that effect, the government introduced several measures, most of which called for the reduction of power by the mammoth industrial associations and their respective ministries responsible for investment decisions. The government responded by returning to the highly centralized system of the past and by taking steps typical of the overheating phase in the investment cycle (more on the nature of that cycle, Bauer, 1978; Ickes 1986). Thus, most of the investment funds that were previously retained at the lower levels – associations – were to be frozen, and unplanned investment projects were to be put under more severe scrutiny by the central agencies.

Executing this investment adjustment depended heavily on the government's ability to circumvent the entrenched special interests – who had developed considerable skill in sabotaging central directives. Industrial lobbies learned how to use political pressure to soften or even reverse decisions made by the government, and how to conceal large-scale activities from the centre. Another complicating factor was that there was not enough information – nor enough processing capabilities – for the central agencies to develop a clear picture of the cumulative results of downsizing or delaying projects already scheduled for full execution. There was thus a risk that too sharp a decline in capital expansion would produce a negative multiplier effect on output that would outweigh any gains for debt repayment from lowered investment (allowing for diversion of goods to foreign markets).

Central intentions were articulated in the 1976–80 national plan, which called for cutting the average annual rate of growth in investment to less than half of that reported in the five previous years. The actual trimming of investment outlays was even more pronounced than expected, with the nominal level of expenditure on gross fixed investment brought to a virtual halt. The annual rate of investment growth was greatly reduced already in 1975 when it fell to 12.1 per cent from 22.3 per cent in 1974; then in 1976, the first year of the 'economic manoeuvre', the level of gross fixed investment was frozen by the government with a negative 0.9 per cent rate reported (table 1.1). In 1977, investment activity picked up, but only by a small margin – 2.7 per cent – to register another decline in absolute volume in 1978 of 4.0 per cent. This adjustment helped to bring the share of investment in the national product from 29.0 per cent in 1975 to 25.9 per cent in 1978.

With all the brakes imposed by the Gierek government, the very high absolute level of investment activity was allowed to continue anyway. This fact has been taken by some economists as evidence that the government was not really in control anymore, while in reality the slowdown achieved during 1975–78 was quite a remarkable accomplishment given the enormous investment momentum of the preceding years and the amount of capital resources needed to finish ongoing projects. It was also commendable if one considers the behaviour of many other leaders in Eastern Europe facing debt problems, while threatened with less risk of internal instability. With the possible exception of Bulgaria, other countries in the region maintained heavy investment patterns, with Hungary reporting an average investment growth rate of 8 per cent throughout 1976–78 (not much different from that experienced in the few years before).[10]

Wage and price policy

Restoring general balance in the economy also required curtailing domestic consumption, especially that of Western goods and those domestic products which relied mainly on imported inputs (e.g., animal feed for meat production). Since worker resentment of price increases was well established, the regime tried to achieve as much as possible through its traditional stabilization measures, namely, reducing increases in nominal wages. The 'economic manoeuvre' programme for recentralization of control initiated in 1976 (and completed in 1977) was intended to aid the government in enforcing this more restrictive wage policy at the enterprise level. The response by workers was strongly negative, since they had become accustomed to substantial annual gains in wages.

At this time workers were probably less concerned about falling into poverty than about protecting their newly acquired higher standard of living. With substantial wage increases, it was difficult for the government to balance the critical (in political terms) market for food. While prices of foodstuffs were increasing less rapidly than the inflation rate, consumers continued to spend a disproportionately large part of their incomes on these goods. This bias in consumption reflected more than mere consumer preference, i.e., high income elasticity of foodstuffs. It was also related to the fact that food substitutes (i.e., durable goods), while greatly increased under the Gierek regime, were still not available in sufficient quantities to meet demand (for more, see Podkaminer 1988).[11]

To cope with these sharp imbalances, across-the-board increases in food prices were announced in mid-1976. Strikes broke out instantly in several old industrial centres, including Ursus and Radom. These protests forced Gierek's government to rescind the new price increases.[12] Industrial unrest did not cease with the price rollback; as many as several hundred strikes took place in 1976–79. As the regime preferred using corporatist measures to using the police force, factory workers were able, in most cases, to win substantial wage increases. In this, the 1976 confrontation between the party and the workers resembled the techniques applied by Gierek's regime to address labour grievances in 1970 (providing further evidence that the communist party had lost its ability to control such a critical economic variable as wages).[13]

As a result of this retreat by the party leadership, nominal wages continued to grow at a hefty rate of 8 per cent in 1976–77, well above the rate of increase in labour productivity and growth in supplies of consumer goods. This imbalance threatened the economy with further aggravation of shortages – under these circumstances, the regime resorted to more aggressive hidden price increases, which, in combination with official price increases, proved effectual. The cost of living index rose by 6.0 per cent on an annual basis between 1976 and 1979, almost three times the 1971–75 rate. The regime succeeded in bringing the rate of growth of real wages to 1.3 per cent a year during 1976–79,[14] far below the rates for 1971–75.[15]

Agricultural difficulties

For successful debt management, it was essential that the government increased its efforts to reap gains from the investment made in the agricultural sector. The government of Gierek made resource allocations to agriculture one of the highest priorities of its overall growth strategy. This commitment to farming was reflected, among other things, in an increase in the number of tractors in use – from 250 per thousand hectares to about 450 units during 1970–75 (with an estimated 20 per cent of the tractor stock idle due to lack of parts and poor maintenance). The use of fertilizers per hectare increased from 124 kilos in 1970 to 183 kilos in 1975, and similarly substantial gains were made in the application of pesticides.

Great concern for upgrading agriculture was also reflected in the diversion of a large portion of Western credit lines to support agriculture. It is estimated that grain and animal feed imports alone absorbed almost one-quarter of Western money borrowed through 1976. By that year Poland imported 6.1 million tons of grain (of which 5.7 million tons were from Western sources), up from 2.5 million tons (of which 1.3 million were purchased for dollars) in 1970.[16] In addition, a considerable amount of credit was spent on expanding the underdeveloped base for processing agricultural products, including the purchase of a number of meat-processing factories and the building of new fertilizer plants. The major purpose of these huge imports was to stimulate meat production, with domestic farms largely being turned into centres for processing foreign inputs into final – including export – goods.

This acceleration in input supplies resulted in strong growth in the farming sector during 1971–73, but then in 1974–75 Poland experienced severe output declines, with grain and meat production falling simultaneously (see table 1.1). The overall disappointing performance could not be squarely attributed to natural adversities, unquestionably periodically present, as during 1974–75. The reason a sizeable inflow of resources to farming did not produce commensurate results can rather be found in unfavourable policies towards the dominant system of private farming, including the policy of providing imported grain mostly to state and cooperative farms. Private farm sale prices were kept too low to fully mobilize resources from individual farmers (in contrast to the heavily subsidized nonprivate farms). The costs of such a policy had to be considerable, given that nonprivate farms experienced only one-half the productivity achieved by private farmers.[17]

In 1977, the government attempted to revitalize private farming by reversing some of its earlier policies. The new measures included the simplification of procedures for the purchasing of land,[18] and introduction of incentives aimed at reducing the outmigration of young people from the countryside – which resulted in a decline of labour input in the whole sector by about 28 per cent between 1970 and 1978.[19] These instruments were accompanied by an increase in prices for slaughter animals and other price revisions which restored profitability to private farming.[20] However, yielding to pressures from the collective farming lobby, Gierek continued to allocate most of the crucial inputs (including Western grain) to the less efficient public sector.[21]

With these half-hearted steps, the output of agricultural products grew only insignificantly during 1977–79. While animal production increased somewhat, grain output did not change, so that the pressure on imports continued to mount. By 1979, grain imports reached their highest level, i.e., 7.2 million tons (with 6.5 millions coming from hardcurrency markets). Moreover, meat supplies proved insufficient in view of rising domestic demand, thus forcing the government for the first time to allocate hard currency for sizeable imports of meat. These additional demands on imports emerged exactly at the moment when the economy more than ever needed savings in hard-currency purchases. In fact, one could call the outcome in agriculture a major failure in the rather carefully engineered adjustment programme to arrest the foreign debt.

Energy conservation

The threat of debt overextension and related defaults on payments forced the regime to consider serious energy conservation measures as well. Firstly, the government had to check the expanding costs of oil imports which were fuelled by a combination of the post-1973 price increases and the sudden increase in domestic demand. This price shock was a more urgent problem for Poland than for the other East European countries because at the time of the first oil-price shock, Poland had been importing, for hard currency, 2.5 million tons of oil annually. This was an amount close to the total dollar oil imports for the rest of Eastern Europe (excluding Romania). Secondly, the regime needed to slow down domestic consumption of coal so as to increase its exports, since coal was traditionally a major source of hard currency.

Portes (1981) and a few other economists have argued that the impact of rising oil prices would have been less severe had the Gierek regime invested less in energy-intensive projects. This is undoubtedly true, since import-led expansion was heavily concentrated on production requiring a relatively high use of energy (such as steel products). It should be noted that some other countries of this region also invested heavily in energy-intensive steel projects. For instance, while investment in steel production quintupled in Poland between 1970 and 1975, Romania also doubled its capital outlays in steel over that period; Czechoslovakia followed a similar path to Poland and Romania, despite a modest overall expansion of its industrial sector.

To save on energy, the Gierek regime sharply raised prices paid by enterprises for fuels and electricity in 1975 and again in 1976. However, due to the general cost insensitivity of enterprises under bureaucratic planning, these price adjustments did not appear to generate major savings. More effective measures were undertaken shortly thereafter, including placing direct restrictions on supplies to industrial users. In addition, Gierek's regime curtailed production levels in several fuel-intensive sectors, including petrochemicals. Some semi-finished projects in that category were simply terminated and others were postponed without firm commitment to resume them – another expression of government resolve.[22]

All these measures helped Poland reduce its imports of fuel in quantitative terms and thus the relative size of the energy bill. The last absolute increase in the quantity of imported oil/gas occurred in 1976, whereas most of Eastern Europe continued to increase its oil imports for several years.[23] However, due to rising oil prices on both the world and Soviet markets, import payments continued to increase (a trend mitigated by the fact that Soviet prices were corrected upward with a time-lag compared to those in the world). With only a modest expansion of hard coal exports, Poland was increasingly unable to cover its oil import expenditures with coal export receipts. As official data indicates, Poland became a net importer of fuels in 1979 for the first time since World War II.

Foreign trade

In order to further stabilize Poland's escalating foreign debt, the Gierek regime also launched a series of general measures in the late 1970s aimed directly at both export promotion and import reduction. The essence of the policy of restoring balanced trade was a return to the pre-1973 detailed plan targets, combined with separate accounts of export transactions and bonuses (for volume increases and higher efficiency as well). While this move may have seemed regressive, one should keep in mind that extraordinary stresses often call for less subtle, more direct, measures. Given the powers acquired by special interests, with their lack of concern for the general equilibrium, reintroducing such authoritative measures seemed quite rational.

This policy change did not produce any sizable acceleration in exports to hard currency markets, but curtailing dollar imports grow proved much more successful. In current prices (= dollars) exports rose by 42 per cent during 1976–9 (from 4.3 to 6.1 billion dollars) and imports went up by 17 per cent in those years (from 7.0 to 8.2 billion dollars).[24] In constant prices exports grew by much less, while imports apparently registered a real decline (mostly due to the sizable import cuts executed in 1976–7, see table 4.1). It must be stressed that none of the East European economies embarked as early in the decade on such deep trimming of imports from the West, even those with already critically high debts (e.g. Hungary[25]).

Even with these import cuts, which were considered by some economists excessive (see for example, Fink 1983), Poland merely succeeded in reducing its trade deficit with Western economies rather than in producing the surplus needed for debt reduction. Debt service payments were mounting at the same time Poland's gross foreign debt owed to Western countries jumped from 8.4 billion dollars in 1975 to 23.7 billion dollars in 1979 (see table 1.2). This was the single largest debt accumulated by any country of Eastern Europe, which, while striking in absolute terms, was not an exceptional rate of debt accumulation by East European standards. (The Hungarian debt, for example, tripled from 2.1 to 7.3 billion dollars in 1976–79; see Tyson 1984.)

In its effort to mobilize exports, Poland was helped by the fact that its investment policy enabled it to supplement a number of traditional exports with more sophisticated products (e.g., cars and trucks, consumer electronics, construction machinery), while at the same time purposely reducing expansion of some of the less promising product areas, including a large part of the machine tool building sector. With this supply-side adjustment, Poland's sales of manufactured goods to Western markets, as documented in the following chapter, grew more rapidly than those of most other East European countries and, except for Hungary, Poland received higher prices than the other East European countries.

A primary impediment to full-fledged export expansion to Western countries was the strong and largely unchecked domestic demand for commodities embodying the latest Western technology, which the Gierek government wanted to use for export promotion to the West. These goods were most desirable for the highly competitive Western markets, but for the same reason were highly sought after at home. As a consequence, an extensive 'black market' for many of these products developed, with prices often double those set by the state administration. Such goods were distributed, through special certificates, in large quantities by the government as a form of inducement. If this domestic demand had been more aggressively restrained, exports to Western markets would have been much higher than the actual levels and thus more adequate to the country's debt-servicing needs.

Technology inflows

The intensive importation of disembodied technology by Poland did not last beyond the beginning of Gierek's economic adjustment in investment in 1976. By the time Poland entered into crisis in 1979, only twelve agreements had been signed (all with Western countries). In 1980, another six licence contracts were signed, concluding negotiations started in the preceding years. In the following five years,

Table 1.2 *Hard currency trade and debt, 1970–1979 (in billion dollars)*

	Exports	Imports	Trade balance	Gross debt	Hard currency reserves
	(1)	(2)	(3)	(4)	(5)
1970	1.1	1.0	.1	1.2	.3
1971	1.3	1.1	.2	1.1	.4
1972	1.6	1.8	−.2	1.2	.4
1973	2.3	3.6	−1.3	2.6	.6
1974	3.5	5.6	−2.1	5.2	.5
1975	4.1	6.9	−2.8	8.4	.6
1976	4.3	7.0	−2.7	12.1	.8
1977	4.7	6.6	−1.9	14.9	.4
1978	5.3	7.4	−2.1	18.6	.8
1979	6.1	8.2	−2.1	23.7	.6

	Cumulative number of licenses		License-based output (percentage of total)		Number of patents granted
	Purchased	Applied	Output	Exports	
	(6)	(7)	(8)	(9)	(10)
1970	142	112	2.1	5.3	321
1971	154	106	1.9	4.4	461
1972	194	114	2.0	4.2	573
1973	245	141	2.7	5.1	331
1974	286	182	3.4	5.3	775
1975	343	216	4.2	4.6	2843
1976	385	238	4.4	4.6	2070
1977	379	257	4.7	5.5	1301
1978	367	270	4.6	5.3	998
1979	344	268	4.8	4.8	–

Sources: (1)–(5) *Economic Bulletin for Europe* (ECE), vol. 43 (1987), New York–ECE, United Nations (p. 125). (6)–(10) *Rocznik Statystyczny*, Warsaw, GUS (various years).

practically no licences were acquired. Payments for remaining licence contracts dropped to an estimated 2.0 million dollars in 1983, and have further declined in the years that followed.[26] To fully appreciate the scale of this decline, it should be stressed that the 1983 figures on licence agreements and payments were already below the low 1973 level.

Some other East European countries also experienced a reduction in licence imports, although not of the same magnitude. To take one example, Czechoslovakia, despite its easily manageable foreign debt, clearly cut down on licence imports after 1979. During 1979–81, the cumulative number of licences in operation dropped from 470 to 403, or by about 15 per cent. Even more drastic was the decline in licence payments, from 66.8 million dollars in 1978 to 27.5 million dollars in 1981, a 60 per cent drop. In contrast, Hungary, with a very high indebtedness, continued its extensive involvement, with the total number of agreements climbing from 379 in 1979 to 519 in 1983, while licence payments in domestic currency showed no signs of decline.[27]

From 1976 to the end of 1978, Poland's imports of specialized and metalworking machines stabilized and then started to decline in nominal terms in 1979, reaching a low around 1982. This downturn – very much like the earlier upturn of 1971 – was quite radical by East European standards. Thus, while Polish imports at current prices declined by 32 per cent between 1976 and 1980, purchases by East Germany increased by 200 per cent, and imports by Hungary and Romania increased by 86 per cent and 45 per cent, respectively. Consequently, Poland's share of total East European imports fell to 26.7 per cent in 1980 (close to that of 24.3 per cent registered by Romania).

In sum, the 'economic manoeuvre' of 1976–79, which aimed at slowing down the pace of consumption while cutting investments, resulted first in a slower rate of economic activity and then in a sudden decline in national product in 1979. In the process, the Gierek regime succeeded in reducing the size of the trade deficit with Western countries, an effort greatly aided by modernization of production based on imported capital. All these steps clearly contributed towards the stabilization of Poland's rapidly increasing foreign debt and reduction of the economic backlash from possible future nonpayments. While pursuing this manoeuvre, however, Gierek paid a political price in terms of growing intra-party opposition and a loss of popularity with the workers and other social groups (Ekiert, 1991).

The prolonged economic crisis

The year 1979 marked the beginning of a yet more difficult period. Debt service payments were rising due to the maturation of debt obligations, and the economy had to start coping with the second oil-price shock. In order to raise money for its debt payments, Poland's government had to introduce more drastic measures than had been applied previously. A viable solution appeared to consist of further cuts in the absolute size of investment, a temporary freeze on consumption, and fresh supplies of foreign credits. However, for this economic package to succeed, the regime needed internal political stability and continued good relations with foreign economic partners, particularly Western creditors – private banks and government agencies.

When Gierek moved ahead with an austerity plan in mid-1980, it became clear that neither of these two requirements would be met. Domestic political disturbances erupted, accompanied by a worsening of foreign political relations – the two developments closely related, for the confrontation between the leaders and the workers triggered a confrontation between the superpowers. Declining cohesion of the party/state leadership and the growing restlessness of the population dramatically reduced his it capacity to manage the inevitable economic crisis. As a result, instead of enduring a few lean years which would have been needed to solve its financial problem, Poland ended up in an extended economic crisis and even deeper financial difficulties. As we will show presently, the intimate correlation of political and economic forces, which used to produce positive synergy, this time 'cooperated' in a negative way.

Lack of control

Many economists have argued that the downturn in Poland's national product by 2.3 per cent in 1979 marked the beginning of an extended period of decline in the basic economic indicators. But the truth is that in the first half of 1980 the economy showed a sharp recovery (marked by a 9 per cent rate of growth in real industrial output). As it turned out, this strong growth could not be sustained because of the damage to food production from widespread spring floods, the worst ever reported in the postwar years. Still, the related losses were not severe enough to produce by themselves a negative rate of growth for the whole of 1980, as other powerful forces were also at work outside of agriculture (see: Kemme 1982; Kemme and Crane 1983).

The final result of this early 1980 recovery depended to a large degree on the regime's ability to curtail real wages, particularly given the expected decline in domestic supplies of food. After an extensive 'demobilization campaign', which presented to the people a gloomy picture of the economy, the regime raised the prices of all basic consumer goods in July 1980. As usual on such occasions, the communist regime promised financial compensations, particularly for low-income groups (including pensioners). However, the move was met with widespread domestic disturbances which caused major short-term output losses and thus undermined the austerity programme. With the compensation actually won by the workers, the rate of growth of real wages was 3.9 per cent in 1980, causing further damage to the plan for economic recovery.

More importantly, the wave of strikes against price increases – and in defence of real wages – gave birth to free (as opposed to official, party-controlled) trade unions, whose power greatly reduced the regime's ability to pursue any further austerity measures. The result was the overthrow of Gierek in 1980 through intra-party manoeuvres, not necessarily by his opponents alone. Gierek's successor, Kania, formerly a member of the Gierek cabinet, tried to hold back real wages through a high rate of inflation. However, the workers, with their new representatives, proved powerful enough to push for wage increases that more than kept pace with price escalation. Thus, in 1981 real wages grew again, this time by 2.3 per cent, as the cost of living increased by 21.2 per cent and nominal wages, as a result of strike threats, by 23.5 per cent (Curry 1980; Touraine et al. 1989).

The strike activity may have also resulted in a long-term downward shift in the production level, because the workers won the right to a shorter (five day) work week. Whereas neither strikes nor this shortening of the workweek had any impact on production in many sectors of the economy, the losses in output in some other sectors were significant. The most critical losses occurred in coal production, a major source of convertible foreign exchange.[28] Coal output dropped by 4 per cent in 1980, and then again by 15 per cent in 1981. The estimated loss of hard currency revenues from the loss of coal output during these two critical years was around 1.8 billion dollars annually, which was close to 15–20 per cent of Poland's debt service obligations to Western countries.[29]

The credit squeeze

Both the uncontrollable wage pressures and the production chaos had a chilling effect on Western creditors, afraid that, with such severe economic imbalances, Poland could not be helped much by fresh money. In early 1980, Poland still had available credits totaling 1.2 billion dollars. The critical change came in 1981, when Western banks started to panic and suddenly withdrew their short-term credit, and the same moves were taken by the East European countries shortly thereafter – even those with reasonable financial exposure. Western governments tried to come up with countervailing assistance, providing around 1.4 billion dollars. But with the large repayments to the Western banks, Poland received only a net of 200 million dollars for the entire year, not enough to arrest the crisis in production (Goldstein 1982).

This credit squeeze forced the Kania regime to open talks on rescheduling the debt, the only way for the country to avoid a formal default – unilateral suspension of payment. After more than six months, talks were concluded, with an agreement that permitted Poland to postpone 2.4 billion dollars in payments due that year. However, no Western long-term plan for solving financial payments was worked out, and no fresh credits were attached. This situation was much different from the conditions of most of the other large rescheduling deals, whether for Yugoslavia in 1981 or for the very heavily indebted countries of Latin America (e.g., Brazil received several billion dollars in fresh money when first rescheduling its huge debt in 1982) (see Cline 1985).

The major reason for this incomplete treatment was that all the negotiations were carried out directly with Western banks, while Western governments remained virtually uninvolved. Western governments did not assume a leadership role since they were uncertain about the outcome of the political struggles between the free unions and the party and therefore had no clear political strategy regarding Poland's crisis. Furthermore, Poland was not a member of the World Bank or the International Monetary Fund (IMF) and hence could not draw on their resources. This made Poland's situation different from that, for instance, of Hungary, which was helped by Western governments and also assisted by the World Bank from 1982 onward.

Given this situation, assistance from the Soviet Union became an important alternative. The Soviet Union did indeed provide some help, but only on a temporary basis. In 1980–81, the total Soviet assistance amounted to 3–4 billion dollars, which included 1 billion dollars in hard currency credits and a nonrepayable grant of 500 million dollars. The rest consisted of trade deficits to the Soviet Union not cleared by Poland, with no considerable direct impact on its ability to service their debt to Western countries. Except for a small emergency shipment of goods by East Germany, the rest of Eastern Europe did not provide any substantial help at all. To the contrary, it put additional pressure on Poland by reducing exports in order to cut their recent trade surpluses.

The Soviet Union did not provide Poland's economy with additional material resources to offset the sizeable losses in Western supplies for the manufacturing sector, but merely kept up current deliveries. The aforementioned uncleared deficits came mostly from higher prices for Soviet oil and other raw materials which were supplied to Poland in more or less the same quantities as in 1979. In fact, other East European countries were allowed similar trade deficits with the Soviet Union, although their economies were performing far better than Poland. These countries were also not beset by the political turmoil which threatened the Soviet position in the region and domestic stability in the Soviet Union as well (Hewett 1985).

Poland's government did not benefit at the time from such forms of special treatment as, for example, the Soviet policy of supplying Bulgaria with energy sources far above its domestic needs, with excess quantities of oil reexported by Bulgaria for hard currency. In 1979, Bulgarian sales of Soviet oil on hard currency markets amounted to 2.4 million tons, almost 30 per cent more than what Poland had to buy for dollars that year with its severe currency shortage. To give another example, while Poland had to clear its trade with the Soviet Union in nonconvertible rubles, Hungary was allowed to run dollar accounts with the Soviet Union. These accounts provided the Hungarian economy with a surplus of about 0.5 billion dollars in 1980, a sum close to the Hungarian trade deficit with Western countries in that year (Marrese 1983).

Further decline

Confronted with a failing austerity plan and no hope for immediate financial assistance from the West, the Kania regime drastically cut both Western imports and domestic investment outlays in 1981. After a relatively modest drop in Western imports in 1980, 1981 witnessed a 34.6 per cent decline of dollar good shipments in constant prices. The sharp squeeze in imports forced a drastic reduction in the number of new projects and a freeze or termination of many ongoing ones. Altogether, total investment outlays in fixed assets dropped by 12.3 per cent in 1980 and by 22.3 per cent in 1981, figures which were unprecedented in the whole post-war period in Poland (and for that matter in the whole of communist East Europe).

To minimize the negative impact of reduced imports and lower investment, the government should have quickly revised its planning priorities and acted accordingly. This did not happen, however, since the Kania regime was preoccupied with political tensions brought about by the several million members of strong free trade unions. Moreover, lower-level officials were confused by the new configuration of political power and preferred to do nothing rather than follow orders and upset the workers, or give in to the workers' pressures and displease their supervisors. Consequently, the cuts were pursued without a clear list of priorities and in a disorderly manner, thus aggravating the shortages (for a very persuasive and detailed discussion of this aspect, see: Nuti 1982).

Left without decisive counterbalancing measures, the economy slipped from a difficult year in 1980, when a 6 per cent drop in the national product was reported, to a fully disastrous year in 1981, when the national product declined by 12 per cent. In 1980, industrial output declined by 0.8 per cent, with agriculture going through an unprecedented loss of 10.7 per cent, while in 1981, the industry registered a loss of 13.2 per cent and agriculture showed an increase of 3.8 per cent. This was in clear contrast with the rest of the area, where only a very few countries – Czechoslovakia, Hungary and Romania – registered absolute declines in their gross material products, these being only very minor and lasting for no longer than one year (while Bulgaria and East Germany did not slow-down at all). Thus, the leadership of Poland saw ample evidence that the crisis was not only escalating but that it was an anomaly as well.

Worsening of economic conditions in Poland was further evidenced in a rise in inflation – from 6.7 per cent in 1979 to 9.4 per cent in 1980, and then to 21.2 per cent in 1981. This situation differed again from that in the rest of Eastern Europe where prices remained either relatively stable, or only one-time acceleration took place (e.g., in Bulgaria and Hungary in 1980). While Poland's inflation intensified in 1981, nominal wages rose even faster, so that real wages rose in 1981, but as indicated these monetary gains were largely statistical. With more money poured in to the economy by households and with production falling already serious shortages were exacerbated. This time, even basic foodstuffs (e.g., cheese, sugar) were missing from store shelves, making daily life far more frustrating and the enormous scale of the economic crisis more obvious to the public at large.

Moreover, the external position of Poland continued to worsen as the real volume of trade registered a large reduction. While total exports experienced a decline, the greatest losses were registered in sales to Western markets, though the latter were most vital for debt control. After increasing from 6.1 billion dollars in 1979 to 7.4 billion dollars in 1980, hard-currency exports declined to 5 billion dollars in 1981, a loss of almost 30 per cent. Imports, in turn, stayed at 8.2 billion dollars in 1980, unchanged from 1979, until 1981 when they fell to 5.8 billion dollars, a reduction of 34 per cent. The trade balance with Western countries continued to be negative, further contributing to the rise in the foreign debt. It increased sizeably, reaching $25.9 billion by the end of 1981,[30] a further indication for the already nervous lendors that Poland's economy was moving rapidly from bad risk to a worse one.

This deterioration in the economy made the undertaking of a complex reform in the bureaucratic system all the more crucial. In fact, both the party and the opposition initiated an ambitious programme of systemic reforms, but the whole issue became as highly politicized as all major economic questions at the time. The programme had been designed in mid-1981, mostly along the lines of the Hungarian system of 1968, highly praised by both sides in the negotiations. One does not know whether this institutional arrangement could have worked under the then-existing economic conditions, but the issue of feasibility was not a major practical obstacle. One politically crucial question, namely, that of who would appoint managers, divided the communist party and the free unions, effectively blocking the introduction of any reform programme for months.

Summary

Making foreign credit lines an important source of capital formation was not the only noteworthy measure taken by Gierek's cabinet to stimulate the stagnant economy it inherited from the previous regime. Other steps – unconventional by the standards of its predecessors – included a decision to energize the workforce and stimulate labour productivity with substantial concessions in terms of consumption increases and more say for workers at the enterprise level. This change in labour relations was one element in a broad set of measures aimed at expanding access to the political scene to extra-party forces. Gierek's government also allowed much of the formal authority concerning resource allocation to be largely delegated to – or captured by – sectoral interests, i.e., ministries, and associations. It was the combination of all these policies which moved the economy away from a 'strong' version of state planning to a 'soft' one, where control over the use of resources was no longer rigid.

This transition towards 'soft' planning seems to have been critical in shaping the behaviour of Poland's economy throughout Gierek's import-led growth strategy. The fact that such a growth strategy was executed, from the beginning, through a soft (= weak) version of state-type planning, could well explain the great acceleration in foreign borrowing – as well as production – early in the period. Much of this acceleration was caused by effective pressures from special interests, including actions taken without prior knowledge by the centre. This softness might have also been important in preventing Gierek's cabinet from fully executing austerity measures needed to arrest the foreign debt before it became unmanageable. Indeed, it was the same special interest groups, operating through the economic system, which undermined the 1976 adjustment aimed at trimming import demand and producing trade surpluses.

When the debt crisis fully surfaced in 1979, even harsher measures had to be taken than those envisioned in the 1976 adjustment programme. For these steps to be implemented within the short time-frame available, the leadership had to recapture some of its authority from the special interests. It also needed the industrial bureaucracy to join in persuading workers to accept a necessary loss of income. However, the opposite happened, as the Gierek government found itself facing not only ever increasing pressure from the industrial lobbies but also from the newly emerged 'free' trade unions. Through self-organization, workers gained even more influence over the economy as well as an avenue for political action. This particular development led to a further softening of the economic system, as widespread strikes and disputes, which surfaced in early 1980, made the government even less capable of redirecting production towards debt servicing.

It thus could be hypothesized that the massive inflow of capital goods imported on credit from international markets was not necessarily misused, this presumably being the major cause of the 1979–82 economic crisis. Given the large amount of foreign credit drawn, some painful repayment problems were unavoidable, forcing the national economy to temporarily slow down, but it could be that the imported capital prepared the economy to cope reasonably well with the debt problem anyway. Sales to hard-currency markets that would have been required to prevent the debt crisis from becoming as bad as it was, and the 1980 undeclared default of payments, could have failed to occur primarily because of the competing domestic demands on exportable goods – including goods based on recently imported technology and thus most suitable for sale abroad and commanding better prices as well.

It would then follow that, if it not had been for adverse political developments and related loss of central authority over economic affairs, Poland probably would have been able to resolve her internal and external imbalances more in the manner of Hungary or, to take a more controversial case, Romania, both of whom had been growing rapidly – with the help of large trade deficits – in the early 1970s. The prolonged strikes and the near disintegration of decisionmaking bodies in 1980–81 pushed Poland into an escalating crisis, which could be arrested only by finding a solution to political instability first. Given the inability to compromise, forceful imposition by one of the parties in the conflict was the only option available. Such a solution was the late 1981 shift from civilian to military rule, allowing the party/state to sway the power balance in its favour so that placing the economic crisis under control became a practical possibility.

2   Impact of technology imports on national economy

Much empirical research has been devoted to the question debated here of whether the Gierek import-led strategy was helpful in building Poland's export capacities and thus avoiding an economic crisis on the scale of 1979–82. While no conclusive evidence was produced at the time of the crisis, the view that the growth strategy failed to accomplish such economic goals gained great currency. It was not the knowledge of massive misallocation of imports – and credits used to pay for them – that gave credence to this view, but rather the fact that from the very outbreak of the crisis, intra-party factions found it a potent instrument in their efforts to oust the Gierek regime. This view was also well received by the workers, generally distrustful of the party leaders' ability to run economic affairs properly. With the departure of Gierek's regime, there was virtually nobody left to challenge this opinion on ineffective import use.

What helped to solidify the negative assessment of import-led policy outside of political circles, in the academic literature, was again not so much the supporting evidence as the fact that it conformed with the general understanding that the economic system of state planning, as operated under Gierek, was extremely inefficient. Gierek's strategy was doomed to fail because such a system makes it impossible to identify the least costly – in terms of lost opportunities – options. Under such a system, political interference takes precedence over economic calculations, whether done correctly or not, so that politically over-represented, well-established producers effectively block the flow of imports to new lines of production. Wherever imports are located under this particular system, there are few incentives for efficient use of them, so that waste is permitted, leaving large quantities of foreign capital either uninstalled or improperly utilized.

In this chapter we attempt to offer a critical review of the existing body of quantitative research on the effects of the import-led strategy, and then introduce our own evidence to show that, on balance, these findings speak against the dominant view on factors behind the crisis. What transpires from our analysis is a favourable assessment of the effects of the import-led growth, consistent with our preliminary findings in the opening chapter. Judging by the productivity trends, capital imports had a visible positive impact, implying that whatever the built-in inefficiency, it did not neutralize the technological advantage of foreign capital. There is certainly evidence of major structural changes during the period in question – reflected in the export-product mix as well as in higher quality of tradables – this latter suggesting that state planning did allow for some flexibility.

The effect of Western imports on productivity

One convenient statistical method of determining the impact of imported technology on export potential in a given economy is the measurement of import contribution to rate of productivity increases and related growth in national product. This kind of analysis offers some insight on how supplies of goods in tradables, providing the basis for exports, are affected by shifting emphasis from domestic to foreign technology. Of course, technology is only one factor behind productivity changes and national product expansion, so that we are confronted with the problem of separating this factor from others (e.g., structural change, human skills). Quantification of inputs of domestic and foreign technology poses a serious methodological problem for estimating the impact of imported capital on productivity as well.

Labour productivity

In this section, we both review and analyse evidence relating to the impact of imported Western technology on Poland's productivity during Gierek's rapid-growth strategy. We begin here with an examination of data on rates of growth of output, which seems to suggest that imports could have a positive impact on levels of productivity. For instance, statistical data compiled by Terrell (1987) reveals that industrial output grew at a slightly higher rate during the 1972–76 period than it did in the preceding decade when imports volumes were much smaller. The average annual rate of growth of output in 1972–76 rose to 9.1 per cent from 7.6 per cent in the 1960–71 period. On the other hand, the reduction of imports after 1976, and even more sharply during the 1979–82 crisis, seems correlated with the negative growth of total industrial output of 1.6 per cent per year over the 1977–83 period.

Among all the industrial branches, the output of the two major branches which were given the highest priority[1] in the modernization of the economy – engineering and chemicals – grew the fastest in both the 1960–83 period and the 1972–76 period. For the 1960–83 period, the average growth was about 6.2 per cent annually: engineering and chemicals grew at 10 per cent and 9.0 per cent respectively. There was little or no change, however, in the growth rate in the 1972–76 period compared with the 1960–83 period in these two sectors, whereas the low priority wood and paper industry almost doubled its rate of output increase. This cross-sector comparison of output growth rates does not indicate that the imported technology had a uniformly positive effect on sectoral output growth.

For the above mentioned total (or sectoral) output acceleration to translate into an upturn in productivity, production increases would have to be stronger than the parallel increases in physical factors, i.e., capital and/or labour. Data gathered by Terrell (1987) again suggests that there might have been some upsurge in productivity because while the rate of growth of total industrial output rose from the 1960–71 period to the 1972–76 period, the corresponding rate for employment (measured in number of workers) was almost halved over these two periods. To be specific, the rate of growth in employment fell from 3.1 per cent annually during 1960–72 to 1.5 per cent during 1972–76, while the import-favoured engineering and chemical sector experienced the sharpest decline in the growth of workforce.

Ascertaining how much of the acceleration in Poland's productivity of labour could be attributed to the technology imports themselves was a task first undertaken by Gomulka (1978). His method is algebraic and based on a generalized vintage-model of economic growth. This class of theoretical models assumes that technology contributes to economic growth not through existing capital stock but rather through the introduction of new vintages of machinery by means of capital expansion. Gomulka's novel approach is to distinguish between two sources of such machinery, domestic and foreign (which he calls 'subvintages', *ibid.*: 3). This is to capture possible differences in the technological level of domestic and foreign supplies of machinery.

The above study assumes that imports of foreign machinery, if technologically superior, have three ways of potentially affecting a given economy. The first is the so-called 'vintage effect', i.e., positive impact of the sheer increase in the volume of capital outlays on output growth. Next, there is the increase in incremental labour productivity on new machines brought from abroad, called 'the direct effect of embodied diffusion', related to more efficient technology incorporated in imported capital. Finally, there is a spillover effect on overall productivity of labour when imported machinery helps – through imitation – to generate supplies of upgraded domestic machinery, this aspect of importation called the 'indirect effect of embodied diffusion'.

To facilitate his estimate, Gomulka (1978) uses a number of empirical studies from several industrial sectors to establish the productivity gap between foreign and domestic machinery (or embodied technology). From this analysis, he concluded that it is legitimate to assume that in 1970, the starting point for the estimate, domestic machinery represented 77 per cent of the productivity of machinery imported from the CMEA, and only 46 per cent of the productivity of Western machinery imports (for comparison, see Poznanski 1988a). Under this assumption, the impact of Western imports becomes a simple positive function of their size (providing that all types of machinery are equally well utilized by domestic enterprises).

The study finds that during 1974–78, the size of the embodied diffusion effect (i.e., both direct and indirect) was considerable. The injection of more productive Western machinery alone – ignoring the vintage effect – increased the average annual growth rates of labour productivity by 1 to 1.5 per cent above the long-run trend (estimated at 5.7 per cent). Gomulka also states that in 1977 the productivity of labour was as much as 7 per cent above the longterm trend line, with this gain being entirely attributable to the impact of the improved composition of the capital stock. The projected impact of imported machinery was found to be possibly even higher during 1978–80, due, among other things, to a considerable rise in the capital/labour ratio (Gomulka 1978: 8).

Gomulka (1986b: 255) also argues that the fact that the import-led strategy was followed by crisis in 1979–82, does not in itself mean that the net effect of imports was negative. By his own estimate, the economic policy of Gierek's regime resulted in very substantial real gains in consumption, something that the workers were promised in the implicit 'social compact' concluded in 1971. In 1980, total consumption was 23 per cent above the hypothetical level of consumption under a balanced-growth scenario (i.e., the simple extension of 1955–70 trends when Western imports were of a modest scale). The dollar value of consumption gain by 1982 exceeded three times the cumulative value of Poland's debt in that year (*ibid.*: 259).

Of course, to properly judge the effects of the import-led strategy on total consumption, one would have to subtract from the pre-1982 gain the losses caused by the outflow of resources to service foreign debt (and related reduction in imports of capital goods needed to maintain machinery stock at its full potential). Gomulka (1986: 260) points to this aspect of calculation and argues that such losses could have exceeded the earlier advances in consumption level. However, even if this were the case, one would still be left with the unanswered question of whether this eventual net loss is related to inherent, system-related waste or improper scheduling of credits, or to the fact that the economy failed to mobilize its entire export potential to meet workable debt payments.

Productivity of capital

Unlike the study by Gomulka, most of the research has focused on the effect of Western technology on fixed assets, rather than on labour. Further, departing from Gomulka's model, where relative productivity of particular 'subvintages' of capital is not estimated within the model but assumed, the other numerical studies apply some form of production function, which allows for such estimation. Green and Levine (1977) were the first to test the Cobb-Douglas (CD) production function for the Soviet Union, assuming a unitary elasticity of substitution between Western and indigenous capital. Their calculations demonstrated that Western machinery imports were indeed more productive – for marginal units employed – than those of domestic origin (and increased industrial output growth rate by approximately 20 per cent).

The results produced by Green and Levine might strike one as very high given the fact that imports of Western machinery by the Soviet Union during 1970–80 represented a relatively low share of her total capital inputs and were a few times lower than those in Poland during Gierek's acceleration programme. One plausible explanation might be that the indirect effect of machinery imports – imitation of borrowed technology by domestic producers – was much stronger in the Soviet Union than in Poland. Assimilation of Western technology could have actually been more extensive in the Soviet Union due, for instance, to her greater involvement in industrial research (reflected in the fact that her share of research expenditure in the national product was twice that of Poland) (also see: Green 1979).

The study by Green and Levine was first challenged by Weitzman (1979), who considered the assumption of unitary elasticity for all inputs – including imported and domestic capital vintages – unrealistic, and departing from the model of Greene and Levine, Weitzman assumed that elasticity between two sources of capital goods is infinite. His quantitative test for the Soviet Union revealed that there is no proof that Western vintages were any more productive than domestic ones. Brada and Hoffman (1985) also raised doubts about the positive impact of imported capital on Soviet productivity by reaching the similar conclusion that indigenous capital was equally, or more, productive than imported capital (though they also admit that a sectoral test revealed that imports stimulated greater productivity of indigenous capital) (*ibid*.: 16).

The production-function estimates of Terrell (1987, 1992) also do not suggest any positive impact by Western technology. The particular value of this study lies not only in its reference to Polish industry during the Gierek period, but also in its providing direct estimates of the relative productivity of both Western and domestic capital.[2] Rather than imposing strong restrictions on the implied elasticities of input substitution, Terrell applies a translog production function to test which is the most constrained specification of this function, and thus what the actual elasticities are. The results show, among other things, that while elasticities of domestic capital in eight main industrial sectors improved after 1971, for Western capital they did not.

Terrell (1992) has also examined the relative difference in marginal products of domestic and foreign capital. The study demonstrates that the differences in the marginal products were quite significant in five of seven industry branches for which data was available. These differences were found to be significant prior to the import-led strategy and continued throughout the whole period of Gierek's intense borrowing. Importantly, the marginal product of domestic capital was found to exceed that of Western capital in three industries, including chemicals, which were among the priority recipients of imports. This implies, as Terrell posits, that the strategy suffered from considerable capital misallocation and that many industry sectors would benefit from substituting Western imports with internal supplies.

As Kemme (1987) indicates, the growth rate of output per unit of capital declined and became negative in all of industry and in each sector (except chemicals) in 1973–77, as compared to 1961–70. Total output per zloty of fixed assets in industry fell by 2.74 per cent a year during 1973–77 as compared to an annual growth rate of 0.82 per cent per annum in 1961–70. From the fact that the chemical industry was the only branch with a positive growth rate, it may be concluded, as was done by Fallenbuchl (1983: 36), that the industries with a higher share of Western imports outperformed those that had lower allocations of foreign technology. Consequently, one could argue that despite its acceleration the transfer of technology was not excessive but, rather, insufficient for creating a measurable difference in productivity.

Joint-factor productivity

In examining five East European countries (including Poland), Whitesell (1985: 241) established that total (= joint) factor productivity growth was generally above average in the early 1970s and below average in the late 1970s, and that these productivity patterns coincided with changes in the rate of growth of Western imports during that period. Similarly, Kemme (1987) found that Polish industry (as a whole) had a small but statistically significant increase in the rate of growth of joint factor productivity during the 1973–77 period as compared with the 1960–72 period. In contrast, in all three specifications which she estimated for total industry, Terrell (1987) found no change in the level of total factor productivity between the 1972–76 and the 1960–71 periods.

Kemme (1987) found that above-average rates of increase in fixed assets did not have any visible positive impact on total factor productivity in several major sectors of Poland's industry during 1960–77. However, he established that the relative scale of technology imports – measured in terms of the number of licence agreements and cooperative agreements with Western companies – had a positive effect on joint factor productivity in the three out of four sectors which were identified as major recipients. Within this group, the scale of technology imports had a positive impact in metallurgy, chemicals and minerals, but not in electrical machinery. This was an important anomaly, since the latter sector not only received more imported technology but increased its total capital assets by more as well.

To explain the above anomaly, Kemme hypothesized that the electrical machinery industry was more susceptible to misallocation of resources (i.e., demonstrated a lower allocative efficiency). This hypothesis is tested in the more recent study by Kemme (1990), covering the period 1971–83. Econometric estimations are conducted to determine sectoral variations in marginal rates of technical substitution and then the output impact of reallocation of resources needed to equalize these rates is calculated. Substantial losses due to allocative inefficiency are found for the industry as a whole (about 8 to 10 per cent of the output). Moreover, the electrical machinery sector was found to be more wasteful than other import-priority sectors.

Kemme's (1987) findings, from estimating both CES and CD production functions for nine industrial branches, concur with those of Terrell (1987) in showing that total factor productivity did not always rise in those sectors whose fixed assets rose the fastest or those which invested more in Western technology. However, Kemme also argues that in those industries where the rate of growth of total factor productivity accelerated during the mid-1970s, such acceleration was due more to the additional inflow of disembodied technology – licensing – than to increase in the rate of expansion of fixed assets. Kemme (1987) and Terrell (1987) are in agreement that food and tobacco and metallurgy were the only branches (except for minerals in the case of Kemme) which had a higher level (faster growth) of factor productivity in 1972–76 (1973–77) than during the 1960–71 (1972) period.

Terrell (1992) concludes that Western capital, which was imported on a relatively large scale in the 1972–76 period, had no effect on total factor, capital, and possibly labour productivity. These findings, as Terrell posits, support the hypotheses that Poland either imported unproductive (obsolete) Western capital or misused relatively more productive (modern) Western capital. Terrell agrees with Fallenbuchl (1983), who argues that the short-term nature, uneven pace (rapid increase and sudden reductions in the flow), and timing (in terms of world economic situation) of the technology transfer made it very difficult for imported technology to be used efficiently. Kemme, in turn, speculates that the weak impact of imports on certain sectors could be attributed to mismanagement (e.g., wide investment front, frequent lack of complementary productive inputs) (see Kemme and Neufeld 1991).[3]

Interpretation problems

In searching for reasons why little or no impact of technology imports has been detected in some of the above mentioned studies, it is not enough to point to the low effectiveness of import application. To provide a satisfactory explanation for these quantitative results, one would have to demonstrate not only that the absorption of foreign capital was inefficient, but that it was so inefficient as to outweigh the obvious superiority of imported technology. In other words, for imported technology to have weak or no positive – sectoral or overall – impact on the economy, the efficiency of import application would have to be so much worse than that found in the use of indigenous technology that the potential gain from superior capital of foreign origin was cancelled out.

However, while the use of Western technology was undeniably plagued with economic waste, if anything, one could expect the projects based on imported capital to demonstrate higher efficiency than domestic projects. Managers were, of course, less familiar with imported technology than with that internally generated – a fact that could have had a negative impact on differential efficiency of the two technology sources. However, this disadvantage was probably offset to a degree by the Western technical assistance provided to import-based projects. Many licensed production capacities were installed on a turnkey basis or with some supervision from abroad, often extended beyond the plant construction stage through long-term cooperation agreements signed for most major import-related projects.

Another factor which might have helped in increasing the effectiveness of foreign technology (= capital) application over the effectiveness of internal absorption is that import-based projects were under pressure from the central administration to pay for themselves through exports (including hard-currency sales through special state shops). In many cases, sellers of Western technology were required to buy back part of the output, so that there was additional pressure on domestic users of imported technology to apply technology effectively – not only to proceed in a timely manner with plant construction but also to assure a high quality of resultant products as well (e.g., a small car factory built with Fiat assistance was expected to pay for itself with exports and it actually accomplished this goal within a five-year period).

A more difficult element to detect, but one which could have contributed toward higher efficiency of foreign technology application was its backing by unusually ambitious and strongly dedicated managers, most of whom had technical background, as well as by other technocratic people in enterprises (and also in governmental agencies). The struggle for imported inputs reflected not only the insatiable demand typical of all 'shortage economies' (see Kornai 1980), but also the modernization drive of technocrats, aware of Poland's industry falling behind the technological frontier. If so, it could be expected that the same people who pressed for imports would also sincerely try to make the best use of imports.

Examination of optimal export policies

After examining both the sectoral and aggregate impact of technology transfers on factor productivity, we turn to another empirical test to determine whether the import-led policy of Gierek was effective in terms of generating competitive exports. The common view of a bureaucratic economic system such as that operated in Gierek's Poland would suggest that the authorities were not really in a position to identify the optimal strategy for import allocation. There presumably was neither the information available to make optimal choices at the higher levels of decision making nor the incentive for decision-makers to assure that the export effect of imports was maximized. Below we examine various types of quantitative evidence on the allocative rationality in the export promotion policies during all those years in question

Linkage analysis

Optimality of export policy can be analysed at many levels, one of them being the linkage matrix for a whole national economy, one which allows for the quantification of flows – material and financial – among particular sectors of production. This particular approach was undertaken by Svejnar and Chaykowski (1987) in their study of Poland's export policy during 1969–82. The research strategy of the authors is to quantify the basic linkage effects of a given industry's exports – a line of analysis pursued before but only in the context of developing non state socialist nations. A linkage approach enables the researcher to establish whether countries whose state bureaucracies are actively involved in economic prioritizing (such as Eastern Europe), have in fact made choices that would produce the best macroeconomic results.

The study by Svejnar and Chaykowski looks into four inter-sectoral linkages which relate expansion of production in particular export industries with, respectively: household income; value added; capital requirements; and import needs of the whole economy. The first two linkages are helpful in establishing whether actual import-led increases in export production in Poland generated maximum welfare effect. The other two types of linkages make it possible to estimate the degree to which the economy was burdened with additional requirements for imports of capital and material goods with which to maintain production. Such an analysis is, of course, extremely sensitive to the price structure, which presumably was highly distorted and therefore incorrectly reflected relative scarcities within the economy, so that using physical data was the only practical way of escaping potential price related inaccuracies.

With the help of an input-output table for fifteen sectors in the Polish economy, Svejnar and Chaykowski established that at the outset of Gierek's import-led growth in 1969, those industries with the strongest value added/income generation potential were: textiles, footwear, construction, foodstuffs, agriculture, exportable services, and wood/paper. Similar sectors were found to offer the best value added/income effect for the 1977 input–output table, disaggregated for thirty-nine industries. The only important difference was the addition of glass/ceramics as another area suitable for export specialization (while showing that among foodstuffs, meat is not). Analysis of value added/income linkages for the 1982 input–output table (with thirty-two sectors) produced a list of priority sectors almost identical to that derived from the 1977 matrix.

In addition to demonstrating considerable stability over time in the list of industries suitable for export specialization, the study in question found that, apparently, these key sectors did not receive the priority in allocation they deserved. This shows, the authors argue, in the fact that the priority sectors did not experience above average growth in exports for the whole economy in 1970–81. Foodstuffs, for instance, saw their share in total exports fall from 11.6 per cent in 1970 to 8.7 per cent in 1975, and then to 5.5 per cent in 1981 (in the same period, agriculture's share declined from 5.3 per cent to 1.7 per cent). Textiles, another sector deserving priority treatment, was only able to retain its original share (i.e., 8 per cent). In contrast, the machinery industry, with weak linkages, watched its share in total exports increase from 31.8 per cent to 55.2 per cent in 1970–81.

The machine-building industry was not only among those with below-average value added/income linkages, but, as Svejnar and Chaykowski show, it was one of the sectors displaying above-average import requirements. Other industries which needed disproportionally large supplies of imported inputs – capital equipment and materials – were in the engineering and chemicals sectors, all demonstrating faster rates of export expansion than total exports. This focus of the import-led strategy on production lines with rather low potential for welfare gains and high import content, is viewed by the authors as one of the major failures of Gierek's modernization drive. It could be, they argue, that what the economy really needed was more technological upgrading of the existing export sectors than use of imports to change the export structure.

Factor endowments

Unlike the work of Svejnar and Chaykowski, the study done by Murrell (1990b) is an example of direct test of models of foreign trade to determine optimality of export specialization under state-planned economies. A number of hypotheses have been produced on the possible differences between trading behaviour under this kind of economy and the market-type in terms of propensity to trade and comparative advantage. Several of these hypotheses are examined by Murrell for nine countries, among them Poland, using the 1975–83 statistics. As such, the numerical results of this investigation are of potential use in our exploration of empirical evidence of possible suboptimality or deficiencies in Poland's export policy under Gierek.

Murrell's methodological approach is to examine whether state-planned economies follow the basic neo-classical model of trade developed by Heckscher and Ohlin (for an earlier attempt, see Rosefielde 1973). The essence of this test is to determine whether the actual structure of trade is consistent with factor endowments which the Heckscher-Ohlin model claims to be the determining force behind export patterns under competitive or market conditions. The statistical picture produced by Murrell is not one of irrational allocation of resources but rather of following the logic of factor endowments, at least at a high level of aggregation. This would be the case, since, as claimed, socialist planning is subject to a learning curve and contains incentives for trading enterprises to maximize profits from exports.

While the neo-classical factor-endowment model of trade is found eminently applicable to the socialist countries (Murrell 1990: 22), there are a few exceptions to this general rule. These are: Hungary, Poland, and Yugoslavia, with the last showing the greatest deviation from the model's predictions (this includes an extreme bias toward the importation of capital-intensive goods and concentration on exportation of products using fuel and land intensively). Since all three countries at the time operated an unorthodox, reformed type of state planning, one has to doubt whether the generally positive tone of the economic literature on promarket reforms at that time was really justified. Murrell ventures a hypothesis that neither decentralization of decision-making nor price rationalization under state planning help efficiency, and, if anything, these reform measures diminish the rationality of resource allocation.

Testing the neo-classical model of trade, Murrell argues, is insufficient, since it only accounts for static efficiency, pertaining to the use of existing resources at a given price/cost structure (or comparative advantage). To capture the dynamic aspects, he also examines a model consistent with evolutionary economics, representing a broad-gauged alternative to the static neoclassical theory. This model includes elements such as product differentiation, barriers to entry, and large-scale effects (i.e., economies of scale). Murrell's test revealed that the structure of trade in socialist-type economies tends to reflect their weak and strong points in terms of dynamic efficiency (e.g., they were found less competitive in industries which require easy entry but were demonstrably more successful in sectors where production concentration is important for keeping unit costs of production down).

Further, when tested for the socialist countries as a whole, this alternative trade model proved less efficient than the neoclassical one. This would seem to suggest that state-planned economies are better at allocating the given resources than at 'rearranging' them. Murrell goes so far as to suggest that the test indicates that while socialist economies appear to be as efficient in static allocation as capitalist economies, they are inferior in terms of dynamic efficiency (*ibid.*: 4). Since Hungary and Yugoslavia, as well as Poland, turned out to do no better in terms of the evolutionary model than the other, more orthodox, countries, it follows that no dynamic gains should be expected from economic decentralization (for presumably 'natural selection', not delegation of power, is the essence of the drive to dynamic efficiency).

Cumulative advantage

Another way of examining trade data for optimality of state policies under socialist planning is to test the concept of cumulative advantage. The argument here, also in the evolutionary tradition, is that foreign trade structure is determined less by factor endowments as reflected in the current price/cost matrix than by preexisting patterns of commerce. These early patterns need not reflect factor endowments at the respective time, but could be initiated, for whatever reason, including pure chance. Once established in a given location, export production creates positive externalities which stimulate further expansion of that activity, as well as related ones. Consequently, if state planning were to be detrimental to specialization, Poland's trade would have to depart from the structure which was established before the last war under the conditions of market competition.

Whether central planning prevented Poland from achieving trade consistent with its actual advantages can best be tested with data on Polish trade with the Western economies. Analysis of this direction of trade seems most appropriate because the majority of Poland's prewar (precommunist) trade was with the countries of what is now called Western Europe. At the end of the interwar period, Poland's principal trading partner – at least among importers – was Great Britain. Germany, critically important at the outset of this period, lost its dominant position in Poland's trade for primarily political reasons – which fuelled a so-called trade war between the two countries. Outside of Western Europe, Russia was traditionally Poland's most significant trading partner, but, again, for political reasons, the turnover between the two countries was radically reduced in the interwar years.

Our examination of Polish sales to Great Britain after 1928 reveals a remarkable stability in product composition through 1968, when Poland still operated a traditional (here called 'strong') form of state planning. Most notable is the continuous domination of Poland's total exports of foodstuffs, for in 1928, the share of this product category was 42.9 per cent and in 1938, right before the outbreak of the last world war, the respective share was 50.0 per cent (see: Poznanski 1991c). In 1968 foodstuffs represented 51.5 per cent of exports to Great Britain, a percentage that did not change through 1979. The share fell after 1979, reaching a low of 9.5 per cent in 1988, and remained close to that level in 1991 as well. This later trend may, however, be another reflection of the government's concern for giving priority to domestic consumption over exporting for convertible currencies.

The second important category of goods exported to Great Britain in the inter war period was raw materials, particularly wood. In 1928 the share of this group was 40.4 per cent, with wood alone accounting for 37.1 per cent of the total exports, and these shares remained largely unchanged through 1938. In 1968, the share of raw materials fell to 24.3 per cent, though this was still the second largest category of total exports. Significantly, wood continued to represent the single most important subcategory – 16.1 per cent of total exports. By 1988 the share of wood fell to 5.0 per cent, while the share of all raw materials reached 41.9 per cent, very close to the prewar pattern. Copper, whose mining on a large scale began under the Gierek government – out of hope for strengthening the export base – became the dominant category in this group, accounting for 16.6 per cent of total exports.

Lower exports of foodstuffs in 1988 were compensated with expansion in three categories, including manufactures by material. This category represented 9.8 per cent of the total in 1928, 8.9 per cent in 1968, and 17.4 per cent in 1988. Wood products accounted for 6.3 per cent of exports in 1928 and remained close to that level in 1988 (5.7 per cent). Another broad category which showed considerable gain by 1988 was miscellaneous manufactures. In 1928 its share was negligible and in 1938 it accounted for merely 0.7 per cent of exports. However, by 1968 miscellaneous manufactures represented as much as 4.5 per cent, and by 1988 the respective share was 11.4 per cent. One of the major contributors was sales of furniture, whose share increased from 1.2 per cent in 1968 to 3.0 per cent in 1988 – a trend consistent with the cumulative advantage theory (for furniture is related to wood production).

The greatest gain was registered in the category of machinery and transport equipment, almost absent from Poland's exports to Great Britain in the interwar years. In 1968, the share of this group was 2.9 per cent, which increased to 11.5 per cent in 1988, and then to 17.7 per cent in 1991. This shift may reflect the results of technological upgrading undertaken during the import-led strategy of Gierek. That Poland was trying to take advantage of this upgrading seems to be reflected in the fact that the many advanced models of goods easily found their way onto foreign markets. We have established on another occasion (Poznanski 1988a: 593–600) that in certain cases, such as machine-tools, the proportion of the most sophisticated models – numerically controlled – in exports of all types of machine tools was higher than their share in domestic production (with numerically controlled types earning one third to one half higher prices than conventional ones).

These quantitative findings are at least to a degree consistent with the general conclusion of Murrell's study that the ability of state planners, through repetitive learning, to identify areas qualified for specialization was not as limited as suggested by conventional views. Since we found that Poland's trade pattern was more consistent with cumulative advantage before the decentralization of 1971 than after this date, this seems to lend additional support to Murrell's argument about the detrimental impact of economic decentralization (as reflected in Hungarian, Polish, and Yugoslav failure to pass the broad test of the neo-classical factor-endowment model). Our determinations also seem to be in line with the earlier mentioned suggestion of Svejnar and Chaykowski that Poland's trade structure during the Gierek years might have been less in need of change than was the product content in particular categories of exports.

Changes in export supplies for Western markets

These paragraphs continue the analysis of import effects on the national economy through an examination of trade data but our focus is no longer the question of allocative optimality. We examine here whether Poland and the other East European countries improved their export base for trading with the West between 1970 and 1982, the last year of the economic crisis. We intend to determine whether these countries were successful in expanding their exports to Western countries as well as improving the efficiency of those exports with the help of Western technology. In particular, we pose the question of whether these countries have been moving away from exporting low-processed goods toward exporting high-processed goods, earning higher value-added as well as having greater prospects for long-term expansion.

Market shares

A summary measure of changes in a country's export ability is the change in its share of foreign markets. While increasing shares indicate that a given country is making improvements in its competitive advantage, that indicator by itself does not say much about possible sources of the improvement (i.e., more dynamic growth of supplies, lower costs, or higher quality). In the context of this analysis, the most appropriate indicator is the trend in Polish and other East European countries' market shares in the West, for the Western market was the hardest to compete in compared to the regional market, i.e. the CMEA, where trade was allocated through bilaterally balanced state agreements in nonconvertible currencies. Western Europe was at the same time extremely critical for sustaining Poland's ability to repay its debt (because most of the foreign credit was drawn from these countries).

Analysis of the OECD market reveals that, as far as total exports are concerned, Poland and Romania were the only two East European countries whose share increased during the 1970–75 period (table 2.1). Poland's share in OECD imports increased from 0.46 per cent to 0.54 per cent (while Romania's market share increase was .4 percentage points).

Table 2.1 *Export market shares of East European countries in the OECD market for manufactured goods (in percentages)*

	1970	1975	1979	1980	1982
1. Total (SITC-0 to 8)					
Eastern Europe – total	1.54	1.55	1.40	1.30	1.13
Poland	0.46	0.54	0.44	0.40	0.27
Bulgaria	0.10	0.07	0.08	0.07	0.06
Czechoslovakia	0.33	0.28	0.24	0.23	0.21
East Germany	0.18	0.17	0.14	0.15	0.19
Hungary	0.23	0.21	0.22	0.20	0.19
Romania	0.24	0.28	0.28	0.25	0.21
2. Chemicals (SITC-5)					
Eastern Europe – total	1.53	1.51	1.27	1.21	1.52
Poland	0.31	0.30	0.22	0.25	0.15
Bulgaria	0.12	0.08	0.07	0.08	0.10
Czechoslovakia	0.26	0.25	0.24	0.30	0.35
East Germany	0.43	0.44	0.29	0.33	0.42
Hungary	0.18	0.23	0.28	0.30	0.28
Romania	0.23	0.21	0.17	0.18	0.22
3. Manufactured by materials (SITC-6)					
Eastern Europe – total	1.63	1.64	1.78	1.69	1.56
Poland	0.39	0.41	0.49	0.54	0.36
Bulgaria	0.09	0.08	0.09	0.07	0.08
Czechoslovakia	0.48	0.46	0.45	0.39	0.42
East Germany	0.21	0.18	0.20	0.18	0.24
Hungary	0.24	0.23	0.25	0.23	0.22
Romania	0.22	0.28	0.30	0.26	0.24
4. Machinery & transport (SITC-7)					
Eastern Europe – total	0.61	0.82	0.77	0.76	0.53
Poland	0.10	0.27	0.27	0.25	0.13
Bulgaria	0.02	0.02	0.02	0.03	0.02
Czechoslovakia	0.23	0.21	0.16	0.14	0.10
East Germany	0.16	0.16	0.13	0.13	0.12
Hungary	0.05	0.08	0.11	0.12	0.10
Romania	0.07	0.08	0.08	0.09	0.06
5. Miscellaneous (SITC-8)					
Eastern Europe – total	1.75	2.52	2.25	2.12	1.75
Poland	0.29	0.54	0.48	0.44	0.28
Bulgaria	0.09	0.07	0.07	0.07	0.06
Czechoslovakia	0.44	0.47	0.34	0.34	0.28
East Germany	0.33	0.33	0.27	0.27	0.24
Hungary	0.31	0.48	0.44	0.42	0.33
Romania	0.29	0.63	0.65	0.58	0.56

Source: *Foreign Trade by Commodities* (Paris: OECD, 1982) and *Foreign Trade, Analytical Tables* (Paris: OECD, 1983).

It is also useful to narrow one's focus on trends in the West European market because Japan, the United States, and Canada were of marginal importance at that time (e.g., the United States accounted for only 8.3 per cent of Poland's sales to the OECD in 1980). Arguably, Eastern Europe's ability to strengthen its competitive position abroad may be more accurately reflected in West European foreign trade statistics. Counter to the trend in OECD market statistics, the East European share of Western Europe's total imports declined from 2.43 per cent to 2.35 per cent during 1970–75.[4] However, the only country within Eastern Europe to show a gain was Poland (from 0.56 per cent to 0.65 per cent), while the decline in Bulgaria's and Czechoslovakia's share was quite severe.

Returning to the OECD statistics, one can notice that the areas in which Poland achieved the most significant gains in 1970–75 were two categories of manufactured goods: machinery and transport equipment (SITC-7), and miscellaneous manufactures (SITC-8). In the machinery and transport equipment group, Poland almost tripled its share from 0.10 to 0.27 per cent, whereas the shares for all the other countries of Eastern Europe remained relatively stable (except for Hungary and Romania, where it respectively rose from 0.05 and 0.07 per cent to 0.08 per cent for both). For miscellaneous manufactures, Poland, Hungary, and Romania were again the only countries to show large gains in the West European market (i.e., 0.25, 0.17, and 0.34 points respectively). However, Poland's share of the chemicals market remained relatively constant throughout this period (table 2.1).

By 1979, Poland seems to have lost much of what it gained in the 1970–75 period in terms of its total market share in the OECD countries. The 1979 share was almost equivalent to the 1970 level but Poland's performance was better than that experienced by Eastern Europe, whose overall share in 1979 was considerably below its 1970 level (1.40 per cent versus 1.54 per cent). It should also be noted that Poland suffered most of its losses in this period in chemicals and miscellaneous manufactures, while Poland's share of manufacturing goods classified by materials rose substantially, though the shares for the other East European countries rose only slightly. Finally it is most telling that unlike in many other economies Poland's share of machinery and transport equipment remained relatively stable.

Further evidence of improvements in Poland's export potential can be found by analysing the product composition of its exports, in particular by examining shares of machinery and transport equipment, as technologically more complex, in total sales abroad. This category represented 5.8 per cent of Poland's total exports to the OECD in 1970, the second lowest share among East European countries (the lowest share was that of Romania at 5.4 per cent). East Germany and Czechoslovakia, the most technologically advanced and trade-oriented economies of Eastern Europe at the time, reported exports of machinery and transport equivalent to 22.7 per cent and 18.7 per cent of their total exports, respectively.

However, by 1975, when one would have expected the first results of increased technology imports to materialize, Poland's share of machinery and transport equipment in total sales was already 11.6 per cent, twice the initial level (table 2.2). Some gains had also been achieved by the other East European countries, but in all of these cases, their respective gains were much below that of Poland. This helped Poland's market share for machinery and transport equipment to move closer to that of East Germany and Czechoslovakia, particularly since these two countries experienced a reduction in their shares during 1970–75 (i.e., to 21.9 per cent and 17.4 per cent, respectively).

Poland's combined share of machinery and transport equipment showed a further gain, to 14.2 per cent, in 1979, and with this share, Poland clearly showed the most impressive improvement in the commodity structure of exports to Western countries among all the East European economies since 1970 (i.e., the 1979 share was two-and-a-half times higher than that of 1970).[5] In Hungary, also ranked as an aggressive importer of Western technology, the respective share increased rapidly as well, doubling over the period to 12.1 per cent. However, Romania, with comparable rates of Western technology imports, increased its share by only a quarter to 6.7 per cent in 1979.

The positive correlation between large-scale technology imports and exports of machinery and transportation equipment is very clear when the record of these three aggressive importers is compared with less active importers of Western technology.[6] The comparison reveals that Bulgaria experienced some gains in 1970–79; its share increased from 7.1 per cent to 8.2 per cent, or by one sixth, or less than Romania. In East Germany the share of machinery and transport equipment declined modestly, while in Czechoslovakia the loss was substantial. The respective share for the latter dropped from 18.7 per cent in 1970 to 14.8 per cent in 1979, i.e., by one-fifth.

An analysis of trade data for chemicals, machinery and transport equipment combined indicates that among the most successful East European economies during 1970–79 were again Hungary (i.e.,

Table 2.2 *Total exports, exports of machinery and transport equipment (SITC-7) from Eastern Europe to the OECD, 1970–1983 (in million dollars)*

	1970			1975		
	Total	S-7	%	Total	S-7	%
Poland	1061	62	5.8	3174	367	11.6
Bulgaria	240	17	7.1	392	36	9.2
Czechoslovakia	723	135	18.7	1642	286	17.4
East Germany	410	93	22.7	1039	229	21.9
Hungary	536	34	6.3	1250	126	9.2
Romania	554	30	5.4	1692	214	7.2
Eastern Europe	3524	371	10.5	9189	1158	12.6

	1979			1981		
	Total	S-7	%	Total	S-7	%
Poland	5057	718	14.2	3607	537	14.9
Bulgaria	915	75	8.2	850	96	11.3
Czechoslovakia	2757	410	14.8	2729	362	13.9
East Germany	641	352	21.4	2190	348	15.9
Hungary	2547	308	12.1	2503	325	12.9
Romania	3267	218	6.7	3592	267	7.4
Eastern Europe	16184	2081	12.8	15471	1935	12.5

	1982			1983		
	Total	S-7	%	Total	S-7	%
Poland	3316	399	12.0	3267	362	11.0
Bulgaria	805	58	7.2	730	38	5.2
Czechoslovakia	2677	315	11.7	2627	320	12.2
East Germany	2385	370	15.5	2429	321	13.2
Hungary	2304	297	12.9	2340	259	11.0
Romania	2618	194	7.4	2810	182	6.5
Eastern Europe	14105	1633	11.6	14203	1482	10.4

Source: Calculated from *Foreign Trade by Commodities* (Paris: OECD).

increase from 11.5 per cent to 21.3 per cent) and Poland (10.5 per cent against 17.9 per cent). Romania, another aggressive importer of technology, did not show any progress, but the modest importers also did not make any progress, and in Bulgaria, the share increased only temporarily, while, in contrast, both Czechoslovakia and East Germany experienced declining shares for these two manufacturing groups (e.g., a decline in the latter from 38.8 per cent in 1970 to 36.2 per cent in 1979, in both cases the highest share for Eastern Europe). Thus, the inclusion of chemicals does not change the earlier ranking of export progress by the countries in question.

Export unit-values

A useful way of determining how efficient given exports are is to measure unit values, i.e., prices per kilogram (or unit) of products sold abroad. This indicator has several shortcomings, summarized, by Amann and Slama (1976), Amann, Cooper and Davis (1977), and Saunders (1978, 1984) (while Poznanski (1987) has extensively discussed methodology of export-unit values as well). Despite these shortcomings, the indicator has been widely utilized for analytical purposes by economists studying international trade and technological gaps. Not only is this measure relatively easy to use, given the availability of statistical data, but, by and large, it gives the same picture as other indicators of trade efficiency (for more discussion, see Poznanski 1985).

This indicator may supplement the previous ones, with the understanding that more favourable (higher) unit values reflect a superior level of technology of the country in question. Stating that more advanced goods by and large receive higher prices per kilogram or unit does not imply that technological progress always leads to such price rises in a particular product group. The more general argument is that whatever the direction of price changes, the exporters of less advanced (often heavier) models will have to accept lower prices than suppliers of the more attractive newer models, so that the less competitive seller will show lower unit values as a consequence.

To be sure, unit values also reflect demand conditions, hence, exporters supplying booming markets will receive higher prices than those selling identical goods elsewhere. However, demand by itself, regardless of market conditions for specific outlets, is influenced strongly by technology, i.e., by degree of reliability, novelty, etc. This makes it more difficult to distinguish technological from demand factors, and one must also bear in mind that unit values reflect not only changes in technology but also pure price movements – inflation or deflation – on foreign markets. When the rate of those price changes differs over time, then any comparison of unit values for one country in a longer period will be distorted.

However, if unit values for a few countries are compared for one year, then by taking data for one foreign outlet and calculating relative unit values (i.e., with the value for one country taken as a base), we can obtain results that will more or less be free of inflationary (deflationary) distortions. To avoid such price distortions, the following analysis calculates relative unit values for selected individual years (for similar analysis, see Poznanski 1988a). Theoretically speaking, a comparison of an average of two or even three years could prove to be more accurate, as it would allow one to factor out some seasonal fluctuations. However, our quantitative test of this hypothesis for a few commodities shows that there are no significant differences in results, whether drawn from annual or from average data.

The figures on unit values for machinery and transport equipment sold by Eastern Europe (and selected Western countries) to the European Community show that Poland obtained the lowest prices per kilogram in the region in 1970, a likely indication of its technological inferiority. With 0.92 dollar per kilogram, the Polish unit value represented only about 50 per cent of that reported by Hungary (1.80 dollars), almost 25 per cent less than that of East Germany (1.20 dollars), and 20 per cent below the Czechoslovak level (1.15 dollars). Indeed, Poland's unit value was close to that of Bulgaria and Romania, which were at that time considered to be among the least technologically advanced countries in the region.

After 1970, Poland made remarkable progress in improving the efficiency of its trade in machinery and transport equipment, so that by 1978 it was paid 2.99 dollars per kilogram of its goods, ranking only second to Hungary (3.43 dollars). At this point, Polish prices per kilogram were much ahead of all the modest importers of Western technology in Eastern Europe. Poland's unit value for machinery and transport equipment was then almost one third above the East German (i.e., 2.17 dollars) level. Even in 1982, in the midst of the economic crisis, when Poland's unit values were again the lowest in the region, they were still closer to those of many East European countries than they were back in 1970 (for reasons which would require a separate investigation, East Germany was the leader at that point).

Poland's export performance in machinery and transport equipment in 1970–78 also looks favourable when its unit values are compared to those of the individual East European exporters to the European Community relative to the average unit values for all exporters into this market combined. In 1970, Polish unit values represented 36 per cent of such aggregate world unit values, but in 1978 the respective figure was 58 per cent. Hungary showed some decline in relative unit values, but still its figure for 1978 was closer to the world level than that of any other East European country. Romania showed some improvement, but neither Bulgaria nor East Germany reduced its gap relative to the world level in that period of time, thus providing further evidence in support of the thesis advanced here.

Deflated indicators

Poland's initial improvements in relative unit values *vis-à-vis* East European (as well as Western) competitors on hard currency markets in the European community can be attributed partly to the weakening of import restrictions in the West and, one would guess, to her improved marketing abilities. But these two factors do not seem to explain fully the improved price performance by Poland relative to the other East European countries, because there are no grounds to believe that Poland was offered so much better concessions by the West than Czechoslovakia or East Germany. Nor is there reason to believe that Poland dramatically outpaced those countries in marketing skills (though with its greater opening to the world market, opportunities for acquiring such skills were positively enhanced).

A more plausible explanation is that the trends noted reflect primarily the more rapidly increasing competitiveness of Poland's exports relative to many other East European economies. It is more than likely that Poland achieved this edge through aggressive replacement of traditional, low value-added goods with higher priced ones, with the help of licence agreements signed with Western nations. However, it is also possible that some, if not all, of the differential between Polish unit values and those in the rest of Eastern Europe (and the Soviet Union as well, Poznanski, 1987) reflects the fact that Poland faced more favourable price trends for its products sold in the West than the others, either because of the specific mix of the Polish export offers or because of the geographical orientation of its trade – a hypothesis which will be difficult to test.

The complexity of our analysis of the unit values becomes even more apparent when one decides to deflate the already calculated unit values by indexes of export prices paid to Eastern Europe and the

Soviet Union in the West. This could be done in order to make the unit values better reflect changes in competitive – or technological – strength of the particular economies (Montias, 1985). According to the data released by the Polish statistical office, prices for machinery and transport equipment sold in the West almost doubled during 1970–78. Since the unit value tripled in the same period, it looks as if there had been something like a 50 per cent improvement in Polish unit values. This is the plausible magnitude of the competitive improvement, assuming that the official price index is purged of quality changes.

Assuming for the moment that countries in the region were facing on the average the same price trend for machinery and transport equipment sold in the West as Poland, it would seem as if the countries showing unit value index below 200 were experiencing a sort of technological retardation. This would be the case of the Soviet Union (163 index) and East Germany (180 index), but also of Hungary (189 index). This exercise clearly shows that if proper deflation was made for all the East European economies and the Soviet Union, the unit value trends could turn out to be different from those that are presented here. Nevertheless, even after controlling for this factor, Poland (and Hungary and Romania) may have done somewhat better than the other countries in the region.

Market reorientation

Montias (1985) offers a hypothesis that the trends during the 1970s in Poland's export performance indicators do not necessarily reflect increased technological strength of domestic producers, as we have claimed, but rather a shift away from the Soviet trade bloc to Western markets. If such a reorientation really took place, particularly in products of above-average quality, this would then explain the reports of increases in relative unit values of goods sold on hard-currency markets. At first glance, this seems plausible since Poland under Gierek undeniably reoriented its trade from the Soviet bloc to the West, particularly in manufacturing (Fallenbuchl 1983).

One must question, however, whether the shift toward Western markets could have been possible without certain technological improvements – mostly related to technology imports – that occurred during 1970–78. It appears rather unlikely that Poland could have managed to redirect its exports of manufactures by as much as it did without a substantial modernization of its product offerings. Western importers were generally more demanding in terms of quality than their Soviet and East European counterparts. There was also a problem of compatibility, as technical standards for many products were different in the West and East, thus complicating sales of indigenous goods to Western markets (as a rule, requiring more extended and timely post-sale service).

To determine whether Montias' hypothesis is correct, we have calculated the shares of CMEA and Western non-CMEA markets for two groups of Polish exports: those that were heavily injected with Western technology and those where technology imports were less important during 1970–78 (Appendix 3).[7] Of all the twenty three products sampled, among these that have been identified as major recipients of Western technology, eight were found to experience a dramatic shift from the CMEA and other non-Western markets to the West. These products were: washing machines, refrigerators, sewing machines, passenger cars, ships, television sets, tape recorders, and nitrogen fertilizers. In contrast, among those products for which no massive imports of Western technology were designated, again eight products have been identified for which the CMEA markets and the developing countries have remained a major sales area throughout the 1970–83 period.[8]

The data suggests that Western technology imports may have indeed provided Poland with new models of products that were in greater demand in Western markets and thus commanded higher prices. Even if some shift away from the CMEA (and its major segment, the Soviet) market took place, such diversion would be impossible, at least in the magnitude implied here, without technological upgrading of production. While Montias (1985) is correct in stressing the positive impact of the redirection of trade to the West on the increasing market shares of Polish exports in the Western markets in 1970–78, this does not contradict our claim that technology imports played a positive role in opening Western markets to Polish goods.

Summary

The speed of the 1970–75 acceleration of technology imports by Poland exceeded parallel efforts of other East European countries, particularly East Germany and Bulgaria. However, in per capita terms, Polish imports were of comparable magnitude to many other countries in the region (e.g., Hungary and Czechoslovakia). The post-1975 slowdown in Poland's imports was not an exception either, though none of the other East European economies allowed its transfers to be cut as severely as did Poland. The evolution of Polish technology imports from the West hence represented a more pronounced version of a pattern that was observed in many other East European countries as well.

Our analysis of export indicators (market shares, product composition and unit values) shows that the most aggressive buyers of Western technology outperformed the conservative importers throughout the 1970s, which indicates that these inflows generally had a positive impact on trade. For example, Poland, as one of the aggressive importers, rapidly increased its markets shares in Western imports, shifted its trade towards more complex manufactures, and showed large gains in terms of relative unit values. At the same time, more reluctant importers, such as Czechoslovakia, experienced both losses in market shares and declining significance of machinery exports, with their unit values registering at best modest gains.

Even during regional economic disturbances since 1979 when the region was forced to sharply reduce imports, cutting into supplies of even intermediate goods, Hungary was a more successful exporter on Western markets than the conservative borrower-countries. Moreover, manufactured exports from Poland to hard-currency markets often proved more resistant to economic adversities during 1979–82 than exports of these goods from many less credit-oriented East European countries. This suggests that, barring political upheavals, there may be a positive relationship between the scale of Western technology imports and export performance in Eastern Europe during this stage as well.

These findings are absolutely central to the main argument being developed in the book. If it is proven that there were no unusual – given the well known inadequacies of the state-planned system – misallocations or simple waste of imports, then this means that the sources of the 1979–82 economic crisis should be sought less in the foreign sector than domestically. Within this alternative perspective, the focus is not so much on supply-side factors – specifically, economic efficiency of input use – as is stressed in the conventional interpretations of the period in question. The emphasis should be instead on the demand side, i.e., utilization of the final product by competing groups, enterprises, households, etc. Thus, to obtain an accurate explanation of the genesis of the 1979–82 crisis, we would have to extend our investigation and put the domestic sector under closer scrutiny.

3   The constraining role of
       political factors

Our earlier analysis suggests that control over foreign debt under Gierek's government was strongly limited by other macroeconomic developments, in particular by rapid income increases which were often out of line with productivity. These income increases threatened the external balance because they forced the redirection of on-credit imports to consumption and thus diverting production to domestic users and away from foreign markets. We also suggested that these excessive income increases were due the lax wage/price policy, so that this policy should be viewed as being an important factor behind the onset of the debt crisis and its escalation. If one further follows arguments made before, one can assert that this lax income policy should be attributed to what is there called the 'softening' of the state-planning machinery, a change which was found to very much define the whole path of the economy in that period.

Whenever fundamental discontinuities occur, such as the above mentioned system's softening, simple, purely economic models fail to offer reliable answers, and political factors have to be looked into. Admitting politics to an economic analysis is particularly desirable when the state-planning order is discussed, because here discretion over economic resources is largely a function of the political resources amassed by actors. So, for such an economic system to change, the political system would have to alter as well, and this did indeed happen in Poland. Economic reforms were by no means a substitute for political changes, but rather occurred simultaneously in a co-evolutionary fashion (in open defiance of the totalitarian model). This softening of the economic system could well be seen as the outcome of political change identified in the previous chapter, i.e., the shifting of the power balance away from the central authorities.

In this chapter we offer further evidence that the economic crisis of 1979, which extended through 1982, could not take place without a parallel political crisis. It is not very difficult to substantiate the claim that Poland did not enjoy the political stability that all other East European countries had since 1971, and particularly from 1976 on. Poland was the only country of the region to experience both widespread and prolonged disturbances in which the majority of industrial workers participated. Likewise, only Poland underwent a rapid succession in the composition of party leadership during 1980–81, which culminated in an overall change from civilian to military rule. The latter development in particular was a vivid sign that, for all practical purposes, the traditional political system, still operational in most of the region, had itself been further fundamentally damaged (probably beyond the point of repair).

We can identify some major factors contributing to these unusual political tensions, under which Gierek's government had to execute its import-led strategy. First, there was exceptional party weakness and/ or a severe leadership cleavage that tended to intensify during periods of economic difficulty and/or political challenges to the regime. Secondly, there was a growth of autonomous and increasingly well organized social groups outside party/state control (i.e., Catholic clergy, industrial workers, and intellectuals) to a degree unknown in other East European countries. Finally, there were a number of external political pressures that interfered with internal developments to a larger degree than in the rest of the region, mainly due to the critical role of the country in both Soviet and Western geopolitical strategies.

As will be shown below, on many occasions, these three sources of political tension aggravated one another in an escalating cycle, particularly during the period of open activity by the independent union Solidarity. Intra-party conflicts led some factions, in many instances, to attempt to manipulate certain social groups into those conflicts, thus aiding independent political forces and placing additional pressure on the party. These extra-party political pressures often had the effect of strengthening interference from the Soviet Union, thus making it more difficult for the regime to come to terms with the social opposition. And it is these escalating political conflicts, which made it impossible for the party/state to mobilize fully the export potential for debt repayments when they suddenly accumulated.

The above would suggest that, barring intense political upheavals, there may indeed be a positive relationship between the scale of capital imports and export capabilities, and that with that potential, the economic crisis could be considerably mitigated. This political immobilization of the economic leadership is what distinguished this crisis from those admittedly less serious crises faced by the party/state before. If so, then one could argue that what was responsible for the unusual depth of the actual economic crisis was less the imbalances accumulated in the years before than that not enough was done to alleviate the crisis once it began unravelling – this was largely a crisis from the failure to properly manage it.

New political style: permissible pluralism

Intra-party relationships

One of the major political problems facing Gierek after assuming the highest post in the party was to reconstruct the operational capability of the party in a way compatible with his method of rule. By the end of 1971, he had already removed most of the top members of Gomulka's team (as well as his temporary allies against Gomulka, the faction ranged around Moczar (Dziewanowski 1976). The purge of political opponents, however, was not total, which distinguished this action from those pursued by other communist leaders under similar circumstances. Nor did Gierek try to build the kind of 'coalition leadership' that at that time characterized the Soviet Union under Brezhnev. Instead, he decided to integrate the party around his personal leadership by relying on 'exchange relations,' i.e., power or bonuses for support.

The other important move within the communist party was to systematically replace the low-skilled cadres with young and well trained apparatchiks. The scale of the actual rotation made generational change in the Polish party far more extensive than in almost any other party in the region at that time. As a result, the party leadership in Poland was younger (e.g., the average age of the PUWP Central Committee members was close to forty) and better educated (e.g., almost 80 per cent of the members of the Political Bureau claimed to have university degrees). Predictably, such changes had far-reaching implications for party behaviour, since the arrival of a new cohort of activists meant new personalities and new ways of thinking as well.

The new generation of apparatchiks elevated by Gierek was made up of people who, very much like their leader himself, had little interest in ideological purity. To most of them, a career within the communist party was a job for which they expected to be properly rewarded in material – financial – terms. Members were thus kept loyal to the party not on grounds of unified doctrinal beliefs but rather on the basis of similar economic interests. Once-admired icons of the movement, its heros, became rather meaningless symbols and party-sponsored events diluted into mere rituals. The official ideology of the party was maintained as a facade, needed to preserve an image of continuity and to please more orthodox communist parties in the region. Party ideology, however, continued to be used for communication purposes as no other 'language' commonly understood by the apparatchiks was readily available.

With these changes, the communist party ceased to be a vanguard possessing the highest knowledge of the doctrine and embodying its principles. Accordingly, the party's sense of having an exclusive political mission in history was weakened, and one of the forces integrating its membership was significantly undermined. No longer seen by the workers as the embodiment of societal interests, the party also lost its traditional source of legitimacy. The cadres became a far more acceptable target for close public scrutiny of their real, measurable achievements. Rather than continuing to await some distant promise of a 'perfect society', the public began to expect from the party more immediate, tangible rewards, primarily material.

Party/state relations

Gierek's leadership also moved ahead with important changes in the organization of both the state administration and the communist party. Theoretically, the purpose of the reorganization was to reduce bureaucracy by eliminating overlapping state and party apparatus responsibilities. In addition, administrative reforms sought to strengthen the central party leadership's control of local units, perceived as too strong and independent. Such reorganization also provided an excuse for reshuffling cadres to different jobs, so that Gierek's supporters were placed in key positions of power. The most essential part of these reforms took place in 1973–75, when a three-tiered regional administrative system linking provinces to county and to township was consolidated to two tiers. On the one hand, townships were enlarged and, on the other, province (*wojewodztwo*) units were doubled in number.

These reforms helped the central party authorities to better subordinate the lower-level political ranks, but, at the same time, the party as a whole lost much of its previously firm control over the state administration.[1] The primary reason for this was the aforementioned elimination of the mid-level territorial units (i.e., county committees). At this level, the party had traditionally enjoyed a particularly strong position *vis-à-vis* the state administration (due to its knowledge of local problems and wider political responsibility). Thus, by eliminating these units, the party lost the arm that had been most effective, among other things, in disciplining enterprise managers, who now became almost solely responsible to the powerful associations.

This weakening of the party's control over the administration was reinforced by several changes in planning procedures, among them some shift of authority from the Planning Commission – hitherto kept under firm control of the party leadership – to the industrial ministries. The idea was to turn these ministries into largely self-financing and revenue-maximizing entities (for more information, see Poznanski 1986a). While such moves fuelled the expansionistic ambitions of the state administration, they also weakened the ability of the central party leadership, the only institution concerned with maintaining macroeconomic balances, to prevent the economy from drifting into deep disequilibrium and stagnation.

Party, workers, and the Church

Gomulka's repressive reaction to the 1970 strikes outraged workers and made the communist party appear an alien force instead of the true representative of the people it had traditionally claimed to be. To change this image, the Gierek regime pursued frequent, direct contact with workers (i.e., on-site visits to factories, public discussion of state decisions, new rules on citizen complaints, and regular opinion polling – all from the repertoire of 'corporatist techniques'), but without conceding to their demands for independent representation at the plant level. The regime preferred to keep the existing forms of purely formal worker participation, assuming they would be passive and refrain from interfering in daily decision-making.

Gierek did not consider the legalization of strikes, despite initial promises to this effect, nor did the government resort to repressive measures to discourage further protest. Rather, he opted for a policy of allowing strikes and countering them with economic concessions (i.e., wages). Thus, the regime, in another expression of its own peculiar 'crisis-oriented' mentality, did not consider strikes an unacceptable embarrassment but a fact of life. This attitude to labour disputes represented a substantial departure from traditional communist practice of repressing workers into constant submission (continued in most of the rest of Eastern Europe and the Soviet Union as well).

To help his political image, Gierek's cabinet adopted another innovative policy, namely, 'borrowing' legitimacy from the Catholic Church and using cooperative relations with the clergy to counterbalance intra-party opposition. It was an ingenious move, since Gomulka's political record had been of one confrontation with the Church after another (e.g., condemnation of Church's friendly contacts with West German clergy, obstruction of nationwide commemorative religious celebrations). Gierek found this adversarial policy counter-productive – particularly in taming the growing forces of religious revival. In a major change of course, the regime began coopting the Church by granting a few concessions long-awaited by the Catholic administration – among them permits for building construction, better access to the media, and a higher quota for candidates to the priesthood.

Gierek had little choice in coming to terms with the Church, which at this point had a solid political base among Poles and an increasing ability to pursue an independent line. Much of this newly acquired strength came from the successful attempt by the clergy to extend its support from the traditional base of private farmers to workers. This became possible due, among other things, to a more progressive ecumenical programme and a new focus on the primary importance of work, human dignity, and individual rights. This change also helped the clergy attract intellectuals, many of whom were anxious to find an organization through which to exercise political influence outside the party.

These political successes, to a large degree, reflected the fact that the Church entered the postwar period as an activist institution rather than as an extension of the state as during the interwar period (Osa 1989). It was an activist church in the sense that it allowed great autonomy for priests and parishioners, and it also relied on rather close personal contacts between clergy and believers (in direct contrast to its political opponent – the communist party). The Church turned from a statist to such an activist institution during the war occupation that decimated its episcopate and forced priests to operate under suppression. This transformation prepared the clergy for the postwar communist reality that represented, to a degree, an extension of such oppressive conditions for ecclesiastical work.

To conclude, in political terms, Gierek's expansionary programme of 'renewal' was an attempt to create a new and dynamic political equilibrium that would synthesize and reorient frequently conflicting forces within Poland's party and state administration. For the party's traditionalists, Gierek offered an ambitious investment programme, a return to collectivization of agriculture, and the rejection of genuine market-based economic reforms. For the upward-moving generation of industrial bureaucrats and state administrators, he provided increased access to sophisticated technology and fewer party/political checks on their exercise of discretion over its selection. This redefined balance within the party/state had to be reconciled with contradictory pressures upon it from society.

In fact, society was included in this domestic balance in a type of corporatist arrangement – through a series of positive incentives and various, often modified, restraints. Thus, for industrial workers, there were wage increases and 'dialogues' on a firm-by-firm basis. For the Catholic Church, there was acceptance of its stronger presence on the political scene and moves toward lasting reconciliation. Finally, for intellectuals, there was increased consultation and promises of liberalization in the party/state policies toward culture and education. If conflicts among these forces subsequently undermined Gierek's leadership, their initial convergence was critical to its establishment at the outset of the import-led strategy.

In the economic realm, the new policies of Gierek greatly helped to revitalize the economy. In terms of an average annual growth rate in national product, Poland outperformed all other centrally planned economies with the possible exception of Romania. Together with the large range of semi-liberalization measures, such a performance made Gierek popular outside the party in addition to strengthening his control within it. Gierek's domestic policies and unprecedented activism in the international arena gave him a good reputation among Western leaders, particularly those in Europe. Meanwhile, his continued loyalty to the socialist alliance and his political triumph over the more extreme nationalist elements in the Polish party led by Moczar gave the Soviet Union cause for satisfaction as well.

The beginning of a political crisis: broken contracts

The important changes in the economic course around 1975, when various imbalances had intensified and made further rapid growth questionable, required political adaptation. Arrangements made by Gierek in the early years were predicated on economic expansion. But with the adjustment of 1976–79, fewer and fewer goods were available to 'pay' for necessary political support. Still, Gierek opted not to change his style of rule and seek an alternative mode, such as a return to the repression of the past. Instead, he continued to rely on support from diverse interest groups for which he was no longer able to pay.

Not surprisingly, his economic options grew even fewer, and as a result, the political system became less stable, a fact manifested most plainly in the regime's declining popularity.

Disobedience and dissent

A serious test of the regime's stability came in 1976, when Gierek's cabinet decided to reduce internal economic imbalances by raising prices for all food products and some other consumer goods as well. In response, massive strikes broke out in about 130 factories, most of them large scale and paying above-average wages. Unlike the protests which took place in 1970 and 1971, these actions were nationwide, clearly indicating that tensions between labour and the party had entered into a new phase. Police action was taken to arrest a number of worker activists and many of the strikers lost their jobs. The most effective measure was, however, the decision to roll back prices, after which the workers were released from prison and most of those fired were reinstated at their jobs.[2]

The political costs of the 1976 clash over price increases included growing frustration among industrial workers. The fact that the regime purposely did not use much force against strikers but instead decided to retreat from its price reform, did not earn Gierek the popularity one might have expected (in contrast with the earlier reversal in official policies). On the contrary, Gierek's retreat caused protesters to think that the communist regime was weak and, in effect, encouraged workers to be more militant. In fact, protesters became more vocal in criticizing both the industrial managers and the local party apparatus, while their readiness to back up their complaints with strikes and work stoppages considerably increased (see Bernhard 1987).

The 1976 confrontation also triggered a build-up of various nonparty opposition forces among intellectuals. The scale of this movement, clearly unprecedented in Eastern Europe, and the tactics employed turned out to be crucial factors in the political evolution of Poland. Traditionally, before 1970, the Polish intellectual opposition had tried to reform the political system by appealing to the party (e.g., the so-called revisionist group associated with Brus and Kolakowski). This time, however, the effort was directed more towards the workers, initially taking the form of financial and legal assistance to harassed strike leaders. Later it was redirected toward encouraging political activism among workers, in particular, those who mobilized around the cause of free unions (some clergymen joined intellectuals in this effort as well).

Another major effort by the opposition was the development of an underground press. Illegal publications (including books) were not new to Poland, but this time the opposition succeeded in boosting the number of titles and their circulation far beyond the norms of the past. As a result, the independent press began to pose a real threat to the state monopoly of mass media. Though the regime had a capacity to penetrate and crack down on illegal publishing, it resorted only to limited harassment of those involved in underground publishing. It also made no attempt to punish the readers of such dissenting publications, in sharp contrast to repressive police actions taken under similar circumstances by other communist regimes.

Intra-party conflicts

Gierek's 'repressive tolerance' towards social opposition seemed to make sense as an instrument for reducing domestic tensions. The cost of this policy for Gierek was, however, that it produced a growing dissatisfaction within some party circles. To many of the party apparatchiks, this was an unacceptable display of 'softness' that could later backfire, causing more political damage than the temporary loss of popularity among the population in case of a bold attack on oppositionists. In fact, much of the brutality during the poststrike repression can be attributed to the efforts made by some party circles (including those in the police) to discredit Gierek and at the same time discipline workers (see Staniszkis 1983).

The extended borrowing, facilitated by Gierek's political relaxation in the country, cost him support within the party as well. The increasing dependence of Poland on Western financing was seen by the intra-party opponents of Gierek as politically objectionable as they thought it gave too much leverage over the communist party to Western leaders. In addition, they felt that this shift towards Western economies undermined traditional ties with the Soviet Union, whose strong direct involvement was seen as crucial for the political survival of the communist leadership in general and for many of Gierek's intra-party opponents in particular.

This perception of Gierek's policies by the intra-party opposition differed little from the feelings shared by a growing number of Soviet leaders. At that time, the Soviet regime had lost much of its initial enthusiasm for Poland's energetic efforts to build up Western ties. This was because many specific choices made by Gierek ran directly counter to Soviet priorities. From the Soviet point of view, Gierek's strategy was detrimental to long-lasting Soviet–Polish cooperation agreements (e.g., in the tractor industry), to sales opportunities for Soviet plants (e.g., colour television), and to certain specialization efforts sponsored by the Soviet leaders (e.g., the regional programme for computers, called RIAD).

The greatest political threat from within the party came from the faction led by Politburo member Olszowski, who staged a campaign of critical letters written by several local party chiefs in 1979 directed against Gierek, and then arranged a series of attacks on Gierek's policies at an important party meeting the same year. Olszowski's faction also encouraged some attacks from outside the party, as shown in a highly critical report by a group of reformist marxist intellectuals published in 1979. This fragmentation of the party came at the very moment when Gierek needed a solid political base to execute the regime's 'austerity' programme initiated in 1976.

The political impact of austerity measures eroded the synthesis of forces which Gierek had created through his expansionary policies of the early 1970s. Rather than each group – workers, intellectuals, party hardliners, technocrats, reform advocates, etc. – being the beneficiary of an individual 'deal' engineered by Gierek, each instead found himself the victim of some sort of sacrifice. With each group suspecting its traditional opponents to be responsible for these sacrifices, a struggle ensued to ensure that the burdens of adjustment were shifted from one group to another. Doing so eventually involved a major and direct confrontation between these groups, something which Gierek's leadership, greatly compromised by the deteriorating economic situation, proved powerless to prevent.

Limited conflict

The internal confrontation culminated in mid-1980, when massive strikes again broke out. When faced with workers' protests, Gierek decided to try again his previously successful tactic of negotiated settlement and to keep the confrontation focused on purely economic issues. Nevertheless, it became impossible to prevent the workers from making political demands. Once the separate striking committees opened communication with each other, the party was forced to talk on political issues with the organized workers' representatives. In late 1980, the regime agreed to the workers' most critical and controversial demand – the formation of free trade unions throughout the entire country with a single leadership at the top (i.e., Solidarity led by Walesa).

At the time, the permanent incorporation of independent unions into the political system of Poland seemed feasible. In the first months of the free trade union's existence, the workers clearly insisted on a limited or rather nonpolitical formula of a 'veto committee', that would leave the actual decision-making to the party. While there was a risk that the independent unions might turn into political bodies, properly executed reforms could well have prevented and/or deterred any deleterious consequences. Moreover, the party was able to continue to function for awhile, and thus was still in a position to 'deal' with workers rather than have to resort to further confrontation.

In addition, the Church played an important stabilizing role in the conflict at this point. Clearly, the sympathy of the clergy was with the workers, particularly because the free unions strongly pressed for more religious freedom. However, this was not an unqualified support, since the Church's desire to preserve the basically hierarchical character of society meant many of its interests differed widely from those pursued by the workers. Importantly, the Catholic Church was afraid that continuation of labour unrest would weaken the economy beyond easy (low-cost) repair.

Any move by the communist party to allow even limited independent representation for the workers encountered opposition from the Soviet Union on ideological and political grounds. Nevertheless, had the party quickly produced a workable package and stood firmly behind it, the regime might have been able to withstand Soviet pressures, much as it did in 1956 when decollectivization was pushed through. But, unlike 1956, the party in 1980–81 was threatened by wider social opposition, this time operating within an identifiable organizational structure and with widely recognized leaders. Faced with such a unified structure, the party found it difficult to divide the workers and manipulate them into absorbing internal conflicts.

Also unlike in 1956, the party did not consolidate around new leadership, but quickly entered into heated internal struggles. The initial clashes were between the Gierek team and the fast growing opposition of Olszowski, now backed by Moczar. This group succeeded in causing Gierek's removal in December 1980. He was replaced by Kania, largely due to the strong backing of Jaruzelski, chief of the army and a Politburo member (apparently, the candidacy of Olszowski was openly opposed by Cardinal Wyszynski). However, even after the elevation of Kania, intra-party struggles continued, thus making the working out of a reasonable compromise with the workers unlikely.

Escalation of the crisis

The intra-party fight had a decisive impact on further political developments. The inability of the party to come up with a reform package forced the free unions to resort to various forms of pressure, with strikes proving their strongest weapon. In addition, the anti-corruption campaign launched by the opposition (with many false stories) to dislodge Gierek backfired insofar as it merely undermined the popularity of the communist party further. As a result, the free union Solidarity – now several million members strong – started to radicalize and diversify. Soon the union split into a number of political factions, with a conservative wing, led by Walesa and close to the Church, seeking a compromise with the party; and militant groups – the most prominent figure being Gwiazda – pushing for a full-scale confrontation with the party and an end to Soviet domination (Ash 1985).

In turn, the radicalization of the free union worked as a catalyst for further polarization of the party. Many apparatchiks, particularly those at the lowest levels, got involved in a grass-roots movement calling for the establishment of direct contact between party members (bypassing the traditional vertical command system) and for the gradual replacement of their bosses through democratically held elections.[3] The conservatives responded to the growing aggressiveness of the unions and the radical reformists within the party with even louder calls for a blunt repressive response to both challenges, some even advocating police action and a return to Stalinist-type propaganda (e.g., they initiated the beating of Solidarity activists gathered for a meeting in Bydgoszcz in March, 1981).

This polarization of the party, rather than revitalizing membership, turned out to be self-destructive. Large-scale desertions from the party ranks occurred as the party was now seen by a growing number of its members as politically bankrupt. In the first three months following the registration of the free unions, party membership did not change significantly (e.g., a drop of 50,000 during September–December 1980). Later, however, the number of dropouts began to accelerate, so that by December 1981, membership was down to around 2.7 million from 3.2 million registered in July 1980, or by 17 per cent.

With a weakened party, the centre of power shifted towards the state administration, led by Prime Minister Jaruzelski since February 1981. The elevation of Jaruzelski, joined by a few others from the military who took over several key administrative posts, indicated that the party had decided, or was forced, to pass its authority to the administration and army. As the only (other than the police) intact institution of political establishment, the army was seen as best prepared to protect the party from total collapse (and deal with economic issues as well). That the political role of the military began to increase was evidenced by the election of Jaruzelski to the position of Secretary General of the party in September 1981.

The change in party leadership was directly related to the first national meeting of Solidarity taking place in that month. The meeting proved that radical elements in the free unions would soon be ready to dominate the movement. Walesa, the symbol of workers' resistance and a moderate, was elected chairman of Solidarity by only a slim margin of votes. Radicals called for free elections to the parliament (a political taboo during the first months). In addition, many low-level union activists engaged themselves in removing party representatives from industrial factories and local offices. The party reacted with a tougher line and almost no room remained for negotiations in the months to come.

Foreign interference

To make matters worse, escalating domestic tensions were accompanied by external political interventions, particularly from the Soviet Union. The domestic disturbance invited interference by the Soviet leaders, who were looking to put an end to independent unions. At the same time, they were anxious for an internal solution to the problem that would not involve direct military involvement. They wanted to avoid the high political costs of earlier interventions in Eastern Europe (such as the 1968 invasion of Czechoslovakia, which caused among other things irreversible damage to the West European communist movement).

Thus, the Soviet party embarked on an indirect approach consisting of several measures, including a bloc-wide media campaign of accusations against Solidarity. Frequent private and public reprimands were communicated to Polish leaders when they attempted to make concessions. Occasional economic threats were made, exploiting the fact that Poland, like other East European countries, depended heavily on Soviet supplies of fuels and other raw materials. Moreover, Soviet

leaders held out the ever-present possibility of direct military intervention to suppress the confrontational workers.

Political pressure came also from Western governments, which for
the most part reacted to the crisis in Poland with open sympathy for
Solidarity. Western leaders believed, however, that the collapse of the
communist system in Poland would not be allowed by the Soviet
Union under any foreseeable circumstances. Accordingly, Western
governments urged a compromise solution, i.e., saving both the party
and organized labour. The objective was to bring the crisis to a quick
conclusion but with greater political freedoms institutionalized as far
as possible. This goal largely coincided with the position taken by
Western unions, an important new political player on the Polish scene.
Western unions did not call for a 'class war' between labour and
capital (= the communist party); instead, they demanded that organized labour be provided with the rights traditionally enjoyed in
Western economies.

While Soviet pressure provoked the radical union members into
increasingly erratic aggressive behavior and the open Western support
of free unions bolstered the spirits of militant labour activists as well.
At the same time, within the party, Western involvement strengthened
moderates while Soviet pressures helped the conservatives, thus preventing a shift towards one side or the other. Such external interfer-
ences constrained the options available to both the regime and the
social opposition, thus adding to the explosiveness of the domestic
political situation, so that any form of a peaceful agreement with the
free union became increasingly unattainable.

The nature of political conflicts

An interesting question in the context of the above analysis is how the
political structure of Poland under Gierek differed from that in the rest
of Eastern Europe and the Soviet Union. If there actually were
substantial differences, then the unusual depth of the economic crisis
that followed Gierek's import-led strategy could more legitimately be
attributed to political factors. This would be particularly the case if the
political structure of Poland exhibited more features potentially dis-
ruptive for macroeconomic adjustment than did other communist
states in the region. To effectively pursue this issue, a proper analytical
framework is essential, so we will begin by searching for such a
framework.

State-centred theory

In a comparative analysis of political diversity in communist Eastern Europe during the import-led growth period, Comisso (1986) offered an imaginative typology of non-democratic political systems that seems well suited to our discussion here. This typology distinguishes two such systems or styles of politics – paternalistic and collective – and then identifies their normal and pathological (or perverse) versions. Paternalistic politics can assume either a normal form – kingship – or a perverse one – tyranny, while collective systems can either take the form of collegial or oligarchical leadership, with the former representing a normal – functional – type of polity, and the latter being a perverse – dysfunctional – version.

With the help of this typology, Comisso offers an interesting reconstruction of the postwar evolution of communist politics, concluding that with destalinization starting in the mid-fifties, all countries, including the Soviet Union, moved away from tyranny. By the time the region was adopting an import-led strategy in the seventies, only one country, Romania, as a kingship, retained the paternalistic mode of politics. Of the other countries, Poland operated under an oligarchic system of political leadership while the others, including the Soviet Union, fell into the category of collegial politics. In other words, all these countries had moved closer to democratic-type politics, with only one of them, namely, Poland, boxed into a perverse mode of politics.

It is also hypothesized by Comisso that the two extreme political systems – kingship and oligarchy – predictably produced a more unstable pattern of economic growth, and thus ended up with foreign debts that were more difficult to service. In Poland, we are told, it was unresolved conflicts between political factions which caused excessive expansion based on foreign borrowing. But in Romania, run-away growth was the product of a single-leader obsession with enlarging his power base (also see: Linden 1986). In contrast, the rest of the region, operating under collegial leadership, showed a rather stable growth pattern, since the presence of mechanisms for political compromise generated more moderate economic strategies, accommodating many constituencies in an orderly way.

The above typology is no doubt quite useful in sorting out the political diversity in the communist world of that time, both in a static and dynamic (diachronic) sense. Presenting both the Polish and Romanian political systems as unusual cases is definitely not without foundation either. Description of the political features of the Gierek period as an oligarchic system captures well the vast divisions into uncooperative factions within the party – a phenomenon which we incidentally identified earlier as distinguishing Poland's polity from that of the other communist countries. Personal control exercised by a single leader who operates through a network of family-related cronies, which was so characteristic of Romania, separates this country from the rest of the region (though one also finds elements of paternalism, or familism, in Bulgaria).

Question marks

Fitting individual cases into this typology produces some problems, as well as speculation on probable economic outcomes of particular models of leadership. For instance, it is unclear whether the Romanian system under Ceausescu was more a kingship rather than some form of tyranny. Many accounts portray Romania's political system as the last bastion of true Stalinism, i.e., tyranny. Tismaneanu (1992) describes the regime as being determined by a vision of communism that synthesizes an updated version of Stalinism and xenophobic populism. This is without denying that Ceausescu, unlike Stalin, tended to rely heavily on family ties and tried to develop a dynastic succession.

With countries so politically different as Hungary, East Germany, and the Soviet Union, one also doubts whether they can all be safely put into one category, that of 'collegial' leadership, at least without some strong qualifications. On one hand, there is Hungary with institutiona-lized factionalism, cleverly exploited by Kadar, where reform-oriented and more conservative forces were in constant negotiation. On the other, there is East Germany, where there is little evidence of distinctive factions and intra-party, well structured, compromise-seeking. Divi-sions, indeed, emerged in Khrushchev's Soviet Union, but they were less centred around attitudes toward reform than on appropriation of resources (e.g., heavy industry lobby versus agricultural lobby).

Moreover, there is a considerable difference between the three apparent cases of 'collective leadership' – Bulgaria, Czechoslovakia and East Germany – in their economic behavior during the period in question. Czechoslovakia only reluctantly and with great delay – as the last country in the region – turned to foreign credits to prop up its economy, but Bulgaria and East Germany, the latter in particular, were much more eager to take this path. Only Bulgaria and Czechoslovakia did not allow their foreign debt to reach a risky level, which at least in the latter case was consistent with the traditional preference of its communist leaders for macroeconomic equilibrium. The East German communist party was much less cautious in its approach, so that foreign indebtedness eventually reached high levels, which made its economy nearly as vulnerable to financial dangers as those faced, for instance, by Hungary.

While Bulgaria, Czechoslovakia, and East Germany followed a smoother economic path than the above two economies, another 'collegial' country – Hungary – did not, as it embarked, as demonstrated before, on a massive campaign of borrowing and investing. Still, in terms of credit expansion, Hungary's import-led strategy was on many accounts more tempered than Poland's, and while it did not avoid debt crisis, its expansion was more tempered and the structure of credit it used to prop up the economy was more reasonable (e.g., greater reliance on long-term credits). Hungary appears also to have been more moderate than Romania (and to a lesser degree than Poland) in its ability to avoid massive concentrations of imported resources on high-visibility projects (typical of the early days of Soviet-type forced industrialization).

Bipolar model

One tacit assumption in the typology of political structures outlined before is that political power rests exclusively with the leadership while society is the passive target and executor of certain economic policies,[4] but not an active player involved in formulation of policies or in their practical realization. This is a common assumption in the political literature on communist societies, reflective of the influence of the totalitarian paradigm (easily traced in the economic debates as well, Poznanski 1993c). A similar line of reasoning is advanced by Staniszkis, who made one of the most important contributions to the analysis of the political scene in Poland (e.g., arguing that political protests under both Gomulka and Gierek were largely engineered by factions within the communist party itself; see Staniszkis 1983).[5]

In truth, however, society has been neither uniform nor left without influence over party/state affairs. Thus, properly to understand the reasons for the radicalism of Gierek's early policies and the ineffectiveness of his effort to arrest an unravelling crisis, it is necessary to adopt a bipolar model, in which the party/state and society interact and constrain each other. Within this framework, the 'numerical' aspect of leadership, that is, the number of players at the central – upper – level, and eventually the pattern of their relations are less important than the political weight of communist leadership compared to that of society (with its specific configuration of interest groups and relationships between them) (for more, see: Hankiss 1989, 1990).

This bipolar approach, when applied, demonstrates that Poland not only differed from the rest of Eastern Europe because of its very polarized leadership, but also, and primarily, because here the communist party had to confront a far more volatile society than anywhere else in the region. Nowhere else were industrial workers as well organized or conscious of their objectives (including the desire to expand elements of labour management). In no other country had intellectuals acquired such strength in forming public opinion and influence over the actions of industrial workers (particularly when compared with Bulgaria and Romania, where political opposition was negligible) (Linden 1986)).

The only other society of Eastern Europe that represented a real political power for the party/state to recognize was Hungary, though for rather different reasons. The strength of the society was mostly the product of the 1956 confrontation with the Stalinist communists, resulting in bitter resentment of the party/state when it was reconstituted. As in Poland, Hungarian intellectuals led the critical attacks on the communist regime, but they were more willing to work with it than their Polish counterparts, who viewed any such form of contact as 'sacrilegious'. There was also very little tradition of organized labour opposition in 'collegial' Hungary, like that found in 'oligarchic' Poland.

One could conclude from the analysis above that one reason why Poland, Hungary, and Romania engaged in more aggressive import-led growth could have been that they shared at least one of these two features of political structure: perverseness of top leadership, and/or presence of a 'civil society'. In other words, Poland and Romania had in common pathological types of leadership – oligarchy and kingship, respectively – while Poland and Hungary shared a political situation under which the party/state was confronted with strong societies. This is what distinguished this group from the rest of Eastern Europe, where 'normalcy' of leadership and its dominant position relative to society were the case.

Imperfect pluralism

While the bipolar model seems to more adequately account for similarities in the behavior of Hungary, Poland, and Romania during the early phases of import-led growth, the question remains whether the same model is as useful in explaining differences which emerged between them later. Particularly intriguing is the question of why only Poland proved unable to avoid a sharp economic downturn at the conclusion of its import-led policy. That the more conservative economies of Bulgaria and Czechoslovakia managed to escape an economic crisis of Poland's proportions is quite understandable, but the difference between Poland and Hungary is not as easy to account for. That Hungary, with greater indebtedness on a per capita basis, incurred much milder losses in economic growth than did Poland, suggests that politics – rather than economics – might be behind these differences.

For debt adjustment not to cause great damage to any of these three economies, both political stability and incentives for efficiency were required. Such an adjustment meant that, after years of high rates, real wages earned by state-sector workers had to be sharply reduced and, for such a manoeuvre to be executed without incurring strikes which would damage output, a resolute party/state was needed. In addition, for the economic cost of debt-related austerity to be minimized, a given economy had to have reasonably strong incentives for workers, which would ensure that labour productivity would not be severely impacted by wage reductions.

Given our institutional knowledge of these countries at the time in question, it could be easily predicted that Hungary would manage the softer landing. One could assume that with the presence of collective leadership and a system of checks and balances which allowed compromise, Hungary should have been able to more evenly distribute the pain of austerity felt by various segments of the working people and to reduce the size of the 'negative' multiplier, related to import restrictions. With its highly reformed economic system, placing greater emphasis on profit maximization, Hungary could also count on producers to adopt stronger cost-cutting measures in response to a state-imposed squeeze on imports (Comisso and Marer 1985).

Clearly, Romanian conditions differed from those in Hungary enough to prevent it from achieving an equally smooth adjustment to its excessive level of foreign debt. True, the authoritarian regime of Ceausescu could more easily rely on coercive forces and mass fear as an effective deterrent to labour unrest in the face of a very sharp decline in the living standard. In fact, there was very little popular resistance to real wage reduction and widespread rationing of goods, which here assumed the harshest possible form among all East European economies. However, without a reasonably efficient economic system like Hungary had, Romania was unable to avoid larger losses in industrial output, leaving the regime with little choice but to base its repayment strategy on curtailing domestic absorption more deeply than Hungary did (see Tismaneanu 1992).

The situation in Hungary and Romania contrasted with that of Poland, whose state was weak and divided into factions absorbed primarily with matters of political survival rather than economic adjustment. Not only was Gierek's regime unable to work out a sensible economic compromise at the central level, but it lacked the power to confront worker hostilities (and successfully resist wage pressures). Unlike Hungary, but similarly to Romania, Poland operated a relatively ineffective economic system; though in the Polish case this was because the institutional reforms were inconsequential, while the largely unchanged Romanian system suffered from its Stalinist legacy. Given this systemic inferiority, Poland's adjustment to the debt crisis had to be more costly.

Principal qualifications

When 'bringing' society into the political analysis, as we have done above, one has to be careful not to overemphasize its real role, and, in particular, not to end up replacing the state-centred model with a society-centred approach. Also, one has to be very cautious in defining the nature of state-society conflict, or in other words, in specifying the exact motivation that drove these two parties. Among other things, one should decide whether societal actions were aimed against the whole system – and the state as its key embodiment – or whether they were directed toward more limited objectives, ones which could be met through political compromise with the state, followed by reforms (to be executed by the same state apparatus).

When social protests – strikes, street demonstrations, to name a few – take place, they testify to the instability of a given system. By themselves, however, such acts do not mean that the core of the system is being rejected by the protesters. In fact, nowhere in Eastern Europe were conflicts between party/state and society fuelled by popular pressure to abolish the entire system, nor was the political leadership ready to assist, such demands. Even in the case of the exceptionally vocal Polish workforce, there were no serious attempts made by labour to permanently oust the communist forces (see Ekiert, 1990).[6] Instead, efforts were made to broaden labour representation in order to assure that the economic interests of workers would no longer be taken lightly or ignored by the communist leadership.[7]

A similar pattern of political opposition to the party/state could be found in other East European countries, where society acquired a considerable ability to influence political outcomes.In Hungary too, if one takes a rather general view, the efforts by the political opposition from outside the party were framed in terms of controlling the party rather than doing away with it. While not seeking independent labour representation, the workers of Hungary managed to partially reshape the official unions into their own political tool, mostly to press their economic needs Batt (1988) correctly argues that official trade unions there converted themselves into relatively effective self-appointed defenders of labour interests. Importantly, these new, more assertive trade unions were accommodated by the party, used to bringing into the political process different interest groups, so that the potential for adversary relations was reduced (also see Batt 1991).

Also in Poland, the growing political influence of extraparty forces was for the most part met by the party/state with gestures of accommodation, so that moderation on the part of the opposition was facilitated as well. Rather then seeking head-on confrontation, the party/state tried to give in to the demands of the opposition, as long as concessions did not threaten the elite's survival. This accommodating posture was possible in large part due to the growing deideologization of the party/state, which continued in the midst of the large-scale wave of strikes during 1980–81. This was not another 'socialist revival' or 'normalization', in the name of true socialism but rather an effort on the part of the elite to deal with national problems such as economic growth, inflationary pressures, and the rise in crime. While not experiencing a comparable political crisis, the Hungarian political elite also kept shifting from the communist rhetoric to the language of national interests.

While the struggle between the party/state and labour throughout the decade of Gierek had great political implications, it was influenced more by particular interests than by conflicting ideologies (i.e., ideas). The party/state tried to protect its power base while workers battled for economic compensation, but this was not a static situation. Both sides in the conflict were undergoing reevaluations of their respective positions. The party/state was gradually becoming more disillusioned with the advantages of power – in a hardly ungovernable country – while labour was growing increasingly aware that their wealth hinged on power. Given this dynamic, society was heading for another major political confrontation while leaving the economy in an even more fragile condition.

Summary

The large-scale borrowing initiated by Gierek's government in 1971 was not a substitute for economic reforms, though the direction of certain systemic changes might have been rather questionable. Nor was credit-taking a substitute for political reforms, as many significant shifts in both power distribution and political style took place during these years. We find no clear evidence that the party leaders decided to take the political risk involved in large-scale borrowing from capitalist countries rather than to accept the risk stemming from instilling more market-like elements (or permitting political expression). In fact, this regime was willing to assume high-risk unorthodox policies in many areas, not only with respect to borrowing capital from abroad.

If anything, there seems to be a certain consistency in the measures taken by Gierek's regime with respect to various aspects of economics and politics. Opening towards the world economy required economic reforms which would allow those closer to production to make the right selection of imported equipment. With the opening of the economy, by itself representing a rejection of an important dogma, came the impetus for a broader deideologization of politics. In turn, changes in the political realm were instrumental in promoting economic reforms, if in no other way, then at least by removing the stigma from certain forms of systemic change (see: Bauer 1988).[8] For their part, the economic reforms facilitated the demonopolization of politics, largely through giving more influence to professional staff.

The inflow of foreign resources, rather than helping the regime stifle the systemic and political change, has facilitated it by allowing the party leadership to better meet demands from strengthened sectoral interests (i.e., alliances of branch ministries and associations) and more confident workers. The new political balance created among the political players (including the Church) was not maintained by a common ideology, or even a broad goal, so that feeding conflicting forces with economic resources was an important stabilizing factor. When in 1975 the first symptoms of overborrowing became visible, the true test of this new political equilibrium took place. It was a test of the ability of the various actors to work out a compromise on distributing economic sacrifices.

The economic adjustment begun in 1976, involving a slow-down in the pace of consumption growth as well as cuts in investment, helped the Gierek regime reduce the size of its trade deficit with Western countries, a necessary step towards the stabilization of rapidly increasing foreign debt. But at the same time, the adjustment of 1976 caused the rate of growth of the national product first to decline and then to turn negative in 1979. The regime also saw imbalances between supply and demand on the domestic market for many goods to aggrevate. These are the expected economic trade-offs, and more radical improvements in domestic and external equilibria were possible only at the expense of further deterioration of the overall growth.

The 1980 decision to sharpen the austerity programme, and shift more of the burden of arresting the unravelling economic crisis to consumers, did not work. It provoked mass unrest that the regime found – for the first time in the postwar period – impossible to dissolve quickly. Neither wage concessions nor promises of political concessions, so effective in the early days of Gierek's rule, worked this time. In the midst of political turmoil, the government proved even less successful in pursuing its economic course than before the harsh steps were initiated. As a result, industrial production – as well as the national product in general – registered even deeper decline, while wages were allowed to accelerate. Both these developments made control of the foreign debt even more problematic, as fewer supplies were left for exports.

As political tension brought much of the economy misery, so a political solution was needed to take Poland out of the debt trap before financial overexposure became even worse. This was a new political situation and it required of the party different skills than those applied during earlier confrontations with workers. Given the lack of 'negotiating' procedures and strong external pressures, the conflicting forces – the party and the workers – were unable to find a compromise. Instead, they provoked each other to take an increasingly extreme posture, pushing the country into a grave political crisis. With this political crisis and the economic one evolving simultaneously, reversing economic adversity was impossible without putting the political crisis to rest or at least deescalating it significantly.

Part II

Economic reforms, divided society and 'growth fatigue'

4 Anti-crisis policies and elusive economic recovery

In our effort to reconstruct the developments during the import-led growth of Gierek, we have uncovered a certain causal model, which helps to account for the behavior of Poland's economy in those years. We found that the economic crisis at the end of that period, while accompanied by a debt crisis, seemed largely related to imbalances that emerged in the domestic sector. These imbalances, in turn, could be linked to changes in the economic system as a framework within which government policies were conducted. Changes in the economic system, finally, were traced to the political scene, or shifts in the relative power of particular players, within the party/state and outside of it. In this opening chapter of the second part of the book, we pursue a similar line of analysis to test the validity of that model after the 1981 state of war and provide ground for its further, more specific examination in the other two chapters that make up the rest of this part.

If the causality discovered in the previous part is found in the post martial law period, this would suggest that this period should be viewed, at least in general terms, as an extension of the previous years. The pattern of economic growth in this period seems to actually suggest that we are dealing indeed with a case of continuity in change. When in 1982, following the imposition of martial law, Jaruzelski's government restored direct control over enterprises and imposed harsh monetary measures, it looked as if Poland's economy was on a new long-term track. Total output increases, foreign trade surpluses, and a decline in inflation, registered thereafter, seemed to offer proof of such a change. However, by 1985, overall performance began deteriorating, and in 1989 Poland entered into economic crisis, in a way repeating the scenario played out during the years of Gierek's import-led growth strategy.

As we suggest below, during the post-1981 period – closing the era of state-socialist system and of one-party rule – it became even more evident that Poland did not suffer from a single periodic economic crisis but rather was undergoing more lasting 'growth fatigue', and that similar forces seemed responsible for this inability to provide for sustained and balanced production expansion. Importantly, while an unresolved foreign debt problem contributed to this fatigue by depriving the economy of the means needed for investment, the external sector was again not the primary independent cause. As we demonstrate below, Poland was allowed by its Western creditors to partially service outstanding debts, with its official segment being practically overlooked. Morever, as in the past, Poland did not make a full effort to utilize its export potential to meet obligations to the lenders, permitting the total hard-currency debt to move to even more dangerous zones.

Thus, one is again left with the domestic sector as one where reasons for deteriorating foreign exposure – and overall economic difficulties – have to be sought. Not only does our reconstruction of that period reveal such a connection between domestic sector and overall growth to be present, but much the same political forces which derailed Gierek's economic programme of import-led modernization continued to upset the post-1981 efforts to restart healthy economic growth as well. Again, periodic excess of nominal wage increases over labor productivity rates was allowed, causing diversion of output from exports as well as fuelling additional inflation. Except for the brief period of martial law, the government was relatively easily giving into labor demands for wages. Industrial workers became even more influential than before the 1979–82 crisis, effectively putting themselves in charge of enterprises – for the most part now only nominally owned by the state.

Temporary militarization of the economy

Wage and price control

General Jaruzelski, succeeding Kania in 1981, regained some control of the economy when he imposed martial law in December of that year. After suppressing domestic protest, with only a very few violent confrontations (e.g., in one of the Silesian mines), Jaruzelski was able to restore order in production as well. To that end, a complete ban on strikes was imposed, severe penalties were introduced for absenteeism, and many enterprises were militarized. The government also replaced the majority of industrial managers and other state officials with politically more reliable individuals, many of them from within the military itself. The principal economic rationale behind these measures, to a degree resembling or echoing the 'war communism' period, was to reverse the downward trend in production.

To arrest the economic downturn, the regime also needed to impose on workers a belated austerity programme, and the crashing of the free trade unions provided such an opening. The method chosen by Jaruzelski's leadership was to sharply raise prices without commensurate financial compensation for workers or other social groups. In February 1982, prices of most consumer goods were increased by 300 to 400 per cent, raising the cost of living index some 100 per cent in that year. Even with the wage compensations that followed, real wages dropped by almost 25 per cent as a result of the price reform.[1] While unprecedented, this reduction in purchasing power met with very little worker resistance, for workers were overwhelmed by repressive actions as well as tired of economic chaos – production stoppages for lack of materials and irregular supplies of consumer goods.

In 1982, not only were wholesale and retail prices adjusted upwards, but rules for setting prices were significantly modified as well. Specifically, three types of prices were established: official, regulated, and contractual. Official prices were put directly under state control, while regulated prices were to be determined by enterprises on the basis of state-established rules (these prices were to be derived from costs at which equilibrium is achieved in a given product group). Contractual prices were left to voluntary negotiations between sellers and buyers, though the state kept the right either to temporarily freeze these prices or to set a maximum for annual price increases if justified by macroeconomic needs.

The original 1981 programme made a commitment to the gradual expansion of regulated and contractual pricing, and the programme was followed through. In 1982, around 36 per cent of consumer goods and 43 per cent of investment goods (as well as 26 per cent of state purchases of agricultural products) were sold at contractual prices. These proportions had not changed as of 1984, though by East European standards, Poland's share of goods which were allowed to be priced freely was already very high. Because the state apparatus did not stop its practice of extensive subsidization and taxation of enterprises, prices remained rather passive (i.e., did not enforce efficient operations by state-owned enterprises) (see Jozefiak 1986).

The 1981 programme promised that state intervention in wage determination would be reduced to a minimum. Traditional control of wage funds through limits was to be abandoned in favor of indirect control through taxes. Henceforth, the government would only be allowed to directly set wage schemes, to formulate methods of inflationary compensation (i.e., wage indexing), and to establish minimum wages; the government would also retain the right to determine salaries for managers. Later in 1984, the government also released its control over wage rates for particular jobs – wage schemes were to be negotiated between managers and workers on the basis of enterprise revenues (and on the ability to borrow operating funds from the banks) (see: Gomulka and Rostowski 1984).

The above decentralization of wage-determination system, actually put in place, was unable to operate very effectively, in great part because the state continued to make independent decisions on compensation regardless of individual enterprise performance. For instance, about two-thirds of the wage payment increase in 1983 resulted from so-called central corrections, i.e., state permission to raise wages for specific trades or industry sectors. Apparently, almost three-fourths of the actual wage increase in the state sector came about irrespective of enterprise economic performance, due both to the above-mentioned 'corrections' by the state bureaucracy and to another powerful instrument – tax exemptions bilaterally negotiated with enterprises.

The regime's policy had two outcomes – domestic consumer goods shortages were reduced, and after the aforementioned doubling of prices in 1982, inflation was lowered. However, Poland's inflation – approximately 14.8 per cent in 1984, and 15.0 per cent in 1985 – was still very high by East European standards. Price increases were fueled mostly by wage pressures from the workers, as the Jaruzelski regime, like its predecessors, had gradually begun to yield to popular demands. Strikes were rare but the competition between now illegal but still active 'free' unions and the official unions for popularity made the latter aggressively use informal channels to press for wage increases as well.

Most importantly, the renewed wage and price spiral gradually dissolved the impact of the 1982 austerity measures calling for the curtailment of domestic absorption. For the economy to produce the trade surplus required to arrest the escalating foreign debt, consumption would have to be held to the low 1982 level for several years. During 1983–84, however, the level of total real consumption (excluding expenditure on services) reportedly increased by a cumulative rate of 10.4 per cent, though in per capita terms, this rate was around 7 per cent. Thus, the real per capita consumption in 1984 was about 7.5

per cent below the 1978 pre-crisis level which was close to the per centage difference between the high-1978 and low-1984 national products.

Decision making

Jaruzelski's somewhat unexpected 1982 price reform was presented to the workers not only as an economic necessity in a debt-ridden economy but also as part of a Hungarian-like economic reform. The blueprint for the reform was drawn up under threats from the opposition shortly before the imposition of martial law in 1981, and the opposition assumed that under the shield of martial law, Jaruzelski's regime would abandon the reform programme. The regime's decision to go along with the 1981 programme seemed[2] to indicate that their intentions during these 1981 pre-martial law reform deliberations with the opposition were sincere. Nevertheless, even in the face of substantive steps to implement the programme, the anti-party forces continued to be doubtful about the intentions of Jaruzelski's regime.

The government's hasty legislative efforts to institute numerous systemic changes in 1982 were generally viewed by the political opposition as a calculated manoeuvre aimed at demobilizing popular discontent. Alternatively they were presented as yet more half-hearted efforts that had no chance of surviving and making a lasting difference, as they lacked the necessary political commitment at the central level. In addition, the claim was frequently made that under the existing political circumstances, no major segment of the society would be willing to lend its support to the reform programme. To the contrary, the common expectation was that a great number of entrenched groups would mobilize to subvert any real change.

One important exception in this generally negative assessment of the 1982 reform package was the view expressed by Gomulka (1986b: 249) in 1983. He argued that the Jaruzelski regime was trying to transform Poland's social system into one like that operated by Spain under the dictatorship of Franco, i.e., a combination of relative economic freedoms and strong political restrictions. Another dissenting view was that of Mizsei (1992), who argued, more realistically, that Poland's reforms of that time were in substance very similar to those instituted by the communist leader Kadar in Hungary in 1968 (many years after his brutal suppression of the 1956 anti-communist rebellion which cost thousands of lives).[3]

The actual record of economic reforms initiated by the Jaruzelski government shows that their commitment to bringing market elements into the inefficient state-planning system was strong and that large-scale change did materialize. The radical price/wage decentralization, mentioned earlier, was only one example of substantial real change in the economic system at the time. Equally important was the decision to discontinue the old-fashioned command structure of detailed plan targets addressed to individual enterprises, while retaining direct control over a few strategic areas. As of 1982, state enterprises were allowed to make most of the decisions on production on their own, a ruling which seemed only to formalize the already extensive independence of management from central control gained during the crisis years.

The 1982 reform also called for the number of branch (i.e., industrial) ministries to be reduced, and in fact only half of them were left by 1983. Critical also was the government's decision to eliminate all middle-level organizations or associations in order to bring the remaining branch ministries and their enterprises into direct communication. Enterprises were, however, allowed to voluntarily or obligatorily (i.e., on an order from the respective ministry) set up industrial groups, which were to refrain from taking on a supervisory role with regard to individual members. These legal provisions created room for the existing middle-level entities to reemerge in their traditional functions of controlling agencies equipped with monopolistic power over buyers.

In its effort to shift economic authority away from the central planners, the government of Jaruzelski also allowed for the formation of elements of labour-management at the enterprise (rather than regional or national) level. In late 1981, in response to demands raised by the independent unions, workers councils were formally established, only to be suspended shortly thereafter, i.e., with the imposition of martial law. In mid-1983, workers councils were reactivated, though without many of the attributes envisioned in the original legislation. Importantly, only the councils of small-and medium scale enterprises were permitted to decide on managerial appointments. In large-scale enterprises (i.e., about 1,500 employees), the traditional nomenklatura system was retained.

The desperate situation in the economy required, of course, that, at least initially, certain direct controls over production by the government be retained. This was to be achieved, among other means, by the incorporation of so-called strategic programmes into the existing decision-making process. These programmes were of traditional command-style, requiring state-owned enterprises to deliver a fixed amount of goods linked to direct supplies. About thirty groups of materials and intermediate products were allocated under these plans by the government in 1982 (and up to 115 in 1985).[4] All these supplies were distributed through the state wholesale network – not operating as profit-maximizing entities.

Illusion of recovery

With the new planning system, the government was able to refocus production efforts on a limited number of key targets incorporated in the three-year plan of 1983–85. Priority was given to the mining industry, a critical source of hard currency revenues for Poland. Miners' wages were raised the most (next to the police and military forces), and the industry was given an abundance of material supplies. The hard coal industry started recovering in 1982, when its output reached 189 million tons as compared to 163 million tons in 1981. By 1984, coal production moved closer to the pre-crisis (1978) level of 200 million tons. The production of sulphur – most of which was directed to foreign markets – was also given priority, and by 1985 its output was back to its 1979 peak.

Another positive sign had been the upturn in real gross fixed investment since 1982, when a 12.1 per cent decline was reported. Investment increased by 9.4 per cent in 1983, 11.4 per cent in 1984, and 6.0 per cent in 1985. However, the problems which plagued investment behaviour before the imposition of martial law have not vanished. While a larger flow of investment funds helped accelerate work on particular projects, both construction enterprises and their industrial clients were compelled even less than in the pre-reform period to press for the shortest realistic time-table. The gestation period of investment was in fact lengthened by almost one year, requiring on average almost fifty months for a project to be completed.[5]

Moreover, the amount of investment capital frozen in uncompleted projects increased by another 600 billion zloty during 1983–84. By the end of 1984, these idle resources amounted to 1,600 billion zloty, i.e., almost one and a half times the value of new investment spending in that year. This was still less than during the crisis years of 1979 and 1980, mostly because the investment 'front' was reduced so drastically. The share of unfinished investment in the net material product in 1975, at the close of the most radical upsurge in fixed-capital outlays under Gierek's ambitious modernization strategy, was 24.8 per cent. In 1979 this share reached 33.4 per cent, and in 1980 climbed as high as 38.9

per cent. In 1985, however, the respective share of unfinished invest-ment projects dropped back to 24.8 per cent.

Jaruzelski's policies produced certain improvements in the overall growth of the national economy, including an increase in industrial output. Industrial production had already picked up by the end of 1982, though a 1.5 per cent decline was reported for the whole year. Industrial output grew by 6.6 per cent in 1983, 5.6 per cent in 1984, and 4.1 per cent in 1985. Agricultural production increased as well, with respect to both grain and livestock (see table 4.1). As a result, after bottoming out in 1982, the national product has been increasing since then, i.e., reaching 6 per cent in 1983, 5.6 per cent in 1984, and 3.4 per cent growth in 1985.[6] These rates were among the highest in the region, with all economies faced with adversities of one sort or another.

However, with the low investment outlays and slower project completion, the recovering Polish industry entered a phase of rapid technological deterioration. This trend manifested itself, among other ways, in the fact that, reportedly, machinery in industry was on average about 60 per cent depreciated in 1982. This decapitalization process affected some of the key sectors of industry, including auto-mobile production (where equipment was on average seventeen years old and only an injection of at least 1.5 billion dollars in new machinery could allegedly have prevented an irreversible technological collapse). Paradoxically, this industry was furnished with advanced machinery under Gierek and became one of the success stories in the export promotion of those years.

Export promotion

To cope with the foreign debt problem, the regime of Jaruzelski felt particularly pressed to make an effort to mobilize production for export to Western countries. While the regime abstained from the application of draconian measures, like those implemented around that time in debt-obsessed Romania, it moved ahead with a broad package of indirect measures. This was also a departure from the previous practices of Polish governments which typically reacted to serious balance of payments adversities with tighter control over foreign trade. The 1981 package was designed, as other reforms of that vintage, with the same objective of giving more responsibility to state-owned enterprises and leaving the central planners with the minimum control necessary to assure overall economic balance.

Table 4.1 *Macroeconomic Indicators, Poland, 1980–1989 (annual rates in per cent)*

| | Net Material Product produced (NMP) | Gross Domestic Product produced (GDP)[a] | Total Output | | Gross fixed investment |
			Industry	Agriculture	
	(1)	(2)	(3)	(4)	(5)
1980	−6.0	−5.1	−.8	−10.7	−12.3
1981	−12.0	−10.0	−13.2	3.8	−22.3
1982	−5.5	−4.8	−1.5	−2.8	−12.1
1983	6.0	5.6	6.6	3.3	9.4
1984	5.6	5.6	5.6	5.7	11.4
1985	3.4	3.6	4.1	5.9	6.0
1986	4.9	4.2	4.4	5.0	5.1
1987	1.9	2.0	3.4	−2.3	4.2
1988	4.9	4.1	5.3	1.2	5.4
1989	.3	.2	−.5	1.5	−2.3

	Share of investment in NMP utilized	Inflation (CPI)	Nominal wages	Real wages	Real consumption
	(6)	(7)	(8)	(9)	(10)
1980	23.7	9.4	13.3	3.9	–
1981	20.0	21.2	23.5	2.3	−4.0
1982	17.9	104.5	79.6	−24.9	−24.9
1983	18.6	21.4	22.6	1.2	6.5
1984	19.8	14.8	15.3	.5	3.9
1985	12.2	15.0	18.8	3.8	2.4
1986	12.3	17.7	20.3	2.6	4.9
1987	12.7	25.2	21.7	−3.5	2.9
1988	13.2	60.2	74.6	14.4	3.4
1989	12.3	251.1	260.5	9.4	−.3

Note: a-Plan Econ Data.
Source: *Rocznik Statystyczny* 1991, Warsaw: GUS (pp. xxiv-xxv).

Foreign trade reforms included the 1982 decision to permit industrial enterprises to negotiate directly with foreign entities.[7] In practice, very few enterprises that qualified for trade concessions took advantage of the new rules. This initial reluctance was due to the excessive cost of direct exchange with foreign countries, lack of skilled personnel, and widespread satisfaction with traditional trading arrangements.[8] Another reform allowed the Ministry of Foreign Trade to transform existing foreign trade enterprises into joint-stock firms with at least 51 per cent of the assets belonging to the Treasury. This form of ownership reorganization turned out to be more warmly welcomed by producer-enterprises than the above-mentioned concessions to engage directly in foreign trade transactions.

To motivate enterprises to export to Western markets, the foreign trade reform also offered tax privileges for improved export performance. These privileges were granted with respect to both the enterprise's wage tax and a special fund for worker retraining. An additional pro-export instrument was the foreign currency account, or retention quota, permitting enterprises to keep for themselves a fraction of their hard currency revenues for financing independent imports. To allow for a more competitive allocation of state finances, the regime also introduced foreign currency auctions in 1983, but with little effect. In 1983, the banks were allowed to issue credits for export promotion – another new arrangement – but there was almost no interest in this alternative source of currency among enterprises.[9]

While the exchange rate for domestic currency had been occasionally corrected in the 1970s, the government allowed for a more active exchange rate policy to promote exports only after 1981. However, similar to general pricing rules, exchange rates continued to be based on the average cost (of earning a unit of foreign currency) rather than on marginal costs satisfying supply/demand equilibrium. Consequently, it paid for enterprises – despite a great shortage of hard currencies – to maximize the use of imported goods and materials. Moreover, while the value of the zloty against the dollar diminished in nominal terms by almost two-thirds during 1982–87, rapid increase in domestic prices, mentioned earlier, resulted in only a modest, about one-fifth decline of the real exchange rate.

Debt repayment

The fact that the regime embarked upon a drastic austerity programme and achieved a restoration of production did not encourage Western creditors to reopen financial lines to Poland. The initial Western reaction was to punish the regime for its suppression of the free trade unions with a ban on governmental credits and a refusal to negotiate the rescheduling of both private and government-backed debts. Subsequently, talks on both types of debt were resumed, with the banks in

1983 and with the governments in 1985, however, no significant new credits were obtained (for more detail see Marer 1984a, 1984b; Moscicki 1985; Raczkowski 1985)

Left without fresh financing, Poland had no choice but to extract resources from within the economy and turn its trade deficit into a surplus. Accordingly, the government had to consider further import reductions, a move which almost all East European countries found unavoidable as well.[10] Very similar was the case of Romania, which – unlike Poland – refused to continue its foreign borrowing, for in both countries, initial import reductions were up to 30 per cent, to be followed by a few years of low import levels. In contrast, East Germany, Hungary, and Czechoslovakia reduced total imports (calculated in constant prices) in 1981–83 by about 10 per cent. The first two countries recovered from an absolute drop in the volume of imports in 1985, while Czechoslovakia did so in 1986. In Bulgaria, imports continued to grow without interruption after 1979 (except for 1989).

Poland also managed to revive its exports to hard-currency markets, particularly in the area of raw materials (most notably hard coal) and food, while manufactures showed no signs of recovery. But the post-1982 export revival was rather timid, so that as late as 1985 total exports to Western markets were still below the 1979 level, with sales of manufacturing goods in a continuous decline up to 1985 (a trend which was observable in most of the other East European countries as well).[11] A more dynamic growth in exports to hard-currency markets was held back by low import levels as well as by a strong domestic demand for goods suitable for shipment abroad.

The combined effect of strong hard-currency import restrictions and weak revival of exports to Western markets helped to produce a trade surplus. After a very small surplus generated in 1982 (see table 4.2), Poland registered a surplus of 0.9 billion dollars in 1983, 1.4 billion dollars in 1984, and 1.1. billion dollars in 1985. These surpluses allowed Poland to service part of the foreign debt it owed to commercial banks, though it continued to make no payments on its official (larger) debt to Western governments. Consequently, the total value of the debt continued to increase – it stood at 26.3 billion dollars in 1982 and by 1985 had grown to 29.3 billion dollars.

Even this level of debt service represented a considerable burden on the economy, as it drained industry of resources needed for investment in rapidly depleting capital stock. This was because the payments to foreign lenders caused a negative transfer of financial resources out of Poland. In 1980, for the first time since the outset of large-scale

Table 4.2 *Hard Currency Trade and Debt, 1980–1989 (in billion dollars)*

	Exports	Imports	Trade balance	Gross debt	Hard currency reserves
	(1)	(2)	(3)	(4)	(5)
1980	7.4	8.2	−.8	24.1	.1
1981	5.0	5.8	−.8	25.9	.3
1982	4.5	4.3	.2	26.3	.6
1983	4.8	3.9	.9	26.4	.8
1984	5.3	3.9	1.4	26.9	1.1
1985	5.1	4.0	1.1	29.3	.9
1986	5.3	4.3	1.0	33.5	.7
1987	6.2	5.1	1.1	39.2	1.5
1988	7.2	6.3	.9	39.2	2.1
1989	7.6	7.3	.2	40.8	2.3

	Number of cumulative licenses		License-based output (percentage of total)		Number of patents granted
	Purchased	Applied	Output	Exports	
	(6)	(7)	(8)	(9)	(10)
1980	329	260	5.0	5.3	1962
1981	289	226	3.3	3.5	–
1982	230	186	2.3	2.8	708
1983	181	148	1.7	2.5	–
1984	149	122	1.2	1.9	–
1985	119	95	1.2	1.6	573
1986	99	82	1.0	1.6	–
1987	78	63	1.3	2.3	–
1988	69	57	1.1	2.1	–
1989	59	51	1.5	2.7	414

Sources: (1)–(5) *Economic Bulletin for Europe*, vol. 43 (1991), New York: ECE, United Nations (p.124); (6)-(10) *Rocznik Statystyczny*, Warsaw: GUS (various year)

borrowing, Poland registered a negative transfer – albeit a rather small one. In 1981 Poland received a small net inflow of resources, and the next negative transfer, which occurred in 1982, was above $0.5 billion. In 1983 more than $1.3 billion 'leaked' out of the national economy and Poland continued transferring resources abroad in this range during the following few years.[12]

Eastward reorientation

The inability to purchase many necessary supplies on Western markets forced the Jaruzelski regime to seek alternative sources within the CMEA, particularly from the Soviet Union. While Poland was hard pressed to improve its trade with the Soviet Union – an objective widely stated in the official media – the latter was more than ready to comply. For the Soviet leaders, this was an opportunity to undo what many saw as the overexposure of Poland to the Western economy under the leadership of Gierek. Jaruzelski's regime expected that a return to the Soviet market would be welcomed by Brezhniev, and thus some economic assistance would be forthcoming to gratify Poland.

Although the Soviet Union was satisfied with Jaruzelski's introduction of martial law and his containment of the free trade unions, it discontinued most of its financial assistance. No new hard-currency credits were supplied by the Soviets after 1981 and the regime received no additional supplies of Soviet oil to substitute for dollar-paid non-Soviet deliveries (cut from 3.5 billion tons in 1980 to 500 million tons in 1981–83). Nor was the pressure on Poland's government – or on many other countries in the region – to eliminate outstanding trade deficits with the Soviet Union significantly relaxed to relieve the pain of shortages felt by the industry.

Instead of bailing Poland out, as expected by Western banks at the outset of large-scale lending to the region, the Soviet Union made sure that the need for repayment of Western debts did not hurt Soviet imports. Of greatest concern to the Soviets were Poland's most technologically advanced products based on Western imports, which were more easily salable in Western markets than products traditionally supplied to the Soviet Union. To facilitate this favourable type of trade, in many cases, the Soviet Union provided equipment to complete investment projects that involved earlier purchases of Western equipment by Poland, as was the case in the steel industry.[13]

Also, for the first time, Poland and the Soviet Union began to promote the idea of establishing joint-stock companies involving capital from both countries (a concept agreed upon by Jaruzelski and Soviet leader Chernenko in 1984).[14] The Soviet leadership, increasingly distrustful of the CMEA bureaucracy, decided to look for more effective ways of securing supplies from East European countries. Such joint-stock companies, allowing for co-management by Soviet personnel, seemed like an appropriate solution,[15] and consistent with long-term trends in the world market, dominated by multinational corporations. Except for Poland, Bulgaria and East Germany, two countries processing a number of advanced products sought by the Soviet Union, became prime targets for such bilateral arrangements.[16]

In addition, a joint programme of direct cooperation in industrial research was developed. During 1986, a new long-term programme of technological progress focusing on more direct cooperation between research institutes in both countries was signed. New regulations were then passed in Poland to permit such direct contacts (e.g., creation of joint-director boards involving top managers, relaxation of foreign trade rules for such cooperating organizations). Poland and the Soviet Union each listed approximately 100 research institutes which had become involved in this form of bilateral cooperation.

All these measures made Poland's economy more subordinate to the CMEA, particularly to the Soviet Union.[17] This seemed to be reflected, among other things, in the changing patterns of import utilization. During 1979–82, dollar exports diminished at a slower rate than respective imports of intermediate goods (i.e., materials and parts), meaning that production of exportables was given preference in import supplies. However, during 1982–85, when hard-currency imports began to increase, exports to dollar markets grew at a slower rate, so that for instance, dollar imports of intermediate goods increased by 44 per cent during these years, whereas exports to these markets increased by 9 per cent (see Kaminski 1986). This would suggest that imports from Western countries during 1982–85 were probably disproportionately used to produce goods for domestic markets and/or for the CMEA.

Concluding, the regime of Jaruzelski succeeded in halting the production decline but it did not provide a framework for genuine recovery. The austerity programme was dissipated by continuous wage pressures from the workers. The surprisingly aggressive systemic reforms were partly sabotaged by intra-party traditionalists and elements of the industrial bureaucracy. Because a working mechanism for promoting exports to hard-currency markets had not been developed, severe import restrictions served as the major source of improvements in Poland's balance-of-payments. In a way, the economy under Jaruzelski's rule continued to suffer from most of the same problems which existed right before the transfer of power to the military.

Economics of hardship and systemic reforms

Inflationary overhang

While Jaruzelski was basically concerned with the decline in physical output, his successor Messner, as Prime Minister in 1985, geared his economic policy mostly to aggregate demand (wage-price) management. An economist by training, Messner surrounded himself with a group of other economists (such as Sadowski, the Minister charged with overviewing systemic reforms, and later a deputy Prime Minister), who were also convinced that to cure the economy the excess of money had to be eliminated. Removal of the monetary overhang – the amount of money not spent due to shortage of goods – was expected to create a buyer's market, thus strengthening incentives for efficiency.

The key element of this policy was price management, i.e., direct and indirect control over price[18] formation. With the help of these measures, the government kept price increases within a tolerable level in 1985, and also in 1986 when consumer prices moved up by 17.7 per cent. Subsequently, however, the inflation rate accelerated, reaching as much as 25.2 per cent and 60.2 per cent in 1987 and 1988 respectively. Clearly, the Messner regime lost control over prices, exhibiting rates of growth above those in the rest of Eastern Europe. At this later stage, inflation was driven not only by state price corrections but also, though to a much lesser degree, by self-propelling forces, i.e., the expectations of all parties in the monetary flow that prices would go higher.

The mounting budgetary deficit was one of the major sources of accelerating inflation. The government was aware of the widening gap between revenues and expenditures, and, on many occasions, plans were made to strengthen financial discipline. But political pressures from various groups were hard to resist, thus large subsidies continued to pour into deficit-making enterprises (and state farms). By the middle of 1988 the size of the deficit was as big as the revenues collected (*Zycie Gospodarcze*, no. 26 1989: 1). Under these circumstances, the Polish National Bank – working without any formal ceiling on the money supply – resorted to printing money.

Market disorganization was another cause of high inflation. For instance, because many products in short supply were made available only through hard-currency shops and because many 'grey' transactions (e.g., apartment sales) were conducted only with foreign money, the exchange rate for dollars became artificially high. Poland became, for all practical purposes, a dual-currency economy (like some other heavily indebted semi-developed countries at that time, e.g., Brazil). Considered more stable, the dollar became desirable as a hedge against inflation, yet conversions of domestic currency into dollars only further fuelled price increases.

Still, the most important pro-inflationary force at this point in time was wage demands by industrial workers. Workers had learned that tacit pressure on managers for wage increases was a superior method to industrial action. The regime tried to get wages under control by imposing an unpopular, prohibitive tax on wage increases in state-owned enterprises, but frequent exemptions from taxes and subsidies made this barrier to wages rather weak. Indexation of wages was another instrument Messner tried to bring wage and price increases more in line, but it turned out to be unmanageable and detrimental to efficiency (fixing sectoral wage proportions worked against realloca-tion of labour).

The regime needed political credibility to restrain wage increases, but workers continued to question the legitimacy of the communist leadership, even though the regime of Messner initiated what looked like a reasonable package of reforms. This became most apparent when Messner decided to have a referendum in 1987 on whether the popula-tion was willing to accept some wage reductions and halt on strikes in exchange for even more far-reaching reforms, including political change. Even if not well articulated by the official media, this seemed to be a quite reasonable offer, but it was rejected by the voters and excessive pressures on wages continued to destabilize the economy.

The Messner regime turned out to be much less in control of wages than its predecessor, one obvious reason for this being the termination of military rule. In 1984, nominal wages increased by 15.3 per cent, the lowest increase in years, but they began climbing much faster there-after. In 1988, when workers responded to price reform with strikes, nominal wages escalated by 74.6 per cent. Initially, the combined effect of price increases and wage controls produced low real wage increases, and in 1987 an even slightly negative rate of real wage growth was reported. In 1988, however, real wages increased by 14.4 per cent, clear proof of the regime's failure (see table 4.1).

The comeback of lobbies

Monetary instability was one problem faced by Messner, the other being how to turn the initial recovery executed by Jaruzelski into strong economic expansion. As Jaruzelski's three-year plan approached its end in 1985, the Messner government viewed the work on the 1986–90 national plan as an opportunity to rethink priorities. With investments already approaching their pre-crisis level, the regime had engaged in an investment programme of considerable magnitude, combined with unblocking hard-currency imports. Rates of growth in investment during 1986–88 did not increase above the earlier reported levels, although on average investments expanded at a rate slightly higher than total national product (see table 4.1).

This continuous mobilization of resources for investment should have been helpful in reorienting production towards industrial sectors with high value-added, but it was not. Despite nearly overwhelming evidence that one of the key sources of Poland's economic problems was overexpansion in traditional industries, they were still given highest priority.[19] While the 1986–90 plan allocated as much as 36 per cent of investment to the coal mining and energy sector (with a few new mines being opened in the cost-ineffective, high sulphur coal region of Lublin), the largest increase in investment was planned for another traditional sector, i.e., metallurgy (i.e., 87–108 per cent above 1985 level) (*Zycie Gospodarcze*, no. 43, 1987).[20]

This investment strategy, combined with the protracted inefficiency of the construction sector, was doomed to fail and it did. The very modest growth rate of the national product reported in 1987 was a signal to the regime that the wrong course was chosen, with this low rate only in part due to poor agricultural performance.[21] Under strong criticism from many official circles, Messner decided to eliminate some projects in the mining and steel sectors but not to completely reverse the ill-conceived strategy. This was not only because of the existing conflict of interests in which the traditional industries had an advantage, but also because the amount of funds already committed to the projects in progress was so high that any substantial downscaling would have caused enormous losses (see Blazyca 1989).

The regime also allowed the heavy industry lobbies to partially roll back the 1982 decentralization reform, the details of which were discussed by us earlier. Once abolished industrial associations began to re-emerge in large numbers with new names. In the mining industry, such organizations were set up in 1985 under the name 'qwarectwa' (guilds). In machinery, chemicals, and light industry, so-called 'supervisory councils' (*rady nadzorcze*) were established in 1984 – mostly through unpublished regulations passed by the respective branch ministries. Other middle-level organizations named combinats, socialist concerns, and consortia appeared elsewhere in heavy industry as well.[22]

Clearly, the coal-steel lobby, which originated in the 1950s and still quite dominant under Gierek's regime, continued to enjoy political influence under Messner. Despite the fact that large segments of the frustrated population held this lobby at least partly responsible for the 1979–82 crisis, its power diminished only marginally. Political conditions at the time, including the presence of the strongest independent unions in heavy industry, played a central role in the lobby's favourable position. Specifically, to the strong investment 'hunger' of managers in that sector of the national economy was added a wage hunger helping the former to more effectively argue for preferential treatment.

Economic reform

Another element of Messner's economic policy was the 1986 decision that the second stage of reforms would be launched in 1987, a move that many critics of the government considered an admission that the 1982 reform programme had to be started all over again.[23] This was not the case, however, since many of the elements of the 1982 reform were successfully implemented, deeply transforming the economic system. Still, the government considered the existing arrangements unsatisfactory in light of the weak recovery and persisting internal imbalances. The purpose of the second reform wave was to consolidate earlier changes and add some new elements as well so that the economy could finally break out of the difficulties.

With respect to organization of the central administration, Messner further cut – by more than half – the number of central ministries and released scores of employees. Many state agencies were merged into the Ministry of Industry (although its departments continued to reflect the earlier branch structure, overrepresented by the heavy industries). The banking system was reorganized as well by limiting the functions of the Polish National Bank and turning nine of its regional branches into independent commercial banks (e.g., allowed to determine their own interest rate and service fees). Both reforms resembled the steps taken earlier by Hungary, still the main source of inspiration for Poland's reforms.

With the downscaling of the central administration came further reduction in the role of budgetary investment projects initiated by the government. As a consequence, in 1987, approximately 83 per cent of investment was under the discretion of industrial enterprises, provincial authorities, and the private sector (*Zycie Gospodarcze*, no. 18, 1988: 3). With about 40 per cent of funds financed internally – from profits – enterprises had to rely on bank credit to provide most of the balance of their total spending (while only 8 per cent came from the state budget). At this point, credit money, needed to finance any major project, was still forthcoming from the state banking system, which left considerable room for the government to affect the scope and direction of decentralized investment activities.

The government also allowed for further rationalization of the price structure, to make it more closely reflect domestic supply/demand conditions. By 1987 most of the material supplies were allocated through direct contracts with users – only 25 per cent of materials were distributed by central agencies in that year. Only 35 per cent of prices for industrial equipment supplies were in the category of administrative prices in 1987 (and 65 per cent for consumer goods). The share of subsidies in the national product declined from 28.5 per cent in 1981 to 18.2 per cent in 1982, and then to 15.4 per cent in 1987 (and about 30 per cent of the state budget; see Havrylyshyn and Rosati 1990: 81).

Significant progress was also made in terms of bringing foreign trade prices more in line with world market prices. State-controlled prices in exports to hard-currency markets – where the government was less restricted than in its trade with the CMEA markets – represented 41.7 per cent of total value in 1985 and 8.5 per cent in 1987, while the share of those prices in imports from these markets accounted for 33.4 per cent and 17.0 per cent in the respective years (ibid.: 225). Subsidies on total exports represented 21.1 per cent of the value in 1985 and 9.4 per cent in 1987, with foodstuffs reporting reduction of subsidies from 76.5 to 26.7 per cent – most of this change related to devaluation of the zloty (*ibid.*: 120).

Ownership changes

Even more important was the regime's decision to change the ownership structure of the economy, which was dominated by state property. The communist regime began to change its attitude toward the private sector only after the economy slipped into the crisis of 1979–82. The 1982 reform under the government of Jaruzelski had marks of earlier tactical retreats made in the face of economic adversity all carefully avoiding any encroachments on public ownership. In 1985, however, deep disappointment with the lengthy anti-crisis policy (see Poznanski

1986a) forced the communist regime to look more favorably at the possibility of making permanent changes in the ownership structure (Fallenbuchl 1989; Kaminski 1989b).

The diagnosis at this point was that there was need for a plurality of ownership forms, including a viable private sector. This was not a call for the transfer of state assets to private hands, but rather for granting permission to citizens to set up their own enterprises. Nevertheless, the role assigned to private activities was a subordinate one, namely, to provide for more successful reproduction of the state sector. The government's hope was that within this dual-track approach (Poznanski 1992b), the private sector would offer cheap supplies and stimulate limited domestic competition that would enforce cost reduction in the state sector as well as create low-cost jobs for excess labour to be released from state enterprises.

Accordingly, regulations on setting up new enterprises by citizens were simplified, the burden of accounting was lessened, and permission was given to private enterprises to freely contract with the state sector.[24] To further invigorate the private sector, the government of Messner significantly improved the status of foreign investors, who were already present in large numbers (an uncommon development for the region). These were mostly small-scale joint-ventures with private enterprises, operated by Polish emigrants, allowed from the beginning to enjoy fewer restrictions than other foreign investors (subject to a separate set of legal regulations).

No major ownership reforms were instituted by Messner in the still dominant state sector. At this stage there was still very little debate about large-scale privatization of state enterprises, though the idea of including property rights in the reform programme was gaining ground. Instead, the regime settled for the continued leasing out of certain state enterprises, mostly in broadly defined services, i.e., restaurants, hotels, retail shops, newsstands, car repair (with a major piece of relevant legislation passed in 1986). It was expected that if state enterprises would just be forced to compete, rational economic behaviour would develop through a combination of 'sound' prices, 'hard' (non-negotiable) subsidies, and bankruptcy procedures. These measures resembled those undertaken after 1983 in Hungary, though they were implemented by Poland's regime more conservatively.

This idea to discipline state industry was never fully realized particularly since the regime, like its predecessor, was unprepared to withdraw financial support to deficit enterprises,[25] and, if necessary, to terminate them. It is true that the government initiated financial scrutiny in order to phase out loss-taking enterprises. In 1982, the banks conducted a broad evaluation of the large fraction of enterprises (about 3200 units) and in 1983 restructuring programmes were pre-pared for 143 financially troubled state-owned enterprises, but only one minor enterprise was declared bankrupt in 1984. In 1985, under Messner's leadership, another two were closed, and but a few more in the remaining years[26] of his tenure (see Slay 1990).

Trade shifts

Suspension of martial law and subsequent concessions to the opposi-tion were rewarded by Western countries with a relaxation of eco-nomic restrictions. Most important was the unblocking of Polish efforts to join the IMF, needed not only to gain access to its funds but also to satisfy private foreign banks. The latter viewed such membership as an assurance that under IMF guidance, Poland would introduce economic policies needed to accelerate debt repayment. However, since joining the IMF in 1986, Poland received no financial assistance from this source through 1989 and very small amounts of money from other sources.

The financial situation of Poland differed from that of the other countries in the region, which were able to borrow more freely from Western sources. For instance, Hungary continued borrowing on international financial markets, receiving altogether almost $8 billion in bank loans during 1983–88 (ECE, Economic Survey of Europe in 1988–89: 209). With this new borrowing, the nominal value of Hun-gary's debt increased from $7.7 billion in 1982 to $17.3 billion in 1988 (ibid.: 214). Apparently, as much as two thirds of the credit Hungary received in that period was used for maintaining the consumption level.

Western banks remained particularly cautious with respect to Poland for a number of reasons. To begin with, many Western governments did not find the political situation in Poland satisfactory, as a renewal of social tension was possible at any time. With each sign of political relaxation by the communist goverment, there was another step which Western leaders expected Poland to follow through, so that frictions in inter-governmental relations continued. In addition, neither economic policies nor reform measures – at least their pace – were fully in line with Western expectations of what needed to be done given the dismal state of the economy. The situation was complicated by the fact that the economic information coming out of Poland was confusing.

Most disturbing to the Western governments – and foreign private business – was the fact that Poland was still unable to generate a sufficient trade surplus to start reducing its debt. After falling from $1.4 billion in 1984 to $1.1. billion in 1985, Poland watched its trade surplus stabilize around this lower level until 1987, and then decline to $0.9 billion in 1988. At the same time, the gross debt increased from $26.9 billion in 1984 to $39.2 billion in 1988 (with net debt showing a smaller increase since Poland managed to increase its hard currency reserves from $1.1 billion to $2.1 billion) (see table 4.2).

While there was a growing perception that Poland's government was not strongly committed to debt-repayment, there was little doubt that her potential for raising exports was limited by her rapidly aging industrial facilities. With the deteriorating export offer – in terms of product quality – Poland's goods not only faced difficulties in finding buyers but were confronted with declining prices as well. This downward pressure on export prices was further aggravated by the fact that the other countries of Eastern Europe were also trying to place an increased volume of similar products on the same – mostly West European – market. Under the circumstances, the ability of Western buyers to bargain for lower prices significantly increased.[27]

Such a negative trend in export prices obtained on hard-currency markets can be detected, for instance, in Polish exports of passenger cars (see appendix 4). In 1978, before the crisis of 1979–82, cars exported by Poland to the European Community were paid for at the level representing 52.4 per cent of the prices commanded by West German cars, but in 1986 the respective ratio was only 40.0 per cent. A similar trend can be detected for relative prices of cars exported by the Soviet Union and East European countries, except for Czechoslovakia (e.g., in East Germany, the ratio fell from 34 per cent to 25 per cent). This negative trend occurred even though there was potential in the European Community market for upgrading prices (as demonstrated by Spain, for instance).

The CMEA trade

The lack of improvement in trade relations with Western countries coincided with a deterioration in trade with the Soviet Union after about 1986. The shift of trade orientation eastward executed by Jaruzelski was undermined by a weakening of Soviet demand for imports. The lower rates of production growth reduced the Soviets' interest in imports from Poland. Among the hardest hit by changes in the Soviet Union was the defence industry due to an additional negative development – the curtailment of military expenditure by the Gorbachev leadership. This arms reduction concentrated on conventional forces, at which most of the Soviet orders for Polish industry were targeted.[28]

Poland's trade with the Soviet Union was further hurt by Soviet inability and/or unwillingness to keep oil/gas supplies to Eastern Europe at levels high enough to feed expanding production. Faced with faltering production of oil and negative terms-of-trade, the Soviet leaders curtailed their oil deliveries to Eastern Europe. Soviet oil exports to the region (excluding East Germany) declined from 60.6 million tons in 1985 to 41 million tons in 1988, with Poland being able to maintain its import levels at around 16 million tons. This loss for Eastern Europe was partially compensated with increased gas deliveries, which rose from 19.3 bcm to 23.5 bcm during 1985–88, with Poland raising its imports from 5.9 bcm to 7.5 bcm, an increase much below that reported by Western importers of Soviet gas (see Dietz 1992: 12).

Reforms initiated by Gorbachev in 1987, while helpful, did not promise any immediate revival of Soviet demand for East European goods or an upturn in Soviet energy supplies to the CMEA. While eager to radically reform the domestic economy, Gorbachev did not pursue any serious reform of the CMEA, except for some minor changes (e.g., including the idea of limited convertibility in trade between selected enterprises in the Soviet Union and, say, Czechoslovakia). Despite the serious adverse impact of declining trade with the Soviet Union and mounting imbalances,[29] no strong interest in reforming the CMEA was shown by the East European countries either (who saw little hope for making this bureaucratic trading regime truly effective).

Increasing difficulties in Poland's trade with the Soviet Union resulted in a substantial redirection of trade away from the CMEA and a similar trend would be observed in a few other East European countries as well. In 1986, the CMEA accounted for 46.6 per cent of Poland's trade turnover, with the Soviet Union's share at 27.6 per cent. In 1989, the respective share of the CMEA market was only 35.1 per cent, with the Soviet Union this time accounting for 20.8 per cent. These were the lowest shares for all East European CMEA members, so that, for instance, in 1989, the respective shares for Hungary were 41.8 and 25.1 per cent, and for Bulgaria – 84.0 and 65.2 per cent (for discussion of these trends, see Havrylyshyn and Rosati 1989; Rosati 1992).[30]

To sum up, for most of his tenure, the government of Messner seemed to be improving economic performance, helped in that by the temporary submergence of mass labour unrests. The economy also benefited from the regime's renewed economic reforms initiated in 1982 and then aided with another package of measures in 1986–87. However, the shocks of the 1979–82 crisis apparently had little effect on the domestic economic policies of the government as the heavy industry lobby maintained, or even strengthened, its power over resource allocation. Instead of a radical restructuring, Poland moved ahead with a buildup in sectors, which became part of the problem rather than of the solution (e.g., steel, coal energy). Consequently, at the end of Messner's tenure, the economy lost momentum, even before making up the losses into consumption suffered during 1979–82.[31]

Dismantling the system and renewed crisis

The replacement of the Messner regime with that of Rakowski in mid-1988 marked a significant change in the communist leadership, namely, a sharp shift from a predominantly conservative to a reform-oriented faction. This change was helped by waves of strikes in that year – a response to the decline in living conditions. The turmoil made it easier for Jaruzelski, chief of armed forces and the president, to promote Rakowski through the party ranks and ultimately secure his prime ministership as well. With this appointment, Poland entered the final stage in the dismantlement of the traditional system of state planning and public ownership – this phase to be carried out largely by the communist party itself (see further Poznanski 1993b).

Macroeconomic withdrawal

The most critical step in the economic realm was the Consolidation Plan announced by Rakowski shortly after assuming power, and then approved by the Parliament at the end of 1988. This programme claimed to stabilize the economy and at the same time finally move it from the old-type of system of central command to one based on market forces. This was not to be just another attempt to create a 'mixed economy' where state plan-targets were blended with financial instruments. Still, there was no well defined timetable for the execution of necessary steps, but rather a general commitment to proceed at a controlled pace. The economic – but also political – circumstances under which the government was to pursue the pro-market pro-gramme turned out to be such that run-away changes resulted instead.

Rakowski's initial efforts to quickly stabilize the domestic market concentrated on selective price corrections and some modifications in wage taxation. Two major price adjustments upward for material supplies for industry and for agriculture inputs respectively, were engineered in late 1988, both leading to more inflationary pressure. To slow down related wage increases and restrict prices, new tax schemes were introduced, including a uniform threshold for annual wage increases that were free of taxes. Additionally, a highly progressive scale was introduced for over-the-threshold payments, as well as a limit on the share of wages in enterprises' sales revenues. Even with these highly prohibitive measures, the rate of inflation for 1988 more than doubled compared to that of 1987 (see table 4.1).

When the early measures failed to improve the domestic market balance, Rakowski devised a new approach. In an effort to cool down excessively high inflation, the regime decided to impose a price freeze on all goods in mid-1989 (for detailed analysis, see: Milanovic 1991a). The expectation was that such a move would help to deescalate wage demands and give the government some time to reexamine the wage structure. The policy was, however, soon abandoned out of fear that it might only further deepen economic imbalances (Dabrowski 1992a). In the fast-paced fashion characteristic of Rakowski's regime, the price-freeze policy was replaced in a matter of weeks with a radical policy of quickly decontrolling state-set prices.

Most important was the decision to completely free prices paid to farmers, and at the same time end the freeze on retail prices for agricultural products. In addition, the government decontrolled prices for many of the subsidized industrial supplies for farming, which came mostly from state-sector monopolists. With one stroke, the Rakowski government abandoned one of the pillars of the communist strategy, i.e., control over agriculture and protection of consumers against inflation for foodstuffs. Made in the face of a rapid decline in the availability of food in state-owned shops, this decision was taken with little preparation. There was no time – but also no interest on the government's part – to consult these measures with the workers, and no accommodation was made to compensate consumers for food price increases. Also, while price rules for farm products were changed, the old-fashioned, monopolistic bureaucracy for product procurement was left unreformed.

Another pillar of communist economics – negotiable subsidization and job-guarantees for industrial enterprises – was abandoned by Rakowski's government as well. Early in its tenure, the regime announced its commitment to bankrupt deficit enterprises and allow for open unemployment. This decision was dictated in part by legitimate concern about increasing production efficiency, and thus creating downward pressure on prices.[32] But, the termination of paternalistic relations with state-owned industry also reflected the government's realization that no amount of protection would alter the deep resentment felt by industrial workers. This shift to an adversarial policy was underscored by the announcement that the government had targeted a number of 'flagship' enterprises for possible closure, including a major shipyard.

In this general withdrawal from central control, the government of Rakowski also removed another fundamental element of the state-socialist economy – state allocation of foreign currency. At this point, state-owned enterprises already enjoyed considerable freedom in export and import decisions, though under a tightly controlled foreign exchange system. Among new decisions was the simplification of customs rules which made it easier for state enterprises to contract imports. Even more radical was the set of measures to allow free access for enterprises – but also households – to foreign currency. Rakowski's reforms created foundations for internal – excluding capital accounts – convertibility of domestic currency combined with legalization of private exchange transactions and permission for private parties to establish currency outlets.

Asset transfers

The rapid release of key state controls over the economy was combined by Rakowski with equally unorthodox reform in property rights. There were few signs that the government had ideological objections to radical changes in the ownership structure, while such reforms – a departure from state-dominated property rights – were now seen as economically necessary. The government was faced with the impractical system under which it owned the capital assets but had little control over them. With greatly weakened party units at the enterprise level, the workers turned their factories into labour-managed entities. Under the circumstances, there was no direct advocate for capital – to protect its value and ensure its reproduction. Workers were not a good surrogate for the 'capital hungry' party elite; instead, they demonstrated vested interests in decapitalizing their enterprises.

In its effort to depart from the state-dominated ownership structure, the regime made another important step to stimulate the private sector by removing limits on the number of employees. More importantly, in further departure from traditional practice, the government allowed the private sector to enjoy in many ways better treatment than the state sector.[33] While it is hard to determine whether this move was purposeful or merely the outcome of growing disorder, private enterprises nevertheless ended up with many financial privileges (lower taxes on wages, few restrictions in determining prices for outputs and exclusion from so-called dividends based on value of capital assets; see: Rostowski 1989).

These policies, favourable to private businesses, had a visible impact on the labour market. The outflow of workers from the state sector, only limited during the early 1980s, became substantial during 1988–89.[34] Workers became attracted by higher wages offered by private employeers, and they were also influenced by a growing feeling that opportunities for production growth in this sector were greater than in the state one. The share of the private non-agricultural sector in total employment was 5.3 per cent in 1985, 5.6. per cent in 1986, 6.2 per cent in 1987, 7.0 per cent in 1988, and 10.1 per cent in 1989. Most of this increase took place outside of industry, but still the share of the non-agricultural private sector in industrial employment increased from 3.2 per cent in 1985 to 4.8 per cent in 1989 (as did its share in industrial production).

More importantly, the Rakowski government moved beyond the dual-track concept of ownership reform by calling for a more systematic sell-out of state assets to private hands through stock acquisitions. Privatization of the state sector was to be carried out mostly within the framework provided by two pieces of legislation from 1988–89.[35] The Consolidation Plan allowed the government to force failing enterprises to be converted into joint-stock companies to be owned by healthy state enterprises or holdings (this without the consent of workers' respective councils).[36] The directorship experiment – a rather vague piece of legislation – permitted managers of state enterprises to acquire public assets with which to set up any type of activity outside of their primary duties for their own profit.[37]

Given the spontaneous nature of privatization by 'nomenklatura' managers, it is difficult to establish with certainty the real scope of this type of asset transfer. There were probably more than 2000 such joint stock companies by the end of 1989. While these were mostly small offshoots of large enterprises, a few large-scale enterprises were turned into joint-stock companies as well. Most of the stocks in these larger companies were owned by the state, i.e., Treasury, or were allocated among state-owned-enterprises in the form of cross-buying. The remaining stocks were mostly owned by the nomenklatura (i.e., party appointed managers)[38] but some stocks were also sold to the workers.

This stage of property reforms was again inspired by ownership reforms taking place in Hungary. At this point, Hungary had already been experimenting for a few years with various nonstate forms of property rights, including leasing working capital in state enterprises to their worker collectives (continuing production after official hours on their own account). In 1988, a new piece of legislation – the Law on Corporate Associations – allowed state enterprises to form joint-stock companies and the private sector to establish limited liability companies. State and private enterprises were given universal rights to set up partnerships with foreign companies, including sales of shares to investors from abroad (up to 30 per cent equity in state enterprises, and up to 60 per cent in the private sector).

Economic downturn

These most substantive, not to say, radical economic changes had taken place in a volatile political atmosphere, since Rakowski's government proved strongly committed to reforming not only the economic but the political structure as well. Again, there was no evidence that economic reforms are treated by communist leaders as a substitute for political change, nor that one is actually possible without another. Most significant were steps taken by Rakowski, shortly after assuming power, towards developing an effective formula for power sharing with the anti-communist opposition. The early 1989 roundtable negotiations entered into with a representation of dissenting forces triggered a rapid sequence of major political changes, leading to the near liquidation – perhaps self-liquidation – of the communist party.

Executed under such circumstances, the economic reforms of Rakowski's government – itself overwhelmed by the complexity of economic problems – inflicted significant damage on the economy, including on the state budget. With greatly diminished central capability to control the public sector, 1989 witnessed a breakdown of tax collection – due to a refusal by enterprises to make payments. With no indexation of taxes, real payments made by enterprises could not keep up with the inflation-driven increases in budget expenditure (e.g., producer subsidies). During the conservative regime of Messner, some minor budgetary deficits were allowed; under Rakowski, state budget deficits skyrocketed, approaching 10 per cent of the gross domestic product – on an annualized basis – in mid 1989 (from .3 per cent deficit for the whole of 1988).[39]

The Rakowski government lost control not only over taxes but also over wages, in large part due to intensified labour disputes. During the first three quarters of 1989, a total of 829 strikes in 718 enterprises was recorded with about 325,000 state-sector workers involved (see *Rzeczpospolita*, 24 November 1989). The government also had its hands tied by the 1988 enumeration parity agreement (linking wages of civil servants, farmers, and workers), and the indexation (at the 80 per cent level) agreed upon in the roundtable talks of early 1989 introduced further constraint. As a consequence, real wages were allowed to increase at a rate much higher than production (e.g., the ratio of wage rises to labour productivity increases reached 1.69 during the first three quarters of 1989).

Budgetary deficits and excessive wage increases, in turn, destabilized the domestic market – causing an acceleration in inflation. Almost unlimited monetization of the budgetary deficits (through both money printing and compulsory bank credit financing) was one active mechanism. Implicit subsidization of loss-making enterprises by extension of short-term bank credits – was another vehicle for price acceleration.[40] Through these two mechanisms, the already high inflation degenerated into a condition which could easily have developed into hyperinflation. This condition marked another turning point in the state-planned economy, which for decades appeared to economists to be immune to rapid, even less uncontrollable, price increases.

The credit instruments that the leadership had hoped to strengthen were completely disarmed by the price chaos. The real interest rate – the nominal rate corrected for inflation – became negative in 1988, and then in 1989 as well. This was because the interest rate charged for credit to state enterprises was based on underestimated projected rates of price inflation.[41] Unpredicted changes in the prices of productive inputs – including nominal wages – and uncertain movement in prices for outputs left many enterprises with liquidity problems. Their inability to make payments to other enterprises initiated a chain reaction, and, lacking cash, a majority of enterprises had to curtail production (see: Milanovic 1991a).

Another reason for the downward pressure on production was the slowdown in the coal (and steel) industry. The elimination of compulsory work on Saturdays, which was agreed upon during the roundtable negotiations, resulted in a sharp reduction in the number of miner work-days. The economic situation was further worsened by disruptions in Soviet supplies, particularly those of energy – oil and gas. Exports of these fuels to Poland as well as other East European countries were curtailed as the Soviet Union suffered major losses in its energy sector in that year. Gorbachev was forced for safety reasons to close a few technically unreliable nuclear power stations. Massive strikes by coal miners, complaining about living conditions and wages, cost the Soviet Union very heavily in output losses.

Given all the above, Poland developed renewed symptoms of recession in 1989, a further indicator of the lasting growth fatigue. After reaching a respectable annual rate of 5.3 per cent in 1988, industrial production declined by .5 per cent in 1989. Gross fixed investment reported a decline of 2.3 per cent in 1989, the first contraction in many years. Both declines – in industrial output and capital investment – were related to the results of the mid-year phase, when – under the conditions of power transfer to the post-communist government of Mazowiecki – the positive trends of early 1989 were reversed. For the whole year, the gross domestic product was reported by state sources to increase by only 0.2 per cent, with some other sources claiming this rate to be in low negatives (e.g., Kolodko 1991a, gives a minus 1.5 per cent figure). This placed Poland – with Hungary and Romania – among worst performing economies in Eastern Europe for the year.

While falling into recession, Poland's economy allowed its double imbalance – internal and external – to deteriorate. Internally, the major force behind further disequilibration was the out-of-control increases in wages. With only a modest increase in production during the first half of 1989, nominal wages increased much faster than aggregate output. Only part of this increase was absorbed by accelerated inflation, now actually approaching near-hyperinflation levels, so that real wages increased by about 40 per cent (Kolodko 1991b: 36 puts this rate at 45 per cent), though most of this increase was statistical. Real consumption did not increase, since production could not keep up with the demand for goods and shortages of goods were aggrevated, causing particular damage to the living conditions of those at the bottom of the income ladder.

Under Rakowski's government through mid-1989, and then during the Mazowiecki government through the rest of the year, the economy continued to generate a modest trade surplus. Both dollar exports and imports calculated in current prices increased in 1989, with the corresponding trade surplus at $0.2 billion (down from $0.9 billion in 1988, see table 4.2). However, in volume terms – at constant prices – these exports did not show such a good performance, and the total exports were reported to stagnate for the whole year, the first time since 1982. The 1989 trade surplus – like those in the recent past – was not sufficient to help stabilize Poland's foreign debt, which reached a gross of $40.8 billion. Hard currency reserves increased slightly in this year, up to $2.3 billion (making the net value of the debt proportionally less).

Summary

While the drastic measures taken in 1981 during the martial law helped Jaruzelski, then holding most of the high party/state posts in his hands, to restore basic order in the economy, they did not provide for a successful recovery from the 1979–82 crisis. The resulting improvement in economic performance did not last long, in large part because the austerity programme – restoring more reasonable relation between real wages and labour productivity – began dissolving briefly thereafter (inability to decisively shift investment priorities in favor of export-oriented sectors was another obstacle). Already early under Messner's government established in 1985, major indicators began to worsen, and the efforts made by the next government, that of Rakowski since mid-1988, proved even more problematic – with the economy slipping into another general crisis, marked by severe imbalances, including a near-hyperinflation combined with great shortages.

This disappointing end to the lengthy struggle to revive faltering economy provided convincing proof that the economy sufferered from a chronic, deep rooted inability to mobilize resources for growth. This was a rather surprising outcome for a country which was neither affected by stagnating (or aging) population nor approaching the saturation point of domestic demand. This 'growth fatigue', as we call it, happened in an economy which had hardly completed its industrialization, and where there were still large reserves of labour in private farming (as well as in the state-owned industry where rather extensive overmanning was permitted). With other countries of Eastern Europe not displaying a similarly negative picture of economic growth, communist Poland remained very much a special, or extreme case.

While perserverance of fatigue symptoms indicated a continuity between the late Gierek period and the years of Jaruzelski's leadership, important changes between the two periods cannot be ignored. Importantly, when in 1989 power was handed over to non-communist forces the economy was to a large degree liberalized. Most of the detailed production targets were phased out and enterprises were allowed to secure most of their material supplies on their own. The majority of prices were set by enterprises as well, one important exception being the prices of some basic industrial supplies, such as energy. Determination of wage funds was left to state enterprises while the government relied on taxes to control the size of total payments. Much of central investment was reduced in favour of bank-credit financing of projects selected by enterprises themselves.

This quite radical systemic change went largely unnoticed by the opposition, distrustful of the party/state's ability to pursue economic reform. Such a perception was reinforced by the general refusal to pay attention to information put out by the communist government. Moreover, in the heat of political exchanges, the opposition had a tendency to discount any positive change instituted by the party/state not to help it gain popularity with the public. All this took place in the absence of a clear programme by the opposition on what the final shape of the economic order should be (except for vague references to the 1981 reform design). Opposition was also unclear on whether it should seek a complete elimination of the communist party or rather look for some form of accommodation with permanent restrictions on its powers.

That Poland's economic system was greatly reformed, giving more leverage to state enterprises themselves – specifically to their worker collectives – did not help the distressed economy. The reason is that these reforms left state enterprises in an institutional setting which can be best described as one where most of the old reasonably coherent rules – those of the 'strong' plan – were gone but where new – namely, genuine market-type – rules were not yet solidly in place. This was yet another, possibly even less cohesive, form of 'soft' planning, in which elements of 'weak' state coordination were combined with 'weak' public ownership. This probably further weakened system not only could not produce the kind of growth which was experienced early under Gierk's import-led period but also failed to keep alive a steady recovery and protect it from the crisis that broke up at the end of that period.

5   Foreign trade developments: under-utilized potential

That Poland during the years of Jaruzelski's political rule permitted its debt problems to increase further, and proved unable to return to a sustainable dynamic growth in production, could be viewed by some as additional evidence of the scope of import misuse by Gierek's government. However, we have earlier raised doubts about the import misuse leading to the 1979–82 crisis, suggesting that partial immobilization of export potential may have been a more critical factor behind the output decline. In this chapter we will look for possible signs that this type of immobilization continued into the post-1982 period, indicating that during this stage of development Poland's actual export potential prepared the economy for better performance than it actually achieved.

We have found a comparative perspective most suitable for the task we have taken on in this chapter, including a look at the type of repayment strategies employed by various heavily indebted state-planned economies of Eastern Europe as well as in the largely market-based or mixed-type economies of many developing countries. It follows from this chapter that like a number of countries in Eastern Europe, Poland chose, or was forced, to rely in its repayment strategy on import reductions combined with sluggish, or declining exports to hard-currency markets. While Poland followed this import-substitution version of 'restrictive' adjustment, heavily indebted South Korea and Taiwan did not allow their imports to fall while accelerating exports. Many Latin American economies, in turn, executed rather considerable import reduction, but most of the repayment came from export mobilization (e.g., in Brazil).

Unlike some other East European economies, Poland did not make an effort to mobilize its exports. Its internal statistics also suggest that the existing export potential was not fully mobilized for debt repayment. Shares of exports in total domestic production of many goods critical for raising foreign revenues were allowed to decline, reflecting an overall turn inwards by the economy. In its import reductions, one of the sharpest in Eastern Europe, Poland gave priority to curtailing capital goods, which in itself indicated the presence of strong domestic demands for consumption. Such reductions in capital inflows harmed Poland's ability to meet replacement needs in factories built during the earlier import surge, not to mention efforts to expand or modernize these facilities, and thus enhance the long-term potential for exports as well.

The choice of debt repayment strategies

We begin by comparing Poland's debt management with the behaviour of other Eastern European countries and ten heavily indebted developing countries. Faced with similar problems of servicing debts owed to banks from Western countries, all these economies had no better way for raising revenues for repayment than by selling more to and/or reducing their purchases from the West. Much of the borrowing, in fact, was done with the purpose of penetrating Western markets, which put them in competitive conflict even before the outbreak of the debt crisis (for detailed quantitative evidence, see Poznanski 1986b). The sixteen countries analysed below had a choice of various types of strategies, differing in terms of their reliance on import cuts as opposed to export push, and in terms of means used to accomplish either of these measures.

Alternative strategies

In 1979–80, world financial markets started to change rapidly. As real interest rates rose dramatically, the availability of credit to debtor countries shrank. At the same time, borrowing countries searched for new supplies of credits in order to cover their negative balances of trade (affected by the 1979 increase in oil prices) and to service their maturing debts. The halt in lending by Western bankers to Poland and Romania in 1980, and to the rest of Eastern Europe shortly thereafter, exposed the indebted economies to a credit squeeze. Their ability to service foreign debts began to hinge crucially on creating a trade surplus which could be transferred to the creditors.

While there is a range of options for generating a trade surplus, the underlying economic strategies can be classified as being either expansive or restrictive. Under the expansive strategy, the source of foreign trade surplus is an increase in domestic output of a given country above the existing trend line in the growth of internal consumption and investment. This strategy hence relies on the mobilization of economic reserves (e.g., reallocation of resources to more productive uses), which generates exportable surplus without interrupting imports. For this strategy to work, a country must be able to secure foreign demand for additional exports without worsening its terms of trade.

Within the restrictive adjustment, a country generates surplus through domestic austerity, i.e., a reduction in the rate of growth of consumption and/or investment (also called 'absorption'). While this particular strategy often leads to a slowdown in the rate of economic growth, the debtor country can redirect more of its output to exports. This shift towards exports, if effectively executed, may produce positive rates of growth in supplies of exportables with the overall level of output in decline. The austerity programme may, of course, be accompanied by improvements in the use of economic resources – another potential source of export acceleration.

Restrictive repayment strategy can follow two different approaches (Poznanska 1985). The so-called export-oriented version of this strategy allows for increases in the volume of exports while imports remain unchanged or expand at a rate that is less than that at which exports increase. Under the so-called import-substitution version of restrictive strategy, on the other hand, trade surplus is generated by cutting imports while exports remain unchanged or decline less than imports. In the first case, the squeeze in domestic absorption affects primarily the users of exportable goods, while the latter repayment strategy squeezes mostly the users of imports.

The countries analysed here functioned within two fundamentally different systems, because the developing countries operated in a market-oriented system with mixed (private and state) ownership. Given this difference, devaluation of the domestic currency was a viable option for generating a trade surplus in developing countries but not in the state-planned economics of Eastern Europe. At this stage of their institutional evolution, the countries of Eastern Europe did not work under a convertible currency system and/or competitive domestic prices. State planners in these countries could, of course, lower prices of exports to stimulate sales but, unlike devaluation, such an exercise will not automatically affect imports. Import reduction required separate instruments, such as increases in prices paid by firms or quantitative restrictions on currency allocation and goods supplies.[1]

Developing countries could also improve their balance-of-payments by encouraging inflow of foreign investment. Any increase in net transfer of foreign capital, whether through sales of financial assets (i.e., portfolio investment) or direct investment, would increase the revenue side of that balance. In countries with an established tradition of such investment (e.g., Brazil, Mexico (Poznanski 1986b, 1987)), a net inflow could be successfully stimulated by various liberalization measures and tax incentives. In Eastern Europe, where such operations were new and still rare, acceleration in foreign investment was not a viable short-term remedy to be considered by its policy makers.[2]

Market and centrally planned economies also differ in the instrumentation available for executing domestic austerity, including the execution of a domestic investment squeeze. Governments of developing countries had to use mostly indirect instruments to affect private agents (e.g., aggregate money supply or corporate taxes), and the effects of these actions often take place after a considerable delay. Since the state apparatus in Eastern Europe directly controlled almost all investment means, it could operationalize a given policy more readily (e.g., an investment contraction through freeze of independent funds at the enterprise level).

Planners in Eastern Europe were also generally better prepared to control consumption because they had direct control over wages, employment, and prices.[3] The planners were perhaps slower in recognizing needs for certain actions but once a decision was made the implementation usually came faster than under a market-type adjustment. However, while equipped with powerful instruments, the planners might have been more reluctant to use them for political reasons than the more restrained bureaucracies in the developing countries. Power is so squarely placed in the hands of the party/state that any measures taken can be traced more directly to them, strengthening public resentment (this point is well developed by Bunce: 1992b).

The debt record

By 1980, the majority of the developing countries which we have included in our analysis had accumulated larger absolute net debts than the East European countries. Argentina, Brazil, Mexico, and South Korea alone owed $133.3 billion in that year, with the total for ten countries at $184.7 billion, as compared to Eastern Europe's $66.5 billion. The former had to pay almost $31.1 billion in debt service that year, whereas Eastern Europe's payments amounted to half that amount. In relative terms, only the most indebted East European country, Poland, reported a higher ratio of annual debt service to yearly exports in 1980 (i.e., 1.20), while the other countries in the region reached similar, or even lower ratios than the major borrowers among the developing countries.

By 1984, the net total debt of Eastern Europe declined to $59.4 billion.[4] The sharpest debt reduction occurred in Bulgaria, where the debt was cut by one third (from $4.1 billion in 1980 to less than $1.5 billion in 1984). The only country whose net debt continued to increase was Poland, where it rose from $24.0 billion in 1980 to $25.8 billion in 1984. Unlike Eastern Europe, excluding Poland, the net debts of the developing countries have been increasing continuously since 1980.[5] For instance, the net debt of Argentina and Brazil combined increased from $73.5 billion in 1980 to $126.7 billion in 1984 (and with Mexico and South Korea the total for 1984 was $244.5 billion).

It would appear that Eastern Europe showed a greater ability, and willingness, to reduce its debt than did the developing countries as a group.[6] However, one can observe that Eastern Europe's figures were conditioned by the appreciation of the US dollar in the early 1980s. Around 60 per cent of its debt was held in currencies other than the dollar, the appreciation of which led to a decline in the dollar figure of Eastern Europe's debt. It is estimated that at least one half of the decrease in the total net debt of Eastern Europe in 1980–84 came from the appreciation of the dollar. Since the developing countries held their debts mostly in dollars, dollar appreciation did not result in a similarly strong decline in their debts.

By the same token, the fall of the dollar in 1987 inflated the total East European debt expressed in dollars, though much of that increase was related to both fresh borrowing and an accumulation of unpaid interest. While Poland's debt grew due to unpaid arrears the increases in net debt levels by Bulgaria and Hungary were in large part due to additional, new borrowing.[7] As a result the East European debt increased from 1984 by $31.6 billion (with Poland accounting for $11.9 billion of the increase), to $91.0 billion in 1987, with all countries, except for Romania, reporting increases. While not as affected by dollar depreciation, the debt of developing countries increased from $332.4 billion to $387.9 billion, or by $55.5 billion between 1984 and 1987.

The initial debt reduction by Eastern Europe and subsequent limited real (i.e., corrected for dollar fluctuations) increase of debt volume in the following years made Western bankers reevaluate their initially highly negative perception of the region's financial viability. After almost a full two-year freeze in lending, all countries, except Poland and possibly Hungary, were now considered reasonably 'safe borrowers' again, although no large scale fresh lending resumed before 1985. Between 1985 and 1989, Eastern Europe received credit in the range of $2 to 2.5 billion annually, with the major borrowers being East Germany and Hungary (though these flows were small by comparison with pre-crisis borrowing).[8]

Actual strategies

While Eastern Europe as a group appeared to be more successful in arresting its debt than other crisis-ridden borrowers, to assess which group of countries dealt most successfully with the debt problem it is necessary to evaluate the specific type of policies that were adopted by particular governments and their impact on overall economic growth.[9] It has to be recognized that specific repayment policies carry different costs for different economies, including potential losses for long-run growth prospects and technological progress. This section presents a comparison of adjustment strategies applied in various heavily indebted countries (see Poznanska 1985).

An analysis of export and import indices for the OECD market as a whole during 1980–8 reveals that within our sample, there are only two clear-cut cases of an expansive adjustment strategy – South Korea and Taiwan. These two countries increased both exports and imports in the period 1980–83 and then during 1983–88. Moreover, the growth indices for exports were much higher than those for imports. For instance, the South Korean export and import indices for 1980–83 were 131.5 and 119.0 respectively, while the respective indices for 1980–88, figures were 406.0 and 281.3 (see table 5.1). Further evidence that these countries pursued an expansive strategy is that they continued, with minor interruptions, their strong economic growth.

During 1980–83, the remaining countries, including those in Eastern Europe, followed a restrictive strategy, as evidenced in their import reductions. Exports fell in all countries of Eastern Europe except for East Germany and each economy in the region including East Germany also reduced imports from the OECD. In all cases of export contraction except for Bulgaria, hard-currency import reductions were deeper than export declines (e.g., in Romania the index for exports was 80.2 and the index for imports was 33.1 during 1980–83). Thus, except for Bulgaria and East Germany, the whole of Eastern Europe pursued the import-substitution version of the restrictive policy. At the same

Table 5.1 *Indices of change in exports (EX) to and imports (IM) from the OECD by selected countries*

Country	Index 1983/1980		Index 1988/1980	
Eastern Europe	EX	IM	EX	IM
Bulgaria	74.3	97.0	79.2	151.4
Czechoslovakia	81.6	65.6	118.7	121.0
East Germany	115.4	79.3	130.8	118.7
Hungary	82.9	79.1	146.5	122.3
Poland	59.0	44.5	101.7	76.4
Romania	80.2	33.1	117.4	32.8
Soviet Union	100.6	103.9	95.4	114.8
Developing Countries				
Indonesia	83.5	106.2	76.7	99.8
Malaysia	83.4	119.7	141.9	137.6
Philippines	87.1	98.0	126.8	105.3
South Korea	131.5	119.0	406.0	281.3
Taiwan	133.5	106.1	348.2	298.8
Argentina	90.9	45.8	132.9	42.1
Brazil	111.3	58.6	191.8	95.9
Chile	89.6	50.9	155.5	91.6
Mexico	144.4	57.9	174.4	125.2
Peru	87.1	75.2	72.5	67.0

Source: Calculated from monthly *Statistics of Foreign Trade* (Paris: OECD) (various years)

time, the national product of these countries grew more slowly than right before the outbreak of financial crisis, providing further evidence of a restrictive type of debt-adjustment.

Among the developing countries that followed the restrictive strategy, two of them – Brazil and Mexico – can be identified as adopting an export-oriented version of this strategy, both before 1983.[10] The export and import indices for Brazil during 1980–83 were 111.3 and 58.6, respectively, while for Mexico these indices were 144.4 and 57.9 respectively. Notably, both countries maintained their ongoing export surge to OECD countries through 1988, yet only Mexico returned to a strong import offensive. While Mexico's adjustment programme coincided with a three-year (1981 to 1983) decline or stagnation in their national products, this period was followed by faster economic growth (see Williamson 1990).

The rest of the developing countries – excluding Indonesia and

Malaysia, which are difficult to classify – used the same import-substitution version of restrictive strategy during 1980–83 as did the majority of East European countries at that time. In the Far East, the Philippines took this route, as did Argentina, Bolivia, and Peru in Latin America. For instance, in 1980–83, the Argentinean export index for the OECD was 90.9 and that of imports was 45.8. These figures place Argentina among the extreme cases of this particular strategy among the developing countries, and close to the average for Eastern Europe. But since 1983, most of these countries returned to dynamic exports that helped them to substantially exceed the 1980 level by 1988 (except for Indonesia and Peru).

In the later years, after 1983, the countries of Eastern Europe geared up for export expansion, with most of them by 1988 pushing their exports to the OECD visibly above respective 1980 levels. Using our typology, the pattern detected for the whole period of 1980–88 implies that as many as three countries, Czechoslovakia, East Germany and Hungary, can be considered as pursuing an expansive strategy. However, when compared with South Korea and Taiwan in the same longer period, expansion of both exports and imports in the three East European economies appears relatively limited. While in Hungary, which showed best performance of the three, the 1988/80 index for exports was 146.5 and that for imports was 122.3, the respective indices for South Korea were 406.0 and 281.3 (see table 5.1).

This performance by the three East Europeans was also less impressive than that of Mexico, which shifted to an expansive strategy later in the decade. For the whole of 1980–88, Mexico registered an export index of 174.4 while its respective index for imports was 125.2. Two other developing countries included in our sample also switched to expansive debt-adjustment – Malaysia and the Philippines. Their performance fell close to that of the three East European economies which employed the same type of strategy. Except for Peru, which continued an import-substitution restrictive strategy, the remaining countries in the sample pursued in the later part of the decade an export-oriented version of that strategy (one of these countries being Argentina).

Besides Peru, the only country in our sample which pursued an import-substitution, more passive version of restrictive debt-adjustment strategy during 1980–88 was Poland. The initial decline in Poland's exports was too deep for the successive growth in foreign sales to produce a visible overall increase in those years. The index of export growth was 59.0 for 1980–83, the worst of all countries analysed, with almost none of the latter reporting an index under 80.0. For the longer period of 1980–88, Poland's export index was 101.7, meaning that the economy had barely reached the pre-crisis level of exports by 1988 (of course, given the extremely sharp initial decline, it took an equally strong buildup of exports to produce this result). By 1988, the index for imports was still negative – 76.4, though up from 44.5, the index for 1980–83 (and much higher than in Romania, where the 1983/80 index was 33.1 and that for 1980–88 was 32.8).

With this variety of strategies most of the countries were able to improve their trade balances with the OECD countries and, in the majority of cases, turned their deficits into surpluses by 1983. Only in six cases – Bulgaria, Hungary, Poland, Philippines, South Korea, and Argentina – were the improvements insufficient to produce a cumulative surplus in 1980–83 but then most of them earned surpluses through 1988. Among the countries that achieved a cumulative trade surplus in 1980–83, the East European economies obtained a relatively small surplus ratio to cumulative exports (except for Romania), while among non-East European countries, the best performances were those of Brazil and Taiwan way ahead of Romania. In fact, the performance of the developing countries turns out to be even better than that of Eastern Europe if the whole 1980–88 period is analysed (though this time the ratio of cumulative trade surplus to export for Romania was the highest of all).

Comparing potential and actual exports

Comparison with Romania

The earlier analysis shows that Romania stands out among the East European countries in terms of its ability to produce a trade surplus with Western economies. Thus, by comparing Romania and Poland, one should be able to establish what Poland's repayment record would have been, had it adopted Romania's debt-servicing schedule. This is, of course, a hypothetical scenario and not necessarily a practical one, given the important differences between the two countries, particularly in political terms, as discussed previously. Still, such comparative analysis could be of considerable heuristic value in assessing to what degree Poland's government mobilized the economy for the sake of debt stabilization.

While Poland's gross debt increased by $13.1 billion, Romania's debt dropped from $10.1 billion to $1.9 billion, or by $8.3 billion during 1981–88. Poland reported an increase in its gross debt for each of the years in the same period, with the possible exception of 1988 (while Romania's gross debt declined each year sometimes by as much as $1 billion annually, as in 1983). Romania not only reduced its financial obligations sharply but also was able to erase its entire long-term debt to the commercial banks (Breinard 1990: 11). Romania's successful debt reduction enabled it to achieve a financial status that satisfied the good risk criteria of international lenders, for instance, its gross debt/export ratio dropped to 26 per cent in 1988, the latter considered a healthy figure.

Romania was able to rapidly repay its debt by quickly turning its overall trade balance from negative to positive, while also generating large-scale surpluses with the West. Even in 1981, Romania produced a surplus, and its economy was able to keep it above $1.5 billion from 1982 onwards. In contrast, as we have reported earlier, Poland achieved its first surplus in 1982 and was only able to generate surpluses on average below $1 billion (see Fallenbuchl 1984). While there was no upward trend in the size of trade surpluses by Poland, but rather a sort of stagnation, the amounts of annual payments to service its debt were on the rise (unlike in Romania where similar payments were declining systematically).

To more precisely measure the relative trade performance of the two countries, we have calculated their trade balance/export ratios. In all years since 1981, the surplus generated by Romania represented a bigger fraction of its exports to the West than in the case of Poland. Consequently if one applies Romanian ratios to Polish exports, then Poland's hypothetical sales exceed actual sales by a considerable amount. The cumulative difference for 1981–86 would amount to $3.0 billion, and it would be more than double that for 1981–88 (see table 5.2). Thus, if Poland used all this extra surplus to service its debt, its level would be much less by that amount than actual outstanding financial obligations.

While it is true that the regime of Ceausescu could proceed with very harsh austerity measures (i.e., rationing, energy black-outs, wage freezes, and permanent shortages of some goods) without undercutting its political power (Chirot 1991) and that Poland's rulers were unable to apply such policies for an extended period, it would be incorrect to suggest that Romania was able to produce a larger surplus only because of its more dictatorial regime. One of the factors that enhanced Romania's effort was its administrative continuity, for, in contrast to

Table 5.2 *Convertible foreign trade and hard currency burden, Poland and Romania (in billion dollars)*

	(a) Poland – actual				
	1979	1980	1981	1982	1983
Exports	6.1	7.4	5.0	4.5	4.8
Imports	8.2	8.2	5.8	4.3	3.9
Balance	2.1	−.8	−.8	.2	.9
Current account	−3.4	−2.6	−2.9	−2.1	−1.1
Total debt, gross	23.7	24.1	25.9	26.3	26.4
Gross debt/exports (in %)	388.0	335.0	518.0	584.0	550.0
	1984	1985	1986	1987	1988
Exports	5.3	5.1	5.3	6.2	7.2
Imports	3.9	4.0	4.3	5.1	6.3
Balance	1.4	1.0	1.1	1.1	.9
Current account	−1.2	−.4	−.6	−.4	−.4
Total debt, gross	26.9	29.3	33.5	39.2	39.2
Gross debt/exports (in %)	507.0	574.0	632.0	632.0	544.0

	(b) Romania – actual				
	1979	1980	1981	1982	1983
Exports	5.4	6.5	7.2	6.2	6.2
Imports	6.5	8.0	7.0	4.7	4.5
Balance	−1.1	−1.5	.2	1.5	1.7
Current account	−1.6	−2.4	−.8	.6	.9
Total debt, gross	7.2	9.6	10.2	9.8	8.9
Gross debt/exports (in %)	133.0	147.0	141.0	155.0	143.0
	1984	1985	1986	1987	1988
Exports	6.9	6.2	5.9	7.3	7.3
Imports	4.7	4.8	4.0	4.4	4.0
Balance	2.2	1.4	1.9	2.8	3.3
Current account	1.5	.9	1.4	2.5	2.5
Total debt, gross	7.2	6.6	6.4	5.7	1.9
Gross debt/exports (in %)	104.0	105.4	108.0	78.0	26.0

Table 5.2 (contd)

	(c) Poland – hypothetical				
	1979	1980	1981	1982	1983
Trade balance/exports ratio, Romania (in %)	−29.6	−23.1	2.8	24.2	27.4
Trade balance/exports ratio, Poland (in %)	−34.4	10.8	−16.0	4.4	18.7
Hypoth. balance, Poland	−1.8	−1.7	0.1	1.1	1.3
Hypoth. minus actual balance, Poland	.3	.9	.9	.9	.4
	1984	1985	1986	1987	1988
Trade balance/exports ratio, Romania (in %)	31.9	22.6	32.2	38.3	45.2
Trade balance/exports ratio, Poland (in %)	26.4	19.6	20,7	17.7	12.5
Hypoth. balance, Poland	.3	.9	.9	2.4	3.1
Hypoth. minus actual balance, Poland	.3	.1	.6	1.3	2.3

Sources: Poland: Polish Foreign Trade Performance in 1987, PlanEcon Report, vol. IV, No. S. 20–21, May 20, 1988; Polish Economic Performance During the First Half of 1988, PlanEcon Report, vol. IV, No. 36, September 16, 1988; Romania: Romanian Economic Performance in 1987, PlanEcon Report, vol. IV, No. 9, March 4, 1988; A Review of Developments in Soviet and East European Hard-Currency Trade, PlanEcon Report, vol. III, No. 36–38, September 17, 1987. Both Countries: Economic Bulletin for Europe, vol 40, October 1988, New York: United Nations.

Poland, at no time was the Romanian bureaucracy shaken to the point of losing its ability to manage the economy. Romania's state machinery was, therefore, in a position to force enterprises to export more while using fewer imports, and to do so without implementing any meaningful reforms in the economic system.

A related issue involved here is, of course, the relative social cost to Romania of its faster external debt repayment. One cost which is difficult to measure is that paid by Romanian society in deprivation of political freedoms, since Ceausescu greatly increased police repression during the period in question, although, Poland went through a highly repressive stage as well. Another cost is the greater hardship felt by

Romanian consumers, though one doubts that the subjective difference between the two countries was great (considering the fact that Poland entered into the crisis with a substantially higher standard of living than did the historically more backward Romania).

Finally, there is the question of the long-term economic costs of adjustment for both countries. With its more aggressive debt repayment schedule, Romania necessarily depleted its capital stock more than Poland with regard to these sectors which required imported equipment. Locked in an old-style planning system, Romania faced greater problems with effective utilization of limited resources from abroad. This situation was somewhat mitigated by the fact that its regime was in a position to give higher preference in remaining imports to capital-goods at the expense of consumer-goods. Romania was also helped out by somewhat stronger overall growth reported by official sources, so that domestic capital formation was probably more favorable than in Poland.

Intertemporal analysis

To expand this study on debt, we next look at trends in the export propensity of Polish industry since the economic crisis began in 1979. This is an intertemporal analysis of only selected manufactures in each major group, i.e., processed materials, machinery and transport equipment, and industrial consumer goods. We chose manufactured goods, even though they have never been dominant in Polish exports to the West, because without mobilization of these types of products for exports, successful debt repayment was not likely. Also, this is the sector where, as documented earlier, a large portion of the capital imported by Gierek's regime was concentrated.

Our analysis demonstrates that, at least within the sample, there was a tendency for export/production ratios to decline between the pre-crisis and crisis years. In the case of two out of nine products, rolled steel and cars, the share of exports in the value of domestic production increased between 1978 and 1987. In all other cases, the respective shares declined, sometimes very drastically, as in the case of cement, machine tools, and tractors, where the ratios declined by 50 per cent or more (see table 5.3). Myant (1993) confirms this foreign trade 'closure' of Poland's economy on the basis of more aggregate statistics on the shares of exports in total output of major sectors of the economy.[11]

Moreover, in six out of nine cases, the share of exports to the West in total foreign sales declined. This decline was particularly strong until 1986, not only in the case of the above mentioned six products but also with two other products in the sample. It was the change in 1987 that put the latter two products out of the category that reported diminishing shares during 1978–87. These two products were cement and synthetic rubber and the third product – one that showed regular increases in those years – was shoes (in this case, it came about because of declining total exports, with sales to Western markets remaining more or less unchanged).

These shrinking portions of the total exports which were shipped to Western markets were frequently caused by its preference for CMEA trade, particularly the Soviet Union. For instance, steel-rolled goods and machine tools experienced the deepest reduction in Western market shares, but showed the single largest gain in trade with the Soviet Union. This preference for the Soviet market occurred even though the Polish debt to the Soviet Union represented just a fraction of that owed to the West. With the resultant trade surpluses, Poland was expected to quickly clear its accumulated trade deficits with the Soviet Union (converted into so-called trade credits carrying a nominal interest charge).

The increase in the share of Western markets in the total exports of the few products among those reviewed by us was largely due to the redirection of supplies from developing countries, with no substitution taking place with respect to the CMEA market. After years of promoting exports to developing markets, Poland seemed to be giving up, in part because the ability of its partners to purchase goods had shrunk dramatically (in fact, many of the exports to developing countries were not paid for). Another contributing factor was the increased competition from Western producers, benefiting from their stronger financial standing (Poznanski 1989c).

It is possible that the above analysis in physical units distorts the real picture, since the aggregates in question are composed of types of goods that may differ in terms of quality and prices they command on foreign markets. Thus, if Poland were to sell its higher quality goods of a particular type to the West, then the share of this region in total exports measured in value terms would be higher than suggested by the physical indicators. As indicated earlier, Poznanski (1988a) has provided preliminary evidence that higher quality goods tended to be more targeted for export than lower quality ones. However, further effort is needed to derive a more accurate statistical picture of possible bias in export directions.

Table 5.3 *Domestic output (a), exports total (b), and exports to the West (c), selected goods, Poland*

	1978	1979	1980	1985	1986	1987
Steel, rolled (th. tons)						
a	13,565	13,572	13,551	11,845	12,340	12,410
b	1012	1760	1779	1969	2030	2081
b/a (%)	7.4	12.9	13.1	16.6	16.4	16.7
c	384	738	617	550	354	438
c/b (%)	37.9	41.9	34.7	27.9	17.4	21.0
Cement (mil. tons)						
a	21.7	19.2	18.4	15.0	15.8	16.1
b	2.2	2.0	1.3	1.3	.9	.5
b/a (%)	10.1	10.4	7.1	8.6	5.7	3.1
c	1.6	1.4	1.1	0.4	0.4	0.4
c/b (%)	72.7	70.0	84.6	30.7	44.4	80.0
Synthetic Rubber (th. tons)						
a	125.5	130.0	117.8	126.0	116.0	116.7
b	35.6	41.7	30.7	26.3	30.5	32.9
b/a (%)	28.3	32.1	26.0	20.8	26.3	28.2
c	27.0	29.1	24.8	19.2	17.0	27.1
c/b (%)	75.8	69.8	80.8	73.0	55.7	82.3
Cars (th. units)						
a	326	349	351	283	290	293
b	57	86	113	89	82	96
b/a (%)	17.5	24.6	32.2	31.4	28.7	32.7
c	35	61	94	53	48	56
c/b (%)	61.4	71.0	83.2	65.1	58.5	58.3
Machine-tools (th. units)						
a	39.5	39.3	38.3	57.4	51.9	46.1
b	7.1	7.3	7.4	5.9	5.9	5.2
b/a (%)	18.0	18.6	19.3	10.3	11.3	11.3
c	3.8	4.0	3.5	1.8	1.7	1.6
c/b (%)	53.5	54.8	47.3	31.8	28.9	30.7
Tractors (th. units)						
a	59.5	54.2	57.5	59.0	61.5	59.2
b	10.7	9.7	4.3	3.6	2.5	3.0

Table 5.3 (contd)

	1978	1979	1980	1985	1986	1987
b/a (%)	18.0	17.9	7.5	6.1	4.0	5.0
c	4.0	4.7	2.0	0.8	0.6	1.0
c/b (%)	37.4	45.4	46.5	22.2	24.0	33.3
Sewing machines (th. units)						
a	322.0	364.0	409.0	418.2	439.9	449.5
b	136.7	116.7	185.1	110.4	148.7	152.4
b/a (%)	42.4	32.0	45.2	26.4	33.8	33.9
c	53.9	79.8	19.3	8.8	13.2	39.9
c/b (%)	39.4	68.4	10.4	8.0	8.8	26.2
Bicycles (th. units)						
a	1,625	1,691	1,637	1,402	1,431	1,442
b	563	533	527	252	283	337
b/a (%)	34.6	31.5	32.2	18.0	19.8	23.4
c	458	466	427	187	193	260
c/b (%)	81.3	87.4	81.0	74.2	68.2	77.1
Shoes, leather (mil. pairs)						
a	73.5	72.8	72.4	70.3	67.9	65.6
b	25.9	23.8	25.0	17.1	18.0	18.8
b/a (%)	35.2	32.7	34.5	24.3	26.5	28.6
c	10.1	9.0	10.4	9.9	9.8	10.3
c/b (%)	38.9	37.8	40.0	57.9	54.4	54.8

Sources: Rocznik Statystyczny Handlu Zagranicznego, and Rocznik Statystyczny Przemyslu (Warsaw: GUS) (various years).

Changes in Poland's competitiveness

Economic crisis is often viewed at least in the evolutionary tradition as a source of adjustment that allows an economy to regain stability and resume growth, since only under overwhelming stress (or threat) are the most needed, tough choices made.[12] There was much hope among the Polish leadership that the crisis of 1979–82, while painful, would allow Poland to make such an adjustment, and that improved resource allocation and increased innovation would allow the country to strengthen its trade competitiveness. The government expected that these positive changes would generate a commodity surplus, arrest the growth of its debt, and eventually allow the national economy to resume a normal growth path – the ultimate goal of its overall strategy.

The following analysis attempts to determine whether the economic adjustment in question did in fact prepare Poland for smooth repayment of its Western debts once the large payments were resumed. Due to the structure of the rescheduled obligations, these large-scale payments were likely to occur in the early 1990s, and hence this is the time horizon of our analysis. Of course, many factors were to determine the future change in Poland's competitiveness strength as well as its ability to repay its debt. Our focus is on one of the most important of these factors – the role of continuous Western technology imports in the modernization of Polish export products.

Trade problems

Immediately after 1980, Poland's sales to the OECD countries fell rather considerably as measured by respective market shares. During this period, the absolute nominal value of the OECD trade dropped as well, but not as dramatically as did imports from Poland. Specifically, while total OECD imports from the world declined by about 11 per cent during 1980–82, the decrease in imports from Poland in that period was almost 40 per cent.[13] Even more contrasting trends occurred in the trade of machinery and transport equipment (SITC-7), where total imports by the OECD declined by 2.5 per cent, while shipments from Poland dropped by 47.8 per cent.

With such sharp declines in exports, Poland more than lost what it gained on the Western market during the successful period of the early 1970s. The share of Polish sales in total OECD imports dropped to 0.27 per cent in 1982, only 58 per cent of its share in 1970. On the West European market alone, Poland's respective share declined from 0.55 per cent in 1979 to 0.36 per cent in 1982, meaning further marginalization of its exports. The single sharpest decline was in the market share for chemicals, which in 1982 was less than one-half of its 1970 share (while Poland's shares of Western markets for many other major product categories in 1982 were comparable to 1970 shares).

OECD statistics reveal that the decline in the absolute value of exports to Western markets was not restricted to Poland. Between 1980 and 1983, total sales from Eastern Europe to the OECD countries declined by 21.6 per cent. If Poland is excluded, the respective rate turns out to be minus 13.4 per cent. The only country with positive rates of change in absolute exports of all products was East Germany (an increase of 11.5 per cent during 1980–83). In Hungary, the decline was 11.1 per cent, in Czechoslovakia 18.3 per cent, in Romania 19.8 per cent, and in Bulgaria 26.5 per cent, with the latter three cases registering rates well above the average rate of decline for total OECD imports in that period.

In the machinery and transport equipment area, Eastern Europe experienced an even more severe decline than in its total trade with the OECD economies. The sales of these manufactures diminished by 36.6 per cent during 1980–83 for all of Eastern Europe, and by 28.7 per cent when Poland is eliminated (several times the total decline in imports of machinery and transport equipment by the OECD). Turning to the individual countries, the rate was -21.3 per cent in East Germany, -27.3 per cent in Czechoslovakia, -27.8 per cent in Hungary, and the sharpest decline, -58.7 per cent, in Bulgaria (which by some accounts represented the most successful case of restructuring in favor of modern manufactures, see Brada and Montias 1984).[14]

As a result of these reductions in various exports to Western countries, Eastern Europe suffered further losses in its market share in OECD imports during the early 1980s. The share of Eastern Europe in those imports declined from 1.30 per cent in 1980 to 1.10 per cent in 1983 but when Poland, as an obvious anomaly, is again excluded from the total loss is smaller – 0.04 per cent points. In machinery and transport equipment, Eastern Europe's share declined from 0.76 per cent in 1980 to 0.40 per cent in 1983, and without Poland, by 0.24. Almost without exception, market shares declined for all goods and for machinery and transport equipment in all countries of the region (appendix 2).[15]

Further evidence

At first glance, this pattern of export changes in Eastern Europe right after 1980 does not seem to be related to cross-country differences in the intensity of Western technology imports in the 1970s. Poland suffered the most severe losses in exports, although its imports of Western technology were comparable in size to those of some other East European countries such as Hungary. Romania was another large-scale importer of technology, but its trade performance was considerably worse than Hungary's, the only country that concluded 1982 with a much higher share of the OECD market for machinery and transport equipment than it had in 1970. This was also the case with miscellaneous manufactures, although in this category Romania reported a large gain over the period as well.

There is some evidence, however, that the modest importers lost more of their market share shortly after 1980 than the large-scale importers from the West. For instance, Bulgaria imported relatively limited supplies of technology and, except for Poland, it experienced the most severe cuts in total exports. Bulgaria's losses in exports of machinery and transport equipment were much more drastic than those of deeply troubled Poland. Another modest importer of technology, East Germany, was the only country that by 1982 managed to increase slightly its share in the total OECD imports above the 1970 level, but these slight gains were, however, mostly due to the expansion in exports of non-manufactured goods; chemicals, machinery and transport equipment, and miscellaneous manufactures fell below their 1970 shares.

Hungary was not only able to keep its losses in the share of machinery and transport equipment to a minimum in 1980–83, but it was also the only East European country to show a substantially higher share of these manufactures in 1983 than in 1970 (i.e., 12.1 per cent against 6.3 per cent). Interestingly, the two countries that also reported higher shares of machinery and transport equipment in total exports to the OECD in 1983 than in 1970 were the remaining two large-scale importers of technology, Poland and Romania. In contrast, all modest importers, as well as Czechoslovakia, experienced a period of declining market shares, having a lower market share in 1983 than in 1970. Bulgaria's share dropped from 6.7 per cent to 5.4 per cent, while Czechoslovakia's respective share shrunk by one third (i.e., from 18.7 per cent to 12.2 per cent), and East Germany's share by almost half (i.e., from 22.7 per cent to 13.2 per cent).

The evidence presented above, particularly the superior performance of the Hungarian economy in the face of financial troubles suggests that large-scale imports of Western technology most likely had a positive impact on the ability of the aggressive borrowers of technology to cope more effectively with the economic disturbances[16] particularly in its export of manufactures. One could argue that Poland, had it not been plagued with internal disturbance, would have probably shown a performance more like that of Hungary. Romania, if not for its refusal to accept financial help from international banks and for the unnecessarily severe deflationary policy selected by its regime, would have performed better as well.[17] It could thus well be that large-scale imports had a lasting positive effect but primarily for those who managed to obtain some external assistance, Hungary being a case in point.

Western machinery

Our next step is to assess the impact of Poland's import reductions on the country's export potential in the long-run. These cuts were quite substantial in the category of industrial machinery particularly after 1980, so that in 1983, Poland's index (with 1980 = 100) for imports of these goods (SITC-7.2, 7.3, 7.4) stood at 38.9. Although our earlier analysis indicates that Western machinery imports were not used most productively, Poland's radical reduction of imports of Western industrial machinery and technology might have had a negative impact on the new production capacities created during Gierek's economic expansion. Given the size of the reduction, it is possible that even a simple replacement of parts and equipment, not to mention more substantial modernization, was prevented.

To determine the likely negative impact of the import squeeze on the replacement of Western capital equipment, we calculate the hypothetical replacement needs for equipment installed between 1970 and 1984 and then compare these figures with the actual value of imported machinery. The differences between the two are used as a rough indicator of capital accumulation if imports exceed replacement demand, or depletion in the opposite situation. For reasons of data availability, we restrict our analysis of both aggregate indicators to products classsified in the three special machinery categories of SITC-7.2, 7.3, and 7.4.

We assume that all machinery is depreciated in ten-year periods with one-tenth of the initial capital value depreciated each year, and that the rate of inflation for imported equipment is 5 per cent each year. In addition, it is assumed that there is no possibility to substitute domestic capital for Western capital, even though some such domestic substitutes were available. It is very unlikely that Poland did not use some of the imported equipment to modernize its production of machinery in the three categories mentioned above.[18] However, without a practical way of determining the actual scale of domestic capital suitable for such substitution, as well as not knowing whether internal equipment is identical in terms of quality, the above simplifying assumption becomes a necessity.

The results of our estimate reveal that imports of industrial machinery since 1980 have not been sufficient to meet all the replacement needs for post-1969 capital investment in Western equipment. If we assume that an appropriate share of imports prior to 1980 was being assigned to replacement of imported capital, then the Western-furnished capacity since 1980 has been subject to rapid depletion. The estimate suggests that if all newly imported machinery in 1983 was devoted to replacement, the deficit in supplies for the needed replacements would amount to approximately two-thirds of required imports. Since it is unlikely that all 1983 imports were devoted to replacement, this ratio was no doubt even higher (see appendix 5).

Poland's decline in industrial machinery imports was almost certainly exacerbated by the regime's decision to give priority to importing of materials and components in order to maintain or even expand current output, rather than importing for the purpose of modernizing existing capacities, a move which surely limited Poland's economic alternatives in subsequent years. This choice could be explained by the typical short time-horizon of planners, which under the existing political circumstances, was particularly short. Trying to prove to the society that the imposition of military rule in 1981 was justifiable, the regime sacrificed long-term needs of the economy for short-term indicators of strong recovery.

Had this negative capital accumulation process continued, Poland would have certainly lost some of its competitive production lines. By loss, we do not necessarily mean a full shut-down of those lines, since the regime could have extended the life-span of imported machinery beyond the ten-year period used for our estimates. However, allowing this capital to age beyond the ten-year period was likely to cause the quality of the resultant products to suffer and their unit cost to rise due to the growing maintenance burden as well. Either way, insufficient level of replacement imports had to cause damage to the export capacity, which was greatly expanded – and made more critically dependent on steady foreign supplies – during the import-led strategy pursued by the Gierek administration.

Foreign licenses

In addition to the decumulation of Western-based capital stock, the industry was left with a drastically reduced inflow of disembodied technology. Gierek's 1976 economic adjustment and the anti-crisis measures pursued since 1980 had a negative impact on Poland's imports of Western licences. This withdrawal from licence imports resulted in a rapid reduction in the number of active agreements. Due to the initial expansion of purchases, the number of such agreements increased from 142 in 1970 to 385 in 1976. Since then, however, the number of active licenses fell to 181 by 1983, this due to an almost complete halt on imports of licenses (a trend also reflected in falling royalty payments (see Poznanski 1987).

Declining imports of licenses could also be detected at that time among many other East European countries as well as in the Soviet Union, though none of these economies stopped buying licenses like Poland did. This downward trend is evidenced in the substantial decline in both the number of license agreements (and applications) and related royalty payments by the region as a whole to Western suppliers of technology.[19] However, in some extreme cases, such as Hungary, strong imports of technology from the West continued, though with a smaller number of major projects. The number of licensed products in Hungary increased from 693 in 1981 to 953 in 1985 with 40 per cent of licensed production exported. Hungary bought 52 licenses from Western countries in 1981, and then 87 in 1982, 100 in 1983, 77 in 1984, 132 in 1985, and 82 in 1986 (see Mach 1990).

This decline in licence inflow by Eastern Europe contrasts with increasing or stable imports by the majority of Western countries (e.g., EEC payments to the United States). Even those among the newly industrializing countries that were forced to make painful reductions in machinery imports did not go as far as Poland in curtailing license agreements. For instance, in Mexico, where imports of machinery declined by almost half in 1980–83, payments for licenses remained virtually unchanged (e.g., Mexico paid the United States $154 million in royalties in 1982, $114 million in 1983, and $146 million in 1984) (*Survey of Current Business*, June 1985).

The scale of the license squeeze in Poland cannot be explained simply in terms of a general reduction in Western machinery imports. Even though capital purchases were needed for most of the potential licenses, the cuts were not of such magnitude as to justify the almost complete withdrawal of Poland from licence contracts with Western countries as documented above. Certainly, despite the overall financial situation of the economy, at least some minor contracts would have been feasible. Only if we agree that no licenses were affordable, can one understand why even the sectors with best export prospects and in desperate need of Western technology were ignored.

The reduction in imports of Western technology into Poland was not compensated by increased supplies of technology from the domestic sector. Just the opposite – the crisis undermined research activities. One of the reasons was the elimination of industrial associations in 1982, as the majority of research organizations used to be attached to associations (see: Poznanski 1987) and be financed by them. With the 1981 reform, research institutions became dependent on orders from industrial enterprises, which, however, did not show much interest in supporting product development and process technologies. With only weak support, by 1985, the number of industrial research centers was down to 91.9 thousand from 129.9 thousand in 1980.

Summary

During the final decade of communist rule, Poland's industry, including all export-oriented sectors in manufacturing, underwent a rapid aging process. Consequently, Poland was less and less able to generate a sufficient supply of competitive goods to be sold on Western markets. Since only these markets could serve as a major source of hard-currency revenues (particularly since reexports of oil coming from developing countries to the West could not have lasted much longer. This meant that Poland's economy was very likely to arrive at the second wave of debt payments, predicted at that time to occur around 1990, with a greatly weakened export potential in manufactures.

The economic adjustment, primarily focused on an investment squeeze rather than on the curtailment of consumption was one of the factors contributing to this aging of export production. Giving priority to maintaining current production – and employment – instead of its modernization was another reason for the accelerated aging process. Importantly, this negative development seemed to take place throughout the entire industry, including the critical area of manufacturing. The absence of even one clear case of a major manufactured product making substantial progress on Western markets, can be viewed as an ultimate indication that Poland's government was unable to set priorities for the embattled economy, struggling as it was with particularly severe scarcities and imbalances.

While the difficulties encountered by Poland in arresting her debt and reviving the economy, documented in the previous chapter, could be viewed as a direct consequence of constraints felt by the Gierek regime, our analysis in this chapter suggests that the disappointments of the post-1982 recovery could may have had a lot to do with similar failures of his successors. It appears that, again, the central agencies were not in a position to mobilize the existing export potential and even less to provide for its maintenace. If they were not, this would suggest that the economic system – and various instruments available to the state planners – did not facilitate such redirection of production to foreign markets. If so, this would, in turn, imply that some, or most of the political conditions which caused the 'weakening' of that system under Gierek remained in place, or possibly got even worse, after his removal from a leadership position.

6   Political struggles and economic malaise

With the evidence offered in the previous chapter that many of the problems with the foreign sector may have had their source in the domestic sector, we are going to look in this closing chapter of the second part at the political forces which could have shaped the internal economy. This stage of our analysis should provide a proper context for understanding the debt-repayment difficulties as well as overall economic performance. We look at the politics of economic choice from the imposition of martial law in late 1981 to the collapse of the communist party/state in mid-1989. We have already established that the economic fortunes of the Gierek government were heavily influenced by political developments, many of them outside of government's control. This part of our analysis provides an opportunity to establish whether politics continued to greatly affect economics in the years that followed the cabinet's departure.

We assert below that during the period of martial law the political leadership of Jaruzelski was able to bring about the near-pacification of society – albeit without its conscious cooperation. Direct clashes of the opposition with the military-run political apparatus had proved too costly to rioters, and therefore lost much of their appeal for the public at large. Consequently, forms of dissent changed as organized and visible protests were replaced by less noticeable or structured acts of defiance. The harsh steps taken by the Jaruzelski regime to stabilize the political situation only produced an 'unstable equilibrium,' which was quite easily disturbable. Renewed tensions – not necessarily as confrontational as before martial law – between society and its rulers (but also within each of these two segments) remained an ever present possibility.

While the government confronted the opposition during 1981–82 with great force, its purpose does not appear to have been the full restoration of pre-crisis polity – with party political monopoly and intra-party working after the pattern of 'democratic centralism'. Nor was the purpose of the military action to rebuild a central, command-type control over the economy along the old lines. This was not a typical case of communist normalization, in which political opponents of the system are crushed to effect a return to the status quo, and in which authority lost by the planners is regained. Rather, force was applied to demobilize a 'strong' society to the point where the government could pursue an array of reforms – both political and economic. That this helped to prolong the party's existence was a sort of side-effect.

Whether the party was struggling for political advantage, or to cut its losses, or just to be able to peacefully step down from the political scene, is hard to determine. The thought of giving away power was undoubtably rare under martial law but, with time, a growing segment of the political elite became more open to the concept. The most disenchanted elements within the party/state apparatus were leaving the ranks for the opposition and/or private sector. At the same time, the reform-minded segments within the political leadership were becoming more and more ready to try ideas once considered taboo. The ruled – society at large – wanted substantive reform as well, though they were very reluctant to give the leaders credit for actually bringing about change, thus denying political gains to the party/state reformers.

While retaining its generally restrictive character, the post-1981 system – political and economic – underwent enormous transformation. The economic reforms did not step far outside of the communist practice of the time, for the Jaruzelski regime, by and large, followed the 1968 design of Hungary. In contrast, political change, like the overall political situation in Poland, was without close parallel in the region.[1] The centrality of this political change marked another break-through in postwar communist history, where the political realm tended to be more rigid than the economic one. Consequently, political developments became an even more important force in shaping the whole economy – while under the Gierek regime, domestic politics worked mainly as a constraint on economics during this later phase, politics seemed to drive economics.

If the political apparatus was more interested in a low-cost exit than long-term survival, then their political manoeuvring after 1981 has proved rather successful. Even if the reform programmes were not helpful in preserving a political monopoly, they reduced the potential for violent confrontation with the society. Equally important in lowering the cost of power transfer were the adjustments made by the opposition forces. Conciliatory elements were able to steer the opposition movement away from frontal attacks on the party/state apparatus. These elements permitted political compromises which were often viewed by militant oppositionists as 'collaboration'. One such move was the early 1989 round-table negotiations, which resulted in the rather unexpected transfer of the majority of political power to the non-radical (we would say 'reformist') wing of the anti-communist movement.

These fast-paced political changes had a decisive effect on economics, for being in a highly politicized environment, the economic sphere itself became highly politicized. Absorbed in political manoeuvring, the central apparatus had to divert much of its energy from economic problems – themselves a formidable obstacle. Concerned for keeping political process under control, the apparatus was even less willing to risk resentment from within enterprises by reallocating resources, say in favour of sectors with greater promise for exports. This was also the case with work discipline, so that declining quality of production, theft of state property for resale, or drinking on the job became more permissable. Afraid of a new eruption of worker discontent, the government was also continuously hard-pressed to protect individual consumption – and welfare payments – at the expense of debt-repayment.

The state of war: restoring unstable equilibrium

Military takeover

At the end of 1981, even if the Jaruzelski regime remained ready to seek a peaceful exit from the political confrontation with the free unions, it was left with little room to manoeuvre in search of a compromise. By that time, the greatly fractured party became ungovernable and thus of dubious use in pressuring the independent unions to lessen their demands. Suggestions by some within the party ranks that 'true' communist leaders throughout the region should not refrain from military intervention in Poland were making the opposition less eager to pursue negotiations with the party. As union leadership was losing control over its huge and diverse membership, there was very little of lasting value that regime-union discussions could have produced. Moreover, calls by militants within the free union to establish similar labour organizations throughout the communist bloc, had a chilling effect on the compromise-seeking elements within the party.

Last but not least, the Soviet Union found the situation intolerable and made it clear to Jaruzelski that if the conflict was not soon resolved internally, then an outside intervention would be unavoidable. There was very little Western governments could have done to prevent the Soviet Union from orchestrating the elimination of the independent unions. However, actions were taken to make the Soviet leaders realize that they would have to pay a steep price if they proceeded with punitive steps in Poland, particularly with military intervention. At this point, Soviet relations with the West were already greatly fractured, as manifested by stiff Western restrictions on technology sales and credits (mostly in response to the invasion of Afghanistan by the Soviet army). The West made it clear that further deterioration of global relations would occur if the Soviets intervened in Poland.

Given these conditions, the Soviet leadership, led by Brezhnev, decided to lower the costs of possible crackdown on the opposition by working with the Jaruzelski regime. Brezhnev chose to have the Polish government eliminate the threat from the independent unions, yet there was the risk that elements in the army might join the workers. Thus, for such a strategy to work, the Soviet Union had to demonstrate to the Poles that if their government failed to impose order, then Soviet troops – possibly with those of some other East European armies – would step in. The Soviet leaders provided sufficient evidence that they were fully prepared to move in with military force, as demonstrated by Soviet military manoeuvres along the Polish border and by increased activity of Soviet troops stationed in Poland.

All the preparations for invasion, including the Soviet decision at a later stage to include Czech and East German troops, were known to the military leadership of Poland's regime. From the very beginning, parts of the Polish military were involved in the Soviet preparation for intervention as well as for the alternative 'internal' solution. Because the latter required the use of military – not just police – force, the question was who in Poland, if this option were chosen, would be put in charge of such a repressive action. Finding an effective power centre seemed to be most critical for the smooth execution of this kind of invasion by proxy. As the Polish communist party was too divided and confused to be relied upon, the Soviet leaders decided to work primarily with the military. By choosing such a *modus operandi*, the Soviet Union ran the risk of at least temporarily placing the military above the party on the domestic scene, in conflict with the doctrinal principle giving primacy to the party.

Under the circumstances, Jaruzelski had little choice but to impose martial law, as he did in December 1981. Through a swift police operation, the core of the political opposition, including Walesa, was arrested. The army took up position in major cities and surrounded the most rebellious enterprises, all in direct concert with police forces. Because workers' resistance was brief and sporadic, there was little loss of human life. In only one incident involving a single coal mine were some workers shot by armed police units, and this was by no means a premeditated killing. Other killings took place in various localities where the central command had less control over the police. The relatively non-violent character of the military action was also a result of the fact that army officers were instructed to apply minimal force and to act as a restraint on police units as well as on the protesters.

Power reconfiguration

Because the state of war helped prolong the existence of the communist party, this action has often been seen as an indication that the party apparatus, acting in self-defence, employed the military to crush the political opposition. According to this interpretation, the application of military force was an admission that the communist party had permanently lost its legitimacy and thus found political forms of action inadequate. Consequently, the party had to change from a political organization into one based on violence. Staniszkis (1982) has argued that after martial law, sheer coercion became the only solid foundation for the communist party, as well as for the reproduction of the entire system (this point being restated by Przeworski 1991). It is not that the party was undermined but rather that one form of its monopoly rule – founded on passive acquiescence – was abandoned, to be replaced by another, possibly more lasting, one.

It might be, however, that the party did not direct the military to rescue it, but rather was offered such assistance by the military on terms which the latter set itself. At this critical point, the party was probably too fractured to direct the military to undertake steps potentially unpopular with the people. Even before the confrontation with the free unions, the party was not in a position to simply impose its will on the military, given the considerable independence which the latter had gained over the years, since at least 1975. With the military sector retaining its cohesion – in fact, being the only segment of the party/state apparatus not affected by erosion in its basic structure – the army was in the best position in years to determine the conditions under which its power would be applied in the ongoing party-union struggle.

There seems to be abundant evidence that, as far as the domestic scene is concerned, the imposition of martial law was indeed less a decision by the party apparatus than a measure taken by the military. Whereas the crackdown on the unions provided an opportunity to rebuild the party, the military directorate – a small circle of generals surrounding Jaruzelski – was reluctant to restore the party's previous political prominence. Although the Jaruzelski regime needed the communist party as a functioning organization to stabilize the internal political life, they chose against empowering the apparatchiks with great authority. In their eyes, the communist apparatus had failed to prevent a confrontation with the workers and they doubted whether the party could be turned into a cohesive and effective force again. In fact, the perception was that it would be a waste of political capital to try to fully repair the political image of the party.

Judging by the actions of the military leadership during the period of martial law, the intention was not to extend the role of the party but rather to reduce it in order to facilitate a different political structure. The decision by the military directorate to arrest several high party officials from Gierek's cabinet (including Gierek himself) was one indication of this intention. The military also placed a number of army personnel within the party organization (with Jaruzelski being not only in charge of the army but also serving as party First Secretary). Besides the obvious shift of power to the military and the police, the Jaruzelski regime decided to expand the authority of the state bureaucracy, hoping that, if it were removed from the political control of the party, it would have a better chance to restore order quickly. To facilitate this power shift and a new state-based, rather than party-based, structure, the military directorate strengthened the role of the prime minister and other cabinet members (compare with Walicki 1991).

Not only was the office of prime minister allowed to overshadow the once omnipotent post of party secretariat, but, to further limit the powers of the party, the military directorate decided to strengthen the parliament and expand its legislative authority. This change was signified, for instance, by the fact that the imposition of martial law was eventually voted in by the parliament, as various acts of emergency legislation were asked for by the directorate. To make the parliament more effective, two smaller non-communist parties permitted by the communists to operate during the postwar years – one representing rural areas and the other aimed at urbanites – were allowed a more independent vote in the parliament. Parliamentary debates became more lively and dissenting positions were more willingly tolerated, with the content of these debates being made available to the public at large.

Several concessions were made by the regime to satisfy the 'coalition' – non-communist – parties in parliament. The peasant party, enjoying the support of the Church, won a number of economic concessions for individual farmers, among them the constitutional guarantee that their land tenure (property rights) could not be withdrawn by the state. Additional opportunities for the members of these parties to be promoted to higher, more lucrative posts within the state administration were provided as well. At that time, there were 1.2 million managerial positions (of which 0.9 million positions were held by communist party members, accounting for about half of the total membership) and 250,000 were covered by the 'nomenklatura' system, controlled by the central party organs. In 1984, a decision was made by the Jaruzelski regime to include members of coalition parties among 'nomenklatura' appointments.

This shift from the party to the state – and the partition of the traditional party/state monolith – was also reflected in the imposition of restrictions on access by the party apparatus to the propaganda machine. The party's traditional near-monopoly of the media was undercut by the expansion of government newspapers and by giving state officials more exposure on television. Moreover, the party was prevented from launching an ideological campaign of 'socialist revival', as it had done in the past following political confrontations with the opposition. Instead, the language of patriotism and national interest was employed by the state-controlled media with only very indirect references to the ideals of socialism. The new references were to the spirit of equality and the social safety net rather than to the actual (i.e., real) social system which the communist party originally embodied.

The Jaruzelski regime, as Kolankiewicz (1988) correctly characterizes it, did not so much seek legitimation – moral acceptance – of its power, as validation of it, i.e., broad acceptance on more practical grounds. Jaruzelski thought that by actions – more than by words – the regime could impress on the general public the value of an assertive government. The hope was that with the development of this mindset, the

public might look more favourably upon the controversial martial law
– viewed by only one segment of society as dictated by the 'national
interest' while condemned by most others as betraying the same. Of
course, active support for the leaders was preferable to passive
obedience, so that the regime's ultimate objective was to use the public
desire for stronger rule to eventually legitimize its power.

Thus, if one wishes to generalize, martial law might be viewed not
as a violent response by the party to political threat but rather as a
military takeover which placed the army at the centre of political
activity. This was not the action of an army seeking permanent political
leadership for itself, but rather an emergency measure executed by a
non-political military to fill a disturbing vacuum created by the
disintegration of normal channels of political reconciliation. Judging by
the preference the directorate gave to the state administration and
institution of parliament, this military takeover could be seen as
designed to permanently change the political organization of the
country. It was unclear at this point, however, whether the military
simply sought to implement a one-party system where the party and
the state were more formally separated, whether it wanted to initiate
transition to some sort of political pluralism,[2] or whether it had yet
something else in mind.

Inclusion policy

A further indication that the Jaruzelski regime was not interested in
restoring old-time polity, was its attitude to the opposition forces. The
actions taken here by the Jaruzelski regime constituted an effort to
normalize relations with the opposition by gradually incorporating
various layers of the opposition into the political process (see Kolankiewicz 1988). Rather than relegate these forces outside the polity, the
regime initiated steps towards accommodating a non-threatening presence of the opposition within the broader power structure. The regime
had no basic ideological objection to workers having their own form of
representation. Their real objection was to an ungovernable union
movement, which might present an obstacle to solving Poland's underlying problem, i.e., a rapidly deteriorating economy and related
adverse changes in the geopolitical balance of power.

True, initial repressive steps taken during martial law did not seem
to be geared toward such a type of normalization. However, to create
conditions for reaching a compromise with independent unions, the
military rulers seemed to have little choice but to rely heavily on police

action. The opposition quickly learned that street confrontations were too risky, though there remained scores of those willing to take the risk. The public – struggling with economic deprivation – was tired of unrest under any banner or for whatever cause. Consequently, opposition activists resorted to alternative means such as increasing the volume of anti-communist publications, from regional journals to factory newsletters. Union structures, without being dissolved, assumed a very low profile, basically trying to preserve the network of personal contacts as much as possible. To gain better protection from the police, the opposition began using church facilities and religious events as a vehicle for their own activities.

The regime also found it difficult to rely on sheer force because of political demands from Western countries. With mounting Western pressure, the Soviets were not in a position to make the Jaruzelski regime adopt a more decisive solution. For one thing, they had to deal primarily with Jaruzelski, who was a centrist within the party. Then too, the events of 1980–81 had greatly reduced the ranks of the conservative faction, which might have been expected to work with its Soviet counterpart. Support for the conservative wing was weak, out of fear that adopting a hard line would ruin the party's remaining chances of regaining social acceptance. During the few months that preceded martial law, Jaruzelski made a number of appointments which consolidated his grip on the party leadership and at the same time lessened the likelihood of dissent from pro-Soviet forces.

While not in control of the party, the conservatives pressed the Jaruzelski regime from the very beginning to take a firmer stand. They tried to accomplish this mainly through mass media manipulation and police intimidation and terror – the killing of a popular Catholic priest, Popieluszko, being an example. Such actions, however, proved counter-productive to the hard-line cause and, rather than intimidating, they strengthened the opposition forces. Victimizing a priest was particularly ill-advised as it outraged the deep religious beliefs of the population, giving rise to a highly emotional, nationwide cult of the priest as martyr with the party cast in the role of evil assassin. These excesses also enabled the regime of Jaruzelski to take measures that discredited the intra-party hard-liners (e.g., open trials and harsh sentences for policemen involved in the killing of Popieluszko).

Caught between forces seeking confrontation, the regime settled for another version of 'repressive tolerance', which was significantly harsher than that under Gierek. Even though martial law was lifted in 1983, most of its extraordinary regulations were incorporated into the civil and criminal codes. This allowed the regime to rapidly apply emergency measures in case of another outburst of popular unrest. As long as the level of tension was found acceptable, the regime was ready to proceed with its policy of political relaxation. In fact, along with the lifting of martial law, the Jaruzelski leadership began releasing the jailed Solidarity members. The activists of the de-legalized union were allowed to pursue their work more in the open and with less risk of being harassed. However, conditions for dissenting activities remained difficult enough to cause tens of thousands of activists to take advantage of the then liberalized passport policy and emigrate.

Another important indication that martial law had been imposed to restore political stability rather than to recreate traditional politics that left no room for extra-party activities, was various institutional changes which channeled the released energy of the opposition into a regularized political process. Among these devices to promote political communication was the Patriotic Movement for National Rebirth, established in 1982. The opposition forces refused to participate in what they saw as a 'popular-front' type of organization, patterned after similar arrangements introduced soon after the last war by the communists. The hierarchy of the Catholic Church also ignored it, but, in 1986, when this organization was converted into the Social Consultative Council, the moderate part of the opposition recognized the value of joining it.

Significantly, Jaruzelski's regime decided to stress the need for legalism in state-citizen relations, in order to both reduce the level of social dissatisfaction and depoliticize it. The regime instituted a number of state agencies to whom citizens could address their various legal complaints rather than using the traditional channel: the party. Among these newly created institutions were the Administrative Court and the Office of Ombudsman. In addition, the Constitutional Court was established to examine the legality of government decisions. By opening these channels, the regime not only reduced the power of the party but also imposed stronger barriers on the state administration against arbitrary actions. At the same time, these agencies reduced the need for the independent unions as representatives of diverse societal interests, while forcing their leaders to give more attention to proceduralism and adherence to law.

With all these measures, the military regime temporarily defused political tensions but did not remove the sources of discontent. In contrast to the early Gierek years, no political programme was here produced with the potential to integrate the society around common goals. Thus, the political cycle of confrontations might have begun to escalate again had this fragile balance been upset. While the political system under Jaruzelski was more repressive, the overall political situation was also more unstable. With the changes instituted by the Jaruzelski regime, the opposition was allowed to consolidate, thus making repression – or the threat of it – much more necessary. This repressiveness was in a way a function of the increased openness which the government was willing to tolerate. It might, in fact, be more appropriate to call the political formula under Jaruzelski a 'terror of reform' (see Poznanski 1992b).

A brief return to political 'normalcy'

Political process

The elevation of Messner to the post of prime minister in 1985 (taking one official function away from Jaruzelski) did not slacken the pace of political reform. Among the major initiatives of the new government was its decision to pursue reformed parliamentary elections. Already in 1983, the Front of National Unity – an organization charged with the preparation of fixed lists of official candidates for elections – had been abolished. In 1985, a reformed system for nominations and revised voting procedures was instituted to facilitate parliamentary elections scheduled for that year. The government also decided to abandon the old practice of intimidating people into voting, thus risking a low turnout. In fact, by official accounts, about 6 million eligible voters boycotted the elections. But the reformed system helped to strengthen the parliament, for as many as one-third of elected representatives were from local councils, and thus presumably closer to the voters themselves.

To allow citizens to express their preferences on some of the central issues, the government of Messner also activated the institution of the national referendum. The first such opportunity was offered in 1987, when citizens were asked to consider a new type of 'social compact', under which the government would launch aggressive reforms in exchange for worker restraint. The compact tried by Gierek, where consumption gains were traded for political compliance, could not have worked, since no immediate improvement in goods supplies was possible. The Messner regime could only offer a promise of economic progress to be accomplished through bold reforms, which were expected to produce initial discomfort to workers. In an exercise of democratic politics, the citizens rejected the proposed compact, a defeat which did not prevent the government from pursuing its reform plans anyway.

Although the government failed to get its social compact approved, this was not because the majority of people objected to more aggressive reforms, or to their particular direction. In fact, the idea of entering into this kind of agreement was accepted by more than half of those who participated in the referendum, though this was less than the minimum needed for the measure to pass. The vagueness of the economic reforms which the government wanted people to endorse – with strike freeze promises and wage concessions – worked against the referendum. Moreover, many of the voters were confused by the imprecise formulation of particular points of the referendum and the exact choices they were supposed to make. Those voting against the social compact were often motivated more by a general mistrust of the Messner regime – or the system it represented – than by the merits of the proposed agreement.

The Messner regime also allowed for rapid growth in the number of non-political organizations, a move coinciding with a spontaneous effort by the population to organize itself outside of the traditional structures created by the party. The formation of independent unions was just one example of the widespread effort to withdraw from 'official' society and develop an alternative, 'second' society. While insisting on relegalization of free unions, the opposition sought additional forms of organization outside of state realms. Together with the Catholic Church, the non-communist forces succeeded in gradually creating a system of institutions traditionally reserved only to the party (i.e, theatres, schools). A true measure of the progress made was that by 1987 there were almost 18 million Poles participating in some form of non-political association, with 2,000 such organizations being registered (Kolankiewicz 1988: 174; also Stokes 1993: 102–130)).

Worker representation was further strengthened as well, even though the Messner regime resisted pressures by de-legalized free unions to make them legal again. The government reduced its policing of free union activities, allowing individual organizations to collect dues, hold meetings, and carry on low-key actions with little harrassment. The trade unions created by the communist rulers after the last war – designed to serve as a 'transmission belt' – were disbanded in 1984. Seen by the regime as compromised and ineffective, the traditional unions were replaced with new official unions to be led by

Miodowicz. Unlike the old unions, the new ones were allowed considerable freedom of action in order to gain the credibility needed to compete with free unions. Thus, conditions were created by the regime for the 'official' unions to evolve into alternative representatives of the genuine interests of workers (see: Goodwyn 1991).

While increasing the potential for conflict with society, the policies of the regime assured greater differentiation of interest groups and thus helped to shift some of the conflict away from the state. These civil organizations were intended to divert a percentage of the opposition movement away from purely political activities. For the anti-communist forces, the switch to alternative structures, in turn, was helpful in strengthening their base against future political confrontations with the communist leadership. These structures were also necessary to meet various needs which large segments of society could not satisfy through officially organized channels. While the expansion of the 'second economy' was a mostly spontaneous response to the failing state-sector industry, the 'second society' was a similar reaction to the deficiencies of official political structures.

Partial normalization

Messner's efforts to stabilize the political situation proved relatively successful, with one indication being that the decline in party membership was largely arrested. Total party membership was at 3,092,000 in 1980; at 2,327,000 in 1982; and then up from 2,129,000 in 1986 to 2,322,000 in 1988 (see: Lewis 1988). In the meantime, however, the membership structure had changed, with the share of workers at 46.1 per cent in 1980, but then down to 37.7 per cent in 1982, while the share of intelligentsia increased from 32.5 to 51.9 per cent. The party was losing its 'proletarian' character but at the same time becoming more technocratic – not unequivocably a negative development. Truly worrisome for the party was another fact, namely, that the share of young members (age 18 to 29) was in sharp decline (with this cohort accounting for 24.8 per cent in 1980, 11.1 per cent in 1982, and 6.4 per cent in 1988) (*ibid.*: 32).

Further evidence of normalization pursued by the Messner regime was the surprising resilience of the official unions. When established under Jaruzelski, this organization seemed unable to compete with free unions. However, the official unions not only built up their membership but kept it at a level of 6 million – well in excess of the membership reported by the free trade unions. Apparently, in 1986, as many as one-half of the total labour force was organized into official unions (down from 12 million in the old-time 'transmission-belt' unions). This organization did more than attract just those interested in the various welfare programmes channelled exclusively through the official unions (with free unions offering only small-scale financial support to its members); the less political character of these unions also drew many workers to the official unions.

While the power base of the regime was being solidified, that of the opposition seemed to be eroding. The free unions were hurt in particular by a growing feeling of apathy – impassivity and indifference to political conditions in the country – among the workers (see Mason *et al.* 1991). With the crushing of independent unions in 1981, workers' interest in politics diminished greatly, with this change in attitude apparently hurting the free unions more than the regime. Official opinion surveys, generally assessed as reasonably accurate, showed the already low popularity of the anti-government forces further declining after 1982. For instance, in 1985, about 46 per cent of citizens polled reportedly strongly rejected the anti-communist opposition, while only 6 per cent expressed strong sympathy for it (*Polityka*, no.5, 1986).

Having to share the 'field' with official trade unions and left with a shrinking number of die-hard supporters, the leaders of the free unions were less able to mobilize large-scale labour actions. Even though the risk involved in open acts of protest was less under the Messner regime than during Jaruzelski's rule, workers were far more reluctant to respond to calls by the leaders of free unions. Plant-level interventions of an economic character were most readily participated in by the members – or sympathizers – of free trade unions. A small numbers of workers – mostly young – were also ready to join street demonstrations of a 'commemorative' nature, such as those recognizing the anniversary of the forming of free unions. However, many calls by the leaders to launch massive or general strikes – in order to regain legal status for the free unions – were ignored by workers, as in 1986 and in 1987.

Ironically, when in mid-1988, a wave of strikes swept the industrial sector, this was not in response to calls from free union leaders. On the contrary, these were by and large spontaneous outbreaks which took the leadership of free unions, as much as those in charge of official unions, by surprise. The apparent reason for the strikes was, much as in the past, dissatisfaction with the price reform – 40 per cent increase in food prices and an even bigger jump in energy prices – announced by the government. Political demands were initially limited, but with the activation of free union structures, the focus of the protests shifted towards non-economic issues. While the scale of the strike wave was the widest since the party-union confrontations of 1981–82, these protests were not a replay of the earlier clash. One indication of the difference was that the strike-wave subsided without violent reactions by the Messner regime.

Legitimacy deficit

It is impossible to speculate on the more permanent impact of political changes under Messner, or earlier under Jaruzelski, without first determining the goal of the core opposition forces. One possible answer is that they were motivated mostly by economic concerns, such as redistributive claims on the national product. In other words, the opposition could be viewed as a nationwide, rather than localized – sectoral or plant-level – labour dispute. This kind of conflict had to have had some political implications, at least to the degree the opposition sought institutional guarantees, or procedures, for unobstructed expression of their interests. In addition, such an economically-driven conflict could have had an indirect influence upon the political situation if actions taken by the opposition proved damaging to the economy – for which the general public held its leadership responsible.

The economic element, as defined, was present in the opposition movement, and the form of organization – trade unions – chosen by the industrial workers speaks well to it. Workers had ample reason to press for higher wages, given the constant threat to their pay from a combination of taxes and inflation. The post-martial law period brought about pauperization of workers in the most neglected, underpaid industries, such as textiles and apparel (dominated by a female work force). Members of the intelligentsia – the educated strata – had even more reason for economic dissatisfaction since a large segment of it fell into poverty as well (Marody 1990, 1992). The intelligentsia saw its salaries fall below wages paid to other groups – more specifically, as Hirszowicz (1990: 143–4) reports, while salaries of state employees with higher education were only 20 per cent above the national average in 1981, they were 25 per cent below this average in 1986.

Viewing the opposition as mainly an economic-revindication movement – solvable through economic means – does not fully square with the ample data collected on the state of mind of workers and other groups. Relying on public opinion data for 1984, Bielecki (1987) rejected the notion that workers rebelled during 1981–82 mainly because of economic disappointment. Consecutive polls showed that, despite the dominant rhetoric and appearances (such as the synchronization of many protests with price reforms), redistributive concerns were not the only cause of labour turbulence. The same surveys also suggest that until very late into the Messner period, the public – particularly those with less education and skills – favoured egalitarian income distribution – suggesting that individual desires to enhance income opportunities were moderated by strong ethical concerns.

Another possible interpretation of the opposition's motives is that the conflict, while having strong economic overtones, was of a more fundamental nature – that it was a 'class struggle'. In other words, this was a battle by workers for control over the means of production – then placed in the hands of the political class, i.e., the communist party. This point is stressed, among others, by Burawoy (1989), who claims that labour organized itself for such a struggle on the basis of its negative work experience (marked by frequent production stoppages, poor quality of supplies, or incompetent management, and confusing central targets). Similarly, Laba (1986, 1991) argues that workers were central and acted mostly independently, demanding free unions in 1970, long before the intelligentsia started building bridges to labour. Kennedy (1991) also centres on the idea of 'class struggle,' but, unlike Buravoy and Laba, he claims that workers did not act on their own, for their leadership was made up mostly of educated people.[3]

It is open to question, however, whether workers viewed control over production as the only (or main) solution to their economic grievances. It is true that under Messner, the employee collectives, both those organized within official unions and those which remained in de-legalized (but tolerated) structures, became the effective owners of their enterprises, thereafter only nominally owned by the state. This is a version of property rights which is commonly called the labour-management model, where workers – not managers – exercise control over resources legally in state hands. This does not mean that workers really sought this solution but it could be that they began to get involved in control of enterprises, at least in part, because of the increasing incapacity – or unwillingness – of the planning apparatus to direct production. In other words, they could have been filling a growing gap in the command-chain created by the disintegrating machine of traditional state planning.

While the changes occurring after martial law altered public perceptions on many issues, at no point, including at the end of the Messner regime, did the workers contemplate dispensing fully with state ownership of the means of production (or with state direct involvement in economic decisionmaking).[4] Opinion polls suggest that workers were inconsistent in their desires and expectations about the shape of the new economy. The 1987–88 polls demonstrated that, by and large, workers wanted capitalism but were unprepared to accept all the inevitable consequences of adopting a competitive system (see Kolarska-Bobinska 1989, 1990). Though longing for capitalism, they did not uniformly support private property, and they generally opposed privatization, particularly with respect to medium- and large-scale state enterprises (which happened to provide a majority of jobs in the industrial sector) (also see Marody 1992).

Role of nationalism

To capture the nature of the opposition, one may thus have to look beyond the economic motivation in either of the two forms mentioned above, and search for the answer in nationalism. In this approach, the struggle by the opposition is seen to be directed less against the economic or political system *per se* – itself condemned for its lack of effectiveness – than against it as a powerful instrument of Soviet control over Poland. Thus, the attacks on the communist party arose from a perception that it was protecting a fundamentally flawed system and, even worse, that its leaders were controlled by the Soviet Union. In this hypothesis, the postwar political struggle by the anti-communist opposition could be viewed as an extension of earlier popular attempts – insurrections – to regain national sovereignty (from non-communist Russia).

Malia (1983) was one of the first students of free unions in Poland to stress these strongly insurrectional elements in the movement's programmes, rituals, and symbols. While emphasizing the fundamentally working-class background of the independent unions, Malia argued that the movement absorbed much of the ethos of the earlier uprisings, centred around the gentry, and of the 'gentry democracy' which existed until the country's partition. Walicki (1990: 37) also pointed to the historical continuity – rather than uniqueness claimed by, say, Kennedy (1991) – in the anti-communist opposition. Specific evidence of this continuity was not only the priority attached to national freedom but also to the national will as the only legitimation of political power, this combined with a romantic view of the national calling for patriotic sacrifice.

While most helpful in energizing society for defence of nationhood, this tradition has also led to conformism and lack of political realism. Accordingly, Krol (1990: 74) calls Polish nationalism a surrogate for political thinking and Holzer (1990) argues, in turn, that this lack of political realism was responsible for the early failure of the independent unions during 1980–81. Workers and intellectuals never realized their great political potential, viewing all actions in terms of national, or moral, revival rather than political conflict. The confrontation with the party/state apparatus (still taken as a unity) turned into self-limiting revolution, with the free unions ready to restrain their actions and compromise for the sake of avoiding another national disaster (i.e., a failed uprising causing unnecessary loss of life and decimation of the elite).

In sum, the regime of Messner further restored some of the power enjoyed by the anti-communist opposition, a move possible because the regime regained sufficient control over the society to back away from the harsh measures taken during martial law. These changes in the balance of power were accompanied – and to some degree also facilitated – by institutional changes, shifting politics from arbitrariness to proceduralism. Political reforms also allowed for very rapid growth of various forms of civil-society organizations and authentication of many existing ones. By bringing civil society back – separating state from society – the reformers in the regime were, intentionally or not, creating the foundation for political pluralism. Strong nationalist concerns, while critical in energizing political actions, undermined open dialogue within the opposition, thus undercutting the trend towards liberal polity.

The demise of the communist structure: power transfer

Efforts to stabilize the country politically were only partly successful, since the conditions for a permanent solution were hard to meet. For one thing, the proper cure for economic discontent was economic improvement, but the illusory recovery achieved by Jaruzelski and Messner was not enough to assure a return to lasting political stability. Nor did the conduct of Poland's economy after the 1979–82 crisis offer much hope for a quick turnaround in the years ahead. Moreover, meeting the public (or popular) demand for sovereignty seemed distant, since the country did not have the power needed to free itself from control by the Soviet Union. Consequently, it was dependent on the seemingly unlikely event of internal collapse of the

Soviet Union or a radical change in the geopolitical strategy of its leaders.

Soviet factor

What had appeared for decades impossible – a reversal to Soviet attemps to subordinate Eastern Europe – became possible, however, due to a quick succession of leaders after the death of Brezhnev. Internal struggles and the shifts that followed weakened Soviet resolve in external affairs, but, even more importantly, personal – or generational – changes in political leadership led to a major reevaluation of the Soviet role in Eastern Europe, or Europe in general. The selection of Gorbachev as First Secretary in 1985 signalled a possible major change in the overall course of the Soviet Union. The new appointee's unusually young age and a past marked with boldness were indications that change might be coming (see Bunce 1992a). Even more telling was Gorbachev's speech to party officials some time before his selection for the job, which outlined his plans for Hungarian-type reform of the economic system and deep internal political reform, as well as a redefinition of Soviet hegemonic relations with other communist countries (also see Terry 1989; Malia 1992).

Gorbachev's first practical steps, however, were rather conservative, at least domestically. His 1985 economic measures very much resembled campaigns periodically launched by the other Soviet leaders. To revitalize the economy, Gorbachev enacted a set of measures aimed at improving labour productivity, such as his anti-alcohol policy (i.e., higher prices for vodka, shorter work hours for liquor stores). An anti-corruption campaign was also launched to remove incompetent management, while placing Gorbachev's supporters in key positions. The 1987 package of reforms was more ambitious, and actually resembled some elements of the Hungarian model (though most of the references in the official debate were to the 'mixed' system which Lenin introduced in the 1920s to replace the so-called 'war economy'), but little was actually introduced in 1987 (more see Dawisha 1990).

While implementation was slow (including the legalization of the 'second economy' and allowing for the leasing of land to families), the sheer interest of the Gorbachev regime in making a decisive departure from the traditional state planning mechanism had a strong impact on other leaders in Eastern Europe. To conservative heads of state, such as in Bulgaria and East Germany, the Soviet change of course provided the stimulus for launching similar limited reform programmes – at least on paper – as well. However, in countries such as Poland, with well-advanced systemic reforms, Gorbachev's reform initiatives provided an excuse for experimenting with even more radical concepts of their own. More importantly, these innovations were not directly objected to by Gorbachev's regime, hoping to draw lessons for itself from experiments tried in other communist countries (Kolankiewicz 1988).

Far more significant were the political changes that the Soviet leadership espoused, the earliest indication being the 1985 relaxation of control over the media. To shake up the media, the Gorbachev regime initiated debates on some controversial issues once hidden from public scrutiny. This change alone might have been interpreted as another wave of the periodic shallow liberalization characteristic of newly promoted party leaders. However, other steps taken at the time indicated that the policy shift may have been more than a replay of the traditional communist 'succession cycle' (Bunce 1992a). Among these other steps was the decision to provide more balanced coverage of the capitalist world and to further expose citizens to the real world. Gorbachev's regime also decided to increase foreign travel (once heavily policed contacts with foreign visitors to the Soviet Union were relaxed as well) (also Aslund 1991).

Importantly, liberalization of the media – as well as efforts to modify dogmatic, rigid school curricula – was combined with the regime's willingness to redefine relations between the party and the state and to push for more competitive politics, though without terminating the party's monopoly. Since 1988, the Gorbachev regime was openly talking about the need to shift more power to the government, i.e., the executive branch, and also to strengthen or rebuild the legislative arm, i.e., the parliament. The concept of developing a system based on checks and balances, analogous to that working in advanced industrial democracies, was rapidly gaining ground. The March 1989 elections to the parliament – conducted with multi-candidate lists and less central intervention – followed by the institution of its second house, were clear indications that Gorbachev was committed to this concept.

Compared, for instance, to Poland, Soviet political reforms of that time were at least a few years late, so that one cannot rule out the possibility that in reforming its economy, the Gorbachev regime was not only drawing from the Hungarian model to reform its economy but also looking at Poland and Hungary as sources of ideas for altering the political structure. While moving in the same direction – of separating party/state and downplaying the party – the Soviet Union was not under the same pressure as Poland, where the leaders confronted an organized opposition. It follows that the Soviet regime was either acting in anticipation of an oncoming crisis, similar to that experienced by Poland, or because of other calculations looking into the future. The fact that Gorbachev assumed reforms without any immediate threat to his power made his actions much more credible in the eyes of other communist leaders in the region (Boetke 1993).

By far the most significant of all initiatives of the Gorbachev regime for Eastern Europe was the indication that the Soviet Union was abandoning its traditional geopolitical doctrine of 'limited sovereignty' for Eastern Europe (i.e., tolerating marginal deviations from the Soviet model of communism and allowing for joint interventions by bloc members in case of anti-communist takeovers). Initial vague indications that Gorbachev's regime was changing its position towards Eastern Europe go back to 1985. By 1986 it was apparent that the regime had decided to greatly expand the room for manoeuvring by communist East European leaders. The September 1987 elimination of the special department for Eastern Europe in the Soviet party structure was one important indication of this policy shift. The December 1988 promise by Gorbachev to withdraw nuclear weapons from Czechoslovakia, East Germany, and Hungary was another such signal.

While tensions in parts of Eastern Europe, particularly in Poland, could have contributed to the rethinking of the Soviet foreign doctrine, these concerns were not decisive. Like all other aspects of Gorbachev's reform package, changes in policy towards Eastern Europe were more reflective of the growing Soviet feeling that to remain strong the Soviet Union had to follow an economic rather than ideological calculus. Convinced that the Soviet Union was heavily overpaying with oil and gas exports for imports of poor quality manufactures from Eastern Europe (for evidence to the contrary, see Poznanski 1989b), Gorbachev's cabinet decided to refocus its economic interests on advanced capitalist markets. Eastern Europe was also seen now as upsetting Soviet efforts to improve political relations with the United States (and Western Europe) needed for de-escalation of cost-prohibitive military buildup (Hewett 1988; Nordhaus 1990).

Roundtable negotiations

It was not easy for East European leaders to fully comprehend Soviet intentions, in part because the Gorbachev regime did not speak with one voice. It was even more difficult for political circles to establish how credible or irreversible were the steps taken by the Gorbachev communist regime – what was needed was for the pronouncements to pass the test of real life. When in late 1988, Rakowski, following directions from Jaruzelski, made an offer to the opposition to talk about possible power sharing, there were no serious objections raised by the Soviet Union. It was the opposition at this point that refused to negotiate – as its leaders were caught unprepared. However, both sides eventually began such negotiations in February 1989, again with the qualified permission of the Gorbachev regime (Batt 1991). With this acceptance of the talks with the opposition – known as the roundtable – the Soviet commitment to serious political reforms finally became credible.

While facilitated by Soviet permissiveness, the negotiations were largely the product of an internal dynamic, the opponents' realization that they had little choice but to seek compromise. Since the preeminent concern of the Gorbachev regime was that reform in Poland not get out of hand, this willingness of both sides to shift from confrontation to accommodation made the Soviet decision much easier. Qualified Soviet acceptance of the roundtable negotiations, in turn, had a calming effect on the main parties to this process. Knowing that the regime basically could not count on Soviet support, except possibly in extreme circumstances, Poland's leaders were forced to be more prepared to give in to the opposition. The opposition had to restrain itself so as not to trigger political outcomes which the Soviet regime would still find intolerable.

The regime's programme for power sharing with the opposition called for the opposition's participation in parliamentary elections and then in a coalition government. This was to be accomplished, however, without allowing for the free unions to resume their original form and providing that the communist party – and the allied parties – would enjoy the controlling 'share' of power. Not that the regime objected to independent representation for workers' economic interest; it simply did not intend at this point to reintroduce a nationwide free union movement which would act as a political force. The latter could easily destabilize the political process, and the regime preferred to see the opposition enter the arena as political parties accountable to voters. Insisting on the retention of a controlling 'share' by the pro-regime parties was, in turn, not necessarily an ultimate objective for the regime but probably a temporary safeguard against the possible eruption of political hostilities.

The opposition entered negotiations mostly to gain legality, something they had been trying to accomplish since the imposition of martial law. The unions needed legal recognition more than anything else, since by being unable to operate in the open, they were therefore threatened with political marginalization. Putting this issue on the agenda was critical enough for the opposition to reject the initial offers by the Rakowski regime to organize a roundtable without looking into the issue of legalization. Only when the regime finally agreed to add the legalization issue to the roundtable agenda did the opposition agree to join the talks. Of course, by entering negotiations, the unions risked helping the Rakowski regime gain legitimacy and thus become an even more formidable opponent. The uncertain prospects for relegalization were, however, sufficient for the free unions to take on this political gamble.

For both sides to agree on the stakes was a difficult task, as was acceptance of a 'roundtable' formula – at best an awkward arrangement with hard-to-evaluate political trade-offs. For the regime, which chose this form of negotiations, the difficulty was that talks were to be conducted outside of any established constitutional channels, with representatives of the regime handpicked by Jaruzelski. The advantage of such an auxiliary institution was that it allowed the reform faction within the regime to also hand-pick those elements within the opposition it found easier to work with on the power sharing formula. Jaruzelski was in a position to at least temporarily eliminate radicals, while allowing moderate opposition factions to consolidate (very much as in the Spanish model under the late Franco: see O'Donnell and Schmitter 1986; Karl and Schmitter 1991; Przeworski 1986).

The opposition movement was also faced with a dilemma, since the roundtable formula did not square with the free union's commitment to democratic procedures. Engaging in secret talks by unelected oppositionists leading to the setting up of the roundtable compromised this principle, as did the fact that negotiations on the regime side were conducted under the supervision of security forces (with Kiszczak, minister of internal affairs, officially leading the regime delegation). This conspiracy with the greatly mythologized political enemy ran the risk of alienating ordinary members of the free unions. However, the roundtable had the advantage of working in a controlled environment, without directly involving a diversified and unpredictable membership. Also, in the climate of 'moral politics', it was convenient for the opposition delegation to keep the 'dirt' of real politics from public view (see Gross 1992).

Begun in February, the roundtable negotiations concluded in April, with the opposition taking away major economic concessions. In a way, this was a reverse of the compact that Jaruzelski – through Messner's government – had unsuccessfully offered to the opposition in 1987. Then, the effort was to make the workers agree to austerity – and a strike freeze – in order to facilitate limited economic reforms. Now, sweeping reforms were to come, but wages were allowed to escalate and restrictions on strikes were to be relaxed. Thus, industrial workers were promised major wage increases through generous indexation and wages in the budgetary sphere were to grow at the same rate as those in state industry, and pensioners were assured of full indexation of their income. Farmers were assured that subsidies would be only gradually reduced, that minimum prices for their products would be guaranteed, and that price controls for some inputs would be restored.

On the political side, the accord foresaw parliamentary elections in June 1989, a win for the official side, since the opposition preferred a later date. These elections were to follow a formula which would assure that the party with two satellite factions retain a majority of seats. Since the opposition was reluctant to enter into such a completely 'structured' election, Jaruzelski worked out a compromise. Quotas were to apply to the lower house while for the upper house – to be recreated – unrestricted competition was permitted. Even with such an arrangement, the elections were expected to allow the communist party to form a coalition government under its majority leadership, with the police and military remaining under communist control – this to assure their integrity in potentially volatile periods. The president was to be elected for a four year term by a joint session of both chambers, with the understanding that the office would serve as a powerful counterbalance to the parliament and that Jaruzelski would keep this post.

Power transfer

While the opposition had little time to prepare for the election, the established union networks – and contacts with the Church – allowed it to mobilize considerable forces. To facilitate the elections, so-called Citizen Committees were established in all localities to gather funds and select candidates. Elected President of independent unions in April, Walesa became a popular spokesman for the opposition cause. With free access to the press as agreed at the roundtable, the opposition managed quickly to expand circulation of its once-illegal titles and turn them into a tool for the elections. In contrast, the official side did not fully mobilize its party network for the vote, with two potential spokesmen, Jaruzelski and Rakowski, mostly absent from the scene. Equipped with state-controlled media, the establishment showed only limited interest in using it for propping up its candidates.

When the ballot count was completed, all but one of the contested seats in both houses went to opposition candidates, which gave the opposition complete control over the upper house and 35 per cent in the lower house. Only a very few seats for which official candidates from the 'national list' were running unopposed, were filled, as others failed to meet the requirement that they receive half of the vote in their districts. The rules had to be changed, with the opposition's approval, to facilitate run-off elections, which allowed the three official parties to take their slots. This development – potentially humiliating for the establishment – was followed by another, since with actual seat distribution, electing Jaruzelski for president required that many opposition parliamentarians had to cast their vote for him or abstain. In another gesture of political realism – and respect for the roundtable determinations – the opposition helped to elect Jaruzelski.

After his election in August, Jaruzelski proposed interior chief Kiszczak for the prime ministership, but the candidacy was rejected by the opposition on the assumption that a more acceptable official figure with no connection to martial law be selected. Instead, after some delay, Jaruzelski agreed to the prime minister suggested by the opposition and for the opposition to form a coalition government. Out of three candidates, Mazowiecki was chosen by Jaruzelski for the post. With the large bloc of its own votes – and support from satellite parties – the communist party still seemed to have a chance to secure a substantial share of cabinet positions. However, the defection of the satellite parties to the opposition camp allowed Mazowiecki to form a cabinet with a minority of posts (nine out of twenty-one) filled by communist party members. Lacking a political base – with their party quickly disintegrating – these cabinet members chose to accept the leadership of Mazowiecki.

In addition to quickly engaging in major political reforms, the government of Mazowiecki moved ahead with measures to improve economic conditions. Some short-run steps were taken immediately (suspension of bonuses to workers, effective currency depreciation of 40 per cent, daily balancing of budgetary revenues and expenditures). While these measures were helpful, the real effort concentrated on formulating a comprehensive programme to be implemented starting in 1990. In the process, the choice was made by the government to adopt a 'shock therapy' programme – radical on most fronts. Two pro-shock groups emerged, one led by Beksiak and the other by Balcerowicz, the latter opting for a more restrained version of shock therapy (e.g., using wage tax rather than indexation and calling for privatization of state industry to be delayed). The more cautious version was eventually selected for implementation as the 'Balcerowicz Plan'.

The leadership of Solidarity – some of whom held posts in the government and parliament – was divided over the future of Poland's economy, including the question of whether to adopt a radical or gradual approach. The smaller faction, with openly pro-market rhetoric, was for a radical approach of 'cold turkey' stabilization, which would allow the possibility of a brief rise in unemployment and real income losses to the population. Numerically larger was the faction which thought more in terms of a mixed economy or even a 'third road' (with labour-management as a dominant form) and called for more gradual change. While recognizing the need to stabilize the economy, this segment was greatly concerned about maintaining a well-developed 'safety net' and minimizing job loss. With little time to debate and little basis on which to judge the merits – realism – of alternative approaches, but also driven by a desire to show unity behind 'their' government, the parliament quickly approved the shock therapy.

Summary

The 1981 imposition of a 'state of war' did not lead to another socialist normalization, in which the political monopoly of the party was restored. The opposition faced by Jaruzelski's regime was too strong to be easily defused, forcing them to look for other means of political stabilization. However, there is little evidence that the regime was trying to take full advantage of its power to coerce the free unions into submission. The political outcome of martial law demonstrated that another head-on confrontation by the opposition would most likely fail. Still holding the high moral ground, they could have mustered their forces for such a confrontation, but chose not to. While martial law did not terminate the political conflict, it did, however, change its character, with important implications for the political scene in the coming years.

The essence of the regime's strategy since martial law could be best expressed by the term 'inclusion', i.e., bringing in various extra-party forces, among them organized opposition, to the political process. This kind of inclusion could have led to another form of corporatism (than that tried by Gierek) with the party as benevolent leader. However, this expansion of political space could also have led to competitive politics and possibly marginalization of the communist party. Whether the regime was prepared for the latter outcome from the beginning, and continuously used inclusion as a vehicle for achieving political pluralization, is very unlikely. Importantly, there were too many unknowns for the regime to closely adhere to any single strategy of political change.

For the regime to proceed with inclusion, the opposition had not only to be restrained, but also – or in spite of these constraints – to be willing to accept this formula and cooperate in good faith. Initially, interest among the opposition in working though the channels provided by the regime was limited, but with growing fears among the union leaders that the movement would lose its effective power, a more accommodating strategy began to emerge (Michnik 1985). Rather than to build an alternative society – outside the official limits – the strategy of this group was to capture, piece by piece, the existing structure. The hope of this group, which eventually won, was that in this organic fashion, the opposition would sooner or later meet its objectives, be they some form of co-determination or even a takeover of the political scene for itself (see Ost 1989, 1991).

Thus, the political process underway was one in which both sides – the regime and the opposition – were active players. This should come as no surprise, since each possessed sufficient power to affect the course of events, and, though in conflict over power, each wanted to change the ineffective political system. The above view is a departure from the hypothesis that, at least towards its end, events were out of the regime's control, to the point that the process could best be described as driven from below (see Ekiert 1990[5]). In this view of the political process, the regime not only took its agenda from the opposition but actually followed the pace set by the latter. Yet another perspective, also not corroborated by this study, is that it was the regime, with an at least loosely outlined strategy, which was engaged in reforming the political scene, with the opposition very much following the course (see Kolankiewicz 1988;[6] Staniszkis 1987).[7]

In this, as we see it, 'interactive game', the regime and the opposition developed strategies of accommodation, and not revolutionary confrontation.[8] In this process of give and take, both sides were learning the limits of their power and the benefits of concessionary options. It was compromises made by each side in the conflict which eventually (not by themselves, of course) produced the conditions for the 1989 roundtable, and not deadly threats of violent attacks on the opponents.[9] The roundtable itself was a formula developed to facilitate a compromise over the most controversial aspect of change, i.e., distribution of power. The determinations made during the orderly negotiations, in turn, created conditions for another series of compromises, which helped to minimize the political costs of the disintegration of communist rule. In brief, this whole process could be described as a case of contractarian divestment of state power (as opposed to contractarian vesting of power in a state).

This political evolution was essential for allowing the economic system to assume a more effective form, and with such change, for the economy to return to a viable track, if only in the longer run. The immediate practical consequence of all these unquestionably substantial, political reconfigurations was, however, a further weakening of the economic rules – incentives and structures – in the dominant state-owned sector. What we mean by that is that with power shifting away from the party to the state, and from the state to the society – its civil zones – the central apparatus was becoming increasingly powerless in managing the economy. In the absence of a developed systemic alternative – market mechanism – a stronger state was needed to keep basic economic order, as well as prevent waste, but the political process produced a weaker state. A weaker state meant a weaker economy, this giving additional incentives to the entrenched communist – more in symbolic than practical terms – elite to seek their own withdrawal from the political scene.

Part III

Communist legacy, 'shock therapy' and economic recession

7   Costly transition to 'hard' markets

The communist party's relinquishment of political control in mid-1989 was a watershed event, taking many political participants by surprise. The general reaction to this development was to view it as a revolution of some sort, but due to the absence of violent clashes between outgoing and incoming power groups – a fact that we stressed earlier on numerous occasions – the term 'peaceful revolution' was widely adopted. This was to convey the feeling that although the power transfer was non-violent, the processes which were to follow this event would be quite momentous. The departure of the communist party was expected to be the trigger mechanism for fast-paced formation of both pluralistic, democratic politics and the reintroduction of economic freedoms – and by many accounts, the post-1989 changes have been of such revolutionary proportions (on this point, see Stokes 1991).

With such sweeping changes in the overall social order, an equally rapid improvement in economic performance was expected as well. The final removal of the state-planned system, so ineffective in utilizing resources, that accelerated the party's collapse, promised that the payoffs for economic reforms would be high. This meant, as the reformers generally assumed, that the faster the existing economic institutions were abolished, the sooner rewards would be delivered to society. This view was also often extended to the state-owned organizations – enterprises and ministries – viewed as so ill-prepared to engage in a genuine market operation that it would be better to terminate them in mass as well. It is in this general spirit that the first post-communist government, formed in late 1989 under the prime ministership of Mazowiecki, drafted its economic programmes, and presented them to the public at large.

With the opening of 1990 Mazowiecki's government announced a radical set of measures, labeled 'shock therapy'. The programme called for a sharp deflation to reduce rapidly rising prices, the wide opening of trade to ensure a realistic price structure, and the rapid turnover of state assets to private hands to create forces interested in profit-maximization. These measures were presented to the public as a quick cure which would produce measurable growth improvement within one year, even though there was no solid evidence to back such a promise. Such a simultaneous three-way economic programme had not been tried before except by Chile after 1973, where, despite starting conditions seemingly more favourable than those in 1990 Poland (Edwards 1992), the immediate results were disappointing. It took years for Chile to produce its (at least by regional standards) economic miracle (Corbo 1992).

The initial results of Poland's shock therapy, as we will show below, turned out to be disappointing as well, and far worse than Chile's during a comparable period. Bringing inflation down was an achievement, though the rates of price increases remained high enough to threaten overall economic growth. Maintaining internal covertibility, despite stubborn inflation, was a success as well, as was the expansion of exports, which led to sizeable surpluses and the multiplication of currency reserves in 1990–91. All these improvements helped Poland to obtain substantial official debt cancellation and triggered an inflow of fresh money (Raczkowski 1991). However, therapy deepened the recession throughout all segments of state industry, and private farming showed some losses as well. Household incomes declined substantially in real terms, and unemployment began increasing rapidly, already by the end of 1991 reaching levels which seemed politically unsustainable (Poznanski 1993a).

Signs of economic recovery, led by the construction sector, were first detected in mid-1992, and positive growth continued through 1995. Rates of production growth have been respectable, with much of the expansion later in the recovery coming from manufacturing and with further delay from agriculture as well. Initially, it has been, however, a rather mysterious development. The exact causes of expansion remained unclear considering the minor increase in fixed investment and thus, presumably, only a limited restructuring of existing enterprises (Dabrowski 1992b; Crane 1992). Domestic consumption, another element of the aggregate demand, did not show gains sufficiently strong to explain the turn in production either. Another potential growth stimulant, exports, could not have become a major source of production expansion either, since the volume of foreign sales (measured in constant prices) had stabilized around that time. This lack of clarity about the exact sources of the recovery does not mean that the upward trend in production should be questioned, it reflects, at least in part, a poor quality, or unreliability of statistical sources.

While quite strong and resistant, the economic recovery from the post-1990 decline was in many ways disappointing, or, at least unsatisfactory. Importantly, production upturn has not prevented unemployment from further increases, with indications that majority of those exiting labour market make no reentry (this meaning that unemployment is to large degree structural and so much more difficult to combat). The large number of people living under the poverty line has not diminished despite the recovery in output, while pockets of extremely high incomes have emerged and become widely known to the public. Neither has the state budget been stabilized for good – mostly due to pressing welfare payments – nor inflation has been reduced to levels to be considered safe from the point of view of least fortunate groups of people. The above tendencies, combined with an overall sense of uncertainty about the future course of economy, contributed to the extension of the broadly based social dissatisfaction beyond the initial frustration related to the effects of the 1990 pro-gramme.

It thus appears that the post-1990 transition has not immediately put an end to the 'growth fatigue' which plagued the final years of communist rule. It could well be that the forces which caused this extension are similar to those that depressed growth in the past, that is to say, they are of a systemic nature. As we show, during the first post-shock years, the economic system was allowed to further weaken, mostly due to announcement of the bold but vague 1990 programme of instant 'centralized' privatization and state withdrawal from owner-ship functions – assisting state enterprises. Left with even greater uncertainty over their future status, managers/workers reduced their efforts, causing output to decline beyond what deflation alone would had caused. The mid-1992 recovery, in turn, was in large part due to the strengthening of the system – with privatization becoming more 'decentralized' and slowing down, and with the state more willing to protect enterprises from financial collapse.

These later changes in the economic system can be linked to the political scene, in much the same way as during the pre-1990 period. Changes in the economic system since 1990 closely followed the political cycle, triggered by the collapse of the communist party. The newly formed leadership was left without effective control, thus creating an opening for such radical steps as the announcement of instant privatization. Extensive personnel turnover reduced bureaucratic capability, this – in combination with anti-statist philosophy – causing the 'abandonment' of state enterprises. With more effective political channels being established, the radicalism of ownership reforms has been tempered and the state has had to resume a more interventionist posture. It was their promise to continue this course that enabled the old-time parties to win a large majority of the vote in the late 1993 election and form the Pawlak government.

That the parties built around the anti-communist groups lost the election to those formed from official parties of the communist period is symbolic as it reflects the degree to which the realities of the past are still present. With the vast organizational resources inherited from the past, these reformed old-time political parties continued to have an advantage over their new opponents. Major platform changes were not really necessary, because the surrounding economic reality was not much different than before radical reforms. With privatization proceeding slowly, industry remained mostly state-owned so that the more interventionist position taken by these parties had an obvious appeal to workers. With land still divided into small parcels, farmers sought a more assertive state as well, which is what the coalition parties had long stood for. With a large segment of society continuing to live in poverty, their calls for 'redistributive justice' also served them well.

Radical stabilization and liberalization

The highest priority for Mazowiecki when he embarked on the shock therapy programme was to halt inflation, perceived not only as a serious drag on domestic production but as potentially as destabilizing for internal politics as well. In this choice, the cabinet echoed the communist policy-makers, who were also preoccupied with removing inflationary overhang – because of similar concerns. With extremely rapid inflation came shorter contract periods and reluctance to invest in long-term projects with high social yield. There were also negative welfare effects, i.e., disincentives to labour productivity and adverse income distribution, as inflation divides households into those protected from price rises and those left unprotected (for a good account of inflationary repercussions at this juncture in Poland, see Lipton and Sach 1990a).

Deflationary measures

Once the government of Mazowiecki decided to give priority to stabilizing the economy, the question arose which way to go, the simplest option perhaps being for the government to slow down its own repricing of controlled goods. Much of the price growth at the time was related to increases in officially fixed prices, so that the government could effectively decelerate the rate of inflation on its own. This would allow more time for state-owned enterprises to adjust, as well as cushion possible income effects on those social groups most likely to suffer from the changed price structure. The risk was, of course, that by holding back price increases in state-controlled goods, imbalances would continue and resource misallocation would be prolonged. Still, with officially-fixed prices accounting for about 20–30 per cent of total sales (see: Kolodko 1991a, 1991b), the extent of these deficiencies was probably not unacceptable for the economy.

While retention of limited price fixing may not be a 'clean' solution, or the most desirable from the standpoint of neo-classical policy prescriptions, there seems to be evidence that it may provide an acceptable compromise for economies undergoing transition to the capitalist market. For example, since 1978, China has utilized dual pricing with parallel markets, where similar goods were traded at fixed prices as well as those reflecting supply/demand conditions, all this without incurring high inflation. Not only has inflation been reasonably low – seldom moving into the low double-digit ranges – but China's production has experienced a very high rate of growth, with state-owned enterprises showing strong productivity gains (see: Naughton 1995). This system has fuelled speculation through resale of low-priced goods supplied through state agencies but at the same time has allowed for their reallocation to more efficient users who can afford higher resale prices.

In any event, the government chose to embark on the 'clean' solution, so that when the 1990 reform package was launched, most of the remaining state-controlled prices were freed in one step or sharply corrected upward to clear particular goods markets. The government expected this price reform to generate additional so-called 'corrective' inflation. Indeed, the monthly price index jumped right away to 79.6 per cent, making the fight with inflation more difficult, or at least strengthening an impression that extraordinary measures were necessary to bring it firmly under control. This added to the great confusion over the exact tightness of stabilization measures needed, since there was very little solid data available on the real depth of the internal imbalance and the government was left with conflicting estimates of the outstanding 'inflationary overhang' (with this uncertainty causing policymakers to overshoot rather than fall short).

To cope with inflation, the government initiated a number of harsh measures, including a tight fiscal policy, in an effort to eliminate inherited budgetary deficits. Despite various efforts by Rakowski's cabinet, the deficit increased significantly from mid-1988 to mid-1989, when it reached about 12 per cent of the gross national product. The cause can be mostly found in poorly conceived tax reform, which left the state with rapidly declining revenues. The steps taken in the second part of 1989 by the Mazowiecki team brought more balance to the state budget but the deficit remained sizeable at the end of the year. For the whole year, the deficit was equivalent to 4.3 per cent of the gross national product, not an alarming level. It could well be that the actual deficit, if balances in local budgets are carefully calculated, was less than that mentioned.

For the sake of quickly eliminating the remaining 'inflationary over-hang', further steps were taken to rid the budget of excess spending in early 1990. The government of Mazowiecki accomplished this fiscal tightening through a combination of measures, including the elimination of various tax exemptions. The state collection agencies also showed more resolve in enforcing tax payments by delinquent state-owned enterprises. More effective tax schemes – a value-added system and income tax – were outlined, to be quickly put in place, but the government was unable to implement them quickly. However, even with the existing schemes, the government undid the damage to the state budget caused by the ill-advised reforms of the Rakowski government. This tax extraction was reinforced in the first part of 1990 by the fact that a rapid rise in prices related to 'corrective inflation' sharply increased the profits of state-sector enterprises (with the latter syphoning income from households; see Gajdeczka 1993).

Another measure employed to improve the budget was the deep cutting of subsidies, mostly by way of lifting restrictions on pricing of goods and by officially raising prices of products still under state control (e.g., coal, whose price in late 1989 equalled one tenth of the world price). The share of state subsidies in the budget was reduced more than half between mid-1989 and early 1990, and their share in the gross national product went down from 11 per cent to 7 per cent. This desubsidization policy, in conjunction with earlier mentioned tax increases, helped turn the state budget deficit reported at the end of 1989 into sizeable surpluses in the early months of 1990. By mid-year, however, monthly deficits reappeared at levels like those before the fiscal adjustment took place, so that the surplus for the whole year was about 0.4 per cent of the gross national product.

The fiscal tightening was accompanied by sharp monetary contraction, reflected in the reduction of credit availability for state-owned enterprises – at this point financing the majority of working- and fixed-capital investment with credits from state banks. Bank reserve requirements were raised, administrative credit limits imposed to restrict lending, and interest rates raised sharply as well. The last measure followed the radical correction at the end of 1989, which, like the increase in 1990, failed to lift the real interest rate out of the negative ranges. However, very high nominal rates acted as a deterrent anyway, since enterprises were unwilling to borrow at these rates, not knowing how prices would behave in the long-run (creating pressure on managers to reduce their money holdings, including foreign currency deposits; see Gomulka 1992a: 363).

Nominal anchors

To further facilitate deflation, the government sought a decisive reduction in wages for the state-owned enterprises, which would extend through the initial stage of stabilization. Again, there were a number of possible options for the government to choose from, including the neoclassically 'clean' solution of allowing wages to be set freely in response to supply/demand conditions. This is exactly how the wage setting issue is handled in the so-called orthodox stabilization programmes, but the government decided against this option (as did many other post-communist reformers – an exception being the 1992 Russian version of shock therapy). This wage policy variant was rejected on the grounds that as long as state enterprises are effectively controlled by their collectives – as in a labour-managed model – the motivation to set their wages in accordance with market dictates will not be sufficiently strong.

The other option for Mazowiecki's government was to ensure deflationary wage reductions in a non-market fashion by reaching a social compact with the industrial workers. This seemed to be a logical solution given the great power accumulated by the now legalized unions, as well as the fact that the government viewed organized labour as a major source of political support. Under conditions in many ways similar to those found in Poland in 1990, Mexico in 1988 chose such a 'wage pact', signed between a labour-based government, powerful unions, and private employers.[1] This accord proved quite effective, both in calming the wage-price spiral and in helping the economy produce a remarkably strong recovery (Edwards 1992).[2] In

Eastern Europe, the Bulgarian government negotiated a social compact limiting wage demands as part of its stabilization programme, resembling in many ways that of Poland.

Rather than trying one of the above variants, Mazowiecki's government opted to continue the policy of the outgoing cabinet of Rakowski, namely, indexing wages for inflation while imposing taxes on excessive – above the legal limit set by the central agencies – increases in nominal wages. Deviating from this scheme would have been controversial as these rules were agreed upon during the roundtable negotiations of early 1989. During the same talks, workers had obtained substantial wage concessions from the communist government, but to stabilize the economy, Mazowiecki's reform team had felt it necessary to cut wages. Taking advantage of the union's willingness to offer what seemed to be blanket approval for the government actions, a policy of very unfavourable inflationary indexation was adopted and taxes on excess wage payments were raised to prohibitive levels (without any differentiation a cross enterprises or sectors of industry, which would give proper consideration to variations in financial conditions).

The actual wage reductions executed in 1990 through this system were significant, with real wages immediately falling by above 30 per cent, and for the whole year by 24.4 per cent.[3] Real incomes fell by less, in part because welfare payments were not cut as heavily as wages, and real consumption fell by a smaller percentage than incomes. These reductions in real wages were to a degree statistical, since, due to extended shortages present before 'shock therapy', some earnings were not spendable, representing forced savings, and this removal of excess money helped to equilibrate the market for consumer goods, which represented a welfare gain (except for those collecting 'rents' through queuing, such as pensioners). But when speaking of the welfare effect, one must consider the negative results of the fact that since 1990 income disparity increased considerably (with the population under the poverty line increasing from 17 in 1989 to 34 per cent in 1991; Milanovic 1991b, 1993).

Another contractionary instrument of the 'shock therapy' programme was the sharp devaluation of domestic currency – designed to reduce the value of domestic reserves of dollars held by households as well as enterprises. At the end of 1989, the official exchange rate was corrected a couple of times to bring it closer to that of the black market, but only the 1990 devaluation aimed at closing the gap between the two. This series of measures forced the value of domestic currency – as estimated at this point – 50 per cent below its equilibrium level.[4]

Following the 1990 sharp devaluation, the currency was pegged at the new value to serve as a nominal anchor together with wage indexation (typical of heterodox stabilization packages). Concern for inflation, specifically, a desire to avoid the frequent corrections of the exchange rate which usually raise inflationary expectations, was behind the pegging.

While helpful in deflating the economy, deep undervaluation of currency could be problematic for protecting production from decline. As the economy entered 1990 with a minor trade surplus, drastic devaluation was likely to produce an even larger surplus, though a temporary deficit would be more helpful in reenergizing production. Alternatively, the exchange rate could be set at the equilibrium level, so that the economy would continue its trade balance, with the effect on production being neutral (an argument developed by Gotz-Kozier-kiewicz and Malecki 1993). Pegging the currency, quite logical from the point of view of arresting inflation, was also not without draw-backs for production. The choice of this regime (similar to that installed in 1991 by Czechoslovakia) rather than a floating system, had com-pelled Poland's government to reduce the money supply in order to delay revaluations, thus putting downward pressure on the expansion plans by producers.

Production downturn

This type of drastic heterodox stabilization programme with two nominal anchors – real wages and exchange rate (or possibly three, if interest rate is added) – had been tried to date by only a few other countries. One important case that comes to mind is Israel in 1985, which allowed, however, for selective credit by the government to stimulate industrial output in export-oriented sectors. Not surprisingly, such a bold deflationary package, through aggregate demand contrac-tion, stabilized the economy quite quickly. It defused the 'corrective inflation' in a matter of two to three months, reducing monthly rates of inflation to 2–3 per cent in mid-1990. But, then, through the rest of the year, price increases accelerated, and oscillated between 5 to 6 per cent on a monthly basis. Given the initial burst in prices, the average yearly rate of consumer price inflation for the whole of 1990 was close to 585 per cent, more than twice the average price increase of 251 per cent reported in 1989.

As a result, domestic currency regained a dominant position in the cash holdings of households, one of the primary objectives of the shock therapy programme. Households, the primary holders of dollars, were slow in turning their existing dollar deposits to zloty, but a favourable interest rate offered by the banks caused households to keep their additional savings in the latter (with the exchange rate held constant, the effective interest rate on domestic currency deposits was about 60 per cent). State-owned enterprises also switched to zloty by selling their balances to the state banks, this in response to sharp devaluation as well as shortage of the credit needed to finance their current operations. At the peak of the 1989 inflation, households kept more than 60–70 per cent of their liquidity in dollars, depending on the exchange rate adopted for this calculation, while at the end of 1990, less than 30 per cent of their cash holdings were denominated in hard currency.

Lowering inflation – and strengthening domestic currency – was accompanied with a sharp production fall immediately after the application of deflationary measures. The initial decline in industrial production was about 29 per cent, with the light industry and machinery sector suffering the greatest contraction (e.g., textiles reported a 34 per cent decline and machinery a 38 per cent loss). The depth of the early 1990 decline in production throughout the industry – and, for the same reason, of the whole domestic output – greatly exceeded the few per cent decline expected by the government. The greater surprise, however, was that industry did not show signs of quick recovery, ending the year with a total loss of 24.2 per cent (table 7.1). Both the rather unprecedented, virtually instant, decline as well as the flattening of output figures that followed, seemed to indicate that the slump could not have been simply the result of aggregate demand contraction, but very likely of more complex, possibly structural, forces at work as well.

In the face of prolonged stagnation, fiscal/monetary policy was relaxed[5] in late 1990, with a moderate positive effect on production, and the year closed with the gross domestic product down by 11.6 per cent (table 7.1).[6] In early 1991, the government, now led by Bielecki, returned to a highly restrictive policy, out of concern for a rising budget deficit and various signals that higher rates of price increases might be returning. These efforts to lower inflation succeeded, with the average consumer price index brought down to 70.3 per cent for the whole of 1991. While the struggle against stubborn inflation continued, state-sector industrial production declined by 11.9 per cent,[7] with the gross domestic product decreasing by 7.6 per cent for the year. This further deterioration on the supply side made it more apparent that

Table 7.1 *Selected economic indicators, Poland, 1989–1993*

	1989	1990	1991	1992	1993
	a. National Product (annual rate in per cent)				
Gross Domestic Product, produced	0.2	−11.6	−7.6	2.6	4.7
Industry, total	−0.5	−24.2	−11.9	3.9	5.6
Agriculture, total	1.5	−2.2	−2.0	−11.9	2.0
Construction, total	−0.5	−14.5	6.7	3.8	5.0
Gross fixed investment	−2.3	−10.0	−4.5	0.7	2.2
	b. Income and prices (annual rates in per cent)				
Personal consumption	0.4	−13.1	7.4	5.2	3.4
Collective consumption	−14.0	0.2	−6.5	4.5	0.9
Average consumer price index	251.1	584.7	70.3	43.0	36.9
Real wages	9.4	−24.4	−0.3	−2.5	−1.8
Retail trade, real growth	−2.7	−17.4	3.7	−4.5	n.a.
	c. Labour market				
Total employment (annual change in per cent)		−4.0	−5.9	−4.2	−0.6
Total unemployment (in millions)		1.1	2.1	2.5	2.9
Rate of unemployment (in per cent of total)		6.1	11.5	13.6	16.4
	d. Foreign trade (in million current dollars)				
Exports, total	8.5	12.0	14.9	13.1	14.2
Imports, total	7.7	8.3	15.5	16.1	18.8
Trade balance	0.8	3.7	−0.6	−3.0	−4.6
Current account	−1.8	0.7	−1.3	−0.3	−2.3
Foreign debt, gross	40.8	48.5	48.4	47.1	47.2
Foreign currency reserves	2.3	4.5	3.6	4.0	4.1

Source: Economic Bulletin for Europe, ECE (New York: United Nations), vol. 44 (1992) and vol. 46 (1994); *ECE Economic Survey of Europe in 1993–1994* (New York: United Nations); *Rocznik Statystyczny 1994*, GUS, Warsaw, 1994.

either aggregate demand control is too severe, or that there are some detrimental structural forces in action, or that both collude against production.

This recession in production was basically limited to the state sector, while private businesses continued to expand, though the exact extent of that growth is hard to judge (large segments of private activity remained underreported, or not reported at all). Still, the private businesses were unable to fully escape the detrimental effects of the slump in state industry. In 1989, industrial output in the private sector increased by 22 per cent, but in 1990 the respective rate was 8 per cent. Investment in the private sector increased by 2.6 per cent in 1989, but declined by 3 per cent in 1990. Only in employment was there no negative change – in both years the number of workers increased by almost 27 per cent.[8] Given this production slowdown, and because of its limited size, the private sector was not able to single-handedly prevent the economy from slipping into recession.

Decreases in total production were followed by the emergence of open unemployment, quickly reaching a very high level by the end of 1991, when the unemployment rate, with 2.1 million people out of work, was close to 11 per cent. Some urban centres, such as Poznan or Warsaw, with a rate of unemployment less than 2 per cent, fared better than the country as a whole. Labour markets in a few major industrial cities, however, experienced unemployment rates close to 25 per cent (e.g., the coal mining city Walbrzych, or the textile city Lodz[9]), and similarly difficult conditions have been found in many smaller towns in rural areas. These figures were probably exaggerated, since the initially favourable unemployment payments attracted numbers of people who did not work on a regular basis, or at all. Many people registered to collect extra income while continuing their 'hidden' employment in the private sector.

Through 1991 most of the unemployment was the result of not hiring newcomers rather than terminating existing contracts with workers – this reflected in a disproportional share of young people among the jobless.[10] Among those let go, a majority were part-time workers, white-collar personnel, and persons who combined their industrial jobs with farming. This suggests that, at this stage, the shock therapy programme did not bring yet into the open the whole hidden unemployment which riddled state industry under the communist system.[11] As enterprises in the state sector tried to retain their work-force as much as possible, the decline in total employment was much smaller than the fall in total output. The result was that labour productivity sharply declined in 1990, and further declined, though much more modestly, in 1991 as well – a clear indication that the structural adjustment was rather timid.

This combination of falling output and growing unemployment could not leave the state budget unharmed. While contracting production undercut the tax base, rising unemployment – as well as a rapidly growing number of people forced to take early retirement – led to increased demand on social payments. With substantial concessions granted to pensioners, the budgetary expenditure in this category expanded rapidly, so that the share of these payments in the total spending more than doubled. In early 1991, the state budget returned to deficit figures, and for the whole year was as high as 7.6 per cent of the gross domestic product. With such a deficit, almost as severe as before the shock therapy programme began, a serious threat to macro-economic stability was revived. Thus, because of its unusual depth, the recession proved a double-edged sword, on one hand slashing inflation and on the other aggravating it (Wernik 1991, 1992).

With subsidies trimmed on the spending side, the primary way for the government to keep the budget under control was to raise taxes. Tax burdens on state-owned enterprises were indeed increased in 1991, with as much as 91 per cent of their profits taken by the budget (compared with 47 per cent in early 1990). At the same time, the private sector was routinely exempted from many taxes, while massive tax evasion here was tolerated (as the tax service was not prepared to effectively collect taxes from the private sector).[12] State enterprises also had to make up for revenue losses from abolishment of the public monopoly on alcohol and cigarettes (the economic rationale for which is difficult to comprehend). Under the weight of these taxes, and deprived of subsidies, the state sector became largely insolvent, and unable to pursue restructuring – this posing a threat to the state budget in the long-run.

External sector

The 1990 shock therapy provided a positive stimulus for exports to hard-currency markets, with about one-third increase reported in that year – bringing the total exports to about $12 billions. Since total imports were kept down at the same time, a trade surplus close to $3.7 billion was generated, compared to a $0.8 billion surplus in 1989. The year 1990 was the first in more than a decade when a current account balance registered a surplus – $0.7 billion (while in 1989 there was a deficit of $1.8 billion). One decisive factor behind this large improvement was the currency devaluation, but the contraction in domestic demand was another, and possibly the single most important determinant. Many economists reacted to this development by saying that Poland was turning into an export-driven economy (assisted by low wages), while others expressed doubt as to whether the combination of recession and devaluation would be sufficient to sustain the export surge.

Exports continued to grow rapidly during 1991, though at a lower rate than a year ago, pushing the hard-currency figure to $14.9 billion. Confronted with a further decline in domestic demand, enterprises rerouted more production to the foreign markets, but little capacity was added to enhance these sales. Limited adjustment was one factor slowing down exports, with currency overvaluation another, because, given the high rate of inflation, the exchange rate, pegged at a fixed value, had become overvalued by late 1990. In mid-1991, the currency was at least 40 per cent above the equilibrium point, prompting an official devaluation, which was not only belated but also moderate, so that disincentives to export continued. Such strong domestic currency – combined with lower protective barriers – stimulated imports, which increased by 45 per cent, mostly in consumer goods.[13] For the whole of 1991, Poland produced a small trade deficit of $0.6 billion, and a current account deficit of $1.3 billion (marking a return to the pre-stabilization figures).

Steady growth in exports to Western economies has contrasted with the developments in Poland's trade with the CMEA economies. Regional trade, already in trouble in 1989, entered into an open crisis in 1990, largely due to recessionary tendencies in the region. Another contributing factor was that economies most aggressive in reforming their system, such as Hungary and Poland, were increasingly reluctant to conduct their trade with the CMEA in non-convertible rubles (as many East European economies, including Hungary and Poland, had rapidly accumulated ruble surpluses with the Soviet Union). When in late 1990, Soviet leaders decided to unilaterally shift to dollar financing and abolish bilateral protocols, the door was opened to the total disintegration of the CMEA trading regime – a process concluded in 1991. This complicated transacting among the former members even more, as there has not been enough liquidity, or insurance against commercial risk, in these countries to keep trading at the preexisting levels (Brabant 1992).

Under the circumstances, Poland's turnover with the former CMEA collapsed, particularly during 1991–92, since in 1990, a favourable ruble exchange rate helped to sustain most of the transactions with the about-to-disintegrate Soviet Union. Calculating trade with Russia, the key partner in the past, was greatly complicated by rapidly changing dollar/ruble exchange rates. Unofficial trade – through smuggling or using of false documents – has become an important channel which has taken over some of the previous transactions openly conducted between respective governments. It is safe to assume, however, that Poland's exports to the former Soviet Union declined by as much as two-thirds, with a less pronounced decline on the import side (due to the extended interest in Russian oil/gas, iron ore and some chemicals). Poland's trade with former East European members of CMEA contracted as well, though not by as much (while its exchange with Czechoslovakia declined by only a little through 1992).

Confronted with the collapse of the CMEA, Poland not only intensified its efforts to shift exports to Western markets, but allowed a process of 'trade destruction' as well – the latter adding to the recession (Rosati 1992). While extracting figures on the post-1990 volumes of trade – exports and imports – among the former CMEA members has been difficult, separating 'diversion' of trade from its sheer 'destruction' is even more complicated. One easily identified case of trade destruction is, of course, military exports to the former Soviet Union, which almost stopped in recent years – Poland (and Czechoslovakia) being the most hurt among East European suppliers. While Czech makers have been able to secure alternative markets in the world, Poland has not, mostly out of political concerns (i.e., unwillingness to work with countries such as Iraq). Defence production has also been among the areas worst hit by the post-1990 recession (e.g., tank production in Bytom, planes from Mielec).

Economic recovery

While production collapsed, so did investment, with gross investment falling by 10 per cent in 1990, and by 4.5 per cent in 1991. The conditions which emerged during the early stage of the shock therapy programme described above, could be best captured by the term 'bad equilibrium' at a reduced level of economic activity. This is because little reallocation took place from inefficient to productive producers, either through mergers (corporate takeover) or by means of investment in new capacities. Moreover, the most socially profitable long-term investments were sacrificed for less desirable short-term projects

(Calvo and Frenkel 1992: 113). Under the circumstances, it was hard to see how the economy would make a turnaround toward a healthy recovery. Still, in the middle of 1992, the economy showed its first signs of recovery, led by acceleration in the construction sector, and then followed by an upturn in various sectors of manufacturing soon thereafter.

Recovery in the industrial sector in 1992 was strong enough to produce a reasonably high rate of growth in the national product for the year, but poor agricultural output – in large part caused by drought – prevented it from happening (table 7.1). In 1993, industrial output increased by 5.6 per cent, proving that the recovery might be sustainable (though at the end of the year there was a slowdown in production expansion). Since a certain amount of production has been going un- or under-reported, the recovery in industry was likely even stronger. In 1992, there were also the first signals that restructuring was intensifying, as labour productivity began to increase, and then showed strong gains in 1993. This turnaround in labour productivity was in large part facilitated by a continuous rise in unemployment, this time mostly related to phasing out existing jobs in the state sector (in 1993, accounting for about 45 per cent of the registered unemployed, with another 35 per cent coming from the private sector).

Labor productivity growth has been affected not only by job elimination, since indications are that the 'selection process' – elimination of weak and expansion of strong – has finally begun as well. While initially most state-owned enterprises seemed overwhelmed by shock therapy, so that downsizing was almost universally distributed, differentiation in economic behaviour of these enterprises began to be visible in 1992. Microeconomic studies have revealed that around that time about half of all state-owned enterprises were in a strong position to expand, while the rest were just struggling to survive (see Dabrowski et al. 1992, and particularly the widely commented upon survey of Pinto et al. 1993). Many of those enterprises that had been privatized in the meantime have shown great promise as well (including many of the enterprises which were placed on the stock market through public offerings) (also Jorgensen et al. 1990).

It may well be that this restructuring – based on the shift of resources from losers to winners – has been one of the factors responsible for the recovery, but one should also look for possible growth stimulation on a demand side. To begin, it is unlikely that deficit financing has been such a force, as deficits reappeared well before the recovery took place and there has been no visible increase in budgetary imbalance since.

Real wages have been kept very much unchanged since 1990, so that this has not been a source of output stimulation either, though dissavings – particularly in 1993 – have contributed to consumption increases (this decline in savings – an obvious stimulator of production – was caused by low interest paid on deposits as well as currency appreciation). Continuing this process of elimination, there has been an upturn in fixed capital investment, though too modest to make a substantial difference, it has been far less to produce this recent recovery on its own.

We are left with one more variable on the demand side, namely exports, as they could possibly compensate for the apparent lack of substantial upturn in domestic demand components, if one were to trust official statistics on the national account. The 1990 surge in exports created a wide-spread feeling that further export expansion will take the economy out of recession, even with little help from domestic demand (=expenditure). But even with the above mentioned surge Poland has remained a very closed – insulated – economy, as evidenced in low levels of export revenue per capita. Besides, the export increases levelled off after 1991, so that by 1993 the volume of exports (calculated in constant prices) represented 92.8 per cent of the 1990 level. Only in late 1994 did foreign sales pick up, in part due to an activation of markets in the former Soviet Union (particularly Russia) as well as the acceleration of imports by Western Europe, going on through its own economic recovery.

This flattening of exports, around the time when the economy assumed a recovery path, took place despite a number of state instruments introduced in order to stimulate exports. Most important changes were those in the foreign-exchange market, now serving as a principal avenue for controlling external sector by the state. In late 1991, in order to improve faltering exports and remove the small trade deficit, the government abandoned one of its nominal anchors – the fixed-rate exchange system (although originally holding the value of currency constant was planned for about half-a-year). A floating system was put in place, allowing for marginal drifts in the price of domestic currency in response to the changing value of a basket of foreign currencies, followed by a 12 per cent devaluation in early 1992, done reluctantly out of fear that it would accelerate inflation.

We thus have to examine another possible (external) source of recovery, i.e. foreign imports, or so-called deficit financing, either as the main engine of the here analyzed economic expansion or its important supportive force. After the 1990 decline of imports in volume (constant-price) terms, imports showed strong real gains starting in 1991 all the way through 1993. Total imports increased from $8.3 billion in 1990 to $18.8 billion in 1993, in current prices while in volume terms the 1993 imports represented 188.3 per cent of the 1990 imports (with the index of real growth in imports showing 137.8 points in 1991 alone). Stagnating exports and surging imports had to produce deficits in the officially reported trade (with trends in unofficial, mostly cross-border trade only to be guessed about). In 1992, after showing early deficits, surplus was earned in mid-year, but a deficit of $3 billion was recorded for the whole year. In 1993, a large deficit of $4.6 billion was generated, though the economy continued to enjoy sizeable foreign currency reserves (estimated at $4.1 billion).

Costs of economic transition

The immediate outcome of the shock therapy programme – if understood as a complex package going beyond stabilization measures – was sufficiently negative on the production side, i.e., resource utilization and output levels, to trigger a lively discussion about the possible causes. In light of this collapse, the initial optimism about transition gave way to a more sober view that, whether radical or gradual, it must first produce some substantial output losses, if not real, then at least statistical. By implication, even a perfectly flawless execution of reforms carries such a high front-load cost for economies in transition, as most, or all necessary macroeconomic measures – financial tightening and price liberalization in particular – lead to a negative response on the output side. The question is whether this economic pessimism, being just one specific example of such an attitude in theoretical literature at large, is well founded and thus definable.

Transition theory

According to one argument about the unavoidability of temporary deterioration in production, the sources of this phenomenon should be sought in the considerable supply rigidities inherent in state-planned economies. Gomulka (1991) argues, for instance, that for any such economy to be reintroduced to the market system, prices have to be liberalized. When prices are freed from state control and begin disciplining enterprises, the high-cost or ineffective enterprises will have to reduce their production programmes, in itself a rationalizing measure. The cost-effective enterprises should, theoretically speaking, be able to expand production, were it not for the fact that resources idled in deficit enterprises can not be easily recycled (= reallocated) to profit-making producers (e.g. labour, as a result of limited housing, remains relatively immobile in the post-communist economies).

A related criticism of the state-planned economy for raising the costs of transition is advanced by Winiecki (1991), who claims that with any tightening of financial control – or hardening of budget constraints faced by enterprises – massive waste, hidden under state-planning, becomes explicit, and then eliminated, so that production figures will take a downturn. Introducing market forces will phase out unwarranted production, which cannot find buyers at cost-covering prices, with related output loss detracting nothing from consumer welfare. In addition to this statistical production decline, there will be a real, though temporary, decline in output, because of the trimming of excess inventory, another source of inefficiency built into the state planned economies. To the degree that this excess stock is reusable, such trimming will reduce demand for inventory replacement, thereby forcing suppliers to cut production.

Hardening of the budget line during transition is also claimed by Kornai (1993) to have a contractionary effect, though for a different reason. In his framework, the state-run economies are generally characterized by permanent shortages, or excess demand, while market systems exhibit a slack, or excess, supply. The transition process thus involves moving from a seller's to a buyer's market – from a supply-constrained to a demand-constrained – economy. Taking this observation as a starting point, one could argue that for a buyer's market to be established, producers have to allow some of their capacities, previously employed to the peak of their technical efficiency, to stay idle as a buffer against demand in case it changes suddenly. Creating such a reserve, perfectly rational under a demand-constrained economy, would have to temporarily cause overall output decline (whether, as Kornai argues, there was considerable waste in production under a supply-constrained economy in the past or not).

All these arguments are probably not without some merit, but for these theories to work as an explanation of Poland's most recent recession, a number of questions would first have to be answered satisfactorily, like, for instance, why transition in Poland before 1989, when prices were being liberalized, did not produce a comparable production decline. It could well be that no such downturn took place because this earlier price-freeing was executed gradually over a longer period of time. This would imply that the point on supply rigidities –

factor immobility – as a principle cause of presumably inevitable output collapse applies only to radical price liberalization. If so, then the one-step decontrol of remaining fixed prices, as well as the sharp upward correction of others, in 1990 would have to be viewed as a policy error – meaning that this particular argument on the inevitability of a high front-load cost would have to be questioned, at least in its original formulation presented above.

Continuing with the argument on supply rigidities, for it to give a correct explanation of the 1990–91 production contraction, the simple observation that there was such a decline is not a proof. Applying this argument correctly, one would expect that when financial conditions are tightened, only some enterprises would register output losses, while others would see no such losses, unless the shrinking of the cost-inefficient sector leaves the viable producers with reduced sales prospects. If, however, opportunities for sales opened – say, on foreign markets – simultaneously with contraction in high-cost enterprises, this negative side effect on efficient producers should be mitigated. Under such conditions, one could expect even a positive supply response by low-cost producers, this if only there were some under-utilized capabilities prior to the financial tightening. Seeing an industry-wide contraction in production, particularly if equally intense, would then suggest that the supply rigidities could not be the main cause.

Quantitative testing

The first carefully conceptualized test of the above hypotheses on the inevitable deterioration of performance under transition was conducted by Brada and King (1991). The authors separated exogenous shocks to aggregate demand from supply-side shocks, identifying only the latter as a potential cause of 'transition costs' (as opposed to uncontrollable shocks to an economy, or shocks caused by macroeconomic policy errors). This definition is not necessarily consistent with the understanding of that concept by many of those arguing the fatality of a negative production response at the outset of transition. Here, the exogenous shocks have nothing to do with economic reform, while the supply-type factors are reform-related, i.e., linked with a changing incentives structure. Separating these two sources of possible output decline is, of course, complicated by the fact that certain measures are double-edged (as with subsidy reduction, which involves both a fall in aggregate demand and a shift in relative prices).

For their estimations, Brada and King (1991) used a simple aggregate determination model of the Keynesian type. The 1989–90 data on investment, the balance of trade and consumption for a sample of economies in transition, with Czechoslovakia, Hungary and Poland, were utilized. The quantitative test results revealed that apparently the economic recession experienced by all these countries could be fully attributed to demand contraction without recourse to supply-side factors, such as price freeing, and demonopolization, or sales of state assets. Of all the cases, Poland produced the most graphic evidence of the demand-induced nature of the 1990 output decline in the transition economies. The authors concluded from these findings that the initial output losses were not reform-related, thus disproving the claim of 'transition costs'.

The authors further argued that output losses were probably excessive because certain elements of the overall demand were pushed down so far by the respective policy-makers (Brada and King 1991: 51; for a revised interpretation of the output decline, see Brada, 1995). Convinced that any transition involves high front-load costs, post-communist reformers in all these countries, Brada and King argue, paid insufficient attention to the recessionary effects of their aggregate demand management on production. Even in the light of massive production declines or stabilization of output at low equilibrium levels, the reformers were unwilling to relax their highly deflationary packages. Consequently, the ill-conceived theoretical argument on high front-load costs of transition became, on the surface, a self-fulfilling prophecy, which gave reformers confidence that they were pursuing an optimal policy package (Brada and King 1991).

Although the argument by Brada and King on excessive deflation (as well as their argument on the negative impact of another demand-side factor, namely, the collapse of Soviet imports) is most plausible, one wonders whether their econometric tests accurately detect the possible negative role played by the recent reforms in the economic system of respective countries. While by the authors' admission, their model is quite crude, even more elaborate models seldom succeed in estimating the impact of such an obscure, or hardly measurable, variable as an 'economic system'. There are some methods (e.g., adding a dummy variable) that would help to more indirectly quantify the significance of that factor, but it would be difficult to properly assign values to particular countries of Eastern Europe for comparative purposes, given the fluid nature of their rather similar systems.

While the conclusion formulated by Brada and King implies that the recent reforms in the economic systems of Poland, Czechoslovakia, and Hungary were minor and thus had a neutral impact, there seems to be ample evidence that the post-communist governments have not only launched substantial institutional reform packages but that they may have made some errors in this respect as well. It is possible that these economies have suffered from excessive deflation as well as from too hasty and/or misguided reformation efforts which further raised the costs of transition. If these were blunders, then, of course, the point by Brada and King that transition need not be costly may still hold (unless it is assumed that even properly executed systemic reforms lead to periodic loss of output since it takes time for any type of enterprise to learn new rules; see Murrell 1990a, 1991).

Income recalculation

Berg and Sachs (1992) conducted another interesting analysis of sources of post-communist output contraction in Poland to offer a somewhat different view on 'transition costs' from that of Brada and King. Unlike the latter, Berg and Sachs precede their examination of recessionary causes with a recalculation of the official income data to cope with numerous inadequacies of recent statistical reporting. After reexamining the major components of Poland's national product in 1990, they argue that its actual contraction of total output – reflecting transition costs – in that year was not about 12 per cent as officially reported. Rather it was 4.9 per cent, if one recalculates the value of that product through separate quantification of each major segment of aggregate demand (i.e., consumption, investment, inventory, government expenditure and exports). If, however, the national product is recalculated from the supply-side, then, the authors suggest, the loss was closer to 7.7 per cent, still considerably below the official reports.

Berg and Sachs also argue that sharp real wage decline reported in 1990 cannot be taken as an indicator of changes in real consumption, since, as the authors stress, a large portion of the money earned before shock therapy was not matched by supplies of goods. However, since it has never been well established what portion of this unspent money represented an overhang rather than voluntary savings, it is uncertain whether reduction in real wages in that year did not cause some welfare loss for consumers. Berg and Sachs believe that by switching to higher-quality imports, consumers have made considerable welfare gains, which should have at least partially offset the monetary losses from wage cuts.[14] However, one should also take into account the fact that a large share of imports consisted of inferior products, i.e., defective shoes, cars not meeting pollution standards, dated foodstuffs.

The major reason aggregate demand, and thus national product, declined was – according to Berg and Sachs – that state enterprises decided to reduce their uneconomically high level of inventories. With the reduction in inventories by above 50 per cent – from an excessive pre-shock level – in 1990, the statistical national product had to decline considerably as well. Apparently, as much as half of the product decline could be attributed to drop in inventories, reflecting in fact an economic rationalization. It would follow then, that the recession has been primarily caused by liabilities left by the state-planned economy, where, as the authors claim, low costs of maintaining inventories and disorganization of production as well as desire to hedge against inflation, encouraged hoarding of materials.

There are several problems with this argument about the central role of inventory decline in causing the post-1990 recession. To be able to assess the role of inventory reduction, one would need more detail about this aggregate than that taken into consideration by the authors. For instance, one would have to know whether all excess inventories have been reusable, since only such inventories could have caused a decline in aggregate demand and related fall in production. Also, one would have to have a reliable measure of what constitutes a rational level of inventories to be able to establish whether the actual decline in inventories removed not only excess stock but cut deeper (so that inventory rationalization was combined with recessionary panic sell-out needed to improve enterprises' cash flow).

The 1991 output reduction was in turn due, Berg and Sachs claim, to another demand-shock, one stemming from the disintegration of the CMEA.[15] No doubt, the demand-shock related to the breakup of the CMEA in 1991 had some negative effect on production, particularly in the machinery, drug, and textile industries, traditionally heavily or-iented toward the vast Soviet market.[16] However, at the time when demand for Poland's exports in the former CMEA was declining sharply, the overall level of trade with the bloc was already largely reduced. Also, one could expect the economy in 1991 to be recovering from the earlier demand-shock, i.e., the utilization of excessive inven-tories, with this upsurge mitigating the CMEA-related damage to production.

At no time, argue Berg and Sachs, has Poland suffered from supply-type negative shock, except for what they consider an insufficiently energetic pace of state-asset privatization. In particular, they reject the notion that the opening of the economy in 1990 – including currency liberalization – had anything to do with the recession. These measures, the argument goes, facilitated export growth on hard-currency markets and accumulation of reserves which helped to stimulate domestic production and to solidify currency as well. However, maintaining convertibility in the face of real appreciation of currency has been possible because of extended credit restrictions reducing demand for foreign exchange. Thus, the price for strengthening currency was that producers were left with insufficient credit for supply modernization and expansion.

While the acceleration in exports to hard-currency markets can be used as an argument in support of the viability of shock therapy, one has to be aware that the same observation weakens the claim that demand, rather than supply, factors caused the recession. This is because expansion to foreign markets, which resulted in trade surplus, as in 1990, involved a substitution of falling domestic demand for the external one. Since the 1990 trade surplus was about 4–5 per cent of the national product, then, if, we accept the claim by Berg and Sachs that the decline of consumption in real terms was 4–5 per cent, these two changes in aggregate demand cancel each other out. Thus, if a demand-type argument is used to explain the recession, the whole decline in output would have to have been triggered by an inventory reduction and/or investment reduction.

Comparative picture

Dabrowski (1992b) has adopted a comparative approach that supports the postulate by Berg and Sachs that high front-load costs are an inevitable feature of transition and that the radical approach – as adopted by Poland in 1990 – has kept the overall costs at the lowest possible level (also Balcerowicz 1995). Sorting statistical data for 1990–91, the author finds that, without exception, all the post-communist economies entered a recessionary stage, with production losses in all cases considerable, not to say unprecedented. Since this happened in economies which often differed greatly in terms of initial economic conditions as well as specific type of transition strategy selected, it would then follow that recession was inescapable (with the economic experience of the former Soviet republics providing strong additional evidence to support that point; see Dabrowski 1994).

This does not mean, Dabrowski argues, that cross-country differences in reform strategy had no impact on relative economic performance, i.e., depth of recession. Two major groups of countries can be distinguished, namely, the radical reformers and those adopting the gradual approach. In the former category fall Czechoslovakia and Poland; in the latter, all other countries. Overall, the record of the radical reformers is found to be markedly superior to that of economies pursuing a gradual strategy – with the exception of Hungary. Significantly, Poland's economy, subjected to probably the most drastic shock therapy of all, suffered the shortest recession, offering further evidence of the virtues of decisive reform programmes (discounting the case of East Germany, where unquestionably the most drastic shock therapy was implemented, though cushioned by large resources put at its disposal by West Germany).

The universality of recession cannot be disputed nor the observation that Czechoslovakia, Hungary, and Poland have been the least damaged by recession. For instance, in 1990–92, the gross national product of Hungary and Poland declined by about 17 per cent, and that of Czechoslovakia by close to 23 per cent. At the same time, the gross national product of Romania was reduced by approximately 32 per cent, while Albania and Bulgaria experienced an almost 28 per cent decline. During 1989–92, industrial output in Poland fell by about 32 per cent, by almost the same amount in Hungary, and by somewhat less in Czechoslovakia during 1990–92. This data compares favourably with as much as 50 per cent contraction registered by Romania during 1989–92 and a 45 per cent loss in Bulgaria in 1990–92 (see table 7.2).

Looking at the least damaging cases of recent transition, one may be inclined to argue that Poland, with its relatively most radical programme, has actually done better than the other two less-damaged economies. Not only was Poland's recession one of the shallowest, but its economy indeed was the first to enter into recovery and has continued this upturn at least through 1995, while the Czech Republic (after the 1992 split with Slovakia) turned its economy around only in 1993. Hungary, in turn, after experiencing another year of declining national product in 1993, did not show a full recovery in 1994 either. With its considerably larger private sector, Poland seemed to undergo faster restructuring than the Czech Republic, but it is doubtful that its economy did as good a job of modernizing its industry as Hungary with its more gradual, if not gradualist, approach has done (particularly since its industry attracted so much more of foreign interest and capital than Poland). Taking quantitative and qualitative indicators together makes the case for Poland's superior performance more questionable.

Table 7.2 *Main Eeconomic indicators for Eastern Europe, 1988–1993 (annual rates in per cent)*

	Poland	Bulgaria	Czechoslovakia[a]	Hungary	Romania
			(a) Gross Domestic Product		
1988	4.1	2.4	2.3	−0.5	−2.0
1989	−0.2	−0.3	0.7	−1.1	−7.9
1990	−11.6	−9.1	−1.2	−3.3	−8.2
1991	−7.6	−11.7	−14.2	−11.9	−13.7
1992	2.6	−5.7	−7.1	−5.0	−15.4
1993	4.7	−3.8	−0.3	−2.3	1.0
			(b) Industrial output		
1988	5.3	2.2	0.8	−2.3	0.1
1989	−0.5	2.2	0.8	−2.5	−2.1
1990	−24.2	−14.1	−3.7	−4.5	−19.0
1991	−11.9	−22.2	−25.5	−19.1	−18.7
1992	3.9	−15.9	−14.2	−9.8	−22.1
1993	5.6	−6.9	−5.3	3.8	1.3
			(c) Gross fixed investment		
1988	5.4	4.5	4.1	−9.1	−2.2
1989	−2.3	−10.1	1.6	0.5	−1.6
1990	−10.0	−18.5	7.7	−7.1	−35.6
1991	−4.5	−19.9	−26.8	−11.6	−28.1
1992	0.7	−25.2	6.3	−1.5	−2.1
1993	2.2	−29.7	−7.9	−0.7	−0.8
			(d) Rate of inflation (cost of living)		
1988	60.2	2.4	−0.4	15.5	1.7
1989	251.1	6.2	1.4	17.0	n.a.
1990	584.7	19.3	10.0	28.9	n.a.
1991	70.3	254.3	56.7	35.0	165.5
1992	43.0	79.6	11.1	23.0	210.9
1993	36.9	72.9	20.8	22.7	257.4

Table 7.2 (cont.)

(e) Foreign trade (exports)

1988	9.1	2.4	3.2	5.0	7.4
1989	0.2	−2.3	−2.0	0.3	−10.8
1990	15.1	−24.2	−4.2	−4.3	41.5
1991	−1.7	30.1	−8.4	−4.9	4.8
1992	1.4	1.8	8.3	4.4	8.0
1993	n.a.	n.a.	8.0	−6.5	0.3

(f) Gross agricultural output

1988	1.2	–	–	–	–
1989	−1.5	1.2	1.7	−1.3	−5.0
1990	−2.2	−6.0	−3.9	−3.8	−2.9
1991	−2.0	−6.4	−8.0	−5.0	1.2
1992	−11.9	−12.5	−12.8	−22.7	−13.2
1993	2.2	−20.1	−0.8	−6.0	12.2

Note: [a] Since 1991, the Czech Republic only.
Source: Compiled from *Economic Bulletin for Europe ECE* (New York: United Nations); ECE, *Economic Survey of Europe 1990–1991* (New York: United Nations); and ECE, *Economic Survey of Europe in 1991–1992* (New York: United Nations); *Transition Countries: Economic Situation in 1994 and Outlook, Research Reports No. 213* (Vienna: The Vienna Institute for Comparative Economic Studies, 1995).

Whatever the general merit of this claim of the superiority of radical transition, it seems hardly applicable to agriculture. Poland can not be counted now as a radical case, since it entered 1990 with well-established private farming, and its reforms were limited, but Czecho-slovakia can be put in that category again, with its bold attempt to decolectivize its mostly state-controlled agriculture; and so can be Hungary, where cooperatives – dominant form of farming – were declared to be dismantled (for the sake of reprivatization). With its limited reform Poland reported a drop in gross agricultural output by about 15 per cent during 1989–1993, but more radical attempts in the Czech Republic produced an almost 24 per cent loss in output, and Hungary registered a drop close to 33 per cent. The latter figure was close to that of Bulgaria for a comparable period, even though Hungary, with a genuine cooperative system of farming, would appear to be in a favourable position compared to those economies – such as Bulgaria but also Romania – where more traditional, Soviet-type agriculture was retained through 1990 (Lukas 1993).

For the argument on the unavoidability of high front-load costs to hold, however, one would have to make sure that the countries in question tried all potentially available variants (= models) of transition. Also, to draw conclusions on the relative effectiveness of particular types of reform approach, it is imperative that each individual country case be properly identified. Since there is little doubt that certain countries – such as Poland and the Czech Republic – have taken radical measures, the critical question is whether any post-communist country in the region could be legitimately classified as following a gradual reform model. We are frequently told that some did, but for such a judgement to be passed, one would have to have an appropriate, operational definition of reform strategy (for instance, see Murrell 1992; Poznanski 1992a).

It cannot be ruled out that none of the economies truly represents a gradual approach, including what would appear to be the almost unquestionable case of Hungary. While it is true that the Hungarian government avoided a deflationary programme as radical as that of Poland, its monetary contraction was considerable (for instance, there is little difference between the two countries in terms of their initial cuts in farming subsidies). No country has tried a more radical plan for privatization than the Czech Republic, but the approach taken by Hungary does not seem to be less radical than that of Poland, trying to sell/lease state assets at the fastest pace possible. Hungary in 1992 adopted the most draconian bankruptcy law of all countries in the region, while the Czech Republic has been quite lenient to loss-taking enterprises (Mizsei 1995).

Furthermore, there is considerable doubt as to whether post-communist countries other than Hungary which are typically classified as being gradual reformers really belong in that category. We should keep in mind that every approach that is not radical is not automatically gradual, since countries may pursue no clear strategy at all but instead submerge in a sort of chaos, without a strong positive feedback from individual steps. Ill-prepared, or indecisive attempts by the state to reform a system or/and reform policies, fall into this category of neither radical nor gradual approach. Initial reform attempts by Bulgaria and Romania fit this description – rather than that of a gradual reform – and Russia and Ukraine seem to fall in this category as well. Such a chaotic attempt may leave the economy very much unchanged but it can also cause considerable change, and in both cases, depending on circumstances, the economy may suffer.

If one takes this position, then the inferior economic performance of such countries as Bulgaria, Romania or Russia does not necessarily prove that radical, shock-type reforms are a least costly option, and no firm conclusion on the inevitability of high front-load costs is possible. The only reasonable conclusion would be that the radical – coherent – reform may be less costly than an incoherent one, or no reform in the face of adverse new challenges. To gain evidence needed to test this hypothesis on front-load costs one would have to include a truly gradual case, such as that of China. There, by most accounts, transition, initiated around 1978 and accelerated in 1985, has been slow-paced, with the party/state in firm control (though, the property reforms in agriculture are sometimes claimed to be radical, see Brada: 1995). China's economic performance since 1978, with no evidence of rampant inflation (and even less hyperinflation), no signs of recession or explosion in poverty, demonstrates that transition does not have to be costly, if economic changes are executed in a gradual fashion.

Bringing China into comparative analysis is often questioned, mostly on the grounds that given its lower level of development, as well as considering that China has avoided political discontinuity (i.e., the demise of the communist party), its reform approach has not been replicable in Eastern Europe (or in the former Soviet Union). There is no room here for an extensive discussion of the above claim but we would like to signal some problems anyway. For instance, one may wonder why political discontinuity would make, say, slow privatiza-tion, as practiced by China, impossible in Eastern Europe. Also, it is unclear why a higher level of development would rule out, say, step-wise decontrol of prices as a viable option for the region, but would be useful for a less-developed China. But even if the above differences have made the gradual approach less, or not, viable for Eastern Europe, one would like to point to certain obvious, at least general similarities with China, such as the common economic system (and related deficiencies, such as, imbalanced markets, soft-budgeting, low competitiveness, or overrepresentation of wage (= labour) interests). Any such similarities should, of course, justify giving preference to a gradual approach, assuming that systemic features present at the starting point do matter (McKinnon 1993a; Naughton 1995).

Institutional factors behind recession

As we have seen earlier, neither blaming the recession on excessive aggregate demand contraction – deflationary 'overdose' – nor seeking an explanation in exogenous shocks to demand for products, such as inventory reduction and/or regional trade 'destruction', provides a complete, or even satisfactory, explanation of production decline in Poland. Below we seek an alternative explanation by taking a closer look at what happened to Poland's economic system – and pay-off matrix for economic agents – since the 1990 series of reforms were initiated. Ideally, such an exercise in identifying supply-side factors should improve our understanding not only of what triggered the recession but also what made the economy turn around in mid-1992 (for a separate analysis along these lines, placing these questions in a broader historical context, see Poznanski 1993b).

Liquidity crisis

Following the observation by Dornbush and Fisher (1986: 40) that it has been a common weakness of recent stabilization programmes to fail to increase the credit supply, we begin our search for possible supply-type causes of Poland's recession of 1989–91 by looking at the banking sector. The authors believe that an accommodating credit supply would soften the recessionary effects of deflationary measures and allow for selective expansion and/or modernization by a healthier group of enterprises (particularly in export-oriented sectors where overall demand conditions are likely to be more favourable than domestically). Poland's stabilization programme under Balcerowicz falls in this class of deflationary packages, where credit contraction provides an additional brake on inflation, so that, if Dornbush and Fisher are correct, such contraction could have contributed to the post-1990 decline of the national product.[17]

The decline in credit supply since early 1990 was at least in part a deliberate measure taken by Mazowiecki's government in the hope that it would drive inflation down as well as discipline state-owned enterprises financially (a similar approach, largely following Poland's example, was taken by many other post-communist countries, including Czechoslovakia). This credit contraction was envisioned through a combination of interest-rate increases mandated by the government and to a lesser degree by the establishment of lower quantitative ceilings for bank-credit. These were not sophisticated measures, but the government had limited choice, given the backward state of the banking system. As with all other elements of the deflationary programme launched in 1990, the cabinet of Mazowiecki had no solid foundation – empirical data – for determining an 'optimal' interest rate or credit quotas for state-owned banks.

Rather then rely on complex calculations, the reform team adopted a simple rule that the interest rate should be kept at least at the level of the inflation rate, so that credit had a 'real' cost. While this appeared to be a reasonable principle to follow, in the highly inflationary environment of this phase of transition, this rule required that very high nominal interest rates be charged on credit issued to enterprises. Since credits taken at this moment were likely to be paid in a period of lower (though hard to predict exactly how low), inflation rate, this meant that borrowers were faced with a high risk of failing to raise the funds for repayment (Rosati 1993a: 247–9). Thus, those enterprises which had no choice, given their desperate need to service earlier debts, borrowed, thereby sinking into deeper financial trouble, while those with a sounder financial outlook tended to avoid borrowing – thus forgoing output expansion (for a critical account of the interest rate policy, see Gomulka 1994).

It would be too simplistic, however, to examine credit conditions only in terms of particular choices – or errors – made by the government, since, at this point, banks, still state-owned, were the core of the financial system. In fact, with the further removal of budgetary financing as well as state-controlled distribution of materials/equipment, the role of banks in providing liquidity increased. While state-owned banks became more critical in assisting state enterprises financially, their status was changed substantially, as they were left without any guarantee of a bailout. The central bank, now separated from other – so-called 'commercial' – banks, declared its intention to abandon its function of unconditionally bankrolling creditors. By ceasing to be a 'lender of last resort' (see Calvo and Coricelli 1991: 202), the central bank raised the risk of bankruptcy for banks, which by itself – regardless of fixing interest rate and setting ceilings – had to lead to a reduction of the credit volume that banks were willing to offer state enterprises (see Svejnar 1992a).

Another factor which inhibited banks' readiness to lend was that when the state withdrew its direct control from enterprises, the commercial banks were left without its intimate knowledge of conditions present in particular enterprises. This was a considerable loss, since after decades of mostly passive financing – following state directives – banks had limited experience in the market evaluation of credit requests coming from enterprises. While the amount of necessary work increased abruptly, there was no pool of personnel to hire to perform even simple jobs, not to mention some more advanced operations. With the rapid reorganization of industry – emergence of new 'entries' and fragmentation of existing enterprises – the ambiguity over customers' conditions increased. An additional complication for banks came with the intended fast-paced privatization, as it made unclear in whose left hands divested enterprises would be (i.e., who exactly would assume financial responsibility for extended credit lines).

State-owned banks have not only co-determined the volume of credit but they have also affected the allocation of liquidity injected into the economy at the time of the shock therapy programme. The government expected that the credit squeeze would hurt inefficient state enterprises but not viable ones, and thus initiate a 'creative destruction' process (a reference to the evolutionary economics of Schumpeter 1942). But rather than helping to weed out losers, the commercial banks engaged in a 'negative selection process', as they felt compelled to support those enterprises where their exposure was high, in fear of losing already extended funds. The reason is that with not yet modified bankruptcy regulations, prospects for banks to recover 'bad debts' from failed enterprises were quite meagre. Less exposed enterprises were given less attention, including those in the private sector (which, despite its overall vigour, was offered a very small per centage of the total credit issued).[18]

The state-controlled measures – official interest rates and credit ceilings – combined with independent decisions by the banks drove credit supplies down by an uncommonly large degree. Bank credit was almost instantly reduced by 30 per cent, and by the end of 1990 its stock was 50 per cent less than in 1989 (Calvo and Coricelli 1991: 16), with very little relaxation in 1991 (a similar pattern can be found in Czechoslovakia, where shock therapy entailed a 30 per cent decline in credit supply). A collapse of credit supply of that magnitude had to cause a severe 'liquidity crisis' in state-owned enterprises, thus leaving them with insufficient funds to maintain their working capital (needed to pay running costs such as wages and material supplies). It could be reasonably argued that even if there were no change in other variables, this factor by itself would cause enterprises to greatly lower their production level, which they did.

There were ways for enterprise managers to relax the shortage of credit for working capital, one of them being overcharging for their product – which thus added to inflation. Another helpful strategy was to reduce the amount of inventories, including by their re-sale for cash needed to meet the most pressing payments (this reaction, of course, represented a crisis-related cause of inventory adjustment, which we have stressed a while ago in our discussion on possible demand-side sources of recession). Borrowing from other, more successful state enterprises (i.e., securing inter-enterprise credit) was another useful method for improving their liquidity position, as well as 'borrowing' from workers by paying wages below ceilings established by the government (as actually happened during most of 1990, and without any visible resentment by the collectives, who were more concerned with the possibility of their enterprises going bankrupt; see Calvo and Coricelli 1991: 203).

Conditions for bank lending have eventually improved, however, one of the reasons being the 1992 change in bankruptcy regulations which have finally given banks a more effective grip on debt-ridden enterprises. According to this law, banks were allowed to force insolvent enterprises into bankruptcy and then to work out restructuring programmes to bring them back to financial health, if possible. Banks obtained great leverage in the clause which allowed them to acquire equity in exchange for cancellation of outstanding debts. Initially, banks were not ready to swap debts for equity, as they lacked the personnel to manage it, but with time separate departments were established for that purpose. With greatly increased interest in equity – in part related to a phenomenal surge in the securities market throughout most of 1993 and early 1994 – share acquisitions became lucrative, thus helping banks to strengthen their position (with some banks gradually turning themselves into holding companies).

While cleaning the banks' balance sheets has made them better prepared to turn to more aggressive lending, the progressive privatization of the financial sector has been another force working in the same direction. Initially, there was no intention expressed by the government of turning banking over to private hands, but beginning in late 1991, nine state-owned commercial banks were converted into joint stock companies with an expectation that they might be eventually privatized. Shortly thereafter, one of these banks issued shares to the public through subscriptions as well as to a foreign investor by direct sale (accounting for about one-third of the full value of shares; see Montias 1993: 18). In early 1994, another governmental bank, working mostly with enterprises in heavy industry, was privatized as well, again through a combination of public subscriptions and a sale to a foreign company.

Despite these institutional transformations, conditions for borrowers did not significantly change through 1994 and 1995. The central bank reduced refinancing and rediscount rates on several occasions during the last few years, but commercial bank rates did not change proportionally, reflecting their overall conservative outlook. Commercial rates were kept far above the rate of increase in producer prices, thus allowing banks to collect considerable premium (i.e., spread). Thus, changes in the availability of credit could not be one of the factors that was responsible for the mid-1992 recovery in Poland's industry. Nevertheless, the improvement in bank credit allocation among state-owned enterprises – related to the institutional changes mentioned above – could have had a stimulating impact on the economy (as well as the gradual shift of credit allocations towards the private sector, where resources might have been expected to be utilized more effectively) (Poznanski 1996).

Industry deprotection

Another institutional change with potential for hurting production was the trade liberalization – or opening – of 1990, which introduced convertibility and linked domestic with world prices through elimination of most trade subsidies and lowering of import tariffs. In early 1990, average import tariffs were reduced to a nominal rate of 10 per cent, but numerous exemptions introduced in mid-1991 brought the effective level of import protection to about 3 per cent. This lowering of tariffs was partially motivated by the need to offset the depressing impact of devaluation on imports, but these exemptions continued long after the domestic currency appreciated enough to stimulate strong imports. In addition to cutting tariffs to a level unusually low for a developing country such as Poland, there were no (at least through 1991) nontariff barriers against imports, with the exception of restrictions on the imports of alcohol, natural gas, tobacco, and oil.

Poland's trade liberalization measures were much more radical than those of other reform-oriented East European economies such as Hungary. One reflection of Hungary's more cautious approach is that, in 1990, about 30 per cent of domestic production remained highly protected from imports. Average tariffs in Hungary were reduced from 16 to 13 per cent in 1990, but in 1991 a trend to raise tariffs emerged. Hungary maintained some foreign currency licensing for state enterprises and did not allow households to freely convert currency. In Czechoslovakia, while the domestic economy was largely liberalized in 1991 – in shock therapy fashion – a temporary 20 per cent import surcharge was added to consumer goods and other restrictions were kept in place, or imposed, as well (see Gacs 1994: 15).

This deprotection allowed by Mazowiecki's cabinet, and extended under Bielecki's leadership was a controversial measure since so many of Poland's import-competing producers operated in negative value-added ranges. McKinnon (1991) estimated that between 20 to 30 per cent of domestic industry in Eastern Europe falls into this category, meaning that their production costs recalculated at prevailing world market prices exceed the prices paid for their products worldwide (similar results were produced by Houghes and Hare 1992). Considering this structural weakness, McKinnon and many other economists have advocated the application of very high, barrage tariffs as a medium-term solution, with a commitment to their gradual removal over a fixed period (McKinnon 1993b).

One indication that deprotection of the domestic markets has hurt Poland's production and thus contributed to the recession is the strong correlation between the relative import exposure of particular industries and the depth of cross-sector output decline. For example, the textiles and electromachinery industries, the sectors most severely affected by the recession, have experienced some of the highest exposure to foreign competition, as evidenced by their import-penetration ratio. While this ratio for Polish industry as a whole increased from 16 to 25 per cent during 1990–91, it rose from 17 to 28 per cent and from 25 to 38 per cent for textiles and electromachinery respectively (for additional evidence, see Coricelli and Revenga 1991: 20).

This deprotection of industry did not extend much beyond 1991, as pressures for protectionism from within industry began mounting. Given the adverse effects of the recession, enterprises had little choice but to seek some financial relief and obtaining protection from foreign competitors – and raising their profit margins – was one avenue that managers turned to. When shock therapy was launched, it was relatively easy for the government to deprotect industry, because many of the existing channels of influence peddling were severed. This period of political dislocation was rather short, and with the successful rebuilding of links with the government, enterprises became more effective in pressing for protective measures. Increasing in number, foreign investors began using their negotiations with the government on sales of equity to demand import barriers as well. Finally, the government itself gradually discovered that higher tariffs may serve as a useful source of budgetary revenues (aiding a failing system of tax collection).

The first effort to reverse deprotection was made already in late 1991, when the government announced a new custom tariff system. On this occasion, the average tariff was raised to 16 per cent, with tariffs for agricultural products and textiles raised to 25–35 per cent (and lower, under 1 per cent, tariffs applied to raw materials). The government continued to temporarily suspend tariffs on numerous products, and only in early 1992 were many of these tariffs restored and many others increased. To further strengthen protection, in late 1992, the government imposed a 6 per cent tax on all imports subject to duties, a payment to be extended to all imports shortly thereafter. The government eventually turned to setting quantitative restrictions as well (e.g., in passenger cars on the insistence of foreign investors, and in agriculture after the political victories by the peasant party in 1993).

'Property vacuum'

Another possible cause of the initial production contraction can be found in the enterprises themselves – in their motivation system or matrix. Critical for this change was the 1990 curtailment of direct intervention in enterprises (with the exception of wages, which, as mentioned, remained subject to control). This change – partly reflecting the reform philosophy and partly the government's own weakness – increased enterprises' autonomy, but also opened them to greater risks. As this withdrawal from ownership functions seemed, at least at the outset of the 1990 economic programme, to be credible, managers and workers had good reason to believe that they now had to bear all the consequences of their choices. Faced with this new situation, they responded by reducing the scale of their production programme as well as shortening its time horizon (a fact which would explain their reluctance to borrow for purposes other than financing current costs, e.g., wages) (Charemza 1992a).

What could have further increased this exposure to risk was the initiation of legal changes in the ownership status of enterprises, i.e., massive and fast-paced privatization of the state sector. Rapid privatization was made an integral part of the shock therapy programme – in fact, the success of stabilization was seen as contingent on the rapid transfer of public assets to private use. It was assumed that only when in private hands, would enterprises respond properly to the new macroeconomic environment of flexible prices, foreign competition, and repayable credit. While the actual privatization has proceeded slowly, with only a fraction of assets divested by 1993, this does not mean that the process initiated in 1990 has had little positive or negative effect. We would posit that, if anything, privatization indeed has initially been a force that added to the uncertainty felt by enterprises in the state sector, thus contributing to the production contraction during 1990–91.

To comprehend the above point, one would have to recognize the fact that property structure – and related incentives – are not affected only when transfer of assets is completed, but also they can change their behaviour enroute to completion. The government's announcement of its intention to privatize was a material fact with serious implications for enterprises' production programmes. This by itself made managers unsure of whether the new owners would allow them to keep their positions (one of the major elements in their objective, or utility, function). As the initial announcement was followed by a series of rather poorly crafted regulations, managers grew progressively uncertain over what would happen to their enterprises in terms of the exact method of divestment. With no clear rules of what criteria would be used to put individual enterprises up for privatization, the likely timetable for asset transfer could not be known either.

Uncertainty over the ambiguous privatization programme not only caused a reduction in production – idling of some existing resources – but also resulted in decapitalization. Unsure of the payoffs for effort extended, managers chose to slacken their efforts, a rational response – particularly considering the uncertainty caused by a rapidly changing external environment, high inflation, changing price structure and volatile exchange rates. For the same reason, they showed little interest in protecting the value of capital, and even less in expanding its stock through the reinvestment of their profits or borrowing from banks. To the degree the capital could have been sold for cash, managers raised funds through such sales to cover their operating costs – materials, energy, and labour. To divert resources to these needs, maintenance of existing capital was neglected, this further contributing to decapitalization.

Faced with increased uncertainty, managers (and workers) also began, or intensified, the siphoning of capital assets to private uses, for their own gain or to facilitate acquisitions by outsiders. Being in a strategic position, they were able to identify the most valuable, generally small, pieces of public capital to single them out for appropriation, through theft or formation of spin-off entities under their ownership. This, of course, facilitated the privatization process, by speeding it up, and has also been helpful in breaking up over-concentrated enterprises. But this has happened at the risk that by taking out such 'portable' pieces of capital, the total efficiency of the remaining assets might be undermined (particularly in the case of indivisible large units of capital). But this side effect – or opportunity cost – has not been on managers' minds, nor has the state actively intervened to prevent such welfare losses.

Such deterioration of the property structure – with related economic pathologies – could not have lasted for too long, for the employees – managers and workers – at some point had to recognize the limits of such destructive behaviour. Workers had to realize at some point that fast decapitalization, while helping to raise wages in the short-run, threatens them with enterprises closure and thus joblessness. Once the marginal workers, contributing little to value-added, were removed, and opportunities for securing wages for the others exhausted, the concern for protecting workplace became stronger. Those managers who chose not to squander state capital for their own – spin-off – ventures had to come to the realization that decapitalization is counter-productive as well as damaging to their reputation and potential for rehiring (along with the flow of additional income based on the enterprise's future profits).

These changes in attitude have been facilitated by, what we would describe as, consolidation of property rights after the initial announcement of radical privatization in 1990. Paradoxically, at least for the proponents of radical privatization, it was deceleration of this process which, at least at this point, helped to solidify 'shaky' property rights. This general slowdown was in part caused by the limited capabilities of state agencies to process transfers of titles, but resistance coming from within state industry was an important contributing factor as well. Moreover, the whole process has become more decentralized, so that enterprises themselves were allowed to co-determine all major issues, including the choice of a specific mode of divestment (within some general official guidelines). Consequently, uncertainty over future property status has subsided, and with this, interest in maximizing the value of capital has been strengthened.

Important in this process of consolidating property rights in the state-owned enterprises has been the emergence of a new group of stakeholders – the board of directors. In those state-owned enterprises which were turned into joint-stock companies, individuals – mostly from within the ruling elite – were appointed to the board of directors. With bonuses promised to them, they have become interested in the well-being of their enterprises. Another reason for such interest has been the prospect of acquiring shares in their companies and then profiting from their appreciation through the eventual listing of their enterprises on the securities market. It was not uncommon from mid-

1993 to mid-1994 that new issues commanded prices ten time higher than those at which they were originally acquired by managers/ workers in the respective enterprises (these practices have become more difficult after policy changes in mid-1994 in response to the controversial listing of a large commercial bank).

Summary

The post-1990 stage in transition presents economists with two puzzles – the initial drastic recession which was not supposed to happen and then, a robust recovery, which is equally hard to explain. Competing views have developed to address the puzzles, one group stressing the role of demand factors (conditions of sale), and another focusing on supply-side forces (related to institutional conditions of production). To put it differently, changing fortunes of the economy could be addressed either from a macroeconomic perspective or a microeconomic one (looking into types of incentives faced by producers). It follows from our analysis that, while demand conditions have been of some consequence for Poland's economic performance since 1990, the principal determining factors have been of a supply-type nature. Institutional changes have affected the incentive structure at the enterprise level in a way that had caused the initial fall in production, and then its recovery.

The roots of the post-1990 recession can be traced to decisions by the reform team to leave the state-owned banks uninsured and to remove steep import protections, combined with the launching of a haphazard privatization programme. All these changes in the institutional setting greatly increased the level of uncertainty faced by state-owned enterprises, which indirectly affected the private sector as well. The response by state-owned enterprises was to reduce production, well below what deflation of aggregate demand – the core of shock therapy – dictated, thus making the crisis to assume a more structural nature. When the government eventually restored assistance for banks to help them clear their balance sheets, brought back high import tariffs, and eased the pace of privatization, the level of uncertainty subsided. Consequently, enterprises became more interested in production expansion – this being a factor significantly contributing to the mid-1992 recovery (initially led by the non-agricultural private sector, and later joined by the remaining state sector).

This shift in governmental policies – radicalization followed by de-radicalization – corresponded with developments in the political arena. The post-1990 developments are another good example of co-evolution of the economic and political realms. The political disloca-tions following the roundtable negotiations – and elections – in 1989, could well be seen as facilitating the radical steps, known as 'shock therapy'. With the outgoing communist party in disarray and as yet no alternative well-formed parties, it was relatively easy for the people in the position of power to experiment with almost any programme, however radical. They were not compelled to seek broad social acceptance of their programmes, nor was it possible to assess public preference for lack of effective channels of political expression. With the stabilization of the political machinery, the public 'returned' to the scene, so that radical economic programmes have been subjected to closer scrutiny. For the most part, voters have rejected these pro-grammes, forcing a step-wise dismantling of shock therapy, though not its total abandonment.

The 'return' of society, disappointed with burdensome transition was first manifested in the rejection of Mazowiecki after less than a year of staying in power (see: Gross 1992). His follower, Bielecki, relying on a similar configuration of forces – emerged from the round-table – lasted even shorter time, swept out by voters tired of economic hardships (and possibly even more of uncertainty). This loss opened the door to new anti-communist forces – not linked to the round-table – whose platform was critical of the shock therapy pursued by the former governments. The new coalition, in 1992, led by Olszewski, made numerous attempts to reverse the radical measures. When the forces which produced Mazowiecki and Bielecki cabinets returned to power in a matter of months, now under Suchocka, they came without a political mandate to reverse the damage done to shock therapy by Olszewski's cabinet, nor did they make any effort to do so. The elections of 1993, however, brought to power a coalition of the communist era peasant party and reformed (renamed socialist) com-munists, led by Pawlak, expected by the voters to further curtail shock therapy.

Formation of Pawlak's government marked a true end to radical reforming initiated by the Balcerowicz programme of 1990. A vivid symbol of this reversal was the nomination of Kolodko, a chief critic of the shock therapy, to the job once held by Balcerowicz. As a Prime Minister in charge of economic affairs, Kolodko issued, in mid-1994, a document outlining strategy for Poland calling for gradual change (Kolodko, 1995). The programme called for fiscal prudence, this being in line with preferences expressed by his predecessors, but the programme also promised to bring costs of transition down, which was rather a new focus. The latter was to be accomplished through a more conciliatory wage procedure (i.e. well-structured formal negotiations between government, employers and workers), but also through resumption of ownership functions by the state with respect to state-owned enterprises (mostly through the so-called commercialization programme envisioning debt cancellation). Acceleration of investment through lower interest rates and tax incentives (e.g. on home improvements) was made another priority by Kolodko, despite warnings that this would facilitate inflation and extend the existence of deficit-ridden enterprises, in the state sector in particular.

The restoration of communist-era parties was received, by and large with great disbelief by scholars, since these were the forces which the public seemed to totally reject in the mid-1989 political transition. The society, as most scholars claimed, was ready to restore pre-communist politics, when the communists were an insignificant minority. This political transition was to be an essential element of a much broader process of the so-called 'return to history', with the communist period representing a temporary sidetrack, or mis-step. In other words, this was the time for abandoning the 'extreme' and restoring the 'normal', in which there was no room for communist forces. However, with the reemergence of the communist-era parties as a leading force in domestic politics, it seems that the true 'return' made by the society has been rather to the 'present'. Or to express it differently, if the society ever engaged in this journey back to the distant, pre-communist past, it has done so without ever completely leaving the present yet.

To say that this political comeback happened because non-communist forces engaged in some very costly – though possibly necessary – reforms would cover only part of the story. Dissatisfaction with economic conditions might have benefited opposition parties other than the old-time ones staying out of power but it did not. The recent reappearance of the communist-era forces was facilitated by the fact that, although sidestepped early during the political transition, they managed to retain enormous strength. At no point have the former communists – and their allies – ever been really outmatched by their opponents in terms of resources that could be mobilized for routine politics rather than 'extreme' circumstances. Decades of practising statecraft have prepared the former political monopolists to take on almost any challenge. When the parties which launched shock therapy failed to legitimize themselves through the economic prosperity they promised to instantly deliver, it was the former communists and their allies from the past who were in the best position to take power away.

Importantly, similar forces have recaptured the political scene in countries as different as Lithuania in 1992, or Hungary in 1994 and Russia in 1995, and with only limited adjustment in their political agenda. As in Poland, the reform-oriented communists in Hungary, made only minor adjustments in their political platforms before defeating their opponents. It could be ventured that the same has been the case with the former communists in Russia, who retained their emphasis on social equality and national interests. If they did not have to greatly change their political platforms to win decisively, then it would follow that the reality – economic and political – around them probably did not change fundamentally. Contrary to the sentiments prevailing at the time when the communist parties in these countries were giving away control, no 'revolutions' – which bury the past – had taken place in those countries. On a more general note, judging by what happened in these post-communist countries, power centres tend to stay around, and have a tendency to undergo metamorphosis rather than to disappear, or at least they tend to first change their form before they die out.

8 Political coalitions and property reforms

We have argued in the previous chapter that for the stabilization programme to proceed with the least disturbance in production a number of microeconomic measures are needed as support. Among them are tax schedules, contractual laws, government regulations, as well as accounting rules, and, most of all, property rights (Pejovic 1979, 1990). The critical role of the last stems from the fact that property rights give the claimant discretion over productive resources in short supply. As such, this institution is a principal precondition for the formation of capital markets – markets of company shares and finance for investment (Breinard 1991, Brabant 1992). Since property rights determine the costs of transacting – gathering information, risk discounting, and contract coordination – they affect the interests of claimants in asset-value maximization. Property rights determine to what degree claimants to assets feel responsible for respecting their budget constraints, i.e. avoiding overspending and thus risking financial insolvency and bankruptcy (Demsetz 1974; Barzel 1993).

Given the above significance of the ownership structure, this chapter is devoted to further discussion of reforms in property rights initiated since 1990. Because Poland has been, at least initially, in the forefront of the major privatization[1] efforts undertaken thus far in Eastern Europe and the former Soviet Union (see Roncek 1988; Schroeder 1988), its experience is of particular value in studying the region's transition to a capitalist private economy. In fact, since Poland has been first to develop and/or try certain approaches to privatization, its experience has provided important input into many programmes formulated elsewhere in the region. Polish experts, often former state officials, have, for instance, served as advisors to Russian and Ukrainian agencies on issues of privatization (though not necessarily being greatly responsible for the direction divestment has taken in those economies).

A variety of interest groups have been clashing over the final type of privatization to be implemented in Poland. These conflicts have yet to be resolved, making the final property structure difficult to predict. There are as yet only early indications that many of the smaller privatized enterprises may have been acquired through leveraged buyouts, i.e., by the employees, as a form of collective property. Workers have also gained equity through preferential allocation of shares within other forms of privatisation (e.g. public offerings). Given the political strength of organized labour at the outset of the shock therapy programme, the scope of such employee buyouts and share acquisitions has been rather narrow. This is particularly evident in light of the type of property pattern emerging in Russia, where, in a matter of two years, most of the assets have already been captured by the collectives – managers and workers (and in the absence of even a rudimentary secondary market for share, this pattern may continue for quite a while).

Another emerging early trend has been the formation of private spin-off companies by individuals – particularly state managers – who enjoy political influence within the bureaucratic system. This has been an extension of the trends which emerged during the final years of communist rule (a pattern detectable in Hungary from as early as 1986 as well). Public assets have been either syphoned off – at greatly discounted prices or for free – to already existing private ventures, or state-owned enterprises have been broken down, with a portion of them taken over by individuals. The crucial role of 'insiders' in this form of privatization, similar to the patterns present in the above mentioned leverage buyouts, suggests that it has been 'positioning' (politics) rather than 'exchange' (economics) that has been driving the divestment of smaller pieces of public property (Stark 1991, 1992).

While domestic agents have been acquiring small units of state capital, there seems to be a strong tendency for larger blocks of assets to be transferred to foreigners. It was the original intention of the Mazowiecki government to avoid sales of assets to foreigners while providing them with attractive incentives to invest directly in expansion of capital stock (through joint-venture and 'green field' projects). Faced with deep recession, the consecutive governments have become more willing to sell assets to more resourceful and experienced foreign companies. Working under a 'tight' schedule – turning all assets over to private hands in just a few years – has further contributed to the change in government's preference for domestic transfer. At the same time, foreign investors have chosen to take advantage of low sales prices for public assets and to acquire a controlling stake in state enterprises in which they have an interest. Many industrial sectors have already passed largely to foreign control (e.g., motor vehicles, electric engines, household chemicals, food processing).

Despite vigorous efforts by the post-communist governments to privatize the economy, by the end of 1994 an overwhelming majority of capital assets, except for small-scale entities outside of the manufacturing sector, remained state-owned, though under drastically curtailed central control. That the transfer process was slow cannot be atrributed solely to political opposition and lack of consensus on which privatization option to choose. As much, or even more, this slowness reflects the sheer complexity of the transfer operation and such economic obstacles as lack of financing and a small pool of qualified buyers. Since finding the talent necesary to run new, independently created private enterprises, as well as finance them, is less complicated then selling – or even giving away – state-owned enterprises, not surprisingly, the autonomous formation of the private sector has been far more dynamic than privatization.

Although slow, this process of privatization has had a rather significant impact on the overall performance of the economy – a point we made in the previous chapter. Our analysis in this chapter gives an even better sense of the kind of deterioration – weakening – of the institutional framework within which enterrprises and state agencies have had to work. For the bulk of enterprises which have continued to be owned by the state, declaration of the privatization programme has resulted in even greater uncertainty over who is in control of assets. It is very likely that this, so to speak, 'property vacuum' has undermined incentives for the effective use of capital, as managers have become less sure of who will appropriate the benefits of their actions. This demotivation of state-managers, as well as workers, may be one of the factors that contributed to the post-1990 reduction of industrial output (see: Poznanski 1991).

Changing policies towards privatization

The extinction policy

The Stalinization of the Polish economy first started in 1946 with the nationalization of banking, industry, and retail services along the lines of the post-revolutionary programme of the Soviet Union. Rapid nationalization was greatly facilitated by the fact that a large share of the assets in war-ravaged Poland was abandoned by the Germans after their defeat. Having distributed the large private land holdings among the peasants in 1944–45, Poland's communist party – again following the Soviet example – launched a collectivization programme in 1948. While nationalization outside of agriculture was completed in 1949, the forced collectivization of peasants which produced a political uproar in the countryside, proceeded rather slowly.

The nationalization/collectivization programme reflected, above all, the Communist party's desire to maximize its power by gaining control over virtually all assets. Since the Soviet Union supervised the Polish communists, the nationalization programme was, for all practical purposes, instrumental in subjugating Poland to Soviet domination (see relevant remarks on 'two-tiered Stalinism', Bunce 1992b). The elimination of the private sector was also driven by ideology, for the communists had derived from Marxist doctrine a deep resentment of private ownership, which was perceived as being the root of the capitalist menace, and leading both to alienation (i.e., dehumanization of the labour force) and economic inefficiency (e.g., recurrent deep depressions).

Some remnants of the private sector were allowed to exist within the Stalinist-type system, but only as a necessary evil, including the 1956 defeat and extensive reversal of collectivization. As a substitute, many restrictions were imposed on farmers (e.g., compulsory deliveries of products, fixed output prices, centralized distribution of material supplies, and state monopoly of mechanized equipment). In the non-agricultural sector, only small, family-type enterprises were permitted, and these were subject to price controls, strict production licensing, and severe restrictions on access to state credit. In addition to overregulation, the entire private sector – called the 'second economy' – was continuously disrupted by erratic changes in legislation.[2]

Under such circumstances, private businesses could hardly have been expected to operate efficiently though, in general, they were more cost-sensitive and innovative than state-owned units (Dallago 1991: 134).[3] As a result of the uncertainty pervading the private sector, participants refrained from undertaking large investment projects (e.g., land improvement) (Kornai 1990a, 1990b). Activities became excessively focused on rent seeking opportunities, i.e., taking advantage of steep prices in certain highly imbalanced segments of the domestic economy. With so many regulatory ambiguities, widespread corruption swept throughout the private sector. To survive, private farms and enterprises were thus forced to endure ritualized under-the-table payoffs to state purchasing agencies and suppliers.[4]

Changing attitudes

The communist regime's attitude towards the private sector changed only during the economic recovery following the severe crisis of 1979–82. As part of a more general effort to expand private activities, the government became at least conceptually ready to allow for some reforms in the ownership of public capital assets. To argue that the relaxation of restrictions on the 'second economy' was only a tactical retreat in the face of economic difficulties (see Aslund 1989) would be inaccurate. For some members of the party/state elite this was a step backward, to be reversed when the economy recovered. In the minds of many other members, allowing more space for the private sector represented only a belated correction of the excesses made during the period of post-war nationalization. Still other members favoured more permissive policies towards the private sector because of their personal interests, i.e., desire for additional income and opportunities for accumulation of wealth.

The initial impulse was to retain state ownership as the principal form of property rights but to allow for a plurality of ways of controlling public assets. Under Messner's regime, the idea was born of turning state assets into shares to be owned by various state entities. Among other options discussed at that time was to make industrial ministries majority shareholders and to allow for cross-ownership among state enterprises which had been turned into joint-stock companies. Establishing state holdings (see Iwanek and Swiecicki 1987; Gomulka 1992b) in order to obtain shares in state-sector enterprises was another solution, which seemed to promise not only more easily identifiable owners but also the foundation for a quasi security market. Yet another concept was to allow workers to temporarily lease parts of public assets for private gain – through self-organized working groups and other forms as well.[5]

Under the Rakowski government, official deliberations on transforming the public sector gradually shifted towards bolder formulations. In an elaboration of the traditional self-management model, it was proposed that bonds be issued to managers and workers, who would thus become creditors to their particular enterprises. Along similar lines was the suggestion that managers/workers be allowed to acquire a majority stake, though without the right to transfer individual shares to outsiders. The concept of free distribution of shares in state-owned enterprises to their managers and workers was put forward at this time as well. This particular line of reform-thinking reflected an interest in blending state-socialism with market-capitalism and thus creating the so-called 'third road' (or 'market socialism') (Bugaj and Kowalik 1990; Nowacki 1989; Dabrowski, 1989).

While these once ideologically foreign and unacceptable options were debated, the most important turned out to be the concept of facilitating spin-off companies by 'nomenklatura' managers (giving managers an almost free hand in securing segments of their enterprises for private use). Also very important was the willingness of the Rakowski government to relax state monopolies by giving lucrative licenses to members of the elite, including industrial managers (e.g., exclusive rights to import specific goods) and sales of real estate (e.g., apartments and lots) were allowed as well. Still the most significant factor in the expansion of the private sector was the formation of independent, small-scale private entities under relaxed regulations.

With all these efforts by the end of the communist period, the scope of the above-ground, legal, private sector, outside of farming, remained rather small, particularly in manufacturing. The most extensive private activities were in consumer services, which provided more favourable conditions for unreported, low capital-intensive business (here, the share of the private sector increased from 25.0 per cent in 1980 to 42.4 per cent in 1989; see table 8.1). Still, Poland's private sector – legal and illegal – emerged as far more extensive than in any other East European country, with the exception of Hungary (where, unlike in Poland, agricultural land was held mostly by cooperatives, but private activities outside of farming were more developed)[6] (Estrin 1994).

Postcommunist plans

With the formation of Mazowiecki's coalition government, the issue of privatization moved even higher on the priority list. The risky 1990 macroeconomic policy of stabilization was combined with a programme of systemic reform, seemingly unprecedented, and thus itself risky. In its 1990 preliminary programme, the Mazowiecki government decided, or at least declared its intention, to reintroduce a capitalist market based on private ownership within two to three years.[7] The concrete programme submitted to the parliament in mid-1990 called for the rapid privatization of the state sector through public offerings, to be executed in a two-step fashion. Initially, almost all public enterprises would be turned into joint stock-holdings owned by the treasury, and later, they would be transferred, in whole or part, to private individuals through public offerings, with some preference given for sales to workers.[8]

Enterprises divested through such public offerings were to be placed on the stock market, fully operational since 1991, to secure a steady flow of new listings. Public offerings were seen as a principal instrument for establishing a secondary market for shares, meaning that priority was given to establishing an Anglo-Saxon type of market, where most of the capital is circulated through securities. The alternative model, in which banks are heavily involved through cross-ownership into capital formation, was sidestepped. This choice was made even though the latter type of market seemed more suitable for a country with only rudimentary finance, as it facilitated more direct access to and supervision of investors. These were the conditions under which the bank-based system originally emerged during the early industrialization of Germany (and was transplanted to, say, industrialized Japan, with relatively backward capital markets as well).

Since public offerings proved tedious, to further accelerate privatization, the government of Bielecki, successor to Mazowiecki, decided to give priority to the free (voucher) distribution of shares among citizens. This concept had previously been resisted by Mazowiecki, who was afraid that, given the political power of labour unions, such a method would turn capital assets over to worker collectives. Bielecki, like Mazowiecki, was not sympathetic to the labour-management model, which was perceived as just as inefficient as centralized planning. His cabinet hoped, however, that freely dispersed shares would quickly be sold by workers pressed for cash to a new group of resourceful and risk-oriented individuals, i.e., capitalists. This option was also backed by the many proponents of the labour-managed model, who expected instead that the workers, if properly informed and led by their representatives, would by and large retain ownership of their shares (see Kawalec 1990)

The free distribution concept had been fully developed by the Ministry of Privatization – led by Lewandowski (a co-author with Szomburg 1989) of the idea first formulated in 1988) – in mid-1991.[9] The final proposal was presented by Bielecki's government as the so-called 'fast track'[10] privatization programme, which would pool hundreds of large-scale state-owned enterprises in two rounds of conversions, with enterprise collectives given only a limited say regarding joining such a conversion. All adults were to receive vouchers convertible into shares in ten to twelve investment, or mutual, funds, which would be managed mostly by foreign experts. Vouchers, or entitlements, would allow citizens to acquire a large portion – in fact the majority – of the total assets, while the remainder would be allocated to state pension funds, foreign investors, and the state treasury (for a good discussion, see: Grosfeld 1990; Hare and Grosfeld 1991).

To augment the two most favoured methods of privatization – public offerings and vouchers – the Bielecki government decided to permit the transfer of assets to domestic agents through the least preferred technique, liquidation, which was initiated in mid-1991. Through this procedure, enterprises, whether financially solvent or not, would be dissolved and most of their assets offered for lease (with option to buy) to managers and workers of particular enterprises. Other parties would be allowed to participate as well, particularly if capable of providing large units of capital as so-called strategic investor. Procedures for such liquidations were to be simplified and lower-level administrative authorities were to play a greater role here. This procedure was designed mostly to facilitate privatization of small- and medium-scale enterprises, concentrated in the services, transportation, and construction areas (rather than in industry, where large-scale entities dominated) (Gomulka and Jasinski 1994; 230–1).[11]

After mid-1991, there have been only a few important additions to the menu of privatization methods (Mujzel 1992), among them the concept of management contracts. This plan was formulated as an alternative to sales and give-aways, with the goal of stimulating efficiency in state-owned enterprises for as long as they remained in the public domain. The government presented this idea as one which should help restructure enterprises before the actual transfer of assets to private hands. In its 1991 version, long-term management contracts could be extended to both nationals and foreigners on a competitive basis. Contract managers would be rewarded for their efforts through benefiting from the increase in the market value of shares, i.e. they would take a majority of the 'capital gain', with the balance divided between workers and board members – the payments to be made in the enterprise's shares.[12] This concept has never gained much support from within any major political circles, nor has the state bureaucracy been especially persistent in pursuing it.

Another later development has been to allow banks to be more actively involved in the privatization process, mostly by passing a regulation which permitted them to convert bad debts into equity. By the 1992 bankruptcy law, tougher rules were outlined with respect to the rights of lenders to take action against debtor enterprises. By the earlier law, banks had little incentive to declare loss-making clients bankrupt, as there was no easy procedure for them to recover their money. Under this new law, there is no requirement that all unpaid lenders (or suppliers) must agree before bankruptcy procedures can be initiated – a majority vote is sufficient or a decision by one party with a large enough stake. Turning bad debt into equity is one option open to banks under these procedures, while others include more direct involvement in the restructuring of defaulted enterprises and forceful closing-down and selling of fixed assets.

In summary, the efforts to restructure property rights – and create a capital market – undertaken during the last decade of the state-planning system, have been extended into the post-socialist transition. At the time of power transfer from the communist party, the economy possessed a sizeable – though rather fragile – private sector, largely operating underground. The post-1989 reforms – introducing numerous bold acts of legislation – have opened the door to even faster growth of the private sector. Importantly, the limited and mostly uncontrolled transfer of public capital to private use allowed during Rakowski's regime have been augmented with more coherent, transparent programmes for large-scale divestment of state-sector capital. At the end of 1991, the privatization programme assumed a clearly pluralistic format, allowing different methods of asset transfer to be simultaneously pursued – thereby increasing both the flexibility of the process and the potential for creating an awkward and confusing end structure.

Conflicts behind asset transfers

It could easily be assumed that privatization, particularly on the scale attempted by Poland, would have to involve the mobilization of tremendous political forces. Because there are so many variants of property rights and because they differ in the opportunities they offer various social groups to meet their economic needs and enhance their relative political power, serious conflicts are inevitable (see Poznanski 1992b).[13] We identify four principal groups involved in this conflict over assets – the state bureaucracy, managers, workers, and foreign investors. The preferences of these major groups for particular privatization models and the political resources that these groups have utilized to influence the process of divestment are discussed in the following sections.

State bureaucracy

Beginning with the state bureaucracy, one might wonder about its motives, since divestment cannot be viewed as a normal, logical step for an administration to take. Privatization, under most circumstances, involves reduction in the size of the state bureaucracy, and thus is potentially detrimental to the state's power base. States are political creatures and their decisions are mostly politically motivated, so one is puzzled about how privatization could ever lead to strengthening such a power base. This would seem to be possible only when a changing property structure undercuts the political resources of major opponents to the state more than it does those of the state itself. Property reform – including genuine privatization – could also improve the power balance in favour of the state if control of assets, given their scale, drained the financial base on which the state rests. It can be demonstrated that these concerns have indeed been to a large degree driving the property reforms undertaken under communist rule, and after.

For the communist party/state, one of the reasons for privatizing the economy was to limit the rights of workers, which had been greatly enhanced by the 1981 reforms. It is not that the control of enterprises by collectives was unacceptable ideologically, since there is quite a lot of justification for such an ownership alternative in the original Marxist writings (explaining, in part, why Yugoslav communists turned to this variant in 1950–52 when seeking a substitute for Soviet-style central planning). The reasons were more practical, since such an institutional arrangement put the leadership in the impossible position of being responsible for economic performance – jobs, prices, supplies – without having the means to ensure proper allocation of resources. Returning to the traditional property structure was questionable as it required restoration of powerful party units within enterprises loyal to the leadership. Therefore, other types of ownership reforms had to be sought to accommodate downsizing of labour strength relative to that of the party-state.

Such concerns for the shifting power balance may explain why the communist government of Rakowski decided that the most appropriate solution was to turn state enterprises into joint stock public corporations – where state ownership would be combined with an independent board of directors (Milanovic 1989: 7–8).[14] It was assumed that the board would represent the only real locus of decisionmaking, possibly with some input from the worker councils. Such corporations would not have to be responsible to the state bureaucracy – or the communist party officials – other than in meeting their standard financial obligations (e.g., taxes, social security payments) and certain regulatory requirements (e.g., technical standards for products). The government hoped that such professionalization – depoliticization – of state-owned enterprises would be welcomed by the workers and cause them to lessen their direct demands for control over production.

The public corporation solution represented one suitable option – in the broader group of divestment models classified as 'quasi-privatization' (see also Kornai 1990b: 70) – another was holdings. They offered an opportunity for regaining effective control over capital assets without detailed intervention in production (particularly if placed under direct state control). Within this ownership arrangement, the state – for instance, the Treasury – would be able to influence the holdings of their choice through both appointment decisions and evaluations of their market performance through financial rewards/sanctions. The economic advantage of such an institutional formula would be that holdings would be evaluated on the basis of the performance of their portfolios, thus creating an incentive for optimal allocation of capital, with shares, for instance, 'leased' to enterprises in exchange for a predetermined dividend.[15]

Another variant of quasi-privatization proposed in communist Poland was to allow some financial institutions, such as state banks, insurance companies, or retirement plans, to take partial or complete control of the capital in state enterprises. This variant of property rights reforms was clearly inspired by the experience of the advanced capitalist countries, where these financial institutions play a crucial role in the securities market. Respective programmes were outlined, among others by Tardos (1988; 1989) and later by Wasowski (1990), both of them echoing the financial practice in some of the most advanced capitalist economies (particularly the United States). The latter economist argued that giving state insurance companies control over enterprise shares would be particularly valuable as this would greatly attract workers to various welfare schemes (particularly if combined with another privatization method that would enhance current income, i.e., wages).

The post-communist bureaucracy has not completely rejected these ideas, but, to the contrary, has continuously returned to the quasi-privatization option, often for the same reasons the communist rulers did. Facing strong labour unions and unsure of their patience, the governments of Mazowiecki and Bielecki were willing to accept such solutions, at least on a temporary basis, before turning state-owned enterprises private. The so-called commercialization of enterprises, turning them into joint-stock companies operating under commercial code similar to that working in the private sector and permitting additional restrictions on labour representation, is an example of such quasi-privatization adopted by the two governments. The same general scheme was endorsed by Pawlak's government in late 1994, though not necessarily for the same reasons. In this latter case, concern for trimming labour power was less important than the interest in assuring that state-owned enterprises, still in large numbers, are made financially more responsible and thus of a lesser burden to the state budget.

While engaged in divestment far more fast-paced than what the communist leaders were prepared for, the post-communist reformers faced the same dilemma that by reducing their stakes in capital assets, and/or leaving them without close scrutiny, they might undercut the state's financial base. Under central planning, state-owned enterprises were the real 'cash cow', with only a fraction of budgetary revenues coming from the other source, households. There was thus a risk that with divestment, the state might lose this convenient source of money, while being unable to establish a fiscal replacement to that system in the emerging private sector. The concern was that with too much loss in revenues, the state might be unable to provide even the most limited services that any public would expect. This possible shift from over-commitment to undercommitment towards the public (= voters) carried a politcal risk that could not be ignored, and there is evidence that the post-communist reformers have struggled with this dilemma.

It would be incorrect to view the actions of the state bureaucracy as motivated solely by a desire to lessen pressures on the budget and/or to change the balance of power between itself and society at large. Behind each state decision – regulation or allocation – stand individuals and their personal interests, and desire for self-enhancement regardless of the consequences for the state-society balance of power. The privatization process should therefore also be viewed as an opportunity – like any other new governmental programme – for the individuals involved, i.e., the bureaucrats, to pursue their various personal ambitions, financial and other. Consequently, one would expect the bureaucrats to try to maximize such opportunities by manipulating the process of privatization to their advantage.

It has to be kept in mind that the decisions the state takes on general regulations as well as on specific transfers of assets are of great financial consequence to potential new owners. Most critical has been the pricing of assets for sale, but determinations on licensing (i.e., monopoly rights) have been of great consequence as well, as have decisions on debt cancellation, tax exemption, etc. This has opened a venue for trading state 'concessions' for under-the-table payments, stock options, or employment opportunities for the officials involved and their relatives. Putting officials on the boards of privatized enterprises – an option allowed under the existing law – has been another avenue for financial gain. In addition, access to information of potential commerical value to the buyers of enterprises to be privatized has offered an opportunity to state bureaucrats to earn extra income.

Insecure managers

Turning to industrial managers, we find an interest group which suffered considerable loss of power during the last decade of communism. In 1980, they were challenged by the independent unions, who were seeking self-management, including the right to appoint managers. While the power of the unions was curtailed during the period of martial law between 1981–82, nearly two-thirds of the top managers were replaced (*Zycie Gospodarcze*, no. 18, 1989). After the lifting of military rule, the managers were subjected to renewed demands from workers. Following the accelerated erosion of communist power in 1988, many party units in the factories either voluntarily disbanded or were ousted by militant workers. As a result, industrial managers were left with even less protection against worker encroachment on their authority.[16]

The privatization process initiated under Rakowski in 1988–89 was perceived by managers, quite predictably, as a rare opportunity to shift the power balance in their favour. Taking advantage of their political connections, many enterprise managers were able to gain leverage by carving out for themselves and/or their family members the most profitable 'pieces' of their respective enterprises. These spin-off acquisitions frequently involved only small amounts of money, for the managers had succeeded in under-reporting the true value of the capital being privatized, with state funds often misappropriated in order to provide the needed cash. Nomenklatura entrepreneurs were also successful in providing state enterprises with overpriced goods and accepting payment – through double booking – for fictional deliveries.

Conversions into joint-stock companies, while offering fewer opportunities for personal gains than spin-offs, were also beneficial to managers as they greatly decentralized decision making (similar conversions took place in Hungary). The chief gain was that such companies were able to bypass state price controls, as well as benefit from lower taxes and avoid wage limits (i.e., high write-offs for the so-called social fund). Privatization under Rakowski was also used by managers as a mechanism for coping with economic imbalances, for many stocks and bonds[17] were sold by enterprises to other enterprises in order to secure supplies of services and/or goods.

This type of privatization met with strong objections from most of the opposition groups. The nomenklatura enterprises were viewed not only as economic anomalies but also, if not primarily, as a vehicle for unjustified compensation of those very individuals most responsible for Poland's economic stagnation. When the anticommunist opposition formed the Mazowiecki government, one of its first decisions was to prohibit the formation of such enterprises. In this, the main initiative came from the rejuvenated parliament, particularly from among the conservative, nationalistic factions such as the party led by Moczulski – the Confederation for Independent Poland or the Centre Agreement of Kaczynski.

Not all the former critics of communist rule have, however, opposed nomenklatura enterprises, interestingly, some of the most vocal support for 'political capitalism' has come from the party of ultraliberals (e.g., the faction led by Mikke). The ultraliberals have not shown much concern about the means by which an effective capital market is created but only with how quickly it is done. They have objected neither to nomenklatura members buying public assets, nor to anybody else acquiring stocks. They also have had no reservations about an underpriced, or even free, dispersal of shares. Who gets capital first, and at what price, is irrelevant, since once real market competition emerges, only those individuals who possess 'animalistic spirit' and are able to manage money effectively will survive.

The actual efforts made by the post-communist governments to eliminate nomenklatura enterprises have been very timid, and only a few such enterprises have been terminated. For example, of approximately forty joint-stock companies in which the party-appointed managers acquired shares, only three or four were dissolved by the end of 1991. As all enterprises have gained stronger protection through recently enacted legislation, accusations pertaining to earlier irregularities have become far more difficult to enforce. Because many of the nomenklatura enterprises have gone through various legal metamorphoses, it has often been quite difficult for the government to trace their records. Legal moves against 'nomenklatura' companies have been further subverted by the post-communist elite's inability to prevent its own members from using their recently acquired power for the purpose of securing preferential access to public assets (for more on this new, post-communist form of 'political capitalism', see Staniszkis 1991).

Factory workers

Industrial workers are another major political force in the current privatization process. Their power is the result of years of carving out an ever greater role for themselves at the factory level, successive gains frequently being institutionalized. Important elements of worker participation in micromanagement were introduced as early as 1956 under Gomulka's regime, when workers councils were established. As indicated earlier in the book, labour representation was greatly strengthened in the 1982 reform programme during Jaruzelski's tenure, while the mid-1989 decision to legalize the independent trade union Solidarity marked another peak in the expansion of labour influence. At that time, workers enjoyed effective representation through a variety of trade unions as well as by councils that had never been stronger.

Industrial workers have not only developed effective channels for promoting their economic interests but have also acquired a strong identity. In this, they have been supported by decades of communist propaganda proclaiming them to be the 'true' owners of the national wealth. A powerful impression has been etched into the social consciousness that workers have an 'implicit contract' with the party, which is merely the guardian of the workers' wealth. Years of mismanagement by the party/state apparatus have made many workers feel that it is up to them to protect public assets against massive waste. In other words, workers looked at public assets not only from an individual perspective – laying personal claims – but also from the viewpoint of a collective, consisting not only of workers as a group but also of the public at large, or the nation.

While a heterogeneous group, the workers all seemed to have expected that the economic reforms, including privatization, would not hinder their already considerable control of production. When the communist leadership of Rakowski first initiated its privatization programme, the labour opposition expressed significant reluctance. At that time, the major centres of opposition, especially the independent worker unions, continued to insist on the reform formula agreed to before the imposition of martial law in 1981, i.e., genuine self-management and public ownership.[18] Privatization under Rakowski was viewed predominantly as an assault on the worker councils, similar, in terms of its practical consequences, to the measures which followed the 'militarization' of industry during the period of martial law in 1981–82.

When Mazowiecki's government began formulating plans for privatization on a more massive scale, workers' sympathies were still centred on labour-management, and when presented with a specific programme for divestment – the rapid sales of assets (= shares) – workers reacted negatively The criticism of this scheme for a massive public offering campaign reflected in part the union's frustration that they were not closely consulted, and that while the bill promised some shares to the workers, it specifically excluded the wide use of employee stock option plans. Moreover, the bill required that the enterprises must first be transferred to the Treasury, which in turn would automatically strip the worker councils of their powers.[19]

Under the impact of worker's criticism – channelled mostly through trade unions and other formal representations – the government compromised by permitting a number of alternatives to public sales, but refused to give any preference to employee stock enterprises. A number of incentives – such as discounts on share-prices – as well as a considerable discretion in deciding on the form of privatization, this including the right to buy smaller (and medium) enterprises, were introduced.[20] These opportunities have increased workers' interest in privatization, initially mostly in leveraged buyouts, later in allowing sales of their enterprises to other parties as well (particularly from the moment the economy started recovering and the threat of massive layoffs and wage concessions considerable subsided) (Poznanski 1996)

By and large, particularly with respect to large-scale enterprises where the majority of jobs are concentrated, many workers have continued preferring to avoid privatization unless completely sure that they have a dominant voice in the proceedings. This position became evident during negotiations between the unions and Suchocka's government on the content of the 'enterprise pact.' Efforts to pass it through parliament in March 1993 failed because the government was short by a few votes mostly because one party from the ruling coalition, the National Christian Union, took a partisan position. The major objection by this party and many other forces on the opposition side was to the pact's idea of appointing foreign companies (and experts) to manage investment funds in charge of a major segment of Poland's industry, to be privatized through vouchers.

In its compromise version – presented immediately after the vote – the government held firm to the fund formula. However, it offered a financial concession to teachers, clerks, and pensioners by providing them with preference in acquiring shares in the first pool of 200 enterprises. This option seemed to the government a convenient way of meeting the Constitutional Courts' demand that the state budget compensate these groups for real wage cuts administered the year before, which, apparently, were illegal under an existing collective agreement. The government's expectation was that these critical segments of polity would be vocal supporters of the programme and that several other parties represented in the parliament would also join the proponents of the voucher scheme in the forthcoming round of voting.

The appeal of the revised programme of mass privatization was greatly undermined by an unexpected call from within the trade unions for a completely new approach. Elements of the trade union movement linked to Solidarity presented a proposal that all citizens should be issued, instead of vouchers, sizeable and identical sums of low-interest credit. This credit would be available for asset purchases of targeted enterprises by common people at their will rather than through funds. The proposal gained strong support from Walesa, who enjoyed considerable influence over this segment of the labour movement. Issuing credit could have been expected to meet with a better reception from citizens than the voucher scheme, thus promising a political payoff for Walesa. It was commonly believed that Walesa endorsed this alternative programme in order to form a presidential party, or at least to strengthen his – momentarily – dwindling popularity.

Foreign investors

The final group of contestants for state assets is capitalist investors from abroad, potentially having more to offer for asset-value maximization than any of the domestic agents – bureaucrats, workers, or managers, as they all are less experienced at putting capital to productive uses under competitive market conditions. Moreover, foreigners are better endowed, at least theoretically, with financial resources to allocate to the modernization of productive capacities.

While these advantages have been recognized by the postcommunist government, the initial preference, as already mentioned, was to channel foreign investment into joint-venture arrangements. An important economic rationale behind this decision was that the government wanted to expand Poland's capital stock rather than to merely transfer it to new hands.

Critical also to the above choice was the government's desire to use the privatization programme as an instrument whereby it could quickly enlarge the middle class, as yet insufficiently developed to support a strong market (or democratic polity). This initial bias was less a reflection of any general opposition to foreign participation in privatization than of a desire to provide 'breathing space' for the weak domestic capitalist strata during the early stages of transition to a market economy. Another important concern was to avoid creating an impression among the public that privatization meant a sell-out to outsiders and to show that, in fact, control of the domestic economy was not being transferred in excessive amounts to foreign interests (for a discussion of the question of economic sovereignty, see Kornai 1992a: 173–74).[21]

Accordingly, the post-socialist government relaxed almost all restrictions on setting up joint ventures, so that from late 1992 on, no permits for such agreements have been needed.[22] Legal limits on the maximum foreign equity participation share have been lifted as well. Since mid-1992, minimum levels on capital contribution by foreigners have been removed and foreign direct-investors have also been given a free hand in remitting profits earned in their commercial operations. At the same time, formal obstacles have been set up to foreign access to equity, including a requirement that all such purchases be approved by the government. A limit of 10 per cent on foreign acquisitions in state-owned enterprises divested through public offerings was introduced in 1990 (with the Ministry of Finance allowed to raise this limit should it find such an increase appropriate). Also, foreigners were excluded from the 1990 voucher distribution initiative (though not from operations on the secondary market once relevant shares became tradable).

This initial reluctance by the bureaucracy to involve foreigners has since been reversed, in large part because it became apparent that fast-paced privatization cannot rely on domestic agents alone. Initial transfers have also proved to bring in only limited revenues for the budget so that in 1991, the second year of privatization, $130 million in revenues was reported.[23] It was not budgetary concerns alone that were responsible for the change of attitude, but also a growing fear that without immediate economic recovery from the post-stabilization recession, labour discontent might become uncontrollable, and that inflow of foreign capital in any form – including equity acquisitions – would be helpful (not to mention the growing perception that foreign owners are more capable of coping with workers).

Unlike the state bureaucracy, industrial managers have from the very beginning been sympathetic to the transfer of state assets in their enterprises to foreign investors. Largely abandoned by the state apparatus, managers have found foreign companies a suitable replacement in their struggle to regain authority *vis-à-vis* workers. A useful strategy has been to bring in a 'front' company from abroad to cover up for actual appropriation of state assets by managers themselves. More often, efforts have been made by the managers to assist foreign agents in gaining ownership of public assets in exchange for retaining executive jobs and/or various sorts of financial satisfaction, such as salary enhancement, preferential shares, etc. (a similar practice has been common in Hungary; see Hunya 1991).

As 'insiders', managers of state-owned enterprises have been able to build enough leverage into the privatization process for potential acquisitors from abroad to take them seriously. By and large, foreign companies have been left with insufficient information to assess the value of assets open to divestment – an important exception being those companies which developed commercial contracts with relevant enterprises in the past. Managers have also proved valuable allies in securing favourable asset sales, or price conditions, given their personal connections with the state privatization bureaucracy. Last but not least, managers have been able to offer the professional skills needed to efficiently operate enterprises after they have been divested to foreign parties.

The sale of Poland's state assets to foreign buyers, on the other hand, has not been welcomed by the majority of workers, as many of their early reactions have shown. The rocky negotiations which prevented the possible foreign purchase of a Gdansk shipyard, or the rejection by workers of an Italian offer to buy a section of the helicopter enterprise in Swidnik,[24] both occurring in 1990, provide good examples. This initial resistance reflected the workers' general apprehension about the possible loss of influence in the daily decision making in their privatized enterprises, as well as fear that foreign owners might proceed with closures of whole enterprises. Workers were also suspicious of their workplaces – considered to be their implicit property – being sold to foreign buyers at a fraction of the perceived market value.

The initially strong resistance among workers to foreign acquisitions has gradually subsided, a primary reason being that many workers have found the alternative solutions impractical in the short run, given the growing threat of financial insolvency of their enterprises. Rather than oppose transfers of assets or object to sale-prices, workers have increasingly turned to bargaining over the extent of their representa-tion and job/wage packages after completion of divestment. In 1992, one of the most visible conflicts involving 'outsider' privatization was that of the copper complex in Lubin, with workers resisting the very idea of sale. However, in the case of the car plant Tychy, workers were agreeable to asset sales but spent almost half a year pressing – including through strikes – for higher compensation (determined as a per centage of total unit production costs).

Foreign investors responded to these shifting interests among domestic actors with a change in their own strategy – switching from joint ventures to equity acquisitions. This new focus has also reflected growing recognition by companies from abroad that making contribu-tions in kind to establish joint ventures is much hampered by the vacuum created in property rights. With the ambiguities of the privatization programme and disintegration of lines of command, state-owned enterprises have been left without a clearly identifiable management with whom potential foreign investors could cooperate in a joint venture format. Purchases of equity in public enterprises have thus become a useful means by which foreign investors could clarify the property structure before money is committed to targeted plants.

Summarizing this section, within a brief period, as we have shown, a complex set of forces have emerged to shape the pace and direction of state asset transfers. Many conflicting interests have clashed over the prevailing privatization model, with the state bureaucracy and man-agers (as well as foreigners) placing a high premium on rapid – compressed to a few-year period – divestment of capital in the state sector. Accordingly, serious consideration has been given to financial schemes which would minimize monetary demands on potential asset recipients, preferably private parties. The workers, in contrast, have been reluctant to support rapid privatization except for leveraged buyouts,or preferential share allocations putting assets in the hands of collectives (with the widespread expectation that privatization will meet certain standards of fairness and equitable distribution).

Early trends in public asset distribution

Grand schemes

Judging by the post-1990 experience with privatization, efforts to execute asset transfers quickly have fallen short of the government's expectations, one reason being that grand schemes – such as mass voucher distribution – on which so much hope rested, have proven difficult to implement. This voucher approach, at least initially, looked like one of the most promising to those who sought a radical departure from the state-socialist economy (good example, see Blanchard et al. 1991). The wholesale, equitable give-away of public assets seemed to offer a clean break with the confused ownership structure left behind by the communist leadership, which made it impossible to determine whose claims to property should be recognized. The concept also appeared to effectively address such practical problems as the lack of personal savings among the public and the impossibility of adequate valuation of assets in the absence of a developed capital market.

But a closer look at the free-distribution formula has revealed that while cutting through some complexities, it also poses problems. There seems to be a trade-off between equity and the efficiency of the voucher system, i.e. the ability to form strong interest in maximizing capital value. True, a society-wide distribution has the advantage of expanding the pool from which the best qualified shareholders can be identified. However, by giving assets away, the government forfeits the possibility of screening out ill-equipped actors – unprepared to make informed decisions and take reasonable risks – at an early stage of capital reallocation. Consequently, a voucher system may create scores of passive share owners, uninterested and/or incapable of ensuring that funds are prudently managed and/or that a secondary market for shares works effectively.

Importantly, it is not necessarily the case that the mass voucher dispersion has to assure an egalitarian distribution of equity ownership, and that therefore this system would be popular with the public and thus useful in building political support not only for the scheme but for the entire privatization programme as well. There is a risk, for instance, that by combining voucher dispersion with establishment of funds to manage shares, capital assets may end up in the hands of a very few. There are indications that the Czechoslovak effort to create 'democratic capitalism' through vouchers has resulted in entrusting the majority of capital wealth to a very few funds.[25] Apparently, of about 400 funds which emerged since 1991 – in a highly unregulated environment (Dyba and Svejnar 1992: 22) – about nine obtained control over 70 per cent of all vouchers issued during the first round (of two) of bidding for shares.[26]

Moreover, there are other methods of gaining workers' support for privatization than simply giving away shares or leasing state property at a nominal price. One alternative, adopted by Mexico, might have been suitable for Poland since the political scene in both countries is dominated by strong trade unions and populist sentiments. However, rather than endorse the concept of 'popular capitalism', as attempted by Poland, Mexico decided to divest state assets through conventional public offerings, with proceeds from sales put into a special fund that finances local projects – schools, hospitals, roads – in the most needy areas. Significantly, due to the strong appeal of this programme, the government's popularity in Mexico (initially under the presidency of Salinas) has been historically high.

Obviously, free distribution helps to bypass the shortage of personal savings needed to quickly sell – at market price – vast state-owned assets. However, this potential advantage becomes less relevant if a gradual, rather than radical, approach to asset divestment is adopted. In other words, the voucher scheme is not an answer to an inherent problem but rather a means of coping with a policy-set target. The voucher system is also of lesser practical value if a given economy enters into transition with hidden inflation, i.e., forced savings. This is exactly the condition which prevailed in most of the communist countries prior to 1989, and Poland, as documented earlier, was definitely in that category. Under these circumstances, shares could be offered to the public for cash – rather than free – thus helping not only to privatize the state sector but also to eliminate supply/demand imbalances (and inflationary pressures as well).

It was the choice of Poland's leadership in 1990 not only to privatize rapidly but also to combine this reform with drastic confiscatory devaluation, so that the voucher system has indeed become particularly attractive to the government. Bold stabilization efforts of 1990, as well as earlier measures by the communist regime to remove 'monetary overhang', have destroyed much of household monetary holdings, possibly even pushing these holdings below the equilibrium level. As mentioned earlier 'inflationary taxes' first shifted 'empty' money from the households to state enterprises, only to then be confiscated by the state budget. But following the 1990 stabilization, households have been rebuilding their money holdings, so that the pool of savings to be mobilized for privatization purposes has increased as well (Crane 1993a).

Even if the savings level is relatively low, there still seem to be workable alternatives to dispersing shares in state-owned enterprises for free. Financial constraint can be alternatively relaxed through credit-type facilities (for further discussion, see Kornai 1992a; Bolton and Roland 1992). One advantage of such credit-based privatization is that, if liberally applied, it would help to maximize the pool of participants while setting up a screening mechanism to weed out ill-prepared individuals. A drawback of this alternative financial scheme is that, to function well, it would require an effective banking system, free of political interference, a condition not met by post-communist Poland. However, in Hungary, when faced with a choice between long-resisted vouchers and easy credit, the government of Antall decided, in early 1993, to adopt the latter.

As far as valuation of capital is concerned, it is not clear that free-of-charge dispersion offers the most practical solution. While it is true that for successful execution of privatization based on market-type procedures – such as public offerings – a smoothly functioning capital market is needed, this is not necessarily a lesser problem in the case of voucher schemes, since it is uncertain whether such a massive dispersal of shares is capable of producing a working market quickly enough. If it does not, then masses of shares – in the absence of information for their holders to make intelligent choices – will be subject to volatility. Once trading in shares is assumed, prices may plunge, causing panic and contraction in the amount of domestic savings available for investment. Such a turnaround may also produce a political backlash and turn the public against privatization, if not the whole reform programme (Czekaj and Sopocko 1991).

Given these numerous concerns and ambiguities, it is not surprising that the concept of voucher privatization has undergone considerable evolution. In its simple, early version, the give-away privatization scheme was one in which the state first converts enterprises into joint-stock companies, and then allocates bundles of vouchers to citizens. These vouchers are next converted by the owners into shares in the enterprises of their choice within the pool of enterprises targeted by the state for compulsory voucher privatization and shares received in this way to be traded on a secondary market or liquidated (for cash) on demand. Because such a simple version has been found inadequate, other schemes along similar general lines have been developed so that of all the countries of Eastern Europe, Poland has possibly gone through the most protracted process of continuously revising the original scheme and making it increasingly complex.

Although Poland's initial plan was to force state enterprises to divest, during Olszewski's prime ministership, the government concluded that rather than try to impose its voucher privatization projects on enterprises, it was time to negotiate with both workers and managers. At the end of 1992, the concept of a collective agreement – called an 'enterprise pact' – was formulated, under which employee representatives were invited to define for themselves which 'route' of divestment to follow, with the provision that if no choice was made within the time allowed, then the Ministry of Privatization would be free to go ahead with its own selection. A strong representation of workers on boards of privatized enterprises was assured, and negotiations on the privatization format were to be combined with talks about financial restructuring to help enterprises recover from recession (i.e., bad-debt clearance and tax adjustments).

Initially, under the government of Mazowiecki, voucher recipients were expected to have substantial freedom in identifying shares they would like to own and if so desired turn for assistance to institutional intermediaries – funds. The original idea was, thus, to allow voucher holders to either entrust vouchers to funds or to select shares directly in the enterprises of their choice (as under the 1992 Czechoslovak voucher plan). Later, fearing that such freedom could lead to excessive volatility, the government of Bielecki decided that all individual shares must be administered by a handful of investment funds. According to the early plans of Bielecki's cabinet, all voucher holders would be allowed to freely choose among individual funds but the government later decided to offer all citizens an equal amount of shares in each fund.

Over time, the flexibility allowed to managers of funds has been reduced as well, in order to establish further safeguards against speculative fluctuations of share prices. According to the late-1992 version of the voucher programme, shares in the funds would be owned for a year by the Treasury and only then would they be exchanged for vouchers. Contrary to earlier plans, these funds would not be allowed to bid for shares in the enterprises of their choice but instead would begin with portfolios selected by the government. In addition, funds would not be allowed to own majority stake in any single enterprise – a modification intended to prevent collusion between funds and enterprises, where they monopolize pricing and drive up share prices at the expense of consumers.

Even with these numerous changes, the programme for mass privati-zation through vouchers still failed to materialize six years after it was first conceptualized by the post-communist reformers. While the gov-ernment has been adding enterprises to the list scheduled for voucher-conversion, the programme gained parliamentary approval only in mid-1993. At the end of 1993, a total of 183 enterprises which had been turned into Treasury property for the purpose of mass privatization still awaited appropriate legislation.[27] In the meantime, they were formally controlled by state-appointed boards, largely indifferent to ensuring the proper working of respective enterprises. The government succeeded in implementing the programme only in 1995 when the substantive work on naming investment funds and deciding on the final scheme of voucher distribution had begun, so that the whole scheme had a chance at best to be fully executed some time in 1996.

'Spontaneous' privatization

The alternative form of privatization, sales of asset by the state, has also proved impossible to implemented in the form originally conceived, i.e., by fast and state-controlled divesture through public offerings and direct sales, as in Great Britian and Chile. In early 1990, this preferred method of privatization was initiated with a few public sales, with many offerings being oversubscribed (as some of the most profitable enterprises were included in the sale). Still, progress was very slow, so that by the end of 1991 the central administration had sold only eleven enterprises through public offerings and another eighteen to selected investors. By the end of 1992, the cumulative number of sales increased to fifty-two cases, with twelve of these falling in the category of public offerings. Only a few more cases were added to these figures in 1993, and in 1994, when several other were added, the total number of such enterprises reached 141 (Poznanski 1996).

The initial insistence on such centralized transfer was a response not only to the underlying reform philosophy but to the political uproar against nomenklatura enterprises that arose under the last communist government of Rakowski (see Poznanski 1992b). The first Polish non-communist cabinet, headed by Mazowiecki, decided to introduce legal limits to such transfers. However, the opportunity for 'insider' appro-priations had not been eliminated completely, as provisions were made within the law to allow for 'insider' buy outs. The original purpose of this method – conventionally called 'liquidation' – was, as mentioned before, to create an avenue for the dismantlement of state enterprises and the sale of their valuable property – machinery, land, and buildings – to new companies or, alternatively, its lease with option to buy (see Sachs 1991, 1992).

Hungary, despite the political objections raised in some corners, has from the very beginning made privatization through leveraged buyouts even more accessible than has Poland. Enterprises have been given the right to initiate such 'inside' sales with minimal supervision, though the government has carefully tried to prevent illegitimate sales. To facilitate this process, the State Privatization Agency introduced a simplified plan in 1991 to assist the sale of 437 small enterprises. In mid-1992, the government made this so-called 'spontaneous' privatization even easier by giving private consultants (including foreign consulting firms) free rein to sell medium-sized state enterprises as well. Of a total of 2000 state enterprises, consulting firms were given responsibility for the quick divestment of 278 enterprises.

After initial reservations, Poland's government also eventually adopted a more favourable attitude towards 'spontaneous' privatization. Besides an overriding interest in speeding up the asset transfer, the decision to decentralize this process reflected the government's inability to tame the enormous demand for capital at the enterprise level. Pressures from local authorities have also proven difficult to resist, as they have typically operated in tandem with manager/ worker groups. The central bureaucracy has not, however, been overtaken by particular interests at the regional level; rather, this has been a relatively orderly process, at least in comparison with post-1991 Russia, which also engaged in 'spontaneous' privatization. Here, privatization has taken this course basically because the state apparatus at the federal level has disintegrated (the transfer taking mostly the form of 'piracy' (Hanson 1990; Tedstrom 1993; Lane 1995)).

With a more permissive approach, the 'liquidation' process in Poland has become an important avenue for divestment – at least in terms of number of enterprises involved – and a viable complement to other methods where viable – competent and solvent – outside investors have been available. To be more accurate, this privatization through 'liquidation' has proceeded through two principal channels – one covering profit-making and the other deficit-ridden enterprises (see Mujzel 1992). About 1,200 enterprises, all having less than 500 employees, had been processed through liquidation procedures as of mid-1992. Of this total, 700 enterprises were declared bankrupt and stakes (20 per cent of book value) in 500 were sold to collectives, with managers becoming 'strategic investors' in 365 cases.

Since mid-1992, the preference among buyers has shifted slightly away from obtaining a lease (accounting, in 1991, for about 80 per cent of concluded transfers) to the outright purchase of capital stock in part or entirely. Initially, most of the cases involved insiders – with strong representation by managers – from the leveraged enterprises, but, later, partnerships with individuals from outside became more common. Many of the outsiders have been coming from the newly enriched private sector group, offering the cash needed to make payments to the government. Payments have been a principal barrier from the beginning, as few collectives have been in a position to finance the required one-fifth of total asset value. Another obstacle has been caused by the fact that banks have been taken back by the confusing dual ownership status of enterprises so leveraged.

'Spontaneous' privatization has become such an active method of transfers in large part because of the considerable opportunity this underformalized procedure has provided for below-value acquisition of equity. This procedure has also been popular because of its low transaction costs, i.e., ability to negotiate conditions of lease/sale within a narrow circle of interested parties. While the complaint has often been made that 'insider' buyouts lead to the retention of old-time managers – who gained their experience under state-planning – one should not overlook the fact that not all of their knowledge is useless. Much of the 'tacit knowledge' needed for proper daily operation of privatized entities, which the former nomenklatura possess, is not readily replaceable, or duplicable, by newcomers.

Foreign acquisitions

Initially, foreign investors tried to acquire equity through public offerings (e.g., Swarzedz furniture factory, Wedel candy plant, Polcolor TV-tube producer), but with slow progress in those sales – as reported earlier – they turned increasingly to direct negotiations with branches of the government (i.e., the Ministry of Finance or Ministry of Privatization). The advantage of such an approach was not only the greater simplicity of direct sales and lack of equity participation ceilings, but the opportunity to negotiate asset transfers with agencies also responsible for many related decisions (e.g., tax holidays, credit facilities, sales licenses). Consequently, while numerically, in terms of units transferred, 'spontaneous' privatization has become the dominant venue, by volume standards – size of equity – it is the foreign investors who have emerged as the first major equity benefactors.

Statistical data on foreign involvement in Poland's privatization has not been very accurate, but there can be little doubt that, at least with respect to legal transfers, foreign interest has indeed played the key role. Of the fifty-two state-owned enterprises sold both through public offerings and direct sales by mid-1992, as many as twenty-eight involved foreign participation. Importantly, many of these enterprises exceeded $100,000 in sale value, with the total of such larger enterprises in the pool equal to thirty-two. Among them was Kwidzyn paper mill, which attracted about $100 million – at the time the single largest state-equity acquisition. Since then, however, a few more, some even larger, transactions have been made (e.g., Warszawa steel mill which went for $200 million, or Fiat's purchase of Tychy car plant for $800 million).

Purchases of equity in state-owned enterprises have been concentrated in a few industries, among them in power-generating equipment. ASEA Brown-Boveri has managed to acquire stakes in a large segment of this sector (including the mid-1992 acquisition of equity in Elfa, Lodz). A large share of the cosmetic industry – controlled by mono-producer Pollena – has been sold to foreign investors as well. With the sale of the second largest (after Kwidzyn) paper mill in Swieck, this branch of industry has also become dominated by foreign interests. It seems that by 1995, most of the entire motor vehicle industry was targeted for foreign control as well; in addition to the already mentioned sale of Tychy small-car plant, the government agreed in that year to sell the sedan-car plant in Warszawa to Daewoo and the truck and bus factory in Jelcz, and another plant making delivery cars, in Poznan, to a German-controlled company.

In almost all cases, foreign acquisitions of state property have involved majority equity. Most of the foreign companies have been able to ensure from the start at least 80 per cent equity participation (e.g., 90 per cent in the case of Tychy car plant, and 80 per cent in the case of Kwidzyn). In those cases where foreign investors were forced – or opted – to assume minority participation, subsequent purchase of shares allowed many of them to raise their portion above 51 per cent (e.g., this was the strategy adopted by Gerber in the baby food plant in Rzeszow, and Pepsi with respect to the Wedel plant). Even in those sales which resulted in minority ownership, the foreign companies typically managed to negotiate an instant controlling vote on the board of directors (a good example being Pepsi's contract with Wedel).

Increasing interest among foreign companies in Poland's equity has proven instrumental in accelerating the inflow of capital to Poland. At the end of 1991, the volume of foreign direct investment was under $300 million, a miniscule amount for a country of Poland's size. However, in mid-1992 foreign investment totalled about $800 million (with 23 per cent coming from Germany) and with the investments which followed, this figure reached $1600 million in early 1993. Of this amount, at least two-thirds could be attributed to equity sales, a pattern similar to that of Hungary – which happened to attract relatively more foreign capital than Poland.[28] In 1991, sales to for-eigners generated $700 million – not all of the income collected by the Hungarian government – which represented 60 per cent of the total value of foreign investment made in that year.

Another indication of the key role played by foreign investors in Poland is that this type of asset transfer became a major source of revenue from privatization. By mid-1992, about one half of the income from asset sales – equal to $250 million – came from the transfer of the above mentioned Kwidzyn mill. If all revenues from sales to foreigners through the rest of 1992 were added, this share would reach about four-fifths. As such, these proceeds have become an important means of balancing the state budget. This pattern of privatization revenues is similar to that reported by Hungary. Here, in 1991, the State Privatiza-tion Agency received about $420 million in proceeds, of which 90 per cent came from sales to foreigners (equally high was the respective per centage for the 1992 revenues, with the total amount of proceeds increasing to more than $800 million).

Private sector

With privatization primarily benefiting foreign investors, the expan-sion of the domestic private sector has to a large degree been left to indigenous growth, i.e., 'entries' by private agents and expansion of already established entities. In other words, in the early stage of full-scale transition to capitalist markets, the two major sources of increase in the private segment of the economy have been through transfer of assets to foreigners and independent capital formation by domestic agents. Interestingly, the critical role of this independent expansion of private activities has been as much a surprise to the reformers as the central role assumed by foreign investors in divestment of public capital. This is because the original programmes assumed that asset transfers – and not the independent entries – would be the dominant source of internal growth in the private sector.

Separating these two sources is complicated, since statistics do not distinguish newly established private businesses in terms of their origin. However, one can detect the actual importance of independently created private business by comparing the number of new private enterprises with that of privatized ones. While the latter has been relatively low – even with smaller units included – as indicated before, the former has been extremely high. At the end of 1991 – before major purchases by foreigners were made – there were already 1.5 million private businesses, triple the level reported in 1989. When referring to these figures, we have to keep in mind that data on private businesses is not very reliable, as many businesses – to avoid taxes – do not register, and a certain number of registered units represent 'front' organizations, set up solely for speculative purposes.

Another indication of the great vigour of capital formation by private agents is the tremendous increase in individually owned businesses, presumably using mostly personal savings, including money pooled by family members. Of the 1.5 million private businesses registered in 1991, there were less than 70,000 non-individual businesses. Of these, about 45,000 were joint stock and limited liability companies, 17,000 cooperatives, and 4,800 joint ventures (Frydman *et al.* 1993: 174). The domination of individual businesses itself suggests that the private sector has been composed mostly of small entities. Within the category of non-individual private property, there were, in 1991, only 2,100 private enterprises where the workforce exceeded 50 (while there were still 319 state-owned enterprises which reported at least 2,000 workers *ibid.*: 175).

The combined effect of privatization and independent 'entries' has produced a very rapid increase in the overall size of the private sector. While it is debatable whether privatization itself has been successful or not, the growth in private activities – and the shift away from a state-dominated economy – has been unquestionably a major success. According to official data, employment in the non-agricultural private sector increased from 1.8 million in 1989 to 3.0 million in 1991, or from 15.8 per cent of the total to 26.3 per cent (for other details see: Mujzel 1992: 16). If the cooperative sector – much reformed since 1982 – is added, then the non-state employment figures are 3.9 million and 4.5 million for respective years, a change from 30.9 per cent of the total to 39.5 per cent (table 8.1).[29]

In 1991, the non-agricultural private sector (with cooperatives counted as well) provided about 24 per cent of total output and in construction alone – 55 per cent. In the retail trade, the share of the private sector had already reached about 80 per cent by the end of 1990

Table 8.1 *Expansion of private sector in Poland, 1989–1993*

	1989	1990	1991	1992	1993
	a) National income produced (in per cent)				
State	69.9	67.7	58.0	50.5	44.7
Private	19.2	32.2	41.0	45.4	47.5
Cooperative, etc.	9.1	–	–	–	–
	b) Total output (in per cent)				
Private share in					
Industry	4.8	11.6	21.3	31.4	36.4
Agriculture	79.0	68.1	–	83.8	88.1
Domestic Trade	4.8	26.3	46.7	86.0	97.2
Consumer Services	42.4	–	–	–	–
	c) Employment (in millions)				
Non-agriculture	12.6	11.6	11.4	–	–
State	8.7	7.7	6.9	6.7	6.0
Non-State	3.9	3.9	4.5	–	4.7
Private	1.8	2.3	3.0	–	3.7
Cooperative	2.1	1.6	1.5	–	1.0
Agriculture	5.0	4.8	4.7	–	3.9
State	0.6	0.5	0.4	–	0.2
Non-State	4.4	4.3	4.3	–	3.7
Private	4.1	4.1	4.1	–	3.7
Cooperative	0.3	0.3	0.3	–	0.0

Source: *Rocznik Statystyczny, GUS*, Warsaw (various years); Slay (1993 table 2.2); Ministry of Privatization data.

(Frydman *et al.* 1993: 174). Private business has not made such significant inroads in industry as it has in the construction or retail trades. This bias against setting up business in industry – requiring larger units of capital and more specific skills – is reflected in the fact that at the conclusion of 1991, of the 1.5 million private businesses listed, only about 340,000 operated in industry (*ibid.*). Still, even with this relatively slower growth, the private sector increased its share of total output in industry from 4.8 per cent in 1989 to 11.6 per cent in 1990, and to 21.3 per cent in 1991 (table 8.1).

The small scale of private industry operations, while not surprising given the early stage of the transition process, is also reflective of enormous legal uncertainties. One of the major problems has been the weak legal protection of private property, in part due to the unresolved question of equity claims by former owners. The reprivatization issue was undertaken by the legislature during Mazowiecki's government, and then intensely pursued by the government of Olszewski. His cabinet was the first to decide that a law on reprivatization must precede any massive transfer of state assets to private hands through vouchers or other means. To avoid legal battles over property, pre-ference was given by the government to partial compensation – rather than full restitution – of the original owners. By mid-1996, the reprivatization question was still unresolved (as in Hungary, where sales of small-scale state entities were also halted; see Bartlett 1992).

An additional barrier to the development of a healthy private sector has been the difficulty of executing tight commercial contracts – the foundation of a genuine market economy. Aside from the still small numbers in the legal profession and their limited experience in commer-cial law, law enforcement has also lacked the capability to persecute breaches of contract among private parties. Under the circumstances, spot transactions rather than routine ones based on written contracts have dominated activities in the private sector. Bilateral cash transac-tions have been most common within the country, even in the case of large scale transactions, and sizeable sums have been taken abroad to purchase imports or deposit in foreign banks. A corollary has been the tendency for private business to engage in operations promising high short term payoffs including illegal or underreported operations (whose scope possibly doubled in recent years).

Summary

The process of privatization has been driven by conflicting forces, with the state being the initial central figure, or animator, pushing for a rapid divestment while looking for allies among foreign investors. During this first stage, the state's principal concern was for the process not to be captured by powerful internal forces and, in addition, there was a strong sense that bridging foreign investors would be the surest way to quickly put public assets into effective uses. Public offerings, which the state chose as its preferable privatization technique, had clearly favored foreigners over domestic buyers as strategic investors. The governments, with roots in the anti-communist opposition, were also willing to offer great concessions to foreigners, not only pricewise but also in terms of assumed liabilities and assurances of market leadership (the most publicized being the case of Fiat car-maker allowed to fix prices in order to reach certain profit margin on internal sales).

This route of privatization has been, however, slowed down by the insiders – managers and workers, once they managed to assure their full participation in the divestment proceedings. In the second stage, privatization has been largely turned over to insiders, who in most cases decided to acquire assets for themselves through leveraged buyouts. This has been done at discounted prices, as reflected in minor revenues provided by that procedure to the state budget. Costs to insiders have been further reduced by the fact that many of the enterprises failed to make payments as agreed in the buyout contracts. With the control gained over the privatization process, insiders have also been able to negotiate favorable conditions for the above mentioned direct sales of their enterprises to strategic investors from outside, both through the access to preferential (initially discounted and through securing their jobs (as well as wage and salary increases).

Finally, during the third phase, the center of gravity in the privatization process has moved away from insiders (who earlier replaced the state in that role) to new players – holdings of domestic origin. Low prices of assets have made it attractive to many financially sound larger entities – commercial banks and enterprises – to engage in equity acquisitions, either for purely financial gain or, more often, to expand their economic standing (= power). Leading producers in many industrial sectors have decided to use this opportunity to reestablish their most viable of old ties with suppliers and customers – often from among the former members of the once banned so-called associations. This has been accomplished largely outside of the state's view, through swapping of debts for equity or an outright purchase of shares in other enterprises. But this time, the state, in the hand of the post-1993 coalition, has been favorable to this active involvement of domestic organizations in the divestment proceedings.

The process of privatization – under the changing leadership of various interest groups – has turned out to be the most complex element of the whole institutional change, and this explains why that process has been a relatively slow one. While the original expectation by the Mazowiecki reform team was that most of the assets will be privatized in three–four years, six years later most of the assets have remained in the state's hands, particularly in industry and banking. By mid-1995, about one fifth of the capital assets in industry has been privatized, with more than 4,000 enterprises still awaiting privatization (and most of the large-scale enterprises included in that pool). Moreover, the state has retained considerable holdings in many divested companies, including those listed on the securities market. More than two third of bank assets has been retained by the state, with all but one of the large-scale commercial banks falling in that category. In ownership terms, the economy at this point could be, at best, called a mixed one, though the direction of change has clearly been towards the one dominated by the private ownership.

Under these circumstances, the initial idea of turning rapid privatization into an instrument for creating a security-based capital market has not materialized (for additional analysis see: Corbett and Mayer 1991; Poznansk 1996). A small number of enterprises has been brought to the securities market with the total capitalization at about three per cent of the gross national product by the end of 1994. So far, securitization has been mainly a method for raising budgetary revenues through sales of shares rather than a vehicle for raising fresh capital. The latter practice has began since the 1993 bull market but the amounts of capital raised through new share issues have been small. At least small by comparison to the credit issued by the commercial banks, which in the meantime have managed to consolidate their position as major suppliers of funding for the purpose of investing. Rather than seeing a shift to the Anglo-Saxon model of the capital market, one finds this sector evolving towards a continental model, with additional evidence coming most recently, when the banks have engaged in large-scale cross shareholding with their customers.

Without any doubt, most of the progress in making the economy more private has been accomplished not due to the official privatization but rather because of incredible number of mostly small-scale entries by private actors. This has happened with very little stimulation from the state, which has simply removed legal obstacles to setting up such businesses. This expansion of the private sphere has also been facilitated by the state's tolerance of massive tax evasions, for much of the new growth in that area has gone underground. The private sector is not only shifting its tax burden to state-owned enterprises, but it takes advantage of the latter entities through a number of corrupt mechanisms. Most of the current financial abuses indeed occur in the contacts between the private and the public sector. All these transfers to the private sector have a positive impact on its further expansion but at the same time they proliferate certain pathological behaviors, which, if prolonged for an extended period, may permanently distort the emerging capitalist market.

9   The paradox of continuity in change

Building on our empirical findings about the pattern of post-1989 developments as well as on previous determinations on earlier years going back to 1970, this final chapter of the book attempts to offer a new, broader perspective on Poland's development – seen as an important case in the region. The initial phase of Gierek's import-led economic strategy and the period of Jaruzelski's anti-recession policy, as well as the most recent stage of radical reforms by postcommunist leaders, might look like distinct, isolated events because so many major changes occured in each of them. This might seem particularly true with respect to the post-1989 years that are viewed by many economists and political scientists as a sort of revolution, but even here one can find a great amount of artefacts from the past. Our analysis in the book indicates, that in many respects all these stages form an integrated whole, which is best captured by the title phrase – protracted transition.

We make an effort to show most critical elements of this continuity in change and not of mechanical continuity – repetition of the past, for this is exactly what we have found in our examination of Poland between 1970 and 1994. It is the stress on continuity in change that distinguishes our own approach from those that are offered – or implied – by both the totalitarian or modernization schools (more see Janos 1986). The totalitarian perspective focuses on continuity while assuming the communist system to be stationary, i.e., unable to change, whereas the latter – i.e., modernization – theory centres on change while at the same time dispenses with history, i.e., continuity. In our own evolutionary approach (for more, see Poznanski, 1995b and 1995e), continuity and change go hand in hand, in fact, social change is seen here as not possible without elements of continuity, because without the latter social processes turns into chaos. Also, thanks to change, elements of the past can be extended despite the altered context within which they happen to operate.

Evidence of continuity in change is presented below by revisiting all the major thematic projects or lines of discourse that make up the bulk of the book, beginning with that addressing the issue of growth fatigue, i,e., momentum loss and increased instability. When all facts are gathered together, it becomes clear not only that symptoms of that fatigue are detectable throughout most of that period but that this turn in performance can be traced to one and the same general source. This source is in the systemic sphere, though it is not, as claimed by a number of economists, institutional rigidity that is at fault. Rather, as our evidence shows, the economic system has been subject to frequent change but this change has produced various weak forms of property rights as well as coordination that have diminished both incentives for expansion and ability to adjust to unexpected – positive or negative – events.

Further indication of continuity in change comes from the line of discourse that deals with the possible connections between the economic system's evolution and political background, i.e., with the political economy of Poland's development. This part of our case study reveals that not only, as just mentioned, has the economic system – seen as a combination of property rights and coordination method – been undergoing change, but so has the political structure, and while the economic system has been weakened, so has the state power. By analogy, thus, one could argue that during the period analyzed the political structure has also assumed various weak forms. These two, as claimed by us, parallel changes are interconnected, because weakening of the state has caused serious problems with both enforcement of property rights and effective coordination. Thus, while both these systems, economic and political, have been undergoing change, the mechanism causing the growth fatigue in all those years has remained the same.

Finally, we encounter the same pattern of continuity in change in our discovery that the lengthy sequence of weak economic – but also political – systems mentioned above meant much more than the deconstruction of communism: it also meant the reconstruction of capitalism. This kind of shift from one general system to another is called in comparative economics 'transition', to separate it from the changes within a given system, that are respectively called 'reform'. It is often said that such a transition to capitalism started only in mid-1989, with the departure of the communist party and the return to free elections. But our study demonstrates that this process of transition has been underway at least from 1970, the staring point of our work. Even with the unquestionable acceleration in systemic change triggered by the post-1989 reforms, this process has not yet been completed. With many elements of the past continuing unchanged or only partially changed, the overall (social) system has assumed yet another transitory – mixed – form.

Alternative explanatory models

We will begin our summary remarks on continuity in change by testing a number of theories that have been developed to account for the peculiarities of Poland's economic growth. Work on these theories was greatly stimulated by Poland's plunge into an economic downturn in 1979–82 which came as a major surprise to theoretical economists. By that time, the view that the state-planned economies were crisis-proof had already been disproved in a number of insightful studies (see: Bauer 1978; Kolodko 1989). Still, the size of the actual decline in production as well as the dimensions of external imbalance and domestic instability were well in excess of what these theories pre-dicted. While the planners' inability to stabilize the economy perma-nently was recognized, it was nevertheless assumed that they had the tools needed to prevent major disruptions in production and suppress inflation as well. In the face of the 1979–82 crisis in Poland, economists have had to rethink the existing paradigms in order to grasp the nature of this development.

Foreign indebtedness

Among the many theories explaining Poland's economic difficulties is one claiming that Gierek's regime made an enormous mistake by borrowing far more than the country could manage to repay. Pouring massive amounts of Western credit into a fundamentally inefficient economy, unable to generate enough exports from the foreign money invested, might have been expected to result in payment difficulties. Thus, in a cyclical fashion, the economy had to pay for its early deficit – financed rapid advances with subsequent decline in production caused by debt repayments. According to this theory, Poland's economy went into a more damaging cycle than did the rest of Eastern Europe because of its far more aggressive borrowing on the interna-tional market (Portes 1981; Montias 1982; Fallenbuchl 1984).

The theory presents the excessive debt accumulation by Poland as a possible explanation of the two main features of the 1979–82 crisis – collapse in production and rise in inflation. The fact that this economic crisis was compounded of these two elements is seen here as quite predictable, for this pattern is typical of most heavily indebted countries, whether state-run or not. In those economies a sudden reduction in foreign lending and/or outflows of national product to meet foreign obligations leave an economy with less to invest in equipment modernization and in output expansion. 'Leakage' of resources abroad to service lenders also tends to push state budgets into deficits which have to be monetized, this leading to additional inflation with further negative effects on production expansion.

Gierek's Poland, as we demonstrate in the book, was indeed aggressive in borrowing abroad – and in importing Western machinery of advanced 'vintage' – if absolute levels are considered, but was not the most credit-driven economy in the region if this involvement is measured on a per capita basis. Moreover, some econometric tests of macroeconomic models conducted by others suggest that, rather than hurting the economy, Western imports may have had a positive impact on Poland's productivity, and thus on total output, so that Poland not only borrowed more but also grew faster, this by itself providing a basis – supplies – for penetrating foreign markets (as long, of course, as the expansion of production was not biased in favour of nontradables). Our own statistical analysis demonstrates that during 1971–79, of all East European countries, Poland probably registered the greatest progress in building up export capabilities suitable for penetrating the highly competitive markets in the developed West. In many respects, Poland emerged with a more formidable export potential than the traditional leaders in hard-currency exports, i.e., Czechoslovakia and East Germany, with the former clearly borrowing less than Poland. Hungary showed a trade advance on Western markets – both in terms of gains in market shares and in unit-value levels – closer to those of Poland, while pursuing a borrowing policy which could also be described as aggressive. This would suggest that Western imports prepared Poland (and Hungary) for servicing, however painfully, their foreign debts.

Without denying that Poland allowed a too rapid debt buildup, our investigation implies that the persistence of her huge debt was less the result of lacking a good supply of hard currency exports than of her inability to mobilize this potential for foreign destinations. This seems to have been the case both during the 1979–82 crisis, and in the post-1982 period until the collapse of communist rule, though not always for the same reasons. At the earlier stage it was a combination of

administrative paralysis and wide-spread labour discontent that undermined exports. In the latter phase, Poland's exports to hard
currency markets, as our data reveals, were hurt by both Western
sanctions (e.g., lack of trade credits) and Soviet demands for hard
(sellable for dollars) Polish goods. Even more important was Poland's
official policy of giving high priority to supplying the domestic market,
in order to calm the political fury of the workers.

With this policy, the last communist governments were unable to
put the brakes on the growing size of foreign debt but this does not
mean that servicing it was an even a greater drag on the economy than
it had been at the outset of the 1979–82 crisis. While debt burden
continued to be an obstacle to both solid growth and stability, its role
in provoking the 1989 crisis was in fact rather secondary or marginal.
Unlike in the years leading to the previous crisis, this time there was no
sudden accumulation of payments, though their level was still well in
excess of the actual payments made. Nor there was there this time any
desire on the part of the government to honour all financial obligations
like that shown by Gierek's regime. Rakowski's government had little
concern for sanctions – a halt on fresh credits – from Western financial
institutions for such were already solidly in place and because credit
sanctions were largely politically motivated, so that the payoff for
more diligent servicing of debt was limited.

When in 1990 the economy entered into an even deeper crisis, this
again had little to do with the foreign debt burden, and less than the
problems encountered by the economy in 1989. Welcomed by Western
politicians, the first postcommunist government of Mazowiecki was in
a position favorable enough to unilaterally suspend payments. Other
forms of financial assistance to back up its radical economic reforms
were provided as well, including a large sum for the purpose of
backing up currency stabilization. Partial repayment was eventually
resumed but with only a few incentives to make the best possible
effort, this because in the meantime the government engaged in
negotiations on official debt reduction. Even more important were the
parallel talks with the commercial lenders, because of the size of the
commercial part of the total debt and also because, unlike the offical
debt, this segment had been serviced by Poland throughout 1989.

The role of foreign debt has become even less important since 1993,
when after lengthy negotiations Poland managed to obtain its first
substantial reduction in its official debt. Left unserviced for years, the
official debt had not bled the economy of resources but it had a
negative impact on its ability to rejoin the international financial

market. To return to that market, Poland also needed some resolution of its commercial debt, and it got it in 1994 (through a Brady-type scheme facilitated with credit lines from the World Bank). The second round of reduction in official debt combined with the reduction in the commercial debt brought the total gross debt in 1994 to $41.9 billion from $47.2 billion in 1993. Due to a parallel increase in currency reserves, the net foreign debt went down from 43.1 billion in 1993 to 35.9 billion in 1994, and the large – unexpected – raise in the 1995 currency reserves caused the net debt to further fall.

Obsolete structure

An alternative to the argument that Poland's problems, as manifested in the 1979–82 crisis, were 'cyclical' is that the economy may have been suffering instead from a 'structural crisis'. Brada and Montias (1984) forcefully argued that the crisis was to a large degree caused by Poland's inability to change its production structure under Gierek's import-led policy. They made a similar point based on a case study of Poland's industrial policies during Gierek's period and in a separate analysis Czechoslovakia was found to have permitted its obsolete structure of industry to have been extended as well. The authors established, however, an important exception in the case of Bulgaria, which apparently used its import-led strategy to focus on a few new export-oriented sectors of production.

It is often asserted that this apparent rigidity of the production structure is a direct result of the intense politicization of economics that occured in Soviet-type societies. Chirot (1991) stresses that the communist parties, when in control of economics, were driven by an ideology designed for the early stages of industrialization, when heavy industries dominated. Since the ideology was not allowed to change, economic efforts continued to be centred on sectors which stopped producing strong 'linkage' effects (in the Rostowian, or Hirschmanian sense). Adding to this rigidity was the fact that powerful party 'lobbies' which were built during the first years of rapid industrialization, when heavy industry was favoured, continued to monopolize power and successfully applied this power to assure priority treatment for their sectors.

In this structuralist theory, the growth slowdown in Poland is said to be caused by the high capital- (and material-) intensity of the dominant heavy industries. This choice of industries in the early post-war phase created extremely high demand for investment funds at the expense of individual consumption. But there was a limit to how far society could be inspired or coerced by propaganda to sacrifice personal consumption for the sake of building a costly industrial base. When pressures for increased wages and consumption by households began eating into investment funds, as they did in the late Gierek period, the rate of growth of these capital-intensive sectors lost momentum, and accordingly the national economy slowed down as well.

The overextended state priority given to heavy industries may also have been a factor in Poland's problems with debt repayment. If Poland's industry was built in direct opposition to its comparative advantage, then it was inevitable that repayment of debts would be difficult. Poland would have to compete in products which did not make intense use of those production factors with which the economy was well endowed. Gaining access to foreign markets would then be jeopardized and there would be a need to undercut prices – provide subsidies – for exports, with the result that their efficiency would suffer. Under these conditions, Poland would, of course, have to sacrifice more domestic resources for debt repayment, and with this, the need to 'tax' the population through inflation would intensify.

However, while there is little doubt that Poland's problems have been in part 'structural', it is less clear that allocative patterns were the major cause of the 1979–82 crisis. This crisis took place at the end of a massive investment expansion, which, as we have indicated earlier, was in large part geared to imported superior technology concentrated in a few not necessarily capital (or energy) intensive areas – among them automatic washing machines, petrochemicals, and passenger cars (but not in machine-tools). Besides, if import-driven Poland was really struck by a structural crisis during 1979–82, why would the conservative importers, such as Bulgaria or Czechoslovakia, be spared such a crisis?

In addition, when judging Gierek's economic strategy, one should keep in mind that the structural problems which the regime encountered at the end of its tenure were not all self-inflicted. With the information available at the outset of import-led growth, the regime was generally correct, for instance, in giving priority to such industries as petrochemicals and steel-making. Rapid expansion of the economy required a sizeable increase in the capacities of these two sectors, unless the country was ready to accept large-scale imports of both types of products. However, with the first oil-price shock of 1973, and then the second one in 1979, the cost structure of these two energy-intensive industries deteriorated, making questionable the rationale behind the original choices. Given the unpredictability of this price shock, the true measure of rationality for the planners was rather the speed and smoothness of their adjustment to the new cost structure.

That Poland did not respond to the first oil shock immediately, but continued with the expansion of energy-intensive production for another few years, was to a degree justifiable because of the artificial prices adopted by the CMEA. In response to world market price changes, the CMEA members agreed that prices for Soviet oil/gas exported to the bloc partners would not be fully adjusted to the new world prices (see Poznanski 1988b). While cushioning the impact of higher energy prices, the agreed-upon lagged price formula created an illusion that Eastern Europe could continue expanding energy-intensive production, like earlier mentioned steel-making and petrochemicals. At the same time, Western Europe was curtailing capacities in these sectors (with the excess supply of related capital goods being shipped to Eastern Europe).

The positive trend in upgrading the technological level of production lasted only through the period of large-scale imports of machinery and was suddenly interrupted by the 1979–1982 economic crisis. While before the crisis Poland benefited from a large-scale net inflow of resources, following the crisis a sizable net ouflow of resources occured. For one, fresh western credits were not forthcoming while partial servicing of the foreign debt was taking place. Moreover, lagged prices set for Soviet oil and gas increased sharply, temporarily surpassing the world market level, this change causing a substantial terms-of-trade loss for Poland. This multiple outflow of resources left Poland with reduced means to allocate in maintenance as well as expansion of capital stock and with less ability to import technology (licences and/or machinery) to support both dimensions of the investment process (see Poznanski 1989b).

This reversal of trend around the time of the 1979–82 crisis had negative long-term consequences for the economy but it would be rather difficult to argue that the aging of industry during the post-1982 elusive recovery should be viewed as the principal cause of the next crisis – that of 1989. With the partial withdrawal from the world market, the national economy found itself under less pressure to upgrade its technological level (with shipments of lower-end and natural resource-intensive goods providing the majority of revenues for servicing the foreign debt). This aging process had a more detrimental impact on the domestic market because it left consumers with impoverished goods from which to chose. The years of import-led policy had unquestionably a strong demonstration effect on consumers so that this new situation caused a considerable amount of dissatisfaction among consumers, thus contributing to political ferment and increasing demands for major systemic change.

The crisis of 1989–1991, similar to the earlier one, resulted in further technological deterioration of industry by bringing investment to an even lower level and pushing imports to their smallest volume in years. However, on one important account, the 1989–91 crisis differed from its predecessor. Unlike the previous one, this crisis had a positive impact on the elimination of the least viable (in technological terms as well) units of capital. Suddenly exposed to sharp foreign competition and left without generous subsidies, producers were forced to sharply downsize their most costly operations or even abandon them entirely. But this drastic change had also forced viable factories into deep financial distress so that not all production restructuring was economically rational. Also, with an ineffective banking system (and with a nonexistent securities market), shifting resources from nonviable operations to those with better prospects was initially relatively limited.

Only during the post-1992 recovery, and particularly since the acceleration of 1994, has the economy begun to upgrade technological level of production in a more active way, i.e., by adding newer vintages of capital and bringing in more current products. This upgrading has been helped by a sharp increase in imports and a rather remarkable gains in exports that facilitated it. A lot of production increase since 1992 has resulted, however, from the activation of capacities which had been depressed by the 1989–91 crisis. Moreover, the scale of investment expansion has been limited given the enormous needs of the greatly outdated industry. The domestic rate of savings remains too low to support the necessary level of capital expansion and the government crowds out a substantial portion of savings anyway (this in order to finance large budget deficits in a noninflationary way). While showing acceleration over time, the inflow of foreign capital has been relatively small and thus unable to substitute for insufficient domestic savings.

Systemic crisis

An alternative explanation of Poland's economic problems at the conclusion of the import-led strategy is that it is not debt overhang or obsolete structure but rather systemic rigidity, or the so understood systemic crisis, which should be considered the main source of the growth fatigue. In this explanation, both excessive indebtedness and rapid aging of production are seen as byproducts, or consequences, of the inadequate pace of systemic – institutional – change. The aggressive borrowing that led to the 1979–82 crisis is said to have been a substitute for economic reforms, because were it not for the lack of systemic changes, the economy would have been able to generate more resources for growth by itself. Also, if not for this lack of systemic reforms, incentives for production improvements would have been much stronger and thus the economy would have been so much less pressed to borrow money abroad in order to pay for the imported technologies.

The above alternative argument is consistent with the view that was dominant at the time of the economic crisis in the comparative system literature, which held that Poland, like other communist states, froze its economic system. One example of that view is the widely recognized theory of the so-called reform cycle (see Brus reprint in Gomulka 1986). It claims that the typical pattern of economic reforms under communism is first to reluctantly allow some change and then to pull back. This is because any reasonable reform would require a decentralization of decision-making that the communist elites were unwilling to accept. Such a delegation of economic authority would undermine their power monopoly, which they felt was extremely vulnerable to even small-scale concessions. Thus, economic-system rigidity paralleled the rigidity of the political structure, built around a single marxist party and party-controlled coercive forces.

It is hard to disagree with the point that the state-centred economic system, in any of its specific versions – traditional or otherwise – had a negative impact on economic performance. In fact, we have made that observation on a number of occasions in the past, particularly with respect to the isssue of incentives for technological change under this sort of economic regime (e.g., Poznanski 1989a). What has to be carefully tested, however, is the suggestion that it is the rigidity of that system – permanently frozen in its original version – which is mainly responsible for the deterioration of economic performance, sometimes of crisis proportions. In theory, the system could be changing and still not result in any strengthening of economic incentives, or even in reducing them, since regressive systemic evolution is a possibility (and this could take place even with decentralization of decisionmaking and expansion of financial instruments).

The popularity of the nonreformability thesis is intriguing given the fact that the communist parties were relentless refomers (for further discussion see Poznanski 1993b). Rather then talking about fear of economic reforms, one might be tempted to think about the communist period as a time of endemic reforms. At least in Poland, the party/state leadership was almost constantly discussing the imperfections of the economic system and trying to modify them. There were a number of culminating moments in this reform-drive, which received attention in the economic literature. However, between, and during, these clusters of reforms, there were other changes made, with different layers of the bureaucracy acting on their own. To assume that all this effort produced nothing of lasting impact does not seem realistic.

It is not realistic for a number of reasons, including that systemic changes, even of a small-scale, are not easily reversible by those who instituted them, i.e., the planners. For reforms in an economic system to be eventually erased those in charge would have to have not only adequate knowledge of systemic conditions but also the capability to execute a return to the starting point. The critic of the state-planned system would be the first to admit that planning authorities are not omnipotent in setting and executing production targets, which makes one wonder why they should be any more effective in pursuing the far more complicated matter of reforming the economic system. It could also be inferred that the authorities would be even less successful in blocking vital systemic changes resulting from the initiatives of other players in the economy. This would be particularly true with respect to modifications of an informal character, which would be harder for the central agencies to detect.

Besides, even if some formal measures were scrapped in the fashion implied by the reform cycle theory, the behaviour of producers and/or households would not necessarily return to its earlier form right away. Reintroducing a past version of the economic system consumes time and getting the players – agents – to assume a past posture takes even more time. With reform efforts undertaken and abandoned in short intervals, these players would find themselves in a constant shift between various rational – consistent with a given version of an economic system – patterns of behaviour. The shorter the cycle of reforms, the more difficult it would be for producers and/or households to complete such a shift. In fact, one could imagine a case where, faced with a fast changing system – and incentive structure, those players would opt to ignore the system entirely, this representing a real change.

The other problem with the rigidity theory is that if the economic order really underwent no major modification then one is confronted with the puzzle of why, after decades of crisis-free growth, Poland suddenly found itself in a deep slump of 1979–82. This is because under the original system, governments were, at least theoretically, equipped with regulatory tools which offered the direct access to enterprises needed to prevent – or at least quickly arrest – production crises, even ones related to foreign indebtedness. With the authority to set prices, control wages, and keep books for enterprises, these governments were also well prepared to combat inflation (better than capitalist states, which must rely primarily on indirect monetary/fiscal measures).

Also if it were true that communist economic (and political) system was rigid by design and impossible to change – short of rejection in its totality – then one is left with another puzzle, namely, why would different countries in Eastern Europe exhibited diversified performance, including the fact that Poland's growth path has been for most of the time, so much different from the rest. One would wonder whether such visible and persistant differences in economic behavior would not be structural, i.e. related to the institutional setting, but the argument on systemic rigidity precludes such a resolution (not to mention that for this argument to hold one would have to conclude that whatever cross-country differences are detectable they would be only of superficial nature rather than of any substance; this including even Hungary which seemingly looked so much different than, say, East Germany before 1990).

To account for these diachronic and/or cross country differences in growth, and, claim at the same time, that systemic factor's played a critical role, then one has to dismiss the theory that Poland's 'rules of the game' remained unaltered. This idea has not been totally foreign to economists, some of whom have departed from the static argument adopting the concept of systemic hybridization. They have argued that the timid, inconsequential reforms pursued by the communists did result in change of the original institutions. What emerged in their place, the arguments goes, was an incoherent 'order' which combined elements of direct control of enterprises with rudimentary market mechanisms (Kaminski 1991). Under this system, where neither plan nor market provided real guidance, 'imperfect' plans lost their traditional ability to mobilize production increases while 'imperfect' markets permitted monopolistic pricing, which resulted in inflation.

Lack of sophistication is one feature of that theory and its rather simplistic application in comparative system analysis is another. Within this theory, systemic change has typically been characterized as single-step discontinuity from a pure plan-type economy to one where the dominant plan is fused with subsidiary market-type elements. To be sure, it is not that the concept of hybridization is not suitable for multiple-step analysis, but simply that it has not been applied in this way. In the hybridization model, one could even envision an argument to the effect that the plan is being systematically replaced by market forces. It could be thus reasonably argued that multiple-step hybridization – with a steady progression of market elements – could acoount for a steadily progressing deterioration of economic performance, as we have found to be the case in Poland beginning, say, at the outset of the Gierek's import-led strategy.

Also, the hybridization model has been used mainly to address the economic side of the overall system and not its political aspect. Unlike in the reform-cycle theory, where economics and politics are tightly knotted, this approach pays little attention to the political framework in which economic institutions function. This aspect of the reform-cycle theory is quite realistic since fusion of politics and economics (see Kaminski 1991) is the defining feature of the state-planned economy. Thus, to make the model of systemic hybridization more realistic one would have to assume that with the changing economic system, the political system had to alter as well. Consequently, one would also have to assume that the political structure would go through at least two stages, for example, move from a complete to a partial monopoly of power – a trend that we have found in our study of Poland.

Transition pains

An alternative to the static argument on the systemic crisis as a source of growth fatigue – a low economic momentum and high instability – is our dynamic argument of what we would like to call a transition crisis (compare with Kornai 1995) of Poland's economic difficulties. What comes out of this case study is a lengthy process of systemic changes that can be traced at least as far back as 1970. We can legitimately call this process a transition, because rather than move in circles – as suggested by the reform cycle theory – the original system has been giving way to its successor, i.e, the market order. The particular pattern of this lengthy transition that we have uncovered has made the intermediate forms increasingly ineffective and this is why one can talk about a transition – rather than systemic – crisis, which we argue brought with it a loss of growth momentum and of relative stability.

To capture the true meaning of the transition changes mentioned above – and their role in undermining the economy – it is necessary to look at that element of Poland's system which has generally been neglected in the above theories – property rights. It is ironic that until very recently this subject has been ignored in most of the post-war debate on the socialist system, since property rights are central to the theories of both the marxist economists and their evolutionary critics (e.g., von Mises, or von Hayek). The debates have instead concentrated on the type and scope of instruments used by the central planners to coordinate state-owned enterprises, (e.g., production targets and material allocation (= targeted supplies).

Economic systems cannot be described simply by looking at means of coordination between single economic agents, i.e., organizations – which take the two basic forms of state control and market competition. Besides these 'external' forms of coordination, economic systems are defined by how individual organizations coordinate their members 'internally'. This perspective is captured by property rights theory, which posits that the particular way of defining property structure – locus of control over resources and allocation of rights to dispose of resources – determines the motivation of economic agents to engage in commercial exchange with other entities and to expand their productive activities.

Any type of imperfection in the area of property rights – legal ambiguities, failures of enforcement, arbitrary taxes – increases transaction costs (as opposed to the commonly recognized so-called transformation, or production, costs) to the resource owner. These transaction costs are always positive, so that certain potential contracting parties may find it cost-prohibitive to conclude their deals. Those possessing resources may not put them to full use if uncertain of their rights, i.e., legal ability to appropriate the effects of their resource utilization. It is the purpose of adjustments in property structure – initiated by states or individuals – to lower transaction costs and open additional opportunities for profitable activities. While such systemic reforms may offer economic benefits, they also cost, so that the choice of a reform path should be subject to economic calculus, too.

There are two basic types of property rights, public and private, each type assuming either a 'weak' or 'strong' version, depending on the degree of specificity, exactness of rights ascribed to a given economic agent, and also on the level of enforceability of claims to particular assets. These four subcategories of property structure can be combined either with state- or market-type 'external' coordination, again with each type taking either a 'weak' or 'strong' version. With these many types of property rights and coordination forms, we obtain sixteen combinations, each representing a different economic system, unique in terms of its weakness or strength with respect to various combinations of coordination and property types.

Kornai (1992b) argues that only combinations of private ownership with market coordination or of state control and public ownership represent strong systems – capable of providing sustained growth and reasonable stability. This is not a disputable point within his typology of economic systems, which does not make this distinction between weak/strong coordination mechanisms and weak/strong property structures.[1] But within our typology, a system is strong only when, for example, a strong market – or, to use more familiar terminology, an 'effective' market – is combined with strong, well-defined and protected, private property. Conversely, if the market is distorted, as by monopoly practices, and private property is exposed to arbitrary seizure, the respective economic order falls into the category of a weak system.

On another occasion, we suggested (Poznanski 1992c) that the relatively good economic performance during the first post-war decades in Eastern Europe (and the Soviet Union) could be satisfactorily explained in terms of property rights theory. At that time, the original system was strong, since as long as people were terrorized or indoctrinated by the official ideology of sacrifice, the political center – the single leader or narrow party circle – had sufficient means to enforce proper economic behaviour by state enterprises with respect to assets entrusted to them. The communist party was thus in a position to realize its ambitions of expanding its power base and national standing through maximization of the value of capital stock (see: Olson 1992).

The traditional system began to erode, as indicated in this book, during the Gierek period, when the cohesive political centre was greatly weakened. Combined with a reduction in the level of coercion, this disintegration of the centre was the prime cause of Poland's growing ungovernability. To be more specific, Gierek's regime weakened the central control over productive inputs – including capital – by dispersing power towards middle-level authorities, i.e., industrial ministries and associations (i.e., clusters of enterprises). This provided for an initial uncontrollable expansion of output, on the basis of

Western credits, to satisfy the needs of industrial lobbies. For the same reason, however, Poland was unable to cool down this economic surge quickly enough in the face of a huge foreign debt to avoid high economic costs.

Ironically, in the face of financial (= debt) insolvency, the economic system was not strengthened but allowed to further weaken. In a state of economic emergency such as this, some form of recentralization by Gierek's government was probably the only practical option at hand. But there was clearly not enough time to allow more decentralization to bring the necessary short-term relief to the heavily indebted economy. Economic authority shifted away from the administration anyway, not because of reforms but due to the erruption of labour protests on a scale never before experienced. Under these political pressures, the political leadership did not consolidate but fractured even more. With this, economic control by the administration, still the main coordinating force, became even more difficult. As a consequence, rather than to go through a brief and shallow crisis, the economy entered in a deep one, lasting from 1979 through 1982. What started mainly as a liquidity crisis turned into a crisis of disorganization, where the national economy simply became unmanagable (= non-governable).

The economic crisis ended in 1983 only under the shield of military rule imposed by Jaruzelski when the badly weakened planning centre gained a firmer hand over economic affairs. The systemic reforms executed in that year, as well as other steps taken since, did not, however, bring the system back to the form it took during the Gierek period. The influence gained by organized labour – or labour in general – in the time of open mass-scale protests was not totally rolled back. What emerged was a less centralized system, resembling the one in Hungary, which at the time was definitely the most decentralized economic system in the region. But while in Hungary economic responsibility was shifted down to competitively appointed managers, in Poland the workers were the winners. This system – a version of labour-management or the so-called third road – proved to be weak, possibly even weaker than that under Gierek, a fact which could easily account for the disappointments of the economic recovery which took place from 1983 on.

The economic system underwent a further transition in 1988, when a number of measures were introduced in a rather hasty manner by Rakowski's government. This change could be likened to what happened in the final years of Gierek's period, when the central administration lost much of its control. This time, however, the loss of authority was not caused by forces external to the government, such as the labour unrests that damagaged the planning centre in the last years of Gierek's period. It was by and large a deliberate, though not fully controlled, withdrawal from many central controls – including ownership functions – left in place after years of decentralization measures taken since 1982. Theoretically, such a withdrawal should have improved the effectiveness of the economic system, but it did not due to the chaotic, inconsequential manner in which these changes occurred. In fact, they further fractured the economic system, thus laying the foundations for the economic crisis that began unraveling in early 1989.

The actions taken by the team of reformers brought in by the first noncommunist government of Mazowiecki in the late 1989 did not reverse the ongoing process of systemic fragmentation but accelerated it. In line with the 1990 reform program, the government reduced its interventions at the enterprise level to a bare minimum. The only significant instrument of direct coordination left in place was wage-setting, a combination of wage limits and taxes. At the same time, the reformist government announced its intention to expeditiously privatize state property, though only modest steps followed. This was enough, however, to upset the expectations above the future legal status of state-owned enterprises and rewards to managers and workers – thus, not only was the coordination weakened but property rights were left even less specified then before. This systemic emplosion caused an increase in uncertainty and enterprises responded predictably by cutting output and raising prices, so that the shallow recession of 1989 turned into a much deeper one that lasted through mid-1992.

This period of suspension – with the state withdrawing from coordination and pushing for rapid though unspecified privatization – did not last long. On the basis of initial evidence that, given its immaturity, the market alone could not lift the whole economy out of recession, the government assumed a more active role in the coordination process (e.g., restoration of high tariffs, selective financial recapitalization). Once the public-sector enterprises felt certain that no sudden change of their legal status was likely to be imposed on them, property structure has became somewhat solidified as well. In addition, the rapidly emerging (mostly through new entries) private sector had been steadily gaining confidence that its assets would not be arbitrarily taken away. These adjustments produced a stronger, yet different hybrid, and it was very much because of these adjustments that the economy entered into a solid recovery.

Mechanism of secular growth fatigue

It follows from or discussion in the previous section that the most intriguing aspect of Poland's economy is the fragility of its economic growth. Our case study provides enough factual detail to enable us to offer a more elaborate explanation of that pheneomenon that the one implied earlier. In this more complex account, our focus is still on systemic determinants but they are linked to the growth pattern with much greater precision. In this type of characterization, the economic difficulties are ascribed mainly to ineffective income policies, i.e., inability to keep real wages in close line with labour productivity. This in turn can be attributed to the weakening of the relevant elements of the economic system that have hurt the central authorities' ability – in the absence of equally effective substitute mechanisms – to tightly control prices and wages. The latter weakness is then tied to contemporaneous deterioration of the political structure.

Growth fatigue

Drawing from different parts of our historical account of Poland's development one could indeed demonstrate that during the period analyzed, the economy has shown a loss of growth momentum as well as greater instability, both, for much of the time, in contrast with other economies in the region. This could be an important conclusion since it would mean that with all the changes in both economics and politics, the entire period under scrutiny here can still be viewed as a unity. If so, this would also suggest that some equally persistent forces – economic or political – could be responsible for the continued fragility of Poland's growth and thus should be searched for. In what follows, we bring together the main facts concerning Poland's production and price behaviour to present a summary view of the growth fatigue phenomenon that we have referred to on a number of occasions in the book.

The sequence of events began with a period of rapid growth during 1971–75, a quite remarkable change from the near-stagnation reported in the proceeding years. At this stage, all sectors exhibited strong expansion, particularly in industry where massive investment concentrated. But later, the Polish economy slowed down considerably and then in 1979 entered into a crisis that lasted through 1982, when the net national product was about a quarter below the 1978 level. The only other country in the region that showed similarly dynamic growth in the first part of the 1970s was Romania, but it managed to avoid a decline in its national product later in the decade. Remaining countries of Eastern Europe experienced a slowdown in their growth rates, but these still remained positive through 1982 (one important exception being Hungary, where there was stagnation in production and a slight decline in effective consumption levels).

Turning to the question of stability, as early as 1971–75, Poland's economy experienced accelerated inflation, though not at alarming levels. These price increases were accompanied by continued shortages of many products (e.g., food). In this period, Poland was the second most inflationary economy in the East European region (after Yugoslavia). With the approach of the 1979 crisis, prices became even less stable and shortages increasingly pronounced (for an interesting account, see Kolodko and McMahon 1987). Admittedly, on average, rates of inflation increased after the mid-1970s throughout Eastern Europe, though many economies in the region – including Czechoslovakia and East Germany – managed to hold prices remarkably stable by any standards. In Yugoslavia, a vastly different economic system allowed for far more discretion at the enterprise level, including the right to engage in independent pricing of goods. Poland, on the other hand, continued to operate a traditional system of administered prices (which meant that inflation was caused primarily by official corrections).

The recovery from the economic crisis of 1979–82 was underway in 1983. The economy demonstrated steady increases which brought the level of the gross national product close to its pre-crisis value by 1988. In per capita terms, however, the 1988 gross national product, calculated in 1970 prices, was only roughly equal to that of 1976, the last year of Gierek's 'investment rush'. Rates of growth during this recovery were generally comparable to those reported by the other East European economies. Given the low starting point of Poland's economy – vastly underutilized production capacities – this could hardly be perceived as a success. Not only was much stronger growth performance expected, but the recovery was not accompanied by the structural adjustment – cost reductions or product change – needed to cope with the foreign debt.

Following the imposition of 'martial law' in 1981 by Gierek's successor Jaruzelski, the rate of inflation was steadily reduced. A one-time drastic increase in prices combined with a wage freeze in 1982 helped remove some of the excess money in circulation. Even though efforts to keep the money supply under control continued thereafter,

Poland remained the most inflationary economy in the region, experiencing double-digit annual rates of price increases (with Yugoslavia, reporting higher rates, Estrin 1992b). As initial progress in lowering the rate of inflation proved impossible to sustain, prices showed another upturn in 1988, reaching a high two-digit annual rate of inflation. During the transfer of power to the opposition forces in mid-1989, inflation, which was then being measured at the three-digit level, soared out of control.

Not yet fully emerged from the 1979–1982 crisis, Poland again found itself in the midst of crisis in 1989. While the 1989 decline was relatively minor, the deterioration of the national economy during 1990–91 – when undergoing the radical 'shock therapy' programme of the post-communist government of Mazowiecki – was of a size comparable to that of the 1979–82 crisis. The national product declined sharply in 1990 and again, by less, in 1991, then stabilized in 1992, pushing the real national output below the 1975 level. This overall decline was largely caused by an even sharper contraction in Poland's industrial output in the state sector which continued through mid-1992, the fourth consecutive year of poor growth performance. Losses of output in agriculture were also unusually deep beginning in 1990, with the sharpest one, by more than one-tenth, taking place in 1992 (with the rest of Eastern Europe showing similar or even worse losses to their farming output).

While recession was arrested in mid-1992, the recovery that immediately followed was rather modest, particularly given the enormous size of the output losses which the economy underwent after 1989. At this early stage, the fundamentals were still very shaky, including only a small increase in real investment through the end of 1993. At this point, most of the growth came from utilization of depressed production capacities as well as low-cost investment. This growth concentrated in services and industry, with the majority of output gains coming from emerging private businesses (conspicuously absent in this early phase of recovery was construction, particularly housing). A critical change came only in 1994, when production growth greatly accelerated and so did investment. Among the few economies in the region that happened to take a positive turn after 1992, Poland was the one that experienced the most impressive recovery.

The early stage of recovery was combined with further success in curtailing the inflation rate, which was cut almost in half during 1992. But even with further reduction in 1993, the rate of inflation remained high – close to that seen at the outset of the 1989–91 crisis. In large part these price increases were fueled by upward corrections in the few goods remaining under governmental control. Even with the drastic price hikes in 1990–91, the additional corrections were substantial. These goods – energy sources, appartment rents, public transportation, railways – while few in number, still counted for a considerable portion of the domestic spending of producers and even more of households. Apparently, as much as one fifth of total inflation was attributable to periodic adjustments in official prices.

The coalition forces with roots in the communist period that won the late 1993 elections provided Poland with new economic leadership that in 1994 turned a weak recovery into a credible rapid growth, which picked up even more in 1995. While this overall acceleration, unusually strong by regional standards, clearly fits the positive trendlines registered in 1992–93, the following years seem to represent yet another distinctive stage. By then it became even more evident that investment – rather than consumption – had assumed the role of principal growth engine. Particularly dynamic was investment in the private sector, apparently almost doubling the volume of capital expenditure in 1995. But the state-owned industry joined the recovery as well, which by that time involved all major segments of the economy, including both construction (particularly with respect to industrial facilities) and agriculture.

The post-1994 stage of recovery has also seen a further decline in inflation (with the first in many years absolute decline in the monthly aggregate price level officially reported in the middle of 1995). This slowdown in inflation came as a surprise to the critics of the coalition's pro-growth policy, and thus of its principal architect Kolodko – the finance minister under both the Pawlak and Oleksy cabinets – as well. The critics argued that higher growth rates and lower price rates are not reconcilable, but they proved to be so. More surprisingly, the inflation rate has been curtailed even though the total domestic money supply expanded rapidly in response to an unexpectedly high inflow of foreign currency that the banking system proved unable to sterilize. Noninflationary financing of the budget deficit has helped to bring inflation down, though at a cost of an increasing public debt.

Wage behaviour

Another element could be added to the model if it were argued that the economic variable most directly responsible for the fatigue is the recurrent – and related to systemic changes – difficulty in keeping real wages in line with labour productivity (see: Sachs 1993:29–31). Improper connection between the two could have such an effect on growth for a number of reasons, one of them being that when wages and productivity are disconnected than workers' motivation suffers. When wage increases are not backed by productivity gains, the economy's ability to divert resources to capital stock expansion may be eroded as well. Excess wages may lead to shortages of goods and thus cause prices to accelerate unless they are controlled tightly by the state. Under such conditions, foreign credit lines may bring relief on both accounts but only on a temporary basis given the need to service the resultant financial debts. At the time of debt repayment, capital funds needed for production expansion may be eroded and inflation may pick up as well.

The impact of uncontrollable wage behaviour can be traced back to the early stages of Gierek's import-led growth programme, when disalignment between wages and productivity induced the government to seek large-scale credits needed to finance imports of goods for the consumer market, and, with some delay, resort to inflationary taxing as well. When borrowing policy led to a dangerously high external debt, bringing wages down – and below productivity – became necessary to generate a trade surplus and begin repayment. Initially, some progress was made in controlling wages but when the country began facing insolvency, pushing wages – and consumption – sufficiently down failed. Capital expenditure – in large part involving imports – was sacrificed, but with this came production slowdown, so that the country was on its way to a debt trap. Only domestic austerity offered a viable solution but wages began running ahead of productivity again, so that rather than ending up in a minor crisis Poland in 1979 entered a major one.

The difficulty that Gierek's regime experienced in bringing wages under control was directly related to the reform changes in the incentive structure initiated in 1971. While his regime did not pursue systemic reforms, which critics of the Soviet-type economic system would find indispensable, Gierek's government did implement substantial changes. Significantly, the regime decentralized economic power by allowing industrial ministries – and some large-scale enterprises – to take much of the control away from the traditional planning centre, i.e., the Central Committee of the communist party and its principal arm, the Planning Office. With this new arrangement, the pressure for wage increases was greatly strengthened, as individual branch ministries, driven by their particular interests, amplified the aggressive demands of the workers.

Runaway wage increases resulted not only from this unprecedented softening of socialist planning (judged by the standards of other East European economies and the Soviet Union), but also, as stressed earlier, from equally sharp changes in party approach to consumption. After years of propagating the puritan model of life devoted to the common goal of building a 'better world', the Gierek regime announced that individual enrichment was acceptable, even desirable. Rather than seeking to mold people according to some predetermined vision of the 'good man', the reformed party yielded to the materialistic impulses of its citizen. Given this change in ideology, the government now ran the risk of losing popularity whenever it could not meet demands for higher consumption levels.

The tendency for wages to temporarily run ahead of productivity was reversed during the last year of the 1979–82 crisis. This helped to remove the effects of wage gains made at the time of falling production (and productivity – because employment remained intact). But demand for higher wages revived shortly thereafter and the government responded to it with wage concessions as well as upward price corrections, though on a much smaller scale than in 1982. In 1987, such a combination produced a small drop in real wages, a relief for an economy whose production registered only a minor gain. But in 1988, real wages reported an enormous – one-seventh – hike, way ahead of productivity gains, so that the inflation rate increased sharply, reaching its second highest level under the postwar planning. This signalled that the economy was probably heading towards another crisis, and in 1989, when the above scenario was repeated, the economy indeed entered into a full-fledged recession.

As during the Gierek regime's economic rule, wage behaviour at that later time had much to do with incentive structure, though in important ways was also different from that existing during the earlier period. Jaruzelski's government – and later on that of Messner – agreed to a set up a participatory system, where crucial choices were left to workers. With this, control over state enterprises had to a large degree slipped away from a divided centre – branch ministries and management of industrial associations – to workers. Predictably, workers used their increased access to decisonmaking to advance their wage interests while paying less attention to other matters. The distractions caused by Rakowski's reforms – allowing managers to siphon assets for personal use – left industrial workers with even more opportunities to push for higher wages irrespective of productivity and they took advantage of them.

Not only did the economic structure facilitate wage escalation as in the Gierek's period but there was also a similarity in the general attitude of the consecutive governments of the Jaruzelski period towards consumption. Given mounting economic problems, these governments were not in a position to continue focusing on consumption. While building a consumer society was no longer feasible, these governments tried to protect their consumers as much as possible. The great interest in keeping inflation low was driven by a desire to spare consumers discomfort. Interest in consumers would explain why the servicing of foreign debt was, as indicated earlier, given a low priority in overall economic policy throughout the whole stage. For the same reason, the government decided to make its partial debt payments through exports of materials and material-based products rather than exports of foodstuffs (so that eventually net exports in that category turned into net imports).

The runaway wages were only brought under control when the first postcommunist government of Mazowiecki executed in 1990 a drastic, about one-quarter, reduction in real wages (comparable in size to that accomplished by Jaruzelski's government at the end of the 1979–82 crisis), and another smaller one in 1991. The correction was achieved mainly by means of accelerated inflation and wage fixing, similar to the steps taken by Jaruzelski several years earlier, though this time the rate of inflation was a few times higher. Also, Jaruzelski's stabilization policy was not accompanied by changes in the economic system as radical as those in the Mazowiecki's package of reforms. While the earlier programme marked the exit from a crisis, this time deflationary measures were followed by a recession that was almost as deep. With the 1990–91 recession came a considerable decline in labour productivity though by less than the decrease in real wages, this helping to arrest inflation.

The curtailment of wages of such proportion could not have happened if not for the fact that the 1990 reform program fundamentally changed the environment in which wages were determined. While wages in the still dominant public sector continued to be controlled, the state severed almost all other ties with its enterprises, e.g., output targets, budgetary subsidies, preferential credits, tax relief, price control. With these changes, for the first time, labour in the state sector had to face almost hard-budget constraint and thus keep their wages in line with productivity. This deep decoupling of workers and the state relieved the latter from powerful wage pressures and the need to apply political force to steer wages. But these reforms also had a negative short-term side effect, because, left to themselves, state-owned enterprises responded to falling wages (and demand) by sharply cutting their production and employment, as well as by raising prices to shift the burden of recesion on the others.

The eventual – possibly excessive – containment of powerful wage demands reflected not only new systemic conditions but also changed policy priorities. The final documents produced during the roundtable talks obliged the Mazowiecki government to adopt a very generous wage policy with unitary indexation and wage parities for major labour groups. It also required that workers be given even more say in their enterprises, to be turned into genuine labour-managed entities. But once in power, the opposition government reversed itself and decided to leave labour to market forces and prevent the labour-managed model – or any sort of 'third way' system – from being implemented. In a way, this was one of the harshest anti-labour positions taken in the region, and in particular contrast with the Czech Republic, where wages losses were also deep but jobs were protected and capital assets were freely distributed as well (as a form of compensation for wage losses).

Even though the second economic crisis ended in mid-1992, real wages continued to fall through 1993, when their level was about one third below 1989 real wages. Real wages kept declining despite the fact that by 1992 labour productivity began to increase. Only in 1994, were real wages allowed to increase though at less than a half of the rate reported for labour productivity growth. Such a change has helped to turn household consumption into another – besides investment – engine of recovery, while posing no serious threat to price stability. This remark applies to both sectors – public and private – keeping in mind that rates of increase in real wages as well as productivity rates were higher in the private sphere than in the public sector. Consequently, wage relations between the two sectors have changed considerably: in 1989 private sector wages were ten points below those in the public sector, but in 1994 the difference was just the opposite.

The shift from possibly excessive wage depression – as another form of wage misbehaviour compared to runaway wages in the communist days – to more balanced wage behaviour since 1994 has occured in a yet another systemic setting. The wage fixing – based on price indices and wage-taxes – by the administration for public-sector enterprises was gradually relaxed after 1992 (by means of reducing tax progression as well as allowing exemptions). In late 1994, this system was replaced with a new scheme of corporatist vintage, wherein three parties – state, workers, and managers – negotiate wages (in line with the procedure already in long use by, for instance, the Czech Republic) (see Hausner 1995). At the same time, state-owned enterprises were given other priviliges that brought their overall system closer to that enjoyed by the private secotr operating under a prewar legal code. While an excess demand on wages was expected by many critics to follow, nothing of that nature actually happened through 1995.

The relaxation of wages since 1994 was possible not only because of the positive trends in production but also because of a policy shift brought in by Kolodko's economic team. The team continued to work with the central bank, led by Gronkiewicz-Waltz on preserving fiscal restraint but with a new focus. Its official – widely publicized – programme called for reducing the social costs of transition by both downsizing unemployment and upgrading wages, particularly for groups that have been trailing behind. Greatly hurt during the 1990–91 recession, farmers were one of the first to benefit from the new policy – on two accounts, i.e., higher tariffs that helped them raise prices for foodstuffs, and financial consolidation that reduced their credit risk. By changing regulations on employment contracts, scores of grossly underpaid low-skill workers in the private sector gained better protection from employers. However, no lowering of extremally high income taxes took place, despite governmental promises to that effect.

Political factor

Our analysis also suggests that the above discussed unusual wage behaviour can be linked to the political framework within which changes in the economic system – and conditions for price/income determination – have been taking place, this representing a final element in our explanatory model. Purely theoretical considerations would be taken into account by any competent student of state-planned economies, given that as indicated before, economics and politics are so closely fused in the communist societies (for analytical account, see Kolakowski 1992). Given this specific feature, all communist systems should be treated by definition as political economies and such a fusion would be particularly tight in the areas considered politically sensitive, with wages definitely in that category (as will be inflation since price stability is high on the preference list of wage-earners in all modern industrial societies).

What also draws attention to the various political ramifications of systemic change is the fact that Poland's political conditions have been for most of the period in question less stable than those of other countries of the region. On many occasions Poland has broken ground for political change elsewhere, often ahead of the Soviet Union, which until very recently, politically dominated the whole region. It is in politics where one finds greatest contrast between Poland and most of the rest of Eastern Europe and the Soviet Union and its successors, while the phenomenon of growth fatigue, or at least its high intensity, is another feature that primarily distinguishes Poland from the rest of the region. It would thus be only logical to infer again that it is in the political scene that important answers to the puzzle of lengthy growth fatigue should be sought.

In trying to understand the possible role of politics in pushing Poland into the series of weak economic systems, it is useful to turn back to the definition of economic systems as combinations of coordination mechanism and property rights. Under the communist system, coordination is direct, through state orders, so that its strength depends on the state's power and ownership is public so that its strength is also a function of state's power (the latter point is one of the major elements of the neo-institutional theory, see North 1979, 1990, 1993). This is the reason why any weakening of state power will contribute to a weakening of such a state-based economic system. But a similar rule applies to the market-type economy, although in this particular case, weakening – or strengthening – of state power plays a less decisive role, for the state is here more of a subsidiary player.

To discuss the role of politics in systemic changes one would need some understanding of what factors account for state power. This is not a very well specified concept in political literature though in wide use, but for the sake of our discussion we only need a general definition. Among those factors making for state power is enforcement ability, i.e., ability to resort to violence. Also important is the state's legitimacy, i.e., the consent of society to the state's application of coercion so that it is not met with costly resistance. And finally, the state's will – desire to reign – is required for coercive resources to be mobilized (more, see Poznanski 1992c). Thus, state power may decrease on one account or more, so that it is theoretically possible for a state to weaken, even mortally, without any loss of its means of violence.

It should thus come as no surprise that when Gierek's leadership decided to change the way the party thinks and works, this had to have some impact on the economic system. By switching away from single-man political control, the leadership invited more internal competition as collective action problems were resolved by party-state players. The relatively monolithic party-state had been transformed into one split into multiple interest groups. These were formed, among other things, around branch ministries and their industrial associations, but also around territorial authorities (particularly in the regions with industrial concentration). With disintegration of the centre came competition – through wages – among various groups for labour, with little concern for overall economic balance. The power left in the hands of structural ministries – such as the ministry of finance - was not enough to counterbalance at all times those destabilizing forces coming from other parts of the formal centre.

Another important political change was that the long-time commitment to marxist ideology was replaced with adherence to party professionalism where personal skills and career matter most. With this came the choice to renounce the use of force as a political tool and rely on the party's ability to earn society's support by solving economic problems. This new approach included a commitment to a steady raise in wages, as well as to bringing in more consumer goods. It became a rule that when faced with labour protests, the leadership would restrain from using force and try to calm the situation by offering wage concessions and/or holding prices down. This is how Gierek's government acted during the 1976 strikes in a few industrial centres, and also during a much more widespread wave of protests in 1980. This means that, while not legal, strikes became a tolerated, and also effective, weapon in the hands of workers with which to press for higer real wages.

The shift of power from the party-state to workers (or society) during Gierek's years left the party-state still in the dominant position, and while this trend continued in the Jaruzelski's period, the logic of this further political change was very different. Martial law imposed in late 1981 by Jaruzelski pushed the balance of power towards the party-state. But this shift was not used to preserve the party-state model, wherein the party – given its authority – is also a state. Martial law was followed by a gradual separation of party and state, intended to make each a more effective force. The direction of change was thus towards a modern state system with a single dominant party, but this process did not produce a strong state immediately, thus undermining wage/price control. A rather weak state was emerging, one left with reduced support from the party apparatus but still suffering a deficit of legitimacy because society continued to view the state as a party too.

Paradoxically, the power gain from workers produced by martial law was not employed to subdue workers – and their multiple trade unions – indefinitely. Instead, this brief, though forceful, confrontation was followed by genuine efforts to appease workers. Not only were economic policies geared to the perceived need of workers, such as employment security, but, importantly, martial law opened a lengthy process of bringing free unions into the formal political process. One reflection of this process was the gradual cooptation of various opposition forces to para-political bodies, while another was the rapid spread of nonpolitical associations. While the free trade unions formed during the clashes of 1980–81 were not legalized, industrial workers were given fair representation, as their enterprises were reformed into labour-managed entities. All this provided workers with opportunities to effectively demand wage increases from a weak state bureaucracy, though in a less confrontational way.

Yet another version of the weak state was produced under the last communist-era government of Rakowski, established in 1988, when efforts to preserve the communist rule in any form were simply given up. Until this point, the communist political system was being weakened mostly because of the erosion of the party-state's ability to coerce as well as because of decline in the legitimacy, or social acceptance of violence. Diminished desire by the party-state to resort to violence, and not just internal incohesion, contributed to the loss of this ability as well. But only under Rakowskis's shortlived government, did the will to rule by whatever means, within the existing structure, evaporate. The events taking place under Rakowski's leadership could thus be best described as withering of the communist-type political system, a process that quickly left both the party and the state in very poor condition, downsized and confused. Not only had the state's ability to control wages/prices sharply diminished, but this macroissue also became largely irrelevant to the self-liquidating state.

In addition, Rakowski's political rule saw a major shift in the state's attitude towards workers, because the traditional concern for their wellbeing ended. Early during the communist reign, the party-state was officially or ideologically committed to improving workers' lifes, and later a similar concern stemmed from interest in keeping social peace. This populist outlook was rejected by Rakowski's government since it wanted not only to release its power monopoly but also to extricate itself from responsibilities towards workers. The necessity of open unemployment, as a disciplining force, was pronounced as an official line, and subsidies for many essentials were removed. The government indicated that it was not going to protect enterprises against bankruptcy, even though very many of them ran deficits.

Workers responded with additional wage demands, which met with little resistance from the ambivalent state.

When Rakowski's government was replaced in mid-1989 with the noncommunist government of Mazowiecki, the pattern of political processes had not changed. Importantly, the new leadership had little interest in rebuilding state power and instead decided to allow it to futher decay. This course of action was largely motivated by the ideology of the reformers rather than by social pressure. It could be that through inertia at least parts of society – having resisted the communist state for a long time – were still seeking reduction of state power, but what mattered most was the desire of Mazowiecki's reformers to leave only a minimum state in place. This was consistent with their ultraliberal (or rather libertarian) economic ideology that saw little need for the state. One important exception was wages, which were put under direct control, a potentially problematic decision given the overall downsizing of the state apparatus.

With the state downsizing also came a rather peculiar situation, where the workers seemed to allow their power, now greater than ever, to be idled. Used to working outside of the political mainstream, unions did not fully enter the party scene. There were temptations to convert union structures into a party, but eventually leaders chose to restrict their activities to shop floor negotiations. By standing largely outside of the political process, workers allowed the newly-formed parties, with labour roots, to choose the economic course of action of their own liking. When this course turned out to bring about instant recession with threats of bankruptcy the workers initially accepted the consequences. Rather than mount a political response, they let their wages slip to assist their endangered workplaces (so that in the first year of recession, wages did not even reach the maximum allowed by the official formula).

The first important sign that this peculiar political vacuum had been filled was the defeat of Mazowiecki's leadership at the polls, with the main charge against it led, in the name of unions, by Walesa. But Mazowiecki's government was, in fact, rejected by a variety of social groups, among them farmers and pensioners. This defeat was mis-understood – or possibly ignored – by the new government led by Bielecki, who tried to continue with the policy of a passive state and painful restructuring. It took two more governments with their roots in anticommunist opposition to slow down the pace of reforms and activate the state before the voters in late 1993 decided to bring back the former communist party and its peasant-party allies to power.

With this change on the political scene, for the first time since mid-1989, calls for a more assertive state began to come from governmental circles, and appropriate steps have followed.

The strengthening of the state by the forces brought to power in the late-1993 elections has not produced, however, a strong state. The reason is that the pattern of shortlived governments has not been broken, anymore than has the tradition of operating in a web of hostile inter-party disputes, wherein almost endless allegations of corruption by persons in power are a favored political weapon. A number of relatively small parties have remained in place, most of them with only rather loosely articulated programs and changing identities, causing voters to feel disoriented and sometimes overreact. The political scene has remained further fragmented by the fact that the office of the presidency was equipped with considerable powers acquired back during the roundtable talks. This has allowed the president – Walesa – to use his office to effectively challenge any government and even bring it down, as has happened with the governments of Mazowiecki and Suchocka, the same fate being shared by the coalition government led by the peasant-party leader Pawlak in early 1995.

It has to be kept in mind, of course, that the comeback of the parties with roots in the communist past has been greatly helped by internal conflicts within their most serious challenger, the conservative parties, many of them with links to the Catholic Church. That they lost the 1993 elections was in large measure due to the fact that, unlike their opponents on the left, they were unable to rally their forces behind a single candidate. The same conservative parties, with some help from the Church, have entered the late 1995 presidental elections in a more cohesive fashion. On the other hand, the coalition has joined the elections greatly fractured, with the peasant party led by Pawlak – a pro-Church party though with communist origins – drifting towards the conservative camp. Poland had been moving to another confrontation at the polls whose outcome has again been unpredictable – another indication of its still unsettled political structure.

Return to capitalist institutions

In the previous section, Poland's growth fatigue has been explained in terms of the disintegration of the communist system, involving the parallel sequence of weak economic and political subsystems. But one could also employ another perspective on this growth fatigue by recognizing that with the appearance of these different weak forms of the state-socialist system, elements of its alternative – pluralistic capitalism – have been reappearing. These elements have also been imperfect, so that one can talk about a series of weak market-type elements as well as of weak forms of civil society developing in the political sphere. This has thus been a dual process, and by stressing one aspect, as we have done earlier in the chapter, the other one can be easily missed. In fact, realization that elements of pluralistic capitalism were gaining ground throughout the whole period in question have come very late and very slowly.

In this step-wise return of capitalism we identify three major trends, beginning with the slow, often hardly visible, shift of central control to self-interested individuals as well as expansion of private property – a phenomenon which we call 'creeping capitalism'. This tendency has been combined with another secular trend, i.e., gradual process of opening the economy to the world market, with the external contacts offering possibly the best opportunity for individuals to accumulate capital, as well as personal wealth in general. Finally, we find that the spread of capitalism has involved a shift towards less egalitarian – more diverse – distribution of wealth, particularly since the 1990 reforms which provided greatly increased opportunities for extraordinary financial gains by some actors while forcing many others into greater economic distress (through a combination of job losses, depressed wages and reduction in welfare services).

Creeping capitalism

While the original design for the state-socialist model called for the communist leaders of post-war Poland to eliminate all forms of market coordination and private property, none of these goals were achieved. From the very beginning, a total shift of control to the centre proved to be impractical, this because of lack of information, for even under the most cooperative environment, not all information can be communicated. Control over vital information has allowed lower level actors to carve niches of private-choice for themselves. These could be used to make adjustments that actually helped to meet directives set by the centre but also hurt them. In both cases, such independent adjustments provided lower-level agents with the opportunity for making private gains.

With time these informal spheres of free action have gained ground, this process, to a degree, being helped by official reforms. Those communist-era systemic reforms that delegated authority down the decision-pyramid, even if shortlived, were conducive to such expansion. Any reversals in the reform course were helpful because they brought in an element of confusion that served lower-level agents to hide their activities. Personal incentives to work outside of official directives – the central plan – increased further with a decline in the level of coercion. With the practice of subverting the system for personal gain reaching all layers of the system, including the centre, interest in applying coercion has subsided. And when in use, coercion was increasingly applied for extracting personal gains as well.

This informal transfer of control to individual players pursuing their personal – rather than collective (or organizational) – interests had certain drawbacks; if exposed, private pursuits were punishable. Besides, access to gains was directly linked to a given position in a decision-pyramid so that there was a considerable element of insecurity. Thus, to move completely outside of the state-owned sector and there apply their experience gained in informal activities became the obvious remedy and pressure on the communist leaders began to mount to open opportunities for legal privately-owned operations. Already under Gierek's government, legal space for such activities was greatly expanded, though only small-scale entities – with limits on employee number – were allowed. Because they found themselves under unfavourable regulations and subject to extortion, the incentive for raising the scale of these private operations was weak anyway.

The real breakthrough came when the Jaruzelski government assumed leadership, and objections to larger private operations were relaxed. This is the point when for the first time concentration of assets in private hands began to accelerate. The government started issuing lucrative trading concessions and production permits in areas where extra profits could be made, often involving foreign contacts where potential for control was limited. These favors were given primarily to the members of political elite, i.e., party bosses, state officials, and the police force. Unlike other private businesses, entities formed in that way could feel secure because the political system provided them also with protection. This marked the real beginning of the formation of so-called political capitalism, where political power is used to acquire private wealth.

This process of converting political positions in the official sector into economic privileges in the private domain further accelerated during Rakowski's government, when additional opportunities for accumulation of assets were provided through new regulations on spin-off companies formed with public capital. From the beginning this process of nomenklatura privatization, as it is commonly called in the literature, was fueled by an increasing sense among the elite that their political positions were endangered, but under Rakowski's cabinet this feeling reached its peak. This inspired the elite to use their remaining time in power to provide themselves with even greater opportunities to build private fortunes and in a matter of month several hundred such spin-offs were formed with little concern for their legality.

With the proliferation of nomenklatura entities – whether newly formed or set up as spin-offs – the once rudimentary market elements expanded into sizable sector, but despite this expansion, this segment of the economic system was still weak. The major source of that weakness was uncertainty over the future of their legal status because they could not know what would happen to them if the opposition took political control. The level of hostility among the opposition to appropriations of assets by the elite was very high, but when the noncommunist government of Mazowiecki came to power only few punitive acts followed. Paradoxically, with their arrival, the pace of asset transfer to the members of the former elite accelerated, in great measure because the government's ability to act in any capacity was severely limited. Besides, it was difficult for liberal-minded reformers in the government to persuade themselves to punish those who were helping them create a private sector.

Also important was the fact that neither the government of Mazowiecki, nor the governments that followed, have moved ahead with a program of mass privatization which would allow a more even distribution of assets. Such a program, giving each citizen a right to free-of-charge acquisition of the same number of shares in state-owned enterprises, has been debated from the very beginning. At the end, in early 1995, under the coalition government of Oleksy, a limited number of such enterprises, accounting for a fraction of the total stock of the nonprivatized entities, was slated for voucher distribution. This was done with great reservation, under pressure from Walesa, who already in an early stage of his presidency promised to support voucher programs (or alternatively to issue credit to all citizens to buy assets). Expanding the finally adopted program to other state-owned enterprises was one of the central points in Walesa's electoral bid in 1995, one that he lost.

These delays in introducing mass privatization initiatives have slowed down the whole process of divesting state assets. No other method could have transferred state-owned capital to private hands rapidly, similarly, for example, to the Czech Republic, where it took three-four years to give most of the capital away. Insufficient private savings and limited processing capability by the state have made other methods, such as public offerings or direct sales, extremely time-consuming. Not surprisingly, by the end of 1994, the value of public assets in state-owned enterprises in the industrial sector transferred to private owners represented slightly more than one-seventh of the initial nominal value of the total capital stock in state hands – though, in terms of relative output, as well as employment, the weight of the privatized enterprises was at that point higher, i.e., about one fifth.

It is not, however, that only through privatization could state-owned companies be forced to start behaving like capitalist entities. Left to themselves, without direction or support, managers – many of them with roots in the old-time elite – in non-privatized companies turned themselves more into capitalist captains of industry. This has been in part out of desire to protect their jobs from elimination in the face of potential bankruptcy. Also important has been the desire to increase their salaries (and bonuses), because under the new rules, they gained more freedom in setting their remunerations. The ultimate objective for them has become, however, the prospect of making financial gains through privatization, i.e., moving to even higher salary scales and, most importantly, obtaining access to preferential shares (with the prospect for multiple gains through initial offerings on the emerging stock market).

With privatization of industry proceeding at a slow pace, the reentry of private ownership – the foundation of the capitalist markets – has proceeded mostly through the formation of new private businesses. Where reforms initiated by Mazowiecki's government made a truly major difference is in the private sector. Unblocking the remaining, still substantial, legal restrictions on private business's access – by allowing complete access to foreign trade operations or leasing of state property – was one of the incentives. Even certain traditional state monopolies, with extra profit margins, were opened to the private sector (e.g., tobacco, liquor). Also, financial burdens on private operations were greatly reduced, though this was not entirely intentional on the government's part. It also reflected the loss of tax-collection capability, or indeed a diminished power to enforce any legal requirements (e.g., product quality, or working conditions).

It is through these new private entries financed with internal savings or informal acquisitions of state assets rather than through official efforts – privatization in various forms – that Poland's economy has been quickly acquiring the features of a market system. Most telling is the trend in the industrial sector, where barriers to entry have been the highest. From a marginal share in 1989, the private sector moved to more than one third of the total industrial output (= sales) at the end of 1994, but its share of total employment at this point was as high as two-thirds. This contribution to the economy was made by the private sector even though its fixed assets accounted for one-sixth of the total, this reflecting productivity differences between private and public companies. But in terms of capital expansion, the private sector out-stripped the public sector by increasing its outlays by a third while the public sector's total investment barely increased at all in 1990–4.

Economic opening

Not only did the communist leaders, in small or large part, uninten-tionally, allow the scope of the private sphere to expand, they also permitted the economy to open to the world market – a process equally inconsistent with the original design of state planning. Se-curing total control over allocation of economic resources and applying collective interest to these choices has proven as unrealistic as the ideologically driven party's attempt to fully insulate the economy from the outside commercial contacts, this to prevent negative impact of market forces left in the capitalist world (such as demand shocks, world inflation, or labour exploitation). Similar to the progressive growth of the private – in a formal or informal sense – spaces, this opening of the economy has proceeded in a rather slow, often invisible, way under pressure from self-interested actors, and, again, the reforms made by the early noncommunist governments had been a great accelerator of that prolonged process.

The decision by Gierek to use massive borrowing from Western sources to fuel the stagnant economy represented probably the first significant break with the traditional practice of self-sufficiency. Whether Gierek's objective was to only briefly expand relations with Western economies – to receive some financing and withdraw after making repayment – or to bring the economy back to the world market on a permanent basis, the consequence of this import-strategy was such that withdrawal to an autarkic economy, or even simply a falling back on the regional bureaucratic-type trading bloc of CMEA, was no longer possible. In brief, Poland's import-driven economy became debt-ridden, its fortunes critically dependent on its ability to receive fresh bank financing, negotiate a restructuring of its payments, and generate export earnings in convertible currencies.

Interestingly, when Gierek's leadership had to finally face the real possibility of insolvency, its response was not to quickly withdraw but rather to come up with a solution that would allow the economy to retain its expanded ties with the world market. At this point, the leadership was prepared to make a major shift in its strategy and allow direct investment on a large scale. Finding it increasingly difficult to attract additional credit – particularly in private banks – Gierek's government considered turning to direct investment. Negotiations were undertaken to allow foreign companies to establish joint ventures with local producers (e.g., with Ford corporation). Politically this was a bold move given the fact that at that time Eastern Europe and the Soviet Union were not ready to try that policy, so that there was no piece of legislation in place to accommodate such arrangements.

When Gierek's government collapsed in the midst of labour unrest, the process of opening the economy was interrupted. Faced with a total ban on fresh credits from Western banks, its successor, Jaruzelski's government, reacted by redirecting domestic production to the Soviet Union and the rest of the CMEA. This relocation, however, was unable to revive industry as it was in great need of Western imports of replacement equipment, spare parts, special materials, etc., which could not be interchanged with CMEA supplies. After a brief effort to return to the CMEA, Poland reassumed its Western orientation, so that by mid-1989, the CMEA share of its total trade volume had dropped dramatically (the only other East European economy which went through a similarly sharp restructuring during those years was Hungary).

The dependence of Poland's economy on the world economy again manifested itself in its great need for foreign credit or other forms of financial (= capital) assistance. Because the slow recovery from the 1979–82 crisis made servicing of the foreign debt quite difficult, new financial sources were needed. More credit was needed to enhance Western imports, almost halved in the aftermath of the 1979 economic crisis but despite its political moderation and strong pro-market orientation Jaruzelski's government was unable to attract more credit, even if just to stabilize Poland's outstanding financial commitments. To reduce repayment pressures, the government set up an entity to buy back at greatly depressed prices its debts on the secondary market (an action going against legal practice). Credit lines were only partially unblocked sometime in late 1987, and only small amounts of money were actually secured.

Because the government was greatly limited in its ability to secure necessary imports, for cash or on credit, private sector found it so much more attractive to bring in foreign goods directly and engage in exports to finance this trade as well. An impoverished consumer market, with limited choice of higher-quality fashionable goods, offered some of the best opportunities for extra profits. But the expanding private production sector, faced with shortages of appropriate equipment and materials, was showing a great interest in accessing foreign markets as well. To satisfy these needs, a huge network of merchants had emerged to personally move goods or ship them in larger quantities, very often through illegal channels. Initially, most of this rapidly growing inflow was coming from other countries of the CMEA bloc, but later on other areas became a source of sizable supplies as well (e.g., Austria, Germany, China and India).

Simultaneously, state-controlled trading enterprises started engaging more aggressively – for personal gain of their employees – in various forms of profitable contacts. Other enterprises that had great exposure to foreign markets, to name those engaged in construction services abroad, began seeking opportunities for individual gains as well. They all became instrumental in setting up numerous joint-venture companies abroad, often to engage in local investing and subcontracting. These, lightly controlled, activities, while extremely helpful in integrating the economy into the world market, were particularly lucrative to the personnel involved. Pressure arose to force the government to allow more self-control, and, indeed, these trade-related enterprises became first to benefit from the privatization wave initiated at the end of the communist rule (as reflected in the conversion of many trading enterprises into joint-stock companies).

It is within this context that Rakowski's government decided to legalize currency, a measure intended to prepare the economy for establishing convertibility. This particular reform followed a number of other steps that were taken over a number of years to open the system. By freeing most of the price-making, Rakowski's predecessors created conditions for linking domestic prices structure to that of the world market. Moreover, systematic steps were taken to reduce subsidization of exports, and to a lesser degree of control over imports (this making price equalization even more effective). While currency remained to be controlled, with only small portion of it left for enterprises to freely allocate, the government engaged in an active exchange rate policy (aimed at reducing an extensive gap between freely traded and officially allocated hard-currencies but also at managing the trade balance).

The process of opening economic system, and thus the economy itself, greatly accelerated under the reform-oriented government of Mazowiecki. Trade liberalization was an integral conceptual element of the general blueprint for rapidly transforming the economy into a market one. There was also another, possibly even overriding, interest in using the opening of the economy as a tool in the struggle against inflation. A combination of radical measures was introduced, among them the decision to allow for partial – excluding capital accounts – convertibility, combined with deep devaluation. Private sector was allowed to engage in all import-export transactions, including in areas typically controlled by states (e.g., tobacco, alcohol). Tariffs were sharply reduced to allow competitive imports to force state-owned enterprises to restructure, but also to prevent them from inflating their prices.

These reforms are often said to worsen the post-1990 recession but it is also true that with these changes came increased export effort on the part of state- and private enterprises. While recession made external markets an obvious substitute for the depressed domestic market, these reforms clearly facilitaed such an adjustment. Expansion of exports in 1990 was indeed phenomenal, exclusively towards under-going an economic recovery Western markets (while exports to the former CMEA members declined sharply). During 1991-3, export growth stabilized but the redirecting of trade away from the defunct regional bloc continued. Another surge in exports came in 1994, and even more so in 1995, when volume of sales increased by more than one-fourth. These were first signs that Poland might have been turning into an export-driven economy.

Welfare commitments

Besides its insistence on non-market economic control and autarkic (or self-sufficient) development, the socialist planning system was de-signed to provide for a tight 'safety net' – combining job security, wage assurances, and stable prices, a comprehensive welfare package by all means. The system inherited by Gierek's regime was not much different from the original design introduced shortly after the war. On the supply side of the labour market, households were generally free to select a job, though voluntary 'exit' from the workforce was not tolerated by the party/state. The demand side was distorted (see Svejnar 1992b: 124), since prices for labour – wage rates – were controlled, and enterprises were not really free to dismiss their workers (except for disciplinary reasons, enterprises were not permitted to lay workers off). Moreover, the system of incentives – linked mostly to the fulfillment of plan targets – encouraged managers to hoard labour (as the easiest factor of production to mobilize when confronted with pressing deadlines).

Under the original system, employees enjoyed not only near perfect job security within their enterprises (or even with respect to their specific job assignment, see Granick 1987), but were also assured that their real wages were not at risk. Workers were not permitted true union representation, nor were they provided with the right to strike, but still there was an implicit agreement by the party/state and the workers, that each annual plan directed enterprises to increase nominal wages, preferably at a steady rate, while trying to hold prices down (particularly for some basic necessities supplied by domestic industry). In addition, workers enjoyed access to subsidized universal pro-grammes, such as free education at all levels, health care, and enter-prise-sponsored vacations.

Gierek's regime was the first to reduce the extent of the 'welfare state', perceived as leaving the party leadership without an effective instrument to stimulate productivity. In particular, the regime decided to allow for greater wage differentials, so that higher productivity could be rewarded and inter-enterprise mobility encouraged. With the widening wage gap, better-paid groups within the labour force began to demand access to more upper-end, luxury goods and greater flexibiity in spending their money as well. To accommodate these needs, the regime allowed for direct imports of many luxury goods, created incentives for private health care and, to give another example, began issuing building permits for individual summer houses.

The changes instituted under Gierek's regime basically allowed for the partial 'exit' of the well-to-do from the 'welfare state', while ordinary people were able to take full advantage of the generously funded social programmes. The threat to the 'safety net' came only with the post-1979 economic crisis, when the communist government began losing its ability to finance all the different programmes at an early level. Still, the regimes did not permit the share of national resources devoted to welfare payments to decline (except for bud-getary payments for temporary sickness and maternity help; see Rutkowska 1991: 15). In other Eastern European countries, such as Hungary and Czechoslovakia, the share of welfare transfers remained relatively stable (at a level comparable to that of the poorer Western European countries (*ibid.*)).

The major change in the post-Gierek communist period was not in the sphere of welfare payments but wage/price security. Jobs were still readily available, for the same reasons as in the past, while the government continued to restrain wage differentials. However, the austerity programme imposed in 1982, followed by governmental efforts to limit wages through highly progressive taxes, left large segments of society with insufficient income to meet their most basic – subsistence – needs. Most affected by poverty were workers in certain underpaid trades (e.g., textile industry), single mothers, and people with fixed incomes (e.g., pensioners) exposed disproportionately more to inflation.

The most critical phase in the dismantling of the 'welfare state' has been the aftermath of the 'shock therapy' programme introduced by Mazowiecki. Not only was massive unemployment permitted to emerge in a short period of time, but, more importantly, many of those laid off were not provided with any form of reliable unemployment compensation or government-sponsored job training. Those workers who have not been laid off have had to accept substantial wage reductions, as enterprises have suffered rapid erosion of their profit margins. Workers' uncertainty has become pervasive, as the post-1990 recession has put the majority state-sector enterprises on what seemed to be the brink of collapse.

Even further, vast, unprecedented income inequality has been permitted, a development strongly related to the expansion of the private sector. While state enterprises' wage funds have been subjected to restrictions, the private sector has been allowed to set wages freely, creating opportunities for some very high incomes. This has been possible in part because of tax incentives for private business and in part due to widespread tax evasion. In the highly distorted market which emerged from the collapse of 'soft' planning, enormous niches for speculative profits or monopolistic rents have been created for the private sector. Novelty-premiums, for those willing to take the risk of introducing previously unknown products, have become another source of extra income, and privatization of state assets has provided an avenue for quick enrichment through shareholding and bonuses for executives (and board members) as well.

While an even larger portion of society has been pushed below the poverty line, welfare payments have, for the first time in the postwar period, been drastically reduced (even though the share of pension payments in the budget expenditure has increased). In an effort to balance the 1990 budget, the government of Mazowiecki decided to cut down subsidies for education, health care, etc. At first, this looked like a temporary measure, but with the renewed threat of budgetary deficits, the government of Mazowiecki, and later those of Bielecki and Olszewski, resorted to further savings (the last government developed a plan to terminate tens of thousands of teachers). At the same time, hospitals could not afford even the most basic medications, and private pharmacies have accumulated piles of unpaid bills for what is left of state-subsidized medicine.

Abandonment of price controls has also disproportionately hit the poorest social groups. As part of the 1990 programme, the post-communist governments have decided to remove price controls for some essentials – subsidies to food products, even the most basic, have been almost completely eliminated and farmers have lost their price guarantees as well. Unlike in many East European countries, the Polish government has also pursued a policy of rapid elimination of subsidies in housing (i.e., rents), support for prices of electricity, and low prices for mass transit. Apparently, faced with wage reductions and rising rents and electricity bills, many households – in some urban sectors in excess of 25 per cent – have stopped making payments.

Summary

We can conclude that while all complex – living – social systems, including communism, are dynamic, they usually undergo change at a slow pace, the evidence of which in Poland's case is abundant.[2] The most obvious proof of that claim, consistent with the essence of the evolutionary paradigm, is that the transition from a state-planned to a competitive-market economy has stretched here over more than two decades and is still far from being finished. This point could be criticized on the grounds that the communist stage of systemic change is not representative because of the apparently unusual conservatism of all hegemonic communist parties. They are said not only to impose a system from design – marxist anti-market model – but also to use their power monopoly to prevent any tampering with it. But even assuming this to be a legitimate reservation, one still finds sufficient evidence of that slowness in Poland by looking at the post-1989 phase of transition, when the communist party's power monopoly was absent.

In the evolutionary paradigm, change is seen not only as slow but also as largely endogenous, i.e., coming from within a given economy rather than from outside. In other words, it is not external shocks but internal dynamics that drive change. In our analysis of economic factors behind Poland's fragile growth pattern we have found that indeed the major sources of it are of internal rather than external origin. This applies, for instance, to the 1979–82 economic crisis which was triggered by the debt crisis but sources of which can be directly linked to the domestic sector (this without neglecting the fact that changes in foreign credit market worsened Poland's liquidity position). Also, the depth of the economic crisis can be largely attributed to the failure by Poland's economy to respond to the external imbalance. This was an internal failure related to the state's loss of ability to manage the economy in the midst of another crisis, the political one.

The process of change is also perceived in the evolutionary perspective as largely indeterministic or random, this because no player in the process has enough information to foresee all elements of a workable system nor enough time to see to it that all these elements are put into action. What that means is that the outcomes of system-building (or tearing down) are largely unintentional, in other words, that they tend to take their own course. Evidence of that is plentyful, beginning with the imposition of the state-planning system right after the war, when, instead of scientific – based on perfect calculations – regulation, a system emerged in which self-interested planners largely improvised. But best documented is the fact that the same planners spent enormous energy on perfecting this system only to see it gradually give in to foreign elements – market mechanisms. Thus, in a way, the collapse of state-planning is such an unintended result.

With this largely nondeterministic character of change comes its nonlinearity, meaning that change does not have to steadily lead to progress, however progress is defined. This would be another point of difference between the here applied evolutionary approach to transition and that of the modernization school, which assumes that the communist – and presumably postcommunist – system were to progress through a series of variants suitable for conditions present at a given time towards a unitary final state. But within the evolutionary view, it is possible for a complete system to be established despite its inferior nature, as was the case with the imposition of state-planning in Poland. Also, working within this framework, one is not surprised that an economic system, even if deliberately reformed to improve its working, may be weakened. The sequence of weak systems that has emerged during Poland's lengthy — protracted – transition seems to fit well this category of regressive institutional change.

Our study also shows that change in a society – including its institutions – proceeds in a coevolutionary fashion, meaning that various elements of the overall systemic order not only interact but also move more or less simultaneously. This nature of institutional change is well reflected in the way economic and political systems have been changing in Poland. Rather then seeing political system as frozen or at best changing at a much slower place than the economic system – a claim made in the totalitarian approach – our study has shown that both of them undergo major changes. Specifically, we have found for the communist period, that while the economic system assumed a series of weak versions, the political system did so also (first losing much of its coercive capability under Gierek, and then suffering a loss of legitimacy during Jaruzelski, only to finally see under Rakowski the communist elite lose its will – desire to rule).

Another element of the evolutionary view of change is that it is animated by diverse individuals rather than monolithic groupings, such as classes – for example, the ruling and ruled classes in the totalitarian approach – or trades and generations as stressed in the modernization view. This is because most of the information needed for systemic change is in the hands – or rather heads – of individual agents and it is their interests that matter most. Our findings for Poland seem to support this view, including the fact that a considerable amount of systemic change has occurred in an informal way, an aspect that comparative economists tend to overlook. This microeconomic mechanism of institutional change has been, for instance, extremely instrumental in the step-wise reinstatement of the market mechanism, a phenomenon called by us 'creeping capitalism'. Though, it is also true that formal programmes, even if not aimed at promoting the market, have often indirectly helped individuals at various levels of decisionmaking to accomplish just that.

By implication, when a single group tries alone to change a given system or, even more, to replace it with another one there is a danger of making costly mistakes, and our study of Poland provides some evidence to support this evolutionary point. In the evolutionary economics such an attempt to impose a systemic solution based on narrow group experience or some sort of blueprint (= perfect design) is called 'constructivism'. We suggest that the 1990 reform programme, known as the shock therapy fits well this category and that the 1990–91 crisis represents in large part the costs that the economy had to pay for excessively ambitious – though well directed – reforms. It is the high cost of these reforms that caused their eventual slowdown as well as partial reversal, so that radical change has been followed by a more gradual one. This substantial shift from one mode of economic reforms to another has been essential for the recovery that the economy has entered in the late 1992.

We have also uncovered another feature of systemic change that seems to agree with evolutionary thinking, namely, that change does not have to mean only conflict among individuals or groups. Rather than view change as conflict – its emergence and resolution – one can look at it as a learning process, where new information is brought in and then spread around. That the latter might really be the right approach is best illustrated by the low level of tension accompanying the most critical point in Poland's protracted transition, which was the departure of the communist party as a hegemony. This event is often called by the name of revolution, but this name, if used with some academic rigor, does not apply to Poland (and possibly even less to other parts of Eastern Europe). That this was a peaceful occurrence, with the power transfer itself rather un-eventful, can be attributed to the fact that a desire for a different type of society – in terms of values and opportunities – was absorbed by a wide spectrum of people among both the rulers and the ruled.

There is also some evidence to support the evolutionary claim that change does not have to mean substitution but may instead involve metamorphosis, i.e., change in agents and not their replacement. Despite its turbulent nature, even the disintegration of a social system, as studied here, has not entailed any large-scale displacement of certain groups by others. We stress in particular that the communist political elite – the party circles and its coercive arm – has been able to preserve much of its influence, though not without its internal conversion. After losing its power monopoly in mid-1989, this elite made a comeback in late 1993 as a coalition of modern parties under a non-marxist program, with another political gain made during the late 1995 presidential elections. Equally remarkable has been the ability of former elite members to transform themselves from guardians of public property into a proprietary capitalist class – this, by using their political influence to appropriate pieces of public assets, but also because of their accumulated experience in managing capital.

Appendix

Appendix 1

Imports of machinery and transport equipment (Total M), specialized machinery (MS), and metal-working machinery (MT), from OECD by Eastern Europe, (1970–82) (million dollars, current prices)

	1970	1971	1972	1973	1974	1975	1976
Eastern Europe							
Total M	1,155	1,365	1,858	2,501	3,152	4,216	4,448
SM	353	331	578	840	1,041	1,284	1,193
MT	131	142	234	354	447	595	847
SM+MT	784	473	802	1,194	1,488	1,879	2,040
Poland							
Total M	232	275	561	1,060	1,497	2,062	1,952
SM	67	73	200	377	448	554	510
MT	31	33	93	159	230	289	320
SM+MT	98	106	293	536	678	843	830
Bulgaria							
Total M	100	117	110	144	225	491	401
SM	28	32	24	48	54	168	155
MT	7	15	13	15	31	43	40
SM+MT	35	47	37	63	85	211	195
Czechoslovakia							
Total M	276	289	304	414	547	668	685
SM	108	110	108	139	186	222	207
MT	25	24	32	43	53	94	118
SM+MT	133	134	140	182	239	316	325
East Germany							
Total M	153	181	219	180	216	332	368
SM	53	48	33	61	72	83	78
MT	13	11	14	13	13	21	23

East Germany (contd)							
SM+MT	66	69	47	74	85	104	101
Hungary							
Total M	135	191	230	273	394	461	524
SM	34	55	65	85	138	135	150
MT	9	11	15	17	23	32	45
SM+MT	43	66	80	102	161	167	195
Romania							
Total M	259	312	434	542	701	674	518
SM	63	86	148	130	143	122	98
MT	46	48	57	107	97	166	97
SM+MT	109	134	205	237	240	288	195

	1977	1978	1979	1980	1981	1982
Eastern Europe						
Total M	4,801	5,591	5,608	5,564	4,531	3,597
SM	1,254	1,404	1,292	1,368	1,045	944
MT	764	989	984	655	496	394
SM+MT	2,018	2,395	2,276	2,023	1,541	1,338
Poland						
Total M	1,834	1,857	1,598	1,805	939	613
SM	439	470	349	407	159	110
MT	322	368	259	183	155	117
SM+MT	761	838	608	580	324	227
Bulgaria						
Total M	334	393	317	437	659	587
SM	116	105	89	106	155	155
MT	37	27	19	38	60	85
SM+MT	153	132	108	144	215	240
Czechoslovakia						
Total M	766	910	878	985	761	725
SM	250	263	257	312	215	223
MT	91	123	109	109	65	65
SM+MT	341	386	366	421	280	298
East Germany						
Total M	301	293	720	538	697	511
SM	69	81	141	139	136	134
MT	26	28	38	70	85	62
SM+MT	95	109	179	209	221	196
Hungary						
Total M	711	978	919	898	943	874
SM	211	295	237	236	262	261
MT	88	80	102	76	60	49
SM+MT	299	375	339	312	322	310

Appendix 1 (*contd*)

	1977	1978	1979	1980	1981	1982
Romania						
Total M	855	1,160	1,176	901	532	287
SM	169	190	219	168	118	61
MT	200	363	335	179	91	16
SM+MT	369	553	554	347	189	77

Source: Calculated from *Foreign Trade by Commodities*, (Paris, OECD) (various years).

Appendix 2

Market shares and relative unit values for exports of major machinery and transport equipment to Western Europe (WE)ᵃ by Poland (P), Czechoslovakia (C), and Hungary (H)

		1978		1982		1984	
		Market share	Relative unit value (WE=100)	Market share	Relative unit value (WE=100)	Market share	Relative unit value (WE=100)
Household	P	1.15	53.4	0.89	50.3	0.59	49.6
Refrigerators	C	0.85	61.1	0.28	45.5	0.55	49.9
	H	2.19	56.1	3.06	58.0	2.78	59.5
Excavating	P	0.13	84.5	0.12	100.3	0.06	138.8
Machines	C	0.04	78.8	0.04	64.2	0.04	90.7
	H	0.01	31.0	0.21	37.8	0.13	39.4
Sewing	P	0.36	26.9	0.73	72.8	0.10	30.1
Machines	C	0.05	79.7	0.10	155.5	0.08	25.2
	H	—	—	—	—	—	—
Machine	P	0.92	13.9	0.24	18.4	0.20	38.5
Tools	C	1.90	14.3	0.88	27.5	0.88	7.4
	H	0.56	21.4	0.44	72.3	0.23	50.8
Typewriters	P	0.14	40.5	—	—	—	—
	C	—	—	—	—	0.03	14.3
	H	0.89	63.1	1.14	32.6	0.19	42.5
Data	P	0.01	83.1	0.00	—	0.00	60.3
Processing	C	0.00	—	0.00	—	—	—
	H	0.02	—	0.17	152.0	0.00	48.2
Ball	P	1.28	43.2	0.98	51.8	0.82	49.8
Bearing	C	3.44	37.6	0.53	47.2	0.41	38.9
	H	0.27	39.4	0.29	47.2	0.36	46.9

Electric	P	1.64	26.8	0.86	9.9	0.75	16.5
Motors	C	2.42	23.7	2.02	12.3	1.86	15.1
	H	1.48	40.3	0.57	19.1	0.40	16.8
Vacuum	P	1.73	59.9	1.81	53.3	1.73	48.0
Cleaners	C	0.68	42.4	0.82	47.6	1.35	42.0
	H	—	—	—	—	—	—
Television	P	0.59	38.9	0.03	50.6	0.07	47.9
Sets	C	0.02	49.7	0.09	35.7	0.05	44.8
	H	—	—	0.25	76.1	0.24	61.8
Radio	P	0.59	74.6	0.34	51.2	0.23	31.8
Receivers	C	0.02	30.5	0.02	38.7	0.01	31.4
	H	—	—	—	—	—	—
Integrated	P	—	—	—	—	—	—
Circuits	C	—	—	—	—	—	—
	H	—	—	—	—	—	—
Tractors	P	0.91	39.5	0.30	43.9	0.42	46.8
	C	2.95	42.0	2.17	40.5	2.23	39.7
	H	—	—	—	—	—	—
Passenger	P	0.30	51.2	0.33	40.5	0.28	40.1
Cars	C	0.18	40.5	0.19	25.5	0.21	30.1
	H	—	—	—	—	—	—
Bicycles	P	1.65	47.9	0.75	43.8	—	—
	C	1.55	43.5	1.82	39.9	0.17	43.3
	H	0.83	49.5	—	—	—	—
Washing	P	0.06	—	0.07	73.5	—	—
Machines	C	—	—	0.01	67.8	0.17	43.3
	H	—	—	0.02	98.2	—	—
Ships	P	2.45	—	2.42	—	9.10	—
	C	—	—	—	—	—	—
	H	—	—	—	—	—	—
Combustion	P	0.32	54.3	0.36	55.8	0.28	54.2
Engines	C	0.08	80.8	0.06	87.7	0.06	152.1
	H	0.02	46.3	0.06	42.4	0.02	85.4

Note: [a] – includes only France, West Germany, Italy, Great Britain, and Austria. A dash means no observation or unreliable data.

Source: Calculated from *Foreign Trade Analytical Tables* (Brussels: Eurostat).

Appendix 3

Share of Western (W) and Eastern (E)[1] markets of Polish exports of selected manufacturing goods (in per cent)

Item		1970	1975	1979	1980	1983
1. Household ovens (units)	W	7.0	0.0	1.7	0.0	1.3
	E	88.0	89.4	97.1	98.8	94.1
2. Washing machines (units)	W	0.0	0.0	0.0	57.9	15.2
	E	57.0	0.0	0.0	0.0	57.7
3. Vacuum cleaners (units)	W	80.0	65.4	70.7	81.7	91.7
	E	15.9	26.1	19.6	13.6	7.0
4. Refrigerators (units)	W	8.2	44.9	69.2	81.4	96.6
	E	90.0	54.2	24.6	14.3	2.1
5. Sewing machines (units)	W	10.9	56.0	68.4	50.8	28.7
	E	87.3	27.0	30.6	40.9	51.2
6. Combustion engines (units)	W	0.2	4.2	0.5	0.2	0.6
	E	49.9	38.3	34.9	34.5	73.1
7. Machine-tools for metal (units)	W	24.7	33.6	62.5	56.3	15.5
	E	46.1	43.9	26.4	28.3	70.5
8. Other machines for working metal (units)	W	0.9	3.6	2.4	0.2	0.0
	E	66.7	68.3	51.3	77.5	94.8
9. Excavators (units)	W	0.0	0.5	6.6	0.0	0.0
	E	89.4	90.0	92.1	91.9	29.6
10. Movers (units)	W	0.0	0.0	6.6	0.0	24.5
	E	86.5	0.0	17.3	38.5	31.9
11. Pumps for fuels (units)	W	28.9	20.5	23.0	0.0	0.0
	E	29.9	52.6	38.7	50.4	68.6
12. Passenger cars (units)	W	11.3	30.8	70.8	83.5	85.6
	E	81.9	47.6	24.2	11.9	12.2
13. Buses (units)	W	0.0	0.0	0.0	0.0	0.0
	E	97.4	87.3	99.5	94.5	83.1
14. Trucks (units)	W	0.0	0.0	6.3	0.0	0.0
	E	98.4	87.7	85.6	78.8	98.9
15. Tractors (units)	W	5.6	15.5	31.9	59.1	30.5
	E	5.8	7.8	0.0	0.0	0.0
16. Bicycles (units)	W	39.5	71.5	87.4	81.0	72.7
	E	27.2	4.1	7.0	7.3	28.4
17. Ships (DWT)	W	0.0	28.3	13.5	63.4	48.0
	E	59.3	57.9	35.9	15.8	4.0

18. Television sets (units)	W	0.2	54.0	497.	25.3	96.8
	E	93.4	0.0	0.0	19.4	2.9
19. Tape recorders (units)	W	0.0	36.4	55.3	0.0	45.1
	E	89.5	61.4	43.9	88.0	53.2
20. Nitrogen fertilizers (tons)	W	13.4	18.5	57.2	54.6	100.0
	E	23.1	11.0	5.4	2.5	0.0
21. Polychloride vinyl (tons)	W	50.0	0.0	72.4	0.0	0.0
	E	39.2	0.0	0.0	98.6	100.0
22. Synthetic fibers (tons)	W	20.8	36.7	5.2	6.8	7.3
	E	22.5	40.3	82.8	84.0	74.5
23. Paint and lacquers (tons)	W	8.5	4.9	5.5	3.2	2.1
	E	82.6	89.6	81.6	82.2	92.3

Note [1] – Eastern countries include: Eastern Europe, the Soviet Union, Cuba, North Vietnam (later Vietnam), Albania.
Source: Rocznik Statystyczny, GUS (Warszawa: GUS), various years.

Appendix 4

Absolute and relative (West Germany=100) unit values in exports of cars to the European Community (absolute in $/kg; relative in per cent in parenthesis)

	West Germany	France	Italy	Soviet Union	East Germany
1986	6.12	5.43	4.69	2.10	1.52
		(88.72)	(76.63)	(34.31)	(24.83)
1985	5.85	5.19	4.51	2.04	1.48
		(88.71)	(77.09)	(34.87)	(25.30)
1984	5.48	4.96	4.24	1.98	1.41
		(90.51)	(77.37)	(36.13)	(25.73)
1983	5.20	4.88	3.90	1.84	1.30
		(93.85)	(75.00)	(35.38)	(25.00)
1982	5.01	4.58	3.59	1.71	1.23
		(91.42)	(71.65)	(34.13)	(24.55)
1981	4.64	4.19	3.39	1.58	1.35
		(90.30)	(73.06)	(34.05)	(29.09)
1980	4.25	4.04	3.50	1.63	1.21
		(95.05)	(82.35)	(38.35)	(28.47)
1979	3.90	3.59	3.24	1.53	1.18
		(92.05)	(83.07)	(39.23)	(30.25)

Appendix 4 (*contd*)

	West Germany	France	Italy	Soviet Union	East Germany
1978	3.59	3.27	2.97	1.53	1.22
		(91.08)	(77.71)	(42.62)	(33.98)
Relative unit values 1978–1986	(100.00)	(97.41)	(98.61)	(80.50)	(73.07)

	Poland	Czechoslovakia	Romania	Brazil	Spain
1986	2.45	2.91	2.89	4.12	5.03
	(40.00)	(47.55)	(47.22)	(67.32)	(82.19)
1985	2.33	2.07	2.82	4.91	4.75
	(39.83)	(35.38)	(48.20)	(83.93)	(81.19)
1984	2.35	1.85	2.96	5.00	4.80
	(42.88)	(33.76)	(54.01)	(91.24)	(87.59)
1983	2.45	1.67	2.74	4.84	4.31
	(47.11)	(32.11)	(52.69)	(96.60)	(82.88)
1982	2.55	1.57	2.89	4.92	3.74
	(50.89)	(31.34)	(57.68)	(98.20)	(74.65)
1981	2.49	1.49	3.21	4.44	3.56
	(53.66)	(32.11)	(69.18)	(95.69)	(76.72)
1980	2.31	1.53	—	—	2.74
	(54.43)	(36.00)	—	—	(64.47)
1979	1.93	1.53	2.02	2.39	2.69
	(49.48)	(39.23)	(51.79)	(61.28)	(68.97)
1978	1.88	1.49	1.95	—	—
	(52.37)	(41.50)	(54.3)	—	—
Relative unit values 1978–1986	(76.38)	(114.57)	(86.92)	—	—

Source: Calculated from *Eurostat, EEC* (various years)

Apendix 5

Poland's imports of industrial machinery[1] from the OECD and replacement needs, 1970–84 (millions of dollars)

	Actual imports	Replacement needs[2]	Difference
	(1)	(2)	(1)–(2)
1970	151	15	136
1971	167	32	135
1972	408	75	333
1973	768	156	612
1974	1,024	270	754
1975	1,339	424	915
1976	1,322	586	736
1977	1,257	732	525
1978	1,289	906	383
1979	1,259	1,081	178
1980	1,020	1,246	−226
1981	552	1,370	−818
1982	402	1,486	−1,084
1983	396	1,608	−1,212
1984	418	1,350	−932

Notes: [1] SITC groups 7–2, 7–3, and 7–4. [2] Assuming a ten year depreciation and five per cent average inflation rate for imports.
Source: Import data from *Trade by Commodities* (Paris: OECD).

Notes

Chapter 1

1 See CMEA Statistical Yearbook (Moscow: CMEA, 1984).
2 Another concern was to create jobs for an incoming wave of labour market entrants (for the nonagricultural workforce was expected to continue growing at 3 per cent annually).
3 Grossman (1983, 1989) provides theoretical arguments on the importance of political leadership (also see Hirszowicz 1980, 1986).
4 See Fallenbuchl (1983), for a discussion of Western efforts to open up Polish markets.
5 Compare with Monkiewicz (1985: 30–1).
6 For additional data, see Poznanski (1988b).
7 The share of Western machinery in total value of investment in machinery increased from 5.9 per cent in 1971 to 8.5 per cent in 1972, and then peaked in 1976, when the respective share was 23.7 per cent. In 1976, Poland reached a share of Western machinery close to that in Hungary in 1971. Hungary's share oscillated between 24 and 28 per cent during the whole period of 1971–79.
8 It is estimated that in 1974 as many as 46 per cent of Western licences were brought as a part of larger deals on complete industrial plants with foreign partners. In 1978, the respective share was even higher at 54 per cent (see Monkiewicz 1985: 64).
9 'Soft' planning is defined here in line with the definition of 'soft' state by Myrdal (1968: 898). Myrdal defines 'soft' state as one where 'policies decided on are often not enforced, if they are enacted at all', and where 'the authorities, even when framing policies, are reluctant to place obligations on people'.
10 See CMEA Statistical Yearbook, Moscow: CMEA, 1981 and National Statistics for Hungary.
11 Podkaminer (1988) argues that shortages of food were caused not by under-equilibrium prices for food but by insufficient supplies of domestic durables. In fact, food (and clothing) were consistently overpriced during 1971–77 and 1978–82, as well as during the post-1982 period. This meant,

as Podkaminer claims, oversubsidization of better-off citizens (with access to cars and other luxuries) at the expense of the lower income segments of society (spending relatively more of their personal budgets on foodstuffs).

12 Gomulka (1986: 211–12) argues that with Gierek's decision to please the striking workers through a freeze on food prices and a promise to raise real wages, 'The politically convenient and economically important freedom to set prices and real wages at levels which the center thought fit was partly lost. (A bid to regain this control was made later on, in June 1976 and in the summer of 1980, but . . . was not successful.)'

13 With greatly increased confidence, workers were able to more effectively put pressure on enterprise management.

14 Real wages dropped by 2.9 per cent in 1978.

15 This development also contrasted with the rest of Eastern Europe, where the slowdown in real wages occurred only around 1980.

16 Trade imbalance in food and grain amounted to 4.3 billion dollars or 24.4 per cent of the total hard-currency trade deficit during 1970–79 (see Gomulka 1986a: 250).

17 The political rationale for the policy shift toward state farms was typical for the Polish leadership, constantly facing a trade-off between economic rationality and ideological obligations. Paradoxically, the very good performance of private farms in 1971–73 made it easier for the regime to undertake the policy. The cause for the policy change appeared to be less Gierek's own initiative than the pressures of agricultural bureaucrats, encouraged by the Soviet Union. The latter had been traditionally wary of the political risk inherent in a large private sector in Polish agriculture. Thus, as in industry, the need to cement a political coalition had a critical impact on economic decisions vis-à-vis agriculture.

18 This was to reverse the declining share of private arable land in the total land used. It went from 75.1 per cent in 1970 to 70.5 per cent in 1975 and to 68.8 per cent in 1977.

19 Almost two million people moved to cities in the 1970–77 period.

20 Changes in relative prices were needed to reverse the decline in relative income of farmers. The ratio of average income in the agricultural sector to that in the nonagricultural sector in 1975 was at 84 per cent of the 1970 ratio, while the 1975 ratio itself was close to 74 per cent.

21 Farm subsidies rose from about 10 per cent of the national income in 1970 to 17 per cent in 1975 and 20 per cent in 1977 (Frydman et al. 1990: 4).

22 In contrast, Hungary's petrochemicals continued to grow at high rates.

23 For example, Romania increased its imports in quantity terms by more than one half and East Germany by one quarter in 1976–79.

24 During 1976–79, the average growth rate for exports to Western markets was 9.3 per cent while for imports, the respective rate was 2.3 per cent (both in current prices).

25 Hungarian purchases, for example, grew around 12 per cent annually in the 1976–78 period.

26 Estimate based on the trend in domestic currency payments for 1980–83 as reported in Table 1.2.
27 See Gueullette (1985).
28 With sharp wage increases triggered by Gdansk negotiations, the government was compelled to divert food – another traditional export – to domestic consumption.
29 Debt service (i.e., amortization and interest payments) amounted to 8.1 billion dollars in 1980, the figure used for the calculation of the relative size of loss from coal production decline. By way of comparison, debt service was at 0.4 billion dollars in 1971; 1.5 billion dollars in 1975; 2.1 billion dollars in 1976; 3.1 billion dollars in 1977; 4.5 billion dollars in 1978; and 6.3 billion dollars in 1979.
30 Debt repayment expected for 1982 was 3.4 billion (*Zycie Gospodarcze*, 1 Nov. 1981).

Chapter 2

1 A ranking of the industrial branches by expenditure on imports of plants, machinery, and equipment from the West during the 1972–77 period indicates that the engineering and chemical industries were first and second, respectively. These two sectors were given a special role in modernizing the economy as they were expected not only to supply new machines and materials for the domestic economy but to contribute to new exports as well. According to the ranking by Fallenbuchl (1983: 122), the above two sectors were followed by less intense importers: metallurgy, light industry, food and tobacco, fuel and energy, construction, wood and paper, minerals, agriculture and printing.
2 Though the study in question is very sensitive to both specification and aggregation of capital-stock data.
3 Kemme and Neufeld (1991) also argue that the impact of technology imports on productivity was diminished because of 'congestion,' i.e., excessive application of capital in production.
4. For details, see Poznanski (1985).
5 For early report of this success, see Fink *et al.* (1984: 5), and Fink (1983).
6 Comparison with Czechoslovakia is also instructive, though a precise interpretation of that particular case is complicated by an unclear picture of the relative involvement of the Czech economy in western technology imports. Additional analysis is needed to determine properly the exact ranking of Czechoslovakia as an importer of western technology. For more information, see Levcik and Skolka (1984).
7 The classification of export products to these categories has been based on the relative (not absolute) scale of licence related technology transfers (see: original data, Poznanska *et al.* 1985).
8 These goods are: household ovens, combustion piston engines (other than foreign cars), machine tools for metals, other metal-working machinery, pumps for liquids, buses, trucks, and tractors. In the case of tractors, large-

scale imports of Western technology took place but the project (i.e., Ursus factory) was not completed by 1978, or by 1983, the last point in our analysis.

Chapter 3

1 As Lewis (1988: 23) points out: 'while making central control more effective, it also brought about a general diminution of local party authority and reduced its influence over government and industry'.
2 Bernhard (1987: 387) conducted a survey of a number of factories taking part in the 1976 strikes to conclude that 'the fact that workers instantly demobilized once they believed that the government had withdrawn the price-rise proposals shows that workers were not prepared to confront the political causes of price reform'.
3 This so-called movement of 'horizontal structures' involving scores of party members that joined independent unions shook the cohesion of the party considerably. The political consequences of that revolt by regular cardholders should not be exaggerated, however, though in some regions, as Lewis (1988: 142) stresses, its impact was most critical.
4 The limits of such a one-actor model focusing on the state as the only source of significant political action are discussed in Hankiss (1989).
5 The literature on corporatism under state-socialism views the party as the sole political actor, which conducts its social projects through various vertically integrated functional groups or officially sanctioned organizations (for an early exposition, see Chirot 1980).
6 Ekiert (1990) argues that at least with respect to pre-1980 collective protests, there is strong indication that they were not aimed against the state idea, or the concept of state (as opposed to the state as a working body). These actions were mostly phrased in the rudimentary language of fairness and economic demands (e.g., proper supplies of goods, price stability).
7 Lewis (1990a: 28) states that the majority of workers wanted to be 'well-governed' by the party.
8 Analysing Polish economic reforms (and those in Hungary), Bauer (1988: 455) also noticed that ideology did not represent an insurmountable obstacle to systemic change. The reason is that institutional reforms were paralleled with 'an ideological "revival" in Eastern Europe: the traditional Stalinist picture of socialism was replaced by a vision of a decentralized, competitive, self-managed, humanized socialism'.

Chapter 4

1 For more, see: Fallenbuchl 1989.
2 The original outline of the reform was published in *Kierunki reformy gospodarczej* (1981, Warsaw: Ksiazka i Wiedza).
3 In a more recent account, Mizsei (1992: 284) argues about 1982 reforms that 'The political atmosphere was very unpleasant indeed at that time; but it

should not distort our perspective when thinking about the reform ... The Polish reform accomplished at that time roughly what the Hungarian reform had done in 1968.'

4 In addition, the government introduced so-called investment orders for projects of priority. There were ten such projects in 1982, but as many as 150 in 1987 (*Zycie Gospodarcze*, no. 29, 1987) (also Kaminski 1989a).

5 1982 unfinished investment projects represented 71.2 per cent of the net material product, and in 1985 – 54.4 per cent.

6 *Rocznik Statystyczny Polski* (Warsaw: GUS, 1988).

7 Specifically, any enterprise with exports exceeding 25 per cent of annual production in a one-year period could now apply for such a concession to the Ministry of Foreign Trade. All products subject to central regimentation were excluded from this new regulation.

8 Out of 110 concessions granted in 1982, only 36 were to state enterprises, while the rest went to private individuals (i.e., small handicraft units) and local (generally small) enterprises.

9 Enterprises were allowed to compete for these resources, but very stiff criteria were applied to the applications, so that only a minor fraction of transactions became financed this way (e.g., 0.02 per cent of total imports in 1983).

10 More, see Poznanski (1986b). As a result of trade difficulties with Western economies, Poland also had to give up many of its cooperation agreements (e.g., with such multinational corporations as Singer, Grundig, Thompson), another potentially important source of technological assistance.

11 See Poznanska *et al.* (1985).

12 According to official sources quoted by Bartosiewicz and Malecki (1991: 11), specific figures for net transfers in consecutive years (all in million dollars) were as follows: 1979 – +202; 1980 – −202; 1981 – +261; 1982 – −555; 1983 – −1310; 1984 – −1259; 1985 – −1305; 1986 – −1272; 1987 – −1260; 1988 – −1217; 1989 – −932; 1990 – +543.

13 E.g., rails in 'Katowice' mill, shapes in 'Pokoj' mill, alloy steel and pipes in 'Jednosc' mill. Another example is the 180 million rubles (plus 20 million dollars) credit to Polish shipyards to accommodate Soviet needs. A veneer factory in Zory received 6.3 million rubles and 3 million dollars to start up production that will be used to repay Soviet credits.

14 In the tractor industry, micromodels for agricultural purposes were chosen for joint manufacturing. Joint production of delivery vans with high pressure engine got into the planning stage, with 30,000 units to be made in the Soviet Union and 35,000 units in Poland. It was decided that electronically operated automatic washing machines would be manufactured in cooperation with the Soviet Union. Colour television sets of a new generation were set to be launched in a joint effort by 1990 (400,000 units total). The scope of Polish-Soviet industrial cooperation, which clearly suffered some losses during Gierek's period, was also increased, including the production of tractors.

15 In 1988, seven joint-ventures between Poland and the Soviet Union were

established, of which four were in Poland. In 1989, fourteen such ventures were finalized on Polish territory and an additional twenty in the Soviet Union, with some of them involving third parties from Western countries.

16 The cosmetics factory Miraculum became the first case of such a jointly-managed entity. Other enterprises designated to become joint-stock companies with the Soviet Union were machine-tool factory 'Avia', chemical apparatus factory in Opole, synthetic fibres plan in Zory, electromagnetic clutch and brake factory in Ostrzeszow, to name a few.

17 According to Kaminski (1986), the share of the CMEA in total turnover increased from 54.9 per cent to 65.2 per cent between 1978 and 1984. Shift towards the Soviet Union was facilitated in part by exchange rate policy. During 1981 and then during 1983–1985, the ruble was overvalued relative to the dollar (with price of each currency determined by the government independently).

18 Formally, the majority of prices continued to be determined by enterprises themselves, but in practice the state held tight control over them (e.g., through a requirement of advance notice about intentions and right to delay price increases). Apparently, about 82 per cent of prices were controlled in 1985 either directly or indirectly (*Zycie Gospodarcze*, no. 41, 1987).

19 Hungary's economy showed a rather similar pattern of concentration on heavy industries. The share of light industries in Hungary's total investment was close to that in Romania, at the time one of the highest in Eastern Europe. The energy sector in Hungary took as large a share of total investment as in Czechoslovakia and East Germany (see Csaba 1989: 17).

20 Kotowicz (1989) provides other indicators of the concentration of investment in those sectors.

21 Since 1982, output in that sector grew at an unusually high rate, so that by 1985 it passed the 1979 level. However, in 1987 agricultural output went back to the 1979 figure. The most severe situation was in animal production, which was 9.5 per cent below that level. And there was very little, or no, growth in 1988.

22 This continued even though the Ministry of Finance came up in 1987 with a package of anti-monopoly regulations to be directed at enterprises supplying more than 30 per cent of goods of a given kind.

23 Gomulka (1986b: 296) remarks that after years of reforms 'the actual economic system may be better described as one of 'informal command planning' rather than of indirect (market-regulated) central planning', indicating a limited success of the 1982 programme.

24 These measures helped to somewhat reverse the Stalinization programme that, in the early fifties, drove the share of the non-agricultural private sector below 4 per cent of total employment. That share remained more or less unchanged through the seventies, after which it quickly crossed the 6 per cent mark, basically as a result of the crisis-related reduction in state construction and cutting of administrative personnel (Aslund 1985: 230). The trend continued under Messner, this time mostly due to incentives created for the private sector.

25 According to Wojciechowska (1988), out of 2,211 enterprises surveyed in 1987, 1,063 enjoyed subsidies or tax relief. On average subsidies amounted to 345 per cent of total profits reported by enterprises (ranging from 0.1 to 1,117 per cent in individual cases).

26 In 1987 there were 100 enterprises that worked on the basis of their own 'restructuring' programmes while an additional 50 deficit enterprises were put under 'commissary' control. Most of them were saved from bankruptcy by merging with more successful enterprises. Many were helped out by their clients who came up with financial assistance.

27 Hungarian analysts also reported a broad deterioration of export efficiency during the post-1979 period. According to Csaba (1989: 21) the value of sales in such large sectors as light industry, engineering and chemicals was below the direct cost of material input from imports.

28 For instance, the helicopter enterprise in Swidnik reported a 42 per cent decline in Soviet demand since 1986 (*Polityka*, no. 46, 1989).

29 An example of trade tensions is the so-called customs war between Czechoslovakia and the Soviet Union in 1988. Soviet tourists converted rubles to koronas at a commercial rate. Rubles accumulated in Czechoslovak banks were then converted to transferrable rubles at a rate less advantageous than the commercial. Thus, Czechoslovakia incurred substantial financial losses (see: Lavigne 1989: 8).

30 *Economic Survey of Europe, 1989* (New York: ECE, United Nations), reports that in 1988 the share of CMEA in total exports of its particular East European members was as follows (figures for the Soviet Union itself in brackets): Bulgaria – 80.9, [62.8] per cent; Czechoslovakia – 73.0, [43.1] per cent; Hungary – 44.6, [24.5] per cent; Poland – 40.7, [24.5] per cent; Romania – 40.8, [24.0] per cent.

31 The increase in the absolute level of consumption was not fast enough to compensate for both population growth (5.7 per cent during 1981–87) and earlier losses. In 1988 the average real consumption of all material goods was still 6 per cent below the 1980 level, and for foodstuffs alone the difference was 8 per cent.

32 The central element in Rakowski's economic programme was also the removal of most of the remaining state controls in material supplies. The proportion of industrial inputs controlled by branch ministries (through subordinate supply organizations) was between 30 to 40 per cent of total sales in this category in 1983 (*Zycie Gospodarcze*, no. 45, 1983). By early 1989, only a handful of key material supplies was distributed centrally, including coal, coke, pulp, crude oil, and special steels. With this decentralization measure came further expansion of prices freely set by enterprises on material supplies.

33 According to some reports, the tax burden at the end of 1989 often represented in the private enterprises only a fraction of financial supplements (e.g., to food purchases) to their owners. Moreover, as much as 40–60 per cent of revenues by the private sector was not reported.

34 During the first half of 1989 alone, as many as 250,000 workers left the state

sector, so that the total number of people so employed exceeded 1.5 million (excluding agricultural production).

35 The shares were to be split in the following way: 80 per cent to the Treasury and 10 per cent to workers and managers respectively, at least in the initial period.

36 The 1989 legislation (i.e., Transformation Law) passed by the Hungarian parliament allowed managers to acquire ownership of their enterprises.

37 The scope of that practice can be judged from a 1990 official study of 152 joint-stock enterprises with the participation of state enterprises in the Katowice region. Among them thirty-eight were managed by directors (a total of sixty-five people) from involved state enterprises, and twelve more were controlled by directors of cooperatives (i.e., their regional layer). Many enterprises had been turned into stock companies and then leased to their directors in exchange for annual dividends. The first was the electronic producer 'Omig' in early 1989, followed by the fashion company 'Telimena', a construction company, and a shoe producer 'Chelmek'.

38 In 1985, the deficit was equivalent to 0.9 per cent of the gross national product, in 1986 it was 1.1 per cent, and in 1987 it reached 0.7 per cent.

39 Milanovic (1991a: 48) argues that the government's inability to resist wage increases was the main cause of Messner's failure to eliminate inflationary overhang.

40 In 1988, the maximum interest rate was set at 30 per cent with the assumption that inflation would be less than this figure, though actual price increases reached about 60 per cent.

Chapter 5

1 See, e.g., Holzman (1987) for discussion.
2 See, e.g., Poznanski (1987).
3 See Tyson (1984) for discussion of this issue.
4 The actual hard currency net debts in the region were as follows:

	1975	1980	1984	1987
Eastern Europe	21.8	66.5	59.4	91.0
in which:				
Bulgaria	2.3	4.1	1.5	5.3
Czechoslovakia	0.7	5.0	3.8	5.3
East Germany	5.4	14.1	12.4	20.4
Hungary	3.3	10.1	9.4	18.0
Poland	7.8	24.0	25.8	37.7
Romania	2.3	9.2	6.5	4.3

Source: Economic Survey of Europe in 1992–1993, the United Nations, Geneva (1993).

5 Net debts for the sample of developing countries were as follows:

	1975	1980	1984	1987
Developing countries	75.7	184.7	332.4	387.9
in which:				
Argentina	4.9	16.8	37.1	43.5
Bolivia	0.8	2.3	3.5	4.1
Brazil	23.4	56.7	89.6	103.5
Chile	4.4	9.4	17.3	17.4
Indonesia	10.4	18.1	26.6	35.7
Malaysia	1.8	5.2	16.1	19.6
Mexico	16.6	41.3	87.6	95.2
Peru	4.4	7.4	10.1	13.0
Philippines	2.8	9.0	14.3	21.6
South Korea	6.2	18.5	30.2	34.3

Source: World Bank, *World Debt Tables* (various years).

6 See also Tyson (1985).
7 Yugoslavia, not covered in this comparison, was able to stabilize its foreign debt during 1984–1987, and then succeeded in reducing its debt to a large degree during 1988–1989.
8 Hungary was receiving around $1 billion a year, mostly from the International Monetary Fund (see Marer, 1985b).
9 Our discussion assumes that debt reduction is *per se* desirable. To the extent that large debts are eventually forgiven by the lendors, this is not a valid assumption.
10 Brazil and Mexico are two of the three newly industrializing countries of Latin America.
11 For all sectors, this share slumped from 12.6 per cent in 1980 to 8.7 per cent in 1984. For fuels, respective shares for these years were 26.9 per cent and 15.6 per cent; metallurgy – 18.1 per cent and 13.0 per cent; engineering – 24.2 per cent and 20.7 per cent; light industry – 12.2 per cent and 6.5 per cent; for agriculture the 1980 share was 2.0 per cent, down to 1.6 per cent in 1984.
12 See, e.g., Schumpeter (1939).
13 Calculated from OECD *Foreign Trade by Commodities* (Paris: OECD, 1982).
14 The newly industrialized countries registered a rapid rise in imports in these categories of goods during this period. See Poznanski (1985).
15 The market shares measured in dollars are affected by the fact that the US currency appreciated in some years (particularly in 1984 when the value of the US dollar increased by almost 30 per cent against some Western European currencies). The appreciation of the US dollar caused a downward bias in dollar-denominated market shares for countries whose export prices are set in terms of Western European currencies. This was the case of East European exporters but, interestingly enough,

not of their newly industrialized competitors, such as Brazil or South Korea.

To separate this effect, we have calculated market shares in European Currency Units (ECU) for the Western European market itself. By this measure, the share of Eastern Europe declined from 1.76 per cent in 1978 to 1.39 per cent in 1983, and moved back to 1.55 per cent in 1984. Again, machinery and transport equipment reported a sharp decline (from 1.01 per cent in 1978 to 0.61 in 1983, and up only to 0.64 per cent in 1984).

Statistics for Western Europe also show that Poland's share in Western Europe's total imports declined sharply during 1978–84, from 0.62 to 0.36 per cent. This decline represented more than four fifths of the Eastern European decline, with Czechoslovakia, Hungary and Romania contributing the balance. Bulgaria showed no change, while East Germany was the only country experiencing an improvement in the market share.

16 More, see Marer (1985a).

17 See interesting analysis by Tyson (1985).

18 Terrell's (1987) analysis shows that it is impossible to determine the elasticity of substitution between domestic and Western capital precisely. However, it is likely that import substitution effect was not very strong, given the fact that such as important segment of the machinery sector as machine-tool production was not given a high priority in technology imports under Gierek's regime.

19 For instance, combined East European and Soviet royalties to the United States reached $50 million in 1977, $33 million in 1979, and $17 million in 1984 (*Survey of Current Business*, June 1985) (a similar trend can be detected from West German data).

Chapter 6

1 There are certain similarities between the anti-crisis programme of Jaruzelski and that pursued by Kadar after the 1956 crisis. Kadar began his term of office with a period of police repression and regressive economic reforms (e.g., his regime launched a programme of forced collectivization of land). Later, however, Hungary experienced a considerable relaxation politically, which went beyond that which existed prior to the clash (see Hirszowicz 1986). The boldest economic reforms of the time were instituted as well (for more discussion, see Marer 1985b). The principal difference between the two cases is that the Jaruzelski regime acted more rapidly; that is, the regressive period was shorter in this case and the reforms that followed were executed far more quickly than in post-1956 Hungary.

2 According to Lewis (1990a, 1990b), the regime wanted coalition politics but without institutional pluralism, i.e., it wanted to work with selected partners.

3 In another interpretation, the intelligentsia is portrayed as the key force responsible for challenging the communist establishment. Grudzinska-Gross (1992: 141) in her very personal account argues that: 'The 1989 velvet revolutions in Eastern Europe were led and carried out largely by dissent

intellectuals.' However, the political history of anti-communist struggle is being rewritten to downplay the role of intellectuals, so that 'in the new interpretation common in Poland and Czechoslovakia, the 1989 revolutions were simply a natural resistance of entire nations opposed to national and religious oppression' (*ibid.*: 145). More on the role of the intelligentsia, see Szelenyi and Martin (1991).

4   Public opinion polls, conducted in 1984, detected popular support for central control of the economy and major distrust of capitalist markets. In one survey, 63 per cent of respondents favoured a state-run system, with industrial workers comprising the most supportive group (see Nowak 1990: 3). Clearly, workers continued to appreciate the benefits of 'free riding' or taking advantage of the state provided by the traditional system.

5   Ekiert (1990: 18) argues that since 1980 the communist party of Poland was no longer able to define the limits of change nor its direction. 'Instead, they were only able to respond to the challenges and processes which developed outside of the political space controlled by the regime.'

6   Kolankiewicz (1988: 157) describes the political situation at this time as one with an 'active state courting a passive population' into reforms.

7   Staniszkis (1987) argues that actions by independent unions were ineffective not only before martial law but also after its imposition. She describes the behaviour of the opposition after the state of war as 'non-transformative rebellion'. In her words, it was a peculiar combination of low-level political disobedience with acceptance of the basic features of the existing system, of which the government was a representative.

8   Among the many authors who refer to the final stage of communist rule as a 'revolution' is Gross (1992: 57), who describes these years as a 'revolutionary period'. For a qualified view, see Ekiert (1990), who argues that 'Only in Poland was the development of a new political society fully realized', so that the country was able to avoid a mass upsurge, while, in contrast, in East Germany and Czechoslovakia, where no political society had a chance to develop, the collapse of the communist party was preceded by a popular upsurge.

9   As Grudzinska-Gross (1992: 146) puts it: 'The coincidence of interests between the opposition and the then-authorities permitted the peaceful transition to post-Communism' (also Ash 1989; Bruszt 1989)

Chapter 7

1   Among East European countries, Czechoslovakia adopted a 'wage contract', Austrian-style, within which workers agreed to some losses in real wages in exchange for generous unemployment payments.

2   Edwards (1992) evaluates Mexico's policy of wage de-indexation as a positive experience and generalizes that 'A fairly democratic society can successfully bring down inflation by working not only through the exchange rate but also by working in the direction of wage, and other, contacts, and by supporting exchange rate anchors through income policies.'

3 At that early stage, at least through mid-1990, enterprises did not even meet the upper limits of wage payments permitted by the government.

4 Such deep devaluation was only partially intentional since, in the absence of a market for currency, the government had no way of precisely determining the equilibrium rate (Crane 1992; Dabrowski 1992b).

5 By mid-1990, the government relaxed monetary restrictions to reverse the economic decline. The interest rate on credit was lowered (from 4 per cent to 2.5 per cent monthly) and credit limits for banks were increased. Government expenditures were expanded to reduce unexpected budgetary surpluses. Moreover, real wages were allowed to increase in the second half of 1990. The economy responded to this aggregate demand expansion with a visible upturn in production, but at the same time, inflation accelerated.

6 The loss in output should be distinguished from the welfare effect, the former being greater than the latter. Elimination of shortages wiped out the welfare loss related to the extended search for goods (proportional to the price gap between the official and black market; see Lipton and Sachs, 1990a). The quality of goods has improved due to expanded imports of consumer goods (though many substandard products have been shipped in as well).

7 Industrial output in the state sector calculated per work-day declined by 25.2 per cent and again by 15.2 per cent in 1991, with the cumulative rate of decline equal to 36 per cent (*Zycie Gospodarcze*, 1992, no.4).

8 See *Informacja Statystyczna GUS*, 8 January 1991.

9 Textile industry employment, mostly concentrated in the Lodz area, declined by 50 per cent through mid-1992.

10 Hidden unemployment in state industry was estimated at 0.9 million in 1991. This means that, if excess labour is eliminated, the rate of unemployment would almost double.

11 There was, however, extensive disguised unemployment, or overmanning.

12 While the private sector has been allowed to expand, no provisions have been made to ensure effective collection of taxes from that sector. There has been no reporting system in place, or collection apparatus, not to mention a 'tax police' (it disintegrated in late 1989), inviting massive tax evasion by the private sector, already common during the communist year). The government has, in response, been increasing the tax burden on state enterprises, whose books have still been under bank control, which makes collection less difficult. While helpful in balancing the state budget, this shift has created a tax bias against the public sector (aggravated by various tax reliefs and other exemptions not available to state enterprises).

13 The deficit was largely due to a rapid increase in imports of consumer goods. In 1991, net imports of consumer goods were $4.7 billion (Gabrich *et al.* 1992: 6; also see Laski et al. 1993).

14 According to Berg and Sachs (1992: 141), real consumption decline in 1990 was about −4.8 per cent and with quality gains, it could be assumed that loss in welfare was nil.

15 Berg and Sachs (1992: 138) state that 'In 1991, the decline is most

importantly related to the collapse of Soviet trade, rather than to the economic reform programme'.

16 In 1989, 10.9 per cent of production of the electric machinery industry was exported to the Soviet Union, and 11.4 per cent in 1990 (Rosati 1992: 91).

17 Calvo and Frenkel (1991) argue that for successful transition, it is essential that effective capital markets be put in place before many other major steps are made. They stress that if price liberalization is executed in the absence of working capital markets, a negative supply-effect is likely. Higher prices of inputs will reduce working capital that will be difficult to build up since lending institutions won't be able to assess the creditworthiness of their clients.

18 It is estimated that the private sector received only 2.7 per cent of the total credit issued during 1990 (see Lipton and Sachs 1990). In 1991, the respective share increased to approximately 10 per cent of the loan portfolio held by state banks. The private sector has been forced to rely on funds available from family members or friends, plus the rapidly expanding 'grey' financial sector, generating only limited amounts of finance.

Chapter 8

1 Privatization is narrowly defined here as the process of transferring state capital to other hands (see Brabant 1992). There are many other definitions of privatization currently in use (compare Vernon 1988; Vickers and Yarrow 1988).

2 In agriculture there were periodic efforts to recollectivize, combined with hardening of conditions for private farming. A case in point is the middle of Gierek's regime when older farmers were forced off their land and the allotment of their sites of excess land to other private farmers was virtually stopped (Poznanski 1986a). Outside of agriculture, there were recurrent efforts to trim the sector, mostly by making it harder to get supplies and by excessive taxes.

3 According to Dallago (1991), in Hungary, private enterprises were limited to thirty workers. However, on average, the existing private enterprises were only about twelve workers strong – a reflection of the inhospitable economic environment.

4 They were also subject to extortion by police, internal revenue, fire department, etc., permitted for the sake of protection against the threat of ultimate liquidation.

5 The concept of 'working groups' was patterned after the Hungarian reforms of 1982–83, whereby a number of new forms of ownership were initiated, including the so-called 'enterprise contract work association' (i.e., a few workers would be allowed to use an enterprise's facilities without assuming risk) and the 'economic contract work association' (which would permit group members to belong to different enterprises and invest their own capital).

6 The legal (tax-contributing) private sector in Hungary was officially

estimated to produce 9.4 per cent of the gross national product in 1988 (Balazs and Laki 1991: 65). The share of this sector in households' expenditures reached 14.6 per cent for the whole of 1989, with the bulk of this expenditure spent on services. In 1988, the share of the private sector in national services output was 63.7 per cent (but only 2.3 per cent in industry; up from 1.3 per cent in 1982) (*ibid.*).

7 The World Bank insisted on the speedy enactment of the July 1990 Privatization Act, making its passage a precondition for a structural adjustment loan.

8 For instance, lower taxes were to apply to that portion of wage payments that is averted to stocks or bonds. Also, a special Bank of Workers' Ownership was created in 1990, a non-commercial institution aimed at financial assistance of employee stocks.

9 Walesa, President since late 1991, was the first to strongly endorse the idea of 'popular capitalism,' i.e., the free distribution of shares. This was the centrepiece of his presidential campaign launched under the slogan of 'acceleration' (see: Lewandowski and Szomburg 1989).

10 The 'fast track' programme called for conversion of about 400 state enterprises into Treasury-owned joint stock companies (accounting for 25 per cent of industrial sales and for 12 per cent of the total industry's employment). Of the listed value of assets, 60 per cent was to be offered for vouchers and thus handed over to the funds, while 30 per cent of the shares was to be allocated to the state.

11 The total number of these buyouts represented less than 10 per cent of the total number of state enterprises this year.

12 The exact division of share enhancement would be: 70 per cent to managers, 20 per cent to workers, and the remaining 10 per cent to the board of directors.

13 Grosfeld (1990; p.16) stresses that: 'the fundamental problem that the reform economists face today [is] the problem of transition. To this, economic theory has no answer. It is a political question' (also see: Comisso 1991; Dewantripont and Roland 1993)

14 This variant shares some similarities with the private joint-stock company, though arguably stockholders in such a company can have more influence over the policies of management than the state with respect to its public corporation (Milanovic 1989).

15 The proposal by Gomulka (1992b) called for the state to provide state investment banks with a balanced packet of shares in various enterprises, representing only a fraction of their value. These banks would have the right to buy and sell shares, with voting rights belonging to the bank managers themselves. Managers would be rewarded with the net earnings on the bank portfolio. It could be assumed that profit-motivated bank managers would buy shares of better performing enterprises, thus allowing those enterprises to raise funds for their development. With that, profit maximization should become a goal of enterprise managers – or worker collectives – as well.

16 As a result, managers often ended up being paid less than their much sought workers, including those in manual jobs. While many managers left public appointments due to unfavourable salaries, others were simply forced out of their jobs by workers. In 1990 alone, about 20 per cent of managers were dismissed.

17 Bonds were introduced with the 1985 law. The new regulation on bonds was passed in 1988 (Czekaj 1989). The Hungarian experience with state-issued bonds has been somewhat different, mostly because supply/demand imbalances were less severe there than in Poland. Nevertheless, in both cases, initial bond transactions were weak due to lack of interest. Hungary issued bonds for 5 billion forints in 1988 but bonds for only 800 million forints were sold. The high rate of inflation, between 9 to 18 per cent yearly, made bonds very unattractive. The government had to buy back the bonds worth a few billion forints.

18 Szelenyi (1989: 273) describes this strategy as 'a bold attempt to build civil society without private ownership'.

19 Independent unions have also engaged in capital acquisitions. They have established a number of joint-stock companies – often using membership fees – to generate revenues for their political activities. The Catholic Church has largely expanded its economic activities during the last several years too, one good example being the self-financed agricultural foundation (e.g., offering credits for water projects).

20 Under the leveraged buyout or 'liquidation' formula, the management and workforce of an enterprise make a downpayment equal to roughly one-third of the estimated value of the enterprise's assets in their enterprise, with the rest of the purchase to be financed by yearly installments spread over a five-year period. When the balance has been paid, the lease holders become the rightful owners of the enterprise.

21 Kornai (1992a) stresses the dilemma faced by post-communist reformers who need foreign participation in divestment but are also aware of the loss of sovereignty. He calls for incentives for foreigners to join the privatization process (particularly in the financial sector) but argues that limitation on the share of foreign ownership is important, since excessive participation reduces the options available to state policymakers.

22 In Hungary, in 1989, two acts – the Hungarian Company Act and the Act of Foreign Investment – allowed managers of state enterprises to negotiate foreign minority joint ventures without state approval. Since 1991, even foreign majority ventures were permitted without state licensing.

23 Compared with $400 million earned from divestment in Hungary, and with $500 million obtained by the Czechoslovak government in the same year.

24 Demand for helicopters from that enterprise fell by 42 per cent between 1986 and 1989, mostly due to lower orders from the Soviet Union. The management decided in 1989 to convert part of the factory to joint stock with Italian producers to make small tractors. This operation guaranteed jobs for only 15 per cent of workers. At the union meeting, the majority of

workers rejected this option and agreed to wait for new regulations to consider turning the enterprise into an employee stock unit (see *Polityka*, no. 46, 1989).

25 To avoid monopolistic manipulation, funds were not allowed to obtain more than 20 per cent of shares in any single enterprise. But collusion between the funds may be difficult to police, with many funds already branching out to use sister funds to acquire additional shares in targeted enterprises.

26 In Czechoslovakia, mass privatization has been conducted in two rounds – the first involving around 40 per cent of assets and the second accounting for 60 per cent of targeted assets. Altogether, 1,492 enterprises will be put up for sale in mid-1992, with the total value of shares estimated at around $10 billion. The stock market – to allow for trading in shares – was to be open when all 'points' are allocated among enterprises.

27 In Czechoslovakia, according to the original programme, the average enterprise was expected to make about 60 per cent of its equity available for conversion into vouchers, but up to 97 per cent have been offered for conversion under the existing regulation (with the remaining 3 per cent to be left as a restitution fund). All citizens were allowed to purchase voucher books for a nominal price (i.e., equivalent to an average weekly wage). These vouchers could be converted into shares in any enterprise listed by the government (expected to represent at least 50 per cent of book value in over 70 per cent of all enterprises). Alternatively, citizens could entrust their vouchers to investment funds (see: Crane 1991; Hare and Grosfeld 1991).

28 According to another source, by mid-1992 there were 286 Treasury joint stock enterprises (up from 115 in early 1992) with 36 so 'commercialized' enterprises actually privatized. The same source placed the total number of privatized enterprises at 542, plus 707 divested through the 'liquidation' procedure (*Zycie Gospodarcze*, no. 32, 1992).

29 In March 1993 the total number of foreign investment projects – tentative, announced, and concluded – was 162, of which 48 fell in the category of acquisitions (i.e., purchases of shares), 46 were joint-ventures, and 68 were green-fields investment. Of all foreign investments, amounting to $556 million in disclosed value, $313.5 million involved acquisitions, with the second largest category being joint-ventures at $170.6 million. By way of comparison, in Hungary, of a total value of $3,163 million, $1,093 million was directed to acquisitions, and $1,141 million to joint ventures. In Czechoslovakia, the respective figures were: $1,390 million for the total value of investment, $880 million in acquisitions, and 444 in joint ventures (*Financial Times*, 28 September 1993).

The total number of joint venture companies with foreign capital in Hungary in early 1990 was close to 1,600. At that time joint-ventures accounted for 5.5 per cent of total production and 11 per cent of Hungary's total investment outlays (see Hare and Grosfeld 1991: 11). The pace of foreign direct investment has accelerated since, so that in mid-1992 the total value of investment actually spent (as opposed to declared) reached $1.3 billion at the end of 1991, and is estimated to exceed $2 billion by mid-1992. The total inflow of foreign capital amounted to 4 per cent of the national product in mid-1992, a very high share by any international standards. It is important to note that while foreign acquisitions have been fewer in numerical terms than domestic sales, the former involved some of the larger state enterprises (e.g., Tungstam lamp factory, electrical plant Orion, Videoton electronic factory).

30 For comparison, in Russia, the private sector – including farming – accounted for 1.6 per cent of total employment in 1990, and for 2.3 per cent in 1991 (Tedstrom 1993: 42).

31 There have also been objections raised to working with a scheme which has never been tested by capitalist countries. Implementation of this system on a large-scale, as attempted by Suchocka's government in mid-1993, could change the pattern of asset transfers identified here.

Chapter 9

1 While Kornai talks about weak and strong linkages between ownership forms and methods of coordination, we talk about weak and strong property structures and coordination forms instead. According to Kornai (1992a: 108), 'a linkage between an ownership form and a type of coordination is strong if it emerges spontaneously and prevails in spite of resistance and countermeasures. It is based on a natural affinity and cohesion between certain types of ownership and certain types of coordination mechanisms.'

2 The inevitability of a slow transformation from socialist to capitalist economy and thus of a slow withdrawal of state interventions is demonstrated by a variety of scholars taking perspectives other than our evolutionary approach. Such point is made for instance by an economic historian Kochanowicz (1993) and in Amsden et al. 1995).

References

Amann, R. and J. Slama, 1976, 'The Organic Chemicals Industry in the USSR: A case study in the Measurement of Comparative Technological Specification by Means of Kilogram', *Research Policy*, no. 5.

Amman, R., J. Cooper and R. Davies, ed., 1977, *The Technological Level of Soviety Industry*, New Haven: Yale University Press.

Amsden, A., J. Kochanowicz and L. Taylor, 1995, *The Market Meets its Match. Restructing the Economies of Eastern Europe*, Cambridge MA: Harvard University Press.

Arendt, H., 1968, 'The Origins of Totalitarianism', New York: Harcourt.

1989, 'Refolution', *New York Review of Books*.

Åslund, A., 1985, *Private Enterprise in Eastern Europe*, London: Macmillan.

1991, *Gorbachev's Struggle for Economic Reform*, Ithaca: Cornell University Press.

Balazs, K. and M. Laki, 1991, 'The Weight of Private Economy in Terms of Money in the Incomes and Expeditures of Hungarian Households', *Acta Oeconomica*, vol. 43, nos. 1–2.

Balcerowicz, L., 1995, *Socialism, Capitalism and Democracy*, Oxford: Oxford University Press.

Bartlett, D., 1992, 'The Political Economy of Privatization: Property Reform and Democracy in Hungary', *Eastern European Politics and Societies*, vol. 6, no. 1.

Barzel, Y., 1993, *Economic Analysis of Property Rights*, Cambridge: Cambridge University Press.

Batt, J., 1988, *Economic Reform and Political Change in Eastern Europe: A Comparison of the Czechoslovak and Hungarian Experiences*, New York: St Martin's Press.

1991, *East Central Europe from Reform to Transformation*, London: Pinter Publishers.

Bartosiewicz I. and W. Malecki, 1991, 'Impact of External Debt and Capital Infllow on Economy Stabilization and Transformation', Working Papers No. 22, Institute of Finance, Warsaw.

Bauer, T., 1978, 'Investment Cycle in Planned Economies', *Acta Oeconomica*, vol. 21, no. 3.

1988b, 'Hungarian Economic Reform in East European Perspective', *East European Politics and Societies*, vol. 2, no. 3.

1991, 'The Microeconomics of Inflation under Economic Reforms: Enterprises and their Environment', in Commander, S., ed., *Managing Inflation in Socialist Economies in Transition*, Washington, DC: The World Bank, Economic Development Institute.

Bernhard, M., 1987, 'The Strikes of June 1976 in Poland', *Eastern European Politics and Societies*, vol. 1, no. 1.

1990, 'Barriers to Further Political and Economic Change in Poland', *Studies in Comparative Communism, vol. 33*.

Bialecki, I., 1987, 'What the Poles Thought in 1981', in: Koralewicz, I., I. Bialecki and M. Watson, eds., *Crisis and Transformation: Polish Society in the 1980's*, London: Berg.

Bielasiak, J. and B. Hicks, 1990, 'Solidarity's Self-Organization. The Crisis of Rationalism and Legitimacy in Poland, 1980–1981', *Eastern European Politics and Societies*, vol. 4, no. 3.

Black, C. 1966, *The Dynamics of Modernization: A Study in Comparative History*, New York.

Blanchard, O., 1989, 'Notes on the Speed of Transition, Unemployment and Growth in Poland', mimeo, MIT, May.

Blanchard, O., et al., 1991, *Reform in Eastern Europe*, Cambridge MA: The MIT Press.

Blazyca, G., 1989, 'Industrial Structure and Economic Problems in a Centrally Planned Economy: The Polish Case', *Journal of Industrial Economics*, no. 28.

Boettke, P., 1993, *Why Perestroika Failed: The Politics and Economics of Socialist Transformation*, London: Routledge.

Bolton, P. and G. Roland, 1992, 'Privatization in Central and Eastern Europe', *European Economic Review*, vol. 37.

Brabant van, J., 1992, 'Divestment of State Assets: Alternative Forms and Timetable', in, Poznanski, K., ed., *Constructing Capitalism: Reemergence of Free Economy and Civil Society in Post-Communist Europe*, Boulder, CO: Westview Press.

Brada, J., 1991, 'The Economic Transition of Czechoslovakia from Plan to Market', *Journal of Economic Perspective*, vol. 5, no. 4.

1995, 'A Critique of the Evolutionary Approach to the Economic Transformation from Communism to Capitalism', in Poznanski, K., ed., *The Evolutionary Transition*, op. cit.

Brada, J. and D. Hoffman, 1985, 'The Productivity Differential between Soviet and Western Capital and the Benefits of Technology Imports to the Soviet Economy', *The Quarterly Review of Economics and Business*, vol. 25, no. 1 (spring).

Brada, J. and A. King, 1991, 'Is There a J-Curve for the Economic Transition from Socialism to Capitalism?', Princeton, unpublished conference paper.

Brada, J. and J. M. Montias, 1984, 'Industrial Policy in Eastern Europe: A Three Country Comparison', *Journal of Comparative Economics*, no. 8.

Breinard, L., 1990, 'Overview of East Europe's Debt: The Evolution of Creditworthiness in the 1980's', *Business Economics* (October).

1991, 'Reform in Eastern Europe: Creating a Capital Market', *Economic Review*, Federal Reserve Bank of Kansas City (January/February).

Bruno, M., et al., 1988, *Inflation Stabilization. The Experience of Israel, Argentina, Brazil, Bolivia and Mexico*, Cambridge MA: The MIT Press.

Brus, W., 1975, *Socialist Ownership and Political System*, London: Routledge and Kegan Paul.

1982, 'Economics and Politics: The Fatal Link', in Brumberg, A., ed., *Poland: Genesis of a Revolution*, New York: Random House.

1986, 'Political System and Economic Efficiency: The East European Context', in Gomulka, S., *Growth Innovation and Reform*, op. cit.

Bruszt, L., 1989, 'The Negotiated Revolution', *Social Research*, vol. 57, no. 2.

Bugaj, R. and T. Kowalik, 1990, 'W kierunku gospodarki mieszanej', *Zycie Gospodarcze*, no. 39.

Bunce, V., 1992a, 'Decline of a Regional Hegemon: The Gorbachev Regime and Reform in Eastern Europe', *Eastern European Politics and Society*, vol. 3, no. 2.

1992b, 'Two-Tiered Stalinism: A Case of Self-Destruction', in Poznanski, K., ed., *Constructing Capitalism: Reemergence of Free Economy and Civil Society in Post-Communist Europe*, Boulder, CO: Westview Press.

Burawoy, M., 1989, 'Reflections on the Class Consciousness of Hungarian Steelworkers, *Politics and Society*, vol. 17, no. 1 (March).

Calvo, G. and F. Coricelli, 1991, 'Stabilization in a Previously Centrally Planned Economy: Poland 1990', *Economic Policy*, vol. 14 (April).

1993, 'Output Collapse in Eastern Europe: The Role of Credit, in Blejer, M. I., et al., eds., *Eastern Europe in Transition: From Recession to Growth*, Washington DC: The World Bank.

Calvo, G. and J. Frenkel, 1991, 'Credit Markets, Credibility, and Economic Transformation', *Journal of Economic Perspectives*, vol. 5, no. 4.

1992, 'Transformation of Centrally Planned Economies: Credit Markets and Sustainable Growth', in G. Winkler, ed., *Central and East Europe Roads to Growth*, Washington: IMF.

Charemza, W., 1992a, 'Market Failure and Stagflation: Some Aspects of Privatization in Poland', *Economics of Planning*, vol. 25, no. 1.

1992b, 'East European Transformation: The Supply Side', in Poznanski, K., ed., *Stabilization and Privatization in Poland*, Boston: Kluver Academic Press.

Chirot, D., 1980. 'The Corporatist Model and Socialism', *Theory and Society* (March).

1991, 'What happened in Eastern Europe in 1989?' in Chirot, D., ed., *The Crisis of Leninism and the Decline of the Left: The Revolutions of 1989*, Seattle: University of Washington Press.

Cline, W., 1985, 'Progress on International Debt', *New York Times*, 15 April.

Comisso, E., 1986, 'Introduction: State Structures, Political Process, and Collective Choice in CMEA States', *International Organization*, Winter.

1991, 'Property Rights, Liberalism, and the Transition from "Actually Existing" Socialism', *Eastern European Politics and Societies*, vol. 5, no. 1.

Comisso, E. and P. Marer, 1985, 'The Explaining Politics of Reform in Hungary', *International Organization*, vol. 40, no. 2.

Corbett, J. and C. Mayer, 1991, 'Financial Reform in Eastern Europe: Progress with the Wrong Label', London: Centre for Economic Policy Research, CEPR Discussion Paper Series, no. 603.

Corbo, J., 1992, 'Economic Transformation in Latin America: Lessons for Eastern Europe', *European Economic Review*, vol. 36.

Coricelli, F. and A. Revenga, 1991, 'Wages and Unemployment in Poland: Recent Developments and Policy Issues', Washington, DC, The World Bank, mimeo.

Coricelli, F. and R. Rocha, 1990, 'Stabilization Programs in Eastern Europe: A Comparative Analysis of the Yugoslav and Polish Programs of 1990', paper presented at the World Bank – World Economy Research Institute Conference, Pultusk, Poland, 4–5 October.

Crane, K., 1985, 'The Creditworthiness of Eastern Europe in the 1980's', Rand Corporation Papers, R-3201–USDP (January).

1988, An Assessment of the Economic Reform in Poland's State-Owned Industry, Santa Monica: The RAND Corporation (May).

1991, *Poland's Economic Performance in 1990: Taking Stock of the 'Big Bang'*, Washington, DC: PlanEcon, Inc.

1992, 'Taking Stock of the Big Bang', in Poznanski, K., ed., *Stabilization and Privatization in Poland*, op. cit.

Csaba, L., 1989, 'The Recent Past and the Future of the Hungarian Reform: An Overview Assessment', in Clarke, R., ed., *Hungary: The Second Decade of Economic Reform*, Chicago: St James Press.

Curry, J., 1980, *The Polish Crisis of 1980 and the Political Survival*, Santa Monica: The Rand Corporation.

1989, 'The Psychological Barriers to Reform in Poland', *Eastern European Politics and Society*, vol. 2, no. 3.

Czekaj, J., 1989, 'Ile warte obligacje', *Zycie Gospodarcze*, no. 15.

Czekaj, J. and A. Sopocko, 1991, Financial Markets in the Period of Transition: Determinants, Perils, Prospects, Working Papers No. 19, Institute of Finance, Warsaw.

Dabrowski, M., 1989, 'Wlasnosc grupowa jako jedna z drog przeksztalcenia wlasnosci panstwowej', in *Propozycje przeksztalcen Polskiej gospodarki*, Warsaw: PTE.

1992a, Interventionist Pressures on a Policy Maker During the Transition to Economic Freedom, *Communist Economies and Economic Transition*, vol. 4, no. 1.

1992b, 'The Polish Stabilization 1990–1991', *Journal of International and Comparative Economics*, no. 1.

Dabrowski, M., 1994, 'Ukrainian Way to Hyperinflation', CASE, Studies and Analyses, no. 15, Warsaw.

Dahrendorf, R., 1989, *Transitions, Politics, Economics and Liberty*, Göteborg.

Dallago, B., 1991, 'Hungary and Poland: The Non-Socialized Sector and Privatization', *Osteuropa Wirtschaft*, vol. 6, no. 2.

Dawisha, K., 1990, *Eastern Europe, Gorbachev, and Reform: The Great Challenge*, New York: Cambridge University Press.

Demsetz, H., 1974, 'Towards a Theory of Property Rights', in E. Furubotn and S. Pejovich, eds., *The Economics of Property Rights*, Cambridge, MA: Cambridge University Press.

Dewantripont, M. and G. Roland, 1993, 'Economic Reform and Dynamic Political Constraints', *Review of Economic Studies*, vol. 59.

Dietz, R., 1992, 'East–West Energy Trade. Recent Trends and Future Prospects', WIIW Reprint-Serie, no. 140 (June).

Dobb, M., 1935, 'The Socialist Theory and the Problem of a Socialist Economy', *The Economic Journal*, (December).

Dornbush, R. and S. Fisher, 1986, 'Stopping Hyperinflation: Past and Present', *Weltwirtschaftliches Archiv*, vol. 122, no. 1.

Dyba, K. and J. Svejnar, 1991, 'Czechoslovakia: Recent Economic Developments and Prospects', *American Economic Review*.

1992, 'Stabilization and Transition in Czechoslovakia', CERGE Working Paper Series no. 7, Prague.

Dziewanowski, M., 1976, *The Communist Party of Poland*, Cambridge MA.: Harvard University Press.

Edwards, S., 1990, 'The Sequencing of Economic Reforms: Analytical Issues and Lessons from Latin American Experiences', *The World Economy*, vol. 13, no. 1.

1992, Central and Eastern Europe in Transition, *Contemporary Policy Issues*, vol. 10 (January).

Ekiert, G., 1990, 'Transition from State Socialism in Eastern Europe', *States and Social Structures Newsletter*, no. 12 (Winter).

1991, 'The State Against Society: The Aftermath of Political Crises in Hungary, 1956–63, Czechoslovakia, 1968–76, and Poland, 1981–89, Center for European Studies, Harvard University, (mimeo).

Estrin, S., 1992a, 'Restructing, Viability and Privatization: A Comparative Study of Enterprises Adjustment in Transition', *Journal of Comparative Economics* (March).

1992b, 'Yugoslavia: The Case of Self-Managing Market Socialism', *Journal of Economic Perspectives*, vol. 5, no. 4.

1994, 'Economic transition and privatization: the issues', in Estrin, S., ed., *Privatization in Central and Eastern Europe*, op. cit.

Estrin, S., ed., 1994, 'Privatization in Central and Eastern Europe, London: Longman.

Estrin, S., M. Schaffer and I. J. Singh, 1994, 'The Provision of Social Benefits in State-Owned, Privatized and Private Firms in Poland', CEPR Working Paper No. 606 (July).

Fallenbuchl, Z., 1983, *East–West Technology Transfer, Study of Poland, 1971–1980*, Paris: OECD.

1984, 'The Polish Economy Under Martial Law', *Soviet Studies*, vol. 36, no. 4.

1989, 'Poland: The Anatomy of Stagnation', in *Pressures for Reform in the East European Economies*, vol. 2, JEC, US Congress, Washington, DC, 27 October.

Fink, G., 1983, 'Economic Effects of the Polish Crisis on Other CMEA Countries', WIIW, mimeo.

1984, I. Grosser and F. Levcik, 1984, *Commodity Composition of East–West Trade*, WIIW Reprint Series no. 48 (August).

Friedrich, K. and Z. Brzezinski, 1965, *Totalitarian Dictatorship and Autocracy*, Cambridge, MA.: Harvard University Press.

Frydman, R., W. Kolodko and S. Wellisz, 1990, 'Stabilization in Poland: A Progress Report', Warsaw (May) (mimeo).

Frydman, R. and A. Rapaczynski, 1992, 'Privatization and Corporate Governance in Eastern Europe: Can Market be Designed?', in Winckler, G., ed., *Central and Eastern Europe: Roads to Growth*, Washington: IMF.

Frydman, R., A. Rapaczynski, J. Earle *et al.*, 1993, *The Privatization Process in Central Europe*, London: CEU Press.

Gabrich, H., *et al.*, 1992, 'Advanced Reforming Countries Might Reach End of Recession', *WIIW Forschungberiechte*, no. 184 (July).

Gacs, J., 1994, 'Trade Policy in the Czech and Slovak Republics, Hungary and Poland in 1989–1993. A Comparison', *CASE Studies and Analyses*, no. 11, Warsaw.

Gajdeczka, P., 1993, 'Inflation Tax, Household Wealth, and Privatization in Poland', in Poznanski, K., ed., *Stabilization and Privatization in Poland*, op. cit.

Gelb, A. and C. Gray, 'The Transformation of Economies in Central and Eastern Europe: Issues, Progress, and Prospects', World Bank, 1991, mimeo.

Glade, W., ed., 1991, *Privatization of Public Enterprises in Latin America*, San Francisco: ICS Press.

Goldstein, E., 1982, 'Soviet Economic Assistance to Poland, 1980–81', in *Soviet Economy in the 1980's: Problems and Prospects*, Joint Economic Committee of the US Congress, Washington, DC.

Gomulka, S., 1978, 'Growth and Import of Technology: Poland 1970–1980', *Cambridge Journal of Economics*, no. 2.

1986a, 'Drogi wyjscia z zadluzenia', *Aneks*, vol. 41–2.

1986b, *Growth, Innovation and Reforms in Eastern Europe*, Madison: University of Wisconsin Press.

1991, 'The Cause of Recession Following Stabilization', *Comparative Economic Studies*, vol. 33, no. 2.

1992a, 'Polish Economic Reform, 1990–91: Principles, Policies and Outcomes', *Cambridge Journal of Economics*, vol. 16.

1992b, 'How to Create a Capital Market in a Socialist Country for the Purpose of Privatization', in Prindl, A., ed., *Banking and Financing in Eastern Europe*, Woodhead-Faulkner.

1993, 'Poland: glass half full', in Portes, R., ed., *Economic Transformation in Central Europe*, op. cit.

1994, 'Lessons from Economic Transformation and the Road Forward', CASE, Warsaw (March).

Gomulka, S. and R. Jasinski, 1994, 'Privatization in Poland 1989–1993: Policies,

Methods, and Results', in Estrin, S., ed., *Privatization in Central and Eastern Europe*, op. cit.

Gomulka, S. and J. Rostowski, 1984, 'The Reformed Polish Economic System', *Soviet Studies*, no. 3.

Gomulka, S. and A. Polonsky, eds., 1990, *Polish Paradoxes*, London: Routledge.

Goodwyn, L., 1991, *Breaking the Barrier: The Rise of Solidarity in Poland*, Oxford: Oxford University Press.

Gotz-Kozierkiewicz, D., 1992, 'Exchange Rate Policy and Economic Growth', *Working Papers* No. 31, Institute of Finance, Warsaw.

Gotz-Kozierkiewicz, D. and W. Malecki, 1993, 'Wspolzaleznosc Polityki Pienieznej i Polityki Kursu Walutowego', Institute of Finance, Warsaw (mimeo).

Granick, D., 1987. *Job Rights in the Soviet Union: Their Consequences*, New York: Cambridge University Press.

Green, D., 1979, 'Technology Transfer to the USSR: A Reply', *Journal of Comparative Economics*, no. 3.

Green, D. and H. Levine, 1977, 'Soviet Machinery Imports', *Survey*, no. 2 (Spring).

Grosfeld, I., 1990, 'Reform Economics and Western Economic Theory: Unexploited Opportunities', *Economics of Planning*, vol. 23, no. 1.

1991, 'Privatization of State Enterprises in Eastern Europe: The Search for a Market Environment', *Eastern European Politics and Societies*, vol. 5, no. 1.

Gross, J., 1992, 'Poland: From Civil Society to Political Nation', in Banac, I., ed., *Eastern Europe in Revolution*, Ithaca: Cornell University Press.

Grosser, I. 1993, 'Shared Aspirations, Divergent Results', *WIIW Forschungberiechte*, vol. 191, Vienna Institute for Comparative Economic systems.

Grossman, G., 1983, 'The Party as Manager and Entrepreneur', in Guroff, G. and F. Carstensen, eds., *Entrepreneurship in Imperial Russia and the Soviet Union*, Princeton: Princeton University Press.

1989, 'Sub-Rosa Privatization and Marketization in the USSR', Berkeley-Duke Occasional Papers on the Second Economy in the USSR, no. 17.

Grudzinska-Gross, I., 1992, 'Post-Communist Resentment, or the Rewriting of Polish History', *Eastern European Politics and Societies*, vol. 6, no. 2.

Gueullette, A., 1985, 'Recent Slowdown in Technology Imports by Eastern Europe: The Case of Hungary', Hoover Institution, mimeo.

Hankiss, E., 1989, 'Demobilization, Self-Mobilization, and Quasi-Mobilization in Hungary: 1948–1987', *Eastern European Politics and Societies*, vol. 3, no. 1.

1990, *East European Alternatives*, Oxford: Clarendon Press.

Hanson, P., 1990, 'Ownership Issues in Perestroika', in J. Tedstrom, ed., *Perestroika and the Private Sector of the Soviet Economy*, Boulder, CO: Westview Press.

1995, 'The Utopia of Market Society in Post-Soviet Context', in Hanson S. and W. Spohn, *Can Europe Work?*, Seattle: University of Washington Press.

Hare, P., 1987, 'Economic Reform in Eastern Europe', *Journal of Economic Surveys*, vol. 1, no. 1.

1990, 'Reform of Enterprise Regulation in Hungary', mimeo.

Hare, P. and I. Grosfeld, 1991, 'Privatization in Hungary, Poland and Czechoslovakia', *European Economy*, no. 5.

Hare, P. and G. Hughes, 1991, 'Competitiveness and Industrial Restructuring in Czechoslovakia, Hungary and Poland', CEPR Discussion Paper, no. 543, April 1991.

Hare, P. and T. Revesz, 1992, 'Hungary's Transition to the Market: The Case Against a "Big Bang"', *Economic Policy*, vol. 14 (April).

Hausner, J., 1995, 'Instytucjonalne uwarunkowania przetargu placowego w gospodarce socjalistycznej i post socjalistycznej (na przykladzie Polski)', Economic Institute, Polish Academy of Sciences, Seminary Materials, no. 2.

Havlik, P. *et al.*, 1994, 'More Solid Recovery in Central and Eastern Europe, Continuing Decline Elsewhere', *WIIW Research Reports*, no. 207 (July).

Havrylyshyn, O. and D. Rosati, 1990, *Polityka Rozwoju Handlu Zagranicznego w Polsce*, Warsaw: The World Bank and Institute of Foreign Trade.

Hayek, F., 1944, *The Road to Serfdom*, Chicago: Chicago University Press.
  1967, *Studies in Philosophy, Politics and Economics*, Chicago: Chicago University Press.
  1988, *The Fatal Conceit: The Errors of Socialism*, Chicago: Chicago University Press.

Hayek von, F., ed., 1935, *Collectivist Economic Planning*, London: Routledge and Kegan Paul.

Hewett, E., 1985, 'Soviet Current Account Surplus with Eastern Europe', Washington DC: The Brookings Institution, mimeo.
  1988, *Reforming the Soviet Economy*, Washington, DC: The Brookings Institution.

Hirszowicz, M., 1980, *The Bureaucratic Leviathan: A Study in the Sociology of Communism*, New York: New York University Press.
  1986, *Coercion and Control in Communist Society: The Visible Hand of Bureaucracy*, Brighton: Wheatsheaf.
  1990, 'The Polish Intelligentsia on a Crisis-Ridden Society, in Gomulka, S. and A. Polonsky, ed., *The Polish Paradoxes*, op. cit.

Holzer, J., 1990, 'Solidarity's Adventures in Wonderland', in Gomulka, S. and A. Polonsky, ed., *The Polish Paradoxes*, op. cit.

Holzman, F., 1976, *International Trade under Communism: Politics and Economics*, New York: Basic Books.
  1987, *The Economics of Soviet Bloc Trade and Finance*, Boulder, Westview Press.

Hrncir, M., 1992, 'Money and Credit in transition of the Czechoslovak Economy', in Siebert, H., ed., *The Transformation of Socialist Economies*, Tubingen: Paul Mohr.

Hough, J., 1986, 'The Gorbachev Reform: A Maximal Case', *Soviet Economy*, vol. 2 (October/December).
  1990, 'Gorbachev's Endgame', *World Policy Journal*, vol. 7 (Fall).

Hughes, G. and P. Hare, 1992, 'Industrial Policy and Restructuring in Eastern Europe', Discussion Paper no. 653, Centre for Economic Policy Research, London.

Hunya, G., 1991, 'Speed of Privatization of Big Enterprises in Central and

Eastern Europe – General Concepts and Hungarian Practice', WIIW Forschunberiechte, no. 176.

1992, 'Foreign Direct Investment and Privatization in Central and Eastern Europe', *Communist Economies and Economic Transformation*, vol. 4, no. 4.

Ickes, B., 1986, 'Cyclical Fluctuations in Centrally Planned Economies: A Critique of Literature', *Soviet Studies*, vol. 37, no. 1.

IF (Instytut Finansow), 1992, 'Raport o Sytuacji Finansowej i Realizacji Polityki Stabilizacyjnej w 1991 Roku', no. 22, Warsaw.

IGS (Instytut Gosporaki Swiatowej), 1990, 'Gospodarka Swiatowa i Gospodarka Polska w 1989 Roku', Warsaw.

Iwanek, M. and M. Swiecicki, 1987, 'Handlowac kapitalem w Socjalizmie', *Polityka*, no. 24.

Janos, A., 1986, *Politics and Paradigms. Changing Theories of Change in Social Science*, Stanford: Stanford University Press.

Jorgensen, E. *et al.*, 1990, 'The Behavior of Polish Firms After the "Big Bang": Findings From a Field Trip', Socialist Economies Reform Unit, Washington DC: The World Bank.

Jowitt, K., 1971, *Revolutionary Breakthroughs and National Development: The Case of Romania, 1945–66*, Berkeley: University of California Press.

1975, 'Inclusion and Mobilization in European Leninist Regimes', *World Politics*, vol. 28, no. 1.

1978, *The Leninist Response to National Dependency*, University of California-Berkeley: Institute of International Studies Research Series no. 37.

1992, 'The Leninist Legacy', in Banac, I., ed., *Eastern Europe in Revolution*, Ithaca: Cornell University Press.

Jozefiak, C., 1986, 'The Polish Reform. An Attempted Evaluation', *WIIW Forschungberichte*, no. 116 (April).

Kaminski, B., 1986, 'Poland's Foreign Trade in the 1980s: Complex Challenges and Simple Responses', in Joseph P., ed., *The Economies of Eastern Europe and Their Foreign Economic Relations*, Brussels: NATO.

1989a, 'The Economic System and Forms of Government Controls in Poland in the 1980s', in *Pressures for Reform in the East European Economies*, vol. 2, JEC the US Congress, Washington, 27 October.

1989b, 'Towards De-etatisation and Democracy: The Challenge of the "Round Table" Agreement', in *Pressures for Reform in the East European Economies*, Joint Economic Committee of the US: Washington, DC.

1991, *The Collapse of State Socialism: The Case of Poland*, Princeton: Princeton University Press.

Karl, T. and P. Schmitter, 1991, 'Models of Transition in Southern and Eastern Europe', *International Social Science Journal*, vol. 128.

Kawalec, S., 1990, 'Employee ownership, state treasury ownership: dubious solutions', *Communist Economies*, vol. 2, no. 1.

Kemme, D., 1982, *The Polish Crisis: An Economic Overview*, in Bielsiak, J. and M. Simon, eds., *Polish Politcs: Edge of the Abyss*, New York: Praeger.

1987, 'Productivity Growth in Polish Industry', *Journal of Comparative Economics*, vol. 11, no. 1.

1990, 'Losses in Polish Industry Due to Resource Misallocation', *Jahrbuch der Wirtschaft Osteuropas*, vol. 14, no. 2.

Kemme, D. and K. Crane, 1983, 'The Polish Economic Collapse: Contributing Factors and Economic Costs', April, mimeo.

Kemme D. and J. Neufeld, 1991, 'The Estimation of Technical Efficiency in Polish Industry: 1961–1986', *Economic Systems*, vol. 15, no. 1.

Kennedy, M., 1991, *Professionals, Power and Solidarity in Poland*, Cambridge: Cambridge University Press.

Kierunki reformy gospodarczej 1981, Warsaw: Ksiazka i Wiedza.

Kiguel, M. and N. Liviatan, 'Stopping Inflation: The Experience in Latin America and Israel and Implications for Eastern Europe', paper presented at the World Bank – World Economy Research Institute Conference, Pultusk, Poland, 4–5 October, 1990.

Kirzner, I., ed., 1992, *Method, Process and Austrian Economics*, Lexington: Lexington Books.

Kochanowicz, J., 1993, 'Transition to Market in a Comparative Perspective: A Historian's Point of View', in K. Poznanski, ed., *Stabilization and Privatization in Poland*, op. cit.

Kolakowski, L., 1971, 'Hope and Hopelessness', *Survey*, vol. 17, no. 3.

1992, 'Mind and Body: Ideology and Economy in the Collapse of Communism', in Poznanski, K., ed., *Constructing Capitalism: Reemergence of Civil Society and Liberal Economy in the Communist World*, Boulder, CO: Westview Press.

Kolankiewicz, G., 1988, 'Poland and the Politics of Permissible Pluralism', *East European Politics and Societies*, vol. 2, no. 1.

Kolarska-Bobinska, L., 1989, 'Poczucie niesprawiedliwosci, konfliktu i preferowany lad w gospodarce', in W. Adamski *et al.*, Polacy 88, Dynamika Konfliktu a Szanse Reform, Warszawa: Centralny Program Badan Podstawowych (reprinted in *Sisyphus Sociological Studies*, vol. 5, 1989).

1990, 'The Myth of the Market and the Reality of Reform', in Gomulka, S. and A. Polonsky, ed., *The Polish Paradoxes*, op. cit.

Kolodko, G.

1991a, 'Stabilizacja inflacji i rynkowa transformacja: Doswiadczenia Polski', in Kolodko, G., ed. *Polityka Finansowa, Stabilzacja, Transformacja*, Warsaw: Institute of Finance.

1991b, 'Polish Hyperinflation and Stabilization, 1989–1990' *Most*, no. 1.

1993, 'From Output Collapse to Sustainable Growth in Transition Economies: The Fiscal Implications', *Working Papers* No. 35, Institute of Finance, Warsaw.

Kolodko, G. and W. McMahon, 1987, 'Stagflation and Shortageflation: A Comparative Approach', *Kyklos*, vol. 40, no. 2.

Kolodko, G., D. Gotz-Kozierkiewicz and E. Skrzeszewska-Paczek, 1992, *Hyperinflation and Stabilization in Post socialist Economies*, Boston: Kluwer Academic Publishers.

Kolodko, G. and M. Rutkowski, 1991, 'The Problem of Transition from a Socialist to a Free Market Economy: The Case of Poland', *The Journal of Social, Political and Economic Studies*, vol. 16, no. 2.

Kornai, J., 1971, *Anti-Equalibirum*, Amsterdam: North-Holland Publishers.

1980, *Economics of Shortage*, Amsterdam: North-Holland Publishers.

1986, 'The Hungarian Reform Process: Visions, Hopes and Reality', *Journal of Economic Literature*, vol. 24, no. 4.

1990a, The Affinity of Ownership and Co-ordination, *Journal of Economic Perspectives*, vol. 40, no. 3.

1990b, *The Road to a Free Economy: Shifting from a Socialist System*, New York: Norton and Company.

1992a, 'The Principles of Privatization in Eastern Europe', *De Economist*, vol. 140, no. 2.

1992b, *The Socialist Economic System*, Princeton: Princeton University Press.

1993, 'Transformational Recession, *Collegium Budapest, Discussion Papers* No. 21 (June).

Kotowicz, J., 1989, 'Ciecia nieuchronne', *Zycie Gospodarcze*, no. 44.

Kotrba, J., 1995, 'Privatization Process in the Czech Republic: Players and Winners', in Svejnar, J., ed., *The Czech Republic and Economic Transition*, op. cit.

Kowalska, M., 1989, 'Odejscie dinozaura', *Zycie Gospodarcze*, no. 46.

Krol, M., 1990, 'The Polish Syndrome of Incompleteness', in Gomulka, S. and A. Polonsky, ed., *The Polish Paradoxes*, op. cit.

Kuklinski, R., 1987, 'Wojna z narodem widziana od srodka', *Kultura*, no. 4.

Laba, R., 1986, 'Worker Roots of Solidarity, Problems of Communism', July–August.

1991, *The Roots of Solidarity*, Princeton: Princeton University Press.

Lane, D., ed., 1995, *Russia in Transition: Politics, Privatization and Inequality*, London: Longman.

Lange, O., 1935, 'On the Economic Theory of Socialism', *Review of Economic Studies*, vol. 4, no. 1.

Laski, K., et al., 1993, 'Transition from the Command to the Market System', *Working Papers* No. 1, The Vienna Institute for Comparative Economic Studies, Vienna (March).

Lavigne, M., 1989, 'Intra-CMEA Relations and Domestic Reforms: Some Inter-actions', Université de Paris, mimeo.

Lavoie, D., 1985, 'Tacit Knowledge and the Revolution in the Philosophy of Science', in Lavoie, D., *National Economic Planning: What is Left?*, Cato Institute, Washington, DC.

Lewandowski, J., and J. Szomburg, 1989, 'Property Reform as a Basis for Social and Economic Reform', *Communist Economies*, vol. 1.

Lewis, P., 1988, *Political Authority and Party Secretaries in Poland 1975–86*, Cambridge: Cambridge University Press.

1990a, 'Non-Competitive Elections and Regime Change: Poland 1989', *Parliamentary Affairs*, vol. 43, no. 1.

1990b, 'The Long Goodbye: Party Rule and Political Change in Poland since Martial Law', *Journal of Communist Studies*, vol. 6, no. 1.

Levcik, F. and J. Skolka, 1984, *East–West Technology Transfer: A Study of Czechoslovakia*, Paris: The OECD.

Linden, R., 1986, 'Socialist Parties and the Global Economy: The Case of Romania', *International Organization*, vol. 40.

Lipton, D. and Sachs, J., 1990a, 'Creating a Market Economy in Eastern Europe: The Case of Poland', The Brookings Economic Papers, January.

1990b, 'Privatization in Eastern Europe: The Case of Poland, *Brookings Papers on Economic Activity*, No. 2.

Lukas, Z., 1993, 'Die Landwirtschaft in den Oststaaten 1992', *Osteuropa Wirtschaft*, vol. 38, no. 2.

McKinnon, R., 1991, 'Stabilization Programs in Post-Communist Eastern Europe', conference paper, University of Washington, The Henry Jackson School of International Studies, 18 June.

1993a, 'Financial Growth and Macroeconomic Stability in China, 1978–92', *Journal of Comparative Economics*.

1993b, *The Order of Economic Liberalization Financial Control and the Transition to a Market Economy*, Baltimore: The Johns Hopkins University Press.

Mach, C., 1990, 'Transfer of Technology – Hungary in the Eighties', *Acta Oeconomica*, vol. 42 (1–2).

Malia, M., 1983, 'Poland's Eternal Return, *New York Review of Books*, vol. 29 (26 September).

1992, 'From Under the Rubble, What?', *Problems of Communism*, (January/ April).

Marer, P., 1984a, 'East Europe's Increased Dependence on World Economy and its Consequences', Indiana University, mimeo.

1984b, 'East–West Commercial Relations and Prospects for East Europe and Yugoslavia', conference paper, ASSA Annual Meeting, December.

1985a, *East–West Technology Transfer: The Case of Hungary*, Paris: OECD.

1985b, 'East European Economies: A Region of Crisis', conference paper, The Annual Meeting of the Association for Comparative Economic Systems, mimeo.

Marody, M., 1990, 'Perceptions of Politics in Polish Society', *Social Research*, vol. 57, no. 2.

Marrese, M., 1983, 'Hungarian Agriculture: Drive in Proper Direction', Northwestern University, Department of Economics, mimeo.

Mason, D. 1985, *Public Opinion and Political Change in Poland, 1980–1982*, Cambridge MA: Cambridge University Press.

Mason, D., Nelson, D. and B. Szklarski, 1991, 'Apathy and the Birth of Democracy: The Polish Struggle',

Michnik, A., 1985, *Letters from Prison and Other Essays*, Berkeley: University of California.

Milanovic, B., 1989, *Liberalization and Entrepreneurship: Dynamics of Reform in Socialism and Capitalism*, Armonk: Sharpe.

1990, 'Privatization in Post-Communist Societies', CECSE, World Bank, Washington, DC, November, mimeo.

1991a, 'Poland's Quest for Economic Stabilization, 1988–1991', World Bank, Washington, DC, mimeo.

1991b, 'Poverty in Eastern Europe in the Years of Crisis, 1978–1987: Poland, Hungary and Yugoslavia', *The World Bank Economic Review*.

Mises L. von, 1920. 'Economic Calculation in the Socialist Commonwealth', in Hayek, F., ed., 1935, *Collectivist Economic Planning*, London: Routledge and Kegan Paul.

1939, *Epistemological Problems of Economics*, New York: New York University Press (1981 edition).

Mizsei, K., 1992, 'Privatization in Eastern Europe: A Comparative Study of Poland and Hungary', *Soviet Studies*, vol. 44.

1995, 'Lessons from Bad Loan Management in the East Central European Transition for the Second Wave Reform Countries', in Rostowski, J., ed., *Banking Reform in Central and the Former Soviet Union*, Budapest: Central European University Press.

Monkiewicz, J., 1985, *Licencje*, Warsaw: Polish Scientific Press.

Montias, M., 1962, *Central Planning in Poland*, New Haven: Yale University Press.

1982, 'Poland: Roots of the Economic Crisis', *The ACES Bulletin*, vol. 24, no. 3.

1985, Comments, conference on The Polish Economy and the Debt, The Kennan Institute, Washington (12 October).

1988, 'Industrial Policy and Foreign Trade in Bulgaria', *Eastern European Politics and Societies*, vol. 2, no. 3.

1991, 'The Romanian Economy: A Survey of Current Economic Problems', *European Economy*, no. 5.

1993, 'Financial and Fiscal Aspects of System Change in Eastern Europe', Yale University, ISPS Working Paper No. 1048.

Moscicki, J., 1985, 'Po umowie paryskiej', *Zycie Gospodarcze*, no. 30.

Mujzel, J., 1989, 'Socio-Economic Reforms in Eastern Europe and Real Socialism', *Communist Economies*, vol. 1, no. 1.

1992, 'Two Years of Polish Economic Transformation and the Problems of Recession', Polish Academy of Sciences, Warsaw, mimeo.

Murrell, P.,1990a, 'Big Bang Versus Evolution: Eastern European Reforms in the Light of Recent Economic History', *PlanEcon Report*, 29 June.

1990b, *The Nature of Socialism: Lessons from East European Foreign Trade*, Princeton: Princeton University Press.

1991, 'Can Neoclassical Economics Underpin the Reform of Centrally Planned Economies?', *The Journal of Economic Perspectives*, vol. 5, no. 4.

1992, 'Evolutionary and Radical Approaches to Economic Reform', *Economics of Planning*, vol. 25, no. 1.

Myant, M., 1982, *Poland, A Crisis of Socialism*, London: Lawrence and Wishart.

1993, *Transforming Socialist Economies: The Case of Poland and Czechoslovakia*, New York: Elgar.

Myrdal, G., 1968, *Asian Drama: An Inquiry into the Poverty of Nations*, New York.

Naughton, B., 1995, *Growing Out of the Plan: Chinese Economic Reform, 1978–1993*, Cambridge: Cambridge University Press.

Nelson, D., 1986, 'Non-Supportive Participatory Involvement in Eastern Europe', *Social Science Quarterly*, vol. 67 (September).

Nelson, R. and S. Winter, 1982, *An Evolutionary Theory of Economic Change*, Cambridge, MA: Harvard University Press.

Newbury, D., 1991, 'Reform in Hungary: Sequencing and Privatization', *European Economic Review* (April).

Nordhaus, W., 1990, 'Soviet Economic Reform: The Longest Road', Brookings Papers on Economic Activity, no. 1.

North, D., 1979, 'A Framework for Analyzing the State in Economic History', *Explorations in Economic History*, no. 2.

1990, Institutions and Credible Commitment', *Journal of Institutional and Theoretical Economics*, vol. 149, no. 1.

Nowacki, S. 1989, 'Rola rynku w gospodarce socjalistycznej', *Zycie Gospodarcze*, no. 17.

Nowak, K., 1990, 'Public Opinion, Group Interests and Economic Reform', Warsaw: University of Warsaw (mimeo).

Nuti, M., 1982, 'The Polish Crisis: Economic Factors and Constraints', in J. Drewnowski, ed., *Crisis in East European Economy: The Spread of the Polish Desease*, London: Croom Helm.

1988, 'Competitive Valuation and Efficiency of Capital Investment in the Socialist Economy', *European Economic Review'*, vol. 32, nos. 2–3.

1991, 'Stabilization and Sequencing in the Reform of Socialist Economies', in Commander, S., ed., *Managing Inflation in Socialist Economies in Transition*, Washington, DC: The World Bank, Economic Development Institute.

Nuti, M. and R. Portes, 1993, 'Central Europe: The Way Forward', in Portes, R., ed., *Economic Transformation in Central Europe*, op. cit.

Nutter, G. W., 1974, 'Markets without Property: A Grand Illusion', in Furubotn, E. and S. Pejovich, eds., *The Economics of Property Rights*, Cambridge, MA: Ballinger Publishing Co.

O'Donnell, G. and P. C. Schmitter, 1986, *Transitions from Authoritarian Rule: Tentative Conclusions about Uncertain Democracies*, Baltimore: The Johns Hopkins Unversity Press.

Olson, M., 1992, 'The Hidden Path to a Successful Economy', in Clauge, C. and G. C. Rausser, eds. (1992).

Osa, M., 1989, 'Resistance, Persistence and Change: The Transformation of the Catholic church in Poland', *Eastern European Politics and Societies*, vol. 3, no. 2.

Ost, D., 1989, 'Towards a Corporatist Solution in Eastern Europe: The Case of Poland', *Eastern European Politics and Societies*, vol. 3, no. 1.

1991, *Solidarity: The Politics of no Politics*, Philadelphia: Temple University Press.

Pejovich, S., 1979, *Fundamentals of Economics: A Property Rights Approach*, Dallas: The Fisher Institute.

1990, *The Economics of Property Rights. Toward a Theory of Comparative Systems*, Dordrecht: Kluver Academic Publishers.

Pelczynski, Z., 1988, 'Solidarity and Rebirth of Civil Society', in J. Keane, ed. *Civil Society and the State*, London: Verso.

Pinto, B., M. Belka and S. Krajewski, 1993, 'Transforming State Enterprises in Poland: Evidence of Adjustment by Manufacturing Firms', *Brookings Paper on Economic Activity*, No. 1.

Portes, R., 1981, *The Polish Crisis: Western Policy Options*, London: Royal Institute of International Affairs.

1983, 'Central Planning and Monetarism: Fellow Travelers?', in Desai, P., ed., *Marxism, Central Planning and the Soviet Economy*, Cambridge, MA: The MIT Press.

Portes, R., ed., 1993, *Economic Transformation in Central Europe. A Progress Report*, London: Center for Economic Policy Research.

Poznanska, J. et al., 1985, 'The Impact of Western Technology on Poland's Economy: 1970–1984', research report, National Council for Soviet and East European Research, Cornell University, mimeo.

Poznanski, K., 1985, 'Competition between Eastern Europe and Developing Countries on the Western Market for Manufactured Goods', in *Eastern European Economies: Slowdown in the 1980's*, vol. 2, Joint Economic Committee of the US Congress, Washington, DC.

1986a, 'Economic Adjustment and Political Process: Poland Since 1970', in E. Comisso and L. Tyson, eds., *Power, Purpose, and Collective Choice*, Ithaca: Cornell University Press.

1986b, 'Patterns of Techology Imports: Interregional Comparison', *World Development*.

1987, *Technology, Competition and the Soviet Bloc in the World Market*, Berkeley: UC- Berkeley, Institute of International Studies.

1988a, 'Economic Determinants of Technological Performance in East European Industry', *East European Politics and Societies*, vol. 2, no. 3.

1988b, 'The Competitiveness of Polish Industry and Indebtedness', in Marer, P. and W. Siwinski, eds., *Creditworthiness and Reform in Poland*, Bloomington: Indiana University Press.

1989a, 'The CPE Aversion to Techncal Innovation', *Economics of Planning*, (October).

1991a, 'Decline of Communism, Rise of Capitalism', Center for European Studies Working Papers, no. 15, Harvard University.

1992a, 'Market Alternative to State Actvism in Restoring Capitalist Economy', *Economics of Planning*, vol. 25, no. 1.

1992b, 'Privatisation of the Polish Economy: Problems of Transition', *Soviet Studies*, vol. 44, no. 4.

1992c, 'Property Rights Perspective on the Evolution of Communist-Type Economies', in Poznanski, K., ed., *Constructing Capitalism: The Reemegence of Civil Society and Liberal Economy in the Post-Communist World*, Boulder, CO: Westview Press.

1993a, 'Poland's Transition to Capitalism: Shock and Therapy', in Poznanski, K., ed., *Stabilization and Privatization in Poland*, Boston: Kluver Academic Publishers.

1993b, 'Restructuring of Property Rights in Poland', *Eastern European Politics and Societies*, vol. 6, no. 1.

1995a, 'Political Economy of Privatization in Eastern Europe', in Crawford, B., ed., *Market, States and Democracy*, Boulder, CO: Westview Press.

1995b, 'Introduction', in K. Poznanski, ed., *The Evolutionary Transition to Capitalism*, Boulder, CO: Westview Press.

1995c, 'The Evolutionary Paradigm of International Political Economy', University of Washington (July), (mimeo).

1996, 'Debt and Equity in Poland's Transition', American Economic Association', convention paper, San Francisco, January 6 (mimeo).

Przeworski, A., 1986, 'Some Problems in the Study of the Transition to Democracy', in O'Donnell, G., P. Schmitter and L. Whitehead, eds., *Transition from Authoritarian Rule: Comparative Perspectives*, Baltimore: The Johns Hopkins University Press.

1991, *Democracy and the Market*, New York: Cambridge University Press.

Quaisser, W., 1986, 'Agricultural Price Policy and Peasant Adjustment in Poland', *Soviet Studies*, vol. 38, no. 4.

Raczkowski, S., 1985, 'Debt Rescheduling: Benefits and Costs for Debtors and Creditors', in Saunders, C., ed., *East–West Trade and Finance in the World Economy*, New York: St Martin's Press.

1991, Comment, in Kolodko, G., ed., *Polityka Finansowa, Stabilizacja, Transformacja*, Warsaw: Institute of Finance, pp. 235–9.

Roncek, L., 1988, 'Private Enterprise in the Soviet Political Debate', *Soviet Studies*, vol. 60, no. 1.

Rodrik, D., 1992, 'Foreign Trade in Eastern Europe's Transition: Early Results', CEPR Discussion Paper no. 676 (June), London.

Rosati, 1992, 'The CMEA Demise: Trade Restructuring and Trade Destruction in Eastern Europe', in Poznanski, K., ed., *Stabilization and Privatization in Poland*, op. cit.

1993a, 'Poland: Glass Half Empty', in Portes, R., ed., *Economic Transformation in Central Europe*, op. cit.

1993b, 'Foreign Trade Liberalization in the Transition to the Market Economy', *WIIW Forschungberichte* no. 193 (March).

1994, 'The Impact of the Soviet Trade Shock on Central and East European Economies', *Empirica*, no. 1.

Rosefielde, S., 1973, *Soviet International Trade in Heckscher-Ohlin Perspective: An Input-Output Study*, New York: Cambridge University Press.

Rostowski, J., 1989, 'The Decay of Socialism and the Growth of Private Enterprise in Poland', *Soviet Studies*, vol. 41, no. 2.

Rutkowska, I., 1991, 'Public Transfers in Socialist and Market Economies, Socialist Economies Research Unit', Research Paper Series, no. 7, Washington, DC: The World Bank.

Sachs, J.,
1991, 'Accelerating Privatization in Eastern Europe: The Case of Poland', Washington, DC: The World Bank (mimeo).

1992, 'The Economic Transformation of Eastern Europe: The Case of Poland', *Economics of Planning*, vol. 25, no. 1.

1993, *Poland's Jump to the Market Economy*, Cambridge, MA: The MIT Press.

1995, 'Postcommunist Parties and the Politics of Entitlements', *Transition*, vol. 6, no. 3.

Saunders, C. 1978, 'Engineering in Britain, West Germany, and France: Some Statistical Comparisons', Brighton: SERU Papers, University of Sussex.

1984, 'Comparative Advantage and Competitiveness in East–West Relations', conference paper, International Economic Association, Budapest-Vienna.

Schaffer, M., 1991. 'A Note on the Polish State-Owned Enterprise Sector in 1990', Center for Economic Performance, London School of Economics, April, mimeo.

1992, 'The Enterprise Sector and the Emergence of the Polish Fiscal Crisis, 1990–91', Centre for Economic Performance, London School of Business (mimeo).

Schroeder, G., 1988, 'Property Rights Issues in Economic Reforms in Socialist Countries', *Studies in Comparative Communism*, vol. 26, no. 2.

1989, 'The Soviet Economy and a Trademill of "Reforms"', in *Soviet Economy in a Time of Change*, vol. 1, US Congress, Washington, DC.

1990, 'Economic Reform of Socialism: The Soviet Record', in Prybyla, S., ed., *Privatizing and Monetizing Socialism, The Annals*.

Schumpeter, J., 1939, *Business Cycles: A Theoretical, Historical and Statistical Analysis of the Capitalist Process*, New York: Harper and Row.

1942, *Capitalism, Socialism and Democracy*, New York: Harper and Row.

Simon, H., 1947, *Administrative Behavior: A Study in Decision-Making Process*, New York: Macmillan Press.

1957, *Models of Man: Social and Rational*, New York: Wiley.

Slay, B., 1989, 'Poland: The Private and Cooperative Sectors in the 1980's', Department of Economics, Bates College, mimeo.

1990, 'Monopoly and Marketization in Polish Industry', *Jahrbuch der Wirtschaft Ost Europas*, vol. 14, no. 1.

Skilling, G. and F. Griffith, ed., 1971, *Interest Groups in Soviet Politics*, Princeton: Princeton University Press.

Staniszkis, J, 1982, 'Martial Law in Poland', *Telos*, no. 54.

1983, *Self-Limiting Revolution*, Princeton: Princeton University Press.

1987, *The Cycles of Dependency*, The Kennan Institute, Woodrow Wilson Center, Washington, DC.

1990, 'Patterns of Change in Eastern Europe', *Eastern European Politics and Societies*, vol. 4, no. 1.

1991, '"Political Capitalism" in Poland', *Eastern European Politics and Societies*, vol. 5, no. 1.

Stark, D., 1991, 'Privatization in Hungary: From Plan to Market or From Plan to Clan', *Eastern European Policies and Societies*, vol. 4, no. 3.

1992, 'Path Dependence and Privatization Strategies in East Central Europe', *Eastern European Poltics and Socieeties*, vol. 6, no. 2.

Svejnar, J., 1989, 'A Framework for the Economic Transformation of Czechoslovakia', *PlanEcon Report*, 29 December.

1992a, 'Microeconomic Issues in the Transition to a Market Economy', *Journal of Economic Perspectives*, vol. 5, no. 4.

1992b, 'Labor Market Adjustment in Transitional Economies', CERG Working Paper Series no. 22, November.

Svejnar, J., ed., 1995, *The Czech Republic and Economic Transition in Eastern Europe*, San Diego: Academic Press.

Svejnar J. and R. Chaykowski, 1987, 'Optimal Export Oriented Economic Policies in Poland', Department of Economics, Cornell University (memeo).

Svejnar, J. and K. Terrell, 'Labor Redundancy in State Owned Transportation Enterprises: Problems and Solutions', Working Paper, INUTD, The World Bank, May 1991.

Swiecicki, M., 1989a, 'Reforma wlasnosciowa', in *Propozycje przeksztalcen Polskiej gospodarki*, Warsaw: PTE.

1989b, 'Uwaga na pulapki', *Zycie Gospodarcze*, no. 23.

Szelenyi, I., 1988, *Socialist Entrepreneurs*, Madison: University of Wisconsin Press.

1989, 'Eastern Europe in an Epoch of Transition: Toward a Socialist Mixed Economy', in Nee, V. and D. Stark, *Remaking the Economic Institutions of Socialism*, Stanford: Stanford University Press.

Szelenyi, I. and B. Martin, 1991, 'The Three Waves of New Class Theories and a Postscript', in Lemert, C., ed., *Intellectuals and Politics: Social Theory in a Changing World*, Newbury Park

Szomburg, J., 1991, 'Dilemmas of Privatization in Poland', paper for the conference on Transitions in Eastern Europe, *Sudosteuropa Gesellschaft*, Munich.

Tardos, M., 1988, 'How to Create Markets in Eastern Europe: The Hungarian Case', in Y. Brada, E. Hewett and T. Wolf, eds., *Economic Adjustment and Reform in Eastern Europe and the Soviet Union*, Durham: Duke University Press.

1989, 'The Property Rights in Hungary', Budapest, mimeo.

Tedstrom, J., 1993, 'Privatization in Post-Soviet Russia: The Politics and Psychology of Reform', in Patterson, P., ed., *Capitalist Goals, Socialist Past: The Rise of the Private Sector in Command Economies*, Boulder, CO: Westview Press.

Terrell, K., 1987, 'Productivity Trends During Import-led Growth Strategy of Gierek in Poland', University of Pitsburgh (mimeo).

1990, 'Technical Change in Socialist Industry: Evidence from Poland', Working Paper No. 262, Department of Economics, University of Pittsburgh.

1992, 'Productivity of Western and Domestic Capital in Polish Industry', *Journal of Comparative Economics*, vol. 16.

Terry, S., 1989, 'The Future of Poland: Perestroika or Perpetual Crisis', Harvard University, Russian Center (mimeo).

Tismaneanu, V., 1992, *Reinventing Politics. Eastern Europe from Stalin to Havel*, New York: The Free Press.

Touraine, A. *et al.*, 1989, *Solidarity: The Analysis of a Social Movement*, Cambridge: Cambridge University Press.

Tyson, L. 1984, *Economic Adjustment in Eastern Europe: Hungary and Romania*, Santa Monica: The Rand Corporation.

1985, 'Debt Crisis and Adjustment in Eastern Europe: A Comparative Perspective', UC-Berkeley, Deparment of Economics (March), mimeo.

Vernon, R., 1988, 'Introduction: The Promise and the Challenge', in R. Vernon, ed., *The Promise of Privatization*, Council on Foreign Relations.

Vickers, J. and G. Yarrow, 1988, *Privatization: An Economic Analysis*, Cambridge, MA: The MIT Press.

Walicki, A., 1990, 'The Three Traditions in Polish Patriotism', in Gomulka, S. and A. Polonski, ed., *Polish Paradoxes*, op. cit.

1991, 'Notes on Jaruzelski's Poland', in Feher, F. and A. Arato, eds., *Crisis and Reform in Eastern Europe*, London: Transaction Publishers.

Wasowski, S., 1990, 'Reforms in Eastern Europe', Department of Economics, Georgetown University, Washington (March), mimeo.

Weitzman, M., 1979, 'Technology Transfer to the USSR: An Economic Analysis', *Journal of Comparative Studies*, no. 3.

Wernik, A., 1991, 'Dostosowanie budzetowe w Polskim programie stabilizacyjnym', in Kolodko, G., ed., *Polityka Finansowa, Stabilizacja, Transformacja*, Warsaw: Institute of Finance.

1992, 'State Budget and Transformation', conference paper, Wilga, June 10–12, Institute of Finance.

Whitesell, P., 1985, 'The Influence of Central Planning on the Economic Slowdown in the Soviet Union and Eastern Europe: A Comparative Production Function Analysis', *Economica*, vol. 52.

Williamson, O., 1990, *Latin American Adjustment: How Much Has Happened*, Institute for International Econmics, Washington, DC.

Winiecki, J., 1991, 'The Inevitability of a Fall in Output in the Early Stages of Transition to the Market: Theoretical Underpinnings', *Communist Economies*, vol. 3, no. 4.

Wojciechowska, U., 1988, 'An Important Lesson: Five Years of Studying the Polish Reform', *Eastern European Economics* (Spring).

Wojciechowski, B., 1977, *Foreign Trade and National Income of Poland*, Warsaw.

1984, 'Przemiany strukturalne a trudnosci importowe Polaski', *Gospodarka Planowa*, no. 9.

World Bank, 1987, *Poland: Adjustment and Growth*, vol. 1–2, Washington, DC.

Index

For EU product safety concerns, contact us at Calle de José Abascal, 56–1°,
28003 Madrid, Spain or eugpsr@cambridge.org.

www.ingramcontent.com/pod-product-compliance
Ingram Content Group UK Ltd.
Pitfield, Milton Keynes, MK11 3LW, UK
UKHW012155180425
457623UK00007B/44